VOLUME II   REVISED EDITION

A HISTORY OF

CHRISTIAN

THOUGHT

From Augustine to the Eve of the Reformation

JUSTO L. GONZÁLEZ

Abingdon Press
NASHVILLE

A HISTORY OF CHRISTIAN THOUGHT, REVISED EDITION

VOL. II

ISBN 0-687-17183-0 (v. 2)
ISBN 0-687-17185-7 (the set)

Library of Congress Catalog Card Number:

74-109679

94 95 96 97 98 99 00 01 02 03 04 — 20 19 18

MANUFACTURED IN THE UNITED STATES OF AMERICA

Preface to the Second English Edition

It has now been more than ten years and ten printings since the first publication of *A History of Christian Thought*—the first volume was published in English in 1970, and the third in 1975. I have been extremely pleased by its widespread use in universities and seminaries. I am also grateful to colleagues who, both in published reviews and in personal correspondence, have suggested ways in which that first edition could be improved. In the preparation of this revised edition, I have endeavored to take account of their criticism and suggestions.

It is still my purpose to produce a book that can serve as an introduction to the subject for readers with little or no theological training, giving them both the basic knowledge needed for further theological and historical studies and a vision of the rich variety of Christian thought through the ages. Therefore, I have sought to avoid sweeping generalizations or purely personal views, which might make the book more interesting to my colleagues, but less useful to my intended readers.

The changes in this new edition are many. Most of them are bibliographical matters, updating references and taking into account more recent research. Where such research has led me to correct my views on a particular subject, this is reflected in changes in the text. Some chapters have been radically reorganized—in particular, the chapter on nineteenth-century Protestant theology. At the suggestion of numerous reviewers, I have also added a chapter on contemporary theology.

Since the first edition was published, I have also become aware of two factors deeply affecting the history of Christian theology, and seldom sufficiently recognized. The first is the liturgical and communal setting in which theology develops. A fuller understanding of medieval theology, for instance, would require a parallel consideration of theological treatises and discussions on the one hand and of the monastic liturgy of the hours on the other. While connections between liturgy and theology appear repeatedly throughout these three volumes, I feel that there is much more work to be done in this area, and I confess that I have not done enough of it to weave the two into a single fabric throughout the entire history of Christianity.

The second factor in the history of Christian theology of which I have become more profoundly aware is the social and economic context and content of theology. This is a field to which I have been devoting much interest in recent years. My studies along these lines have enriched my appreciation for many of the theologians discussed in these three volumes, and deepened my understanding of a number of abstract theological issues. I have referred to economic matters at a few points in this revised edition. However, given the purpose of this book, to serve as an introduction to students who do not necessarily know the more traditional interpretations, I have refrained from rewriting the entire history from the perspective of this particular insight. I hope to do this in two separate works now in preparation—one on the history of Christian views on economics, and another on how the different types of theology that can be discerned in the history of Christianity relate to these and other issues.

To a large degree, history is autobiography—or perhaps one should say that it is the prolegomena to one's biography. In any case, our view of who we are, both as individuals and as a community of faith, depends in large measure on what we understand our history to be. As this revised edition goes to press, it is my prayer that its readers will gain new understandings from it, and thus be aided in what is after all the primary task of the Christian community: being faithful and obedient in the world in which we have been placed.

J. L. G.
Decatur, Georgia
September 19, 1986

Preface to the First English Edition

There is always a certain awkwardness to writing a Preface, for the author is acutely aware that what he writes last may well be what his reader will read first. In this particular case, this awkwardness is compounded by the fact that this is a "Preface to the Second Volume" of a three-volume series, and I therefore feel tempted to use it as an opportunity to sum up what I have done to this point, and to project how I plan to develop the third volume.

This temptation, however, I shall resist, apart from two comments as to the scope and plan of this second volume. The first is that, just as in the first volume I deemed it wise not to include Augustine, but rather to begin with him in this second volume, I now have decided to bring the story of the development of Christian thought only up to the eve of the Reformation, and to leave out of this second volume both the Reformation itself and any detailed discussion of the Renaissance and Humanism. These subjects will be the starting point of the final volume of this *History*. The second comment that I must make is that here again I have attempted to make this *History* fully ecumenical, and have included in it developments within the Eastern churches which are usually passed in silence. If the reader finds that the periodic incursions into Eastern theology interrupt the flow of the narration, it should be a simple matter to read the various chapters dealing with the Eastern and Western churches in an order more suitable to his interests.

Finally, a word of gratitude. Once again, those to whom I owe the possibility of writing this book are too numerous to mention. Therefore, the names that I do mention stand as symbols for all those to whom gratitude is due. The librarians of Yale Divinity School and the Evangelical Seminary of Puerto Rico, Dr. Raymond P. Morris and Miss Wilma Mosholder, have been most kind and generous in their help, the former during a sabbatical which I spent at Yale while preparing the manuscript for this book, and the latter by securing hundreds of volumes which were necessary for my research. To this end, the Theological Education Fund contributed a substantial grant, and for that, too, I am grateful. Although the typing of the manuscript was shared by several persons, the heaviest load was carried by Mrs. Ramonita C. de Brugueras, who also typed the entire Spanish manuscript; Miss F. Elizabeth Adams; and Mrs. June B. Caldwell. I wish to record my indebtedness to them, not only for their work, but also for the interest that they have shown in the project itself.

J. L. G.
Emory University
Lent, 1971

Contents

List of Abbreviations   11

I   The Theology of Augustine   15

II   Western Theology After Augustine   56

III   Eastern Theology Between the Fourth and the Sixth Ecumenical Councils   76

IV   The Carolingian Renaissance   107

V   The Dark Age   143

VI   The Renaissance of the Twelfth Century   157

VII   Eastern Theology from the Islamic Conquests to the Fourth Crusade   195

VIII   General Introduction to the Thirteenth Century   220

IX   The Augustinian Tradition in the
       Thirteenth Century   243

 X   The Dominican School   257

XI   Extreme Aristotelianism   284

XII Eastern Theology to the Fall of
       Constantinople   292

XIII Theology in the Later Middle Ages   304

XIV Dawn or Dusk?   335

Appendix: Suggestions for Further Reading   339

Index of Subjects and Authors   342

List of Abbreviations

ActHung	*Acta antiqua Academiae Scientiarum Hungaricae*
ACW	*Ancient Christian Writers*
AHDLMA	*Archives d'Histoire doctrinale et littéraire du Moyen Age*
AlAnd	*Al-Andalus*
AmBenRev	*American Benedictine Review*
AmEccRev	*American Ecclesiastical Review*
Ang	*Angelicum*
AnnTh	*L'Année Théologique*
AnnThAug	*L'Année Théologique Augustinienne*
AnSacTarr	*Analecta Sacra Tarraconensis*
Ant	*Antonianum*
ArchFrHist	*Archivum Franciscanum Historicum*
ArchPh	*Archives de Philosophie*
ARG	*Archiv für Reformationsgeschichte*
Aug	*Augustinus*
Auga	*Augustiniana*
Augm	*Augustinianum*
BAC	*Biblioteca de Autores Cristianos*
BibOr	*Bibliotheca Orientalis*
BijGesch	*Bijdragen tot de Geschiedenis*
BogSmotra	*Bogoslovska Smotra Ephemerides Theologicae*
BThAM	*Bulletin de Théologie Ancienne et Médiévale*
CD	*La Ciudad de Dios*
CECath	*Cahiers des Études Cathares*
CH	*Church History*
CienFe	*Ciencia y Fe*
CienTom	*Ciencia Tomista*
CollFranNeer	*Collectanea Franciscana Neerlandica*
CommSanct	*Communio Sanctorum*
CSCO	*Corpus Scriptorum Christianorum Orientalium*
CSEL	*Corpus Scriptorum Ecclesiaticorum Latinorum*
CuadEstGall	*Cuadernos de Estudios Gallegos*
CuadSalFil	*Cuadernos Salmantinos de Filosofía*
Denzinger	*Enchiridion Symbolorum Definitionum et Declarationum* (ed. Denzinger and Rahner), 31st edition, 1957

11

DHGE	*Dictionnaire d'Histoire et de Géographie Ecclésiastiques*
DissAbs	*Dissertation Abstracts*
DivThom	*Divus Thomas: Commentarium de Philosophia et Theologia*
DKvCh	*Das Konzil von Chalkedon: Geschichte und Gegenwart* (ed. Grillmeier und Bacht)
DomSt	*Dominican Studies*
DOP	*Dumbarton Oaks Papers*
DS	*Dictionnaire de Spiritualité*
DTC	*Dictionnaire de Théologie Catholique*
EchOr	*Échos d'Orient*
EncCatt	*Enciclopedia Cattolica*
EngHisRev	*English Historical Review*
EphemMar	*Ephemerides Mariologicae*
EstEcl	*Estudios Eclesiásticos*
EstFran	*Estudis Franciscans*
EstudiosFran	*Estudios Franciscanos*
EtAug	*Études Augustiniennes*
EtFran	*Études Franciscaines*
FrancSt	*Franciscan Studies*
FranzSt	*Franziskanische Studien*
FrFran	*La France Franciscaine*
GCFilIt	*Giornale Critico di Filosofia Italiana*
GM	*Giornale di Metafisica*
Greg	*Gregorianum*
GuL	*Geist und Leben*
HistZschr	*Historische Zeitschrift*
HorSem	*Horae Semiticae*
HTR	*Harvard Theological Review*
Hum	*Humanitas*
IntkZtschr	*Internationale kirchliche Zeitschrift*
JEH	*Journal of Ecclesiastical History*
JHP	*Journal of the History of Philosophy*
JKGSlav	*Jahrbücher für Kultur und Geschichte der Slaven*
JMedRenSt	*Journal of Medieval and Renaissance Studies*
JRel	*The Journal of Religion*

LCC	*Library of Christian Classics*
Mansi	*Sacrorum Conciliorum Nova et Amplissima Collectio* (ed. Mansi)
MedSt	*Mediaeval Studies*
MiscFranc	*Miscellanea Francescana*
ModSch	*Modern Schoolman*
Ms	*Manuscripta*
MSR	*Mélanges de Science Religieuse*
NedTheolTschr	*Nederlands Theologisch Tijdschrift*
NSch	*The New Scholasticism*
OgE	*Ons geestelijk Erf*
OrChr	*Orientalia Christiana*
PatMed	*Patristica et Mediaevalia*
PG	*Patrologiae cursus completus . . . series Graeca* (ed. Migne)
PL	*Patrologiae cursus completus . . . series Latina* (ed. Migne)
PO	*Patrologia Orientalis*
RCHist	*Rivista Critica di Storia della Filosofia*
RelCult	*Religión y Cultura*
RET	*Revista Española de Teología*
RevAscMyst	*Revue d'Ascetique et de Mystique*
RevBened	*Revue Bénédictine*
RevEsp	*Revista de Espiritualidad*
RevEstGall	*Revista de Estudios Gallegos*
RevEtAug	*Revue des Études Augustiniennes*
RevStSl	*Revue des Études Slaves*
RevPhil	*Revue de Philosophie*
RevPhLouv	*Revue Philosophique de Louvain*
RevPortFil	*Revista Portuguesa de Filosofia*
RevUMad	*Revista de la Universidad de Madrid*
RFilNSc	*Revista di Filosofia Neoscolastica*
RHPhRel	*Revue d'Histoire et de Philosophie Religieuse*
RnsPh	*Revue néoscolastique de Philosophie*
RQH	*Revue des Questions Historiques*
RRosm	*Rivista Rosminiana*

RScPhTh	*Revue des Sciences Philosophiques et Théologiques*
RScRel	*Recherches de Science Religieuse*
RStLet	*Rivista di Storia e Letteratura Religiosa*
RThAM	*Recherches de Théologie Ancienne et Médiévale*
RThLouv	*Revue théologique de Louvain*
Sal	*Salmanticensis*
Sap	*Sapientia*
Sapza	*La Sapienza; Rivista di Filosofia e di Lettere*
SC	*Sources Chrétiennes*
Sch	*Scholastik: Vierteljahrschrift für Theologie und Philosophie*
SJT	*Scottish Journal of Theology*
SM	*Sacramentum Mundi*
Spec	*Speculum: A Journal of Medieval Studies*
StCath	*Studia Catholica*
StFran	*Studi Francescani*
StMed	*Studi Medievali*
SVNC	*Scriptorum Veterum Nova Collectio*
Theoria	*Theoria: Swedish Journal of Philosophy and Psychology*
ThGl	*Theologie und Glaube*
ThPhil	*Theologie und Philosophie*
ThR	*Theologische Revue*
TLztg	*Theologische Literaturzeitung*
TQ	*Theologische Quartalschrift*
Tut	*Tijdschr voor Theologie*
Viv	*Vivarium*
VyV	*Verdad y Vida*
Wuw	*Wissenschaft und Weisheit*
ZKT	*Zeitschrift für katholische Theologie*
ZschrKgesch	*Zeitschrift für Kirchengeschichte*
ZschrPhForsch	*Zeitschrift für Philosophische Forschung*

I

The Theology of Augustine

Our previous volume took us to A.D. 451, which was the date of the Council of Chalcedon. However, the last chapters of that volume dealt exclusively with the christological controversies that took place in the East, and left aside the development of Western theology after the trinitarian controversy. We must now return to the West and to the end of the fourth century and the early years of the fifth in order to study the theology of Augustine.

Augustine is the end of one era as well as the beginning of another. He is the last of the ancient Christian writers, and the forerunner of medieval theology. The main currents of ancient theology converged in him, and from him flow the rivers, not only of medieval scholasticism, but also of sixteenth-century Protestant theology.

As his theology was not developed in abstract meditation, nor out of the requirements of a system, but rather within the context of the various issues that faced him throughout his life, the best introduction to that theology is through his biography.[1]

---

[1] Good introductions in English are: Eugène Portalié, *A Guide to the Thought of Saint Augustine* (Chicago: Regnery, 1960); Gerald Bonner, *St. Augustine of Hippo: Life and Controversies* (London: SCM Press, 1963); P. Brown, *Augustine of Hippo: A Biography* (London: Faber and Faber, 1967).

His Youth

Augustine was born to a Christian mother and a pagan father in A.D. 354, in the small North African town of Tagaste. The main source for our knowledge of his youth and his conversion is his *Confessions*, a spiritual autobiography in which he attempts to show how God guided his steps since his early years in spite of his own rebelliousness and unbelief. It is therefore a document without parallel in ancient literature, and a very useful source in attempting to discover how his own life helped shape Augustine's theology.[2]

Augustine lived in Tagaste until it was necessary to move to another city in order to continue his studies. This led him first to nearby Madaura, and later—when he was seventeen years of age—to Carthage. There he spent his time not only studying rhetoric, but also in a disorderly life that led to his taking up of a concubine, who a year later gave him his only son, Adeodatus. But in spite of his escapades, Augustine continued his work in rhetoric, and seems to have become one of the most eloquent speakers in the city.

It was at this time, and in order to improve his style, that Augustine undertook the study of Cicero's *Hortensius*. Although he approached this work seeking only beauty of expression, he found in it a forceful call to search after truth.

In the ordinary course of study, I lighted upon a certain book of Cicero, whose language, though not his heart, almost all admire. This book of his contains an exhortation to philosophy, and is called *Hortensius*. This book, in truth, changed my affections, and turned my prayers to Thyself, O Lord, and made me have other hopes and desires. Worthless suddenly became every vain hope to me; and, with an incredible warmth of heart, I yearned for an immortality of wisdom, and began now to arise that I might return to Thee.[3]

---

[2] Doubts regarding the historical accuracy of the *Confessions* revolve mainly around its account of Augustine's conversion. See n. 15.

[3] *Conf.* 3. 4. Trans. J. G. Pilkington (New York: Heritage Press, 1963), p. 33.

This search for truth, however, led young Augustine not to the orthodox Christian faith, but rather to Manichaeism.

Manichaeism

The origin and doctrines of Manichaeism are much better known today than they were thirty years ago, for in recent times the discovery of several important Manichaean documents has served to correct the fragmentary and somewhat distorted vision of this sect which was gleaned from Christian discussions and refutations of it.[4]

Mani, the founder of Manichaeism, was born in Babylon in A.D. 216. It seems that his father was a member of a sect of Gnostic and ascetic leanings, and that it was in such a community that Mani was born and raised. When twelve years of age he received a revelation ordering him to withdraw from the sect in which he had been raised, and twelve years later a new revelation turned him into the prophet and apostle of a new "religion of light." After preaching in Persia, Mesopotamia, and even India, he fell out of favor with the political authorities and was made a prisoner and bound in chains in such a manner that it was not a month before he was dead.[5] For a period his disciples were split, but by A.D. 282 they were already reunited under the leadership of a certain Sisinius. At that time Manichaeism began a period of widespread diffusion eastward into India and China, and westward into Palestine and Egypt. Some time later, its believers were found in all the Mediterranean Basin, where they were gaining followers by ridiculing the doctrines of orthodox Christianity.[6]

---

[4] It is for this reason that Ferdinand Christian Baur's otherwise excellent study, *Das Manichäische Religionssystem* (reprinted from 1831 edition; Göttingen: Vandenhoeck & Ruprecht, 1928) is to be corrected by more recent scholarship. See: L. J. R. Ort, *Mani: A Religio-Historical Description of His Personality* (Leiden: E. J. Brill, 1957); Henri-Charles Puech, *Le Manichéisme* (Paris: Civilisations du Sud, 1949). Puech's chronology is followed throughout this section.

[5] The widespread notion that he was skinned alive seems to be grounded only on the imagination of some ancient authors. See Puech, *Le Manichéisme*, pp. 54-57.

[6] One result of this rapid expansion was that regional differences appeared within Manichaeism. Therefore, a detailed study of the influence of Manichaeism on Augustine must begin by determining the exact nature of North African Manichaeism. See J. Zeiller, "Les hérésies en Afrique entre la paix constantinienne et l'invasion vandle," in *Mélanges à la Mémoire de F. Martroye* (Paris: Société nationale des antiquaires de France, 1940), pp. 101-6; W. H. C. Frend, "The Gnostic Manichaean Tradition in Roman Africa," *JEH*, 4 (1953), 13-26; L. H. Grondijs, "Numidian Manichaeism in Augustine's Time," *Ned-TheolTschr*, 9 (1954-55), 21-42; F. Decret, *Aspects du manichéisme dans l'Afrique romaine* (Paris: Études Augustiniennes, 1970).

Manichaean doctrine follows the ancient Gnostic pattern of attempting to offer an answer to the mysteries of the human condition through a revelation that lets us know our divine origin and frees us from the bonds of matter. According to this doctrine, the human spirit is part of the divine substance, and must return to it in order to fulfill its destiny. Meanwhile, it is subject to a frightful anguish that is simply the result of its union, here on earth, with the principle of evil. On the other hand, the principle of good has been revealed through several prophets, of which the most important were the Buddha, Zoroaster, and Jesus. Mani himself is the continuation of this illustrious lineage of prophets, although he is the last of them. Those who preceded him left only incomplete and partial revelations; but Mani has now revealed the final truth, that truth to which the Buddha, Zoroaster, and Jesus were witnessing. Furthermore, Mani is the incarnation of the Paraclete, and he reveals not only a religious truth, but also a perfect science. This "science" consists almost exclusively of a series of myths regarding the origin and the functioning of the world. In these myths, the center of the stage is occupied by the eternal struggle of two opposed principles, which are called Light and Darkness. Yet, in spite of its mythological character, this so-called science was able to capture the imagination and the trust of such a man as Augustine.

Augustine was never more than a "hearer" of Manichaeism, and he does not seem even to have attempted to join the rank of the "perfect."[7] Because of its dualism, Manichaeism proposed such an ethics of renunciation that it would have been impossible to follow it without almost starving to death. In order to overcome this difficulty, a distinction was made between the "hearers" and the "perfect." The hearers did not lead a life of absolute renunciation, but rather continued sharing in the common life of humankind, although participating in Manichaean worship and doctrines, and contributing with their offerings to the work of the "Church of the Light." The hope of

---

[7] D. Roché, "Saint Augustine et les manichéens de son temps," *CECath*, 1 (1949), 21-50.

such hearers was not that they would go directly to heaven after their death, but that they would be reincarnated in a perfect believer. On the other hand, the perfect were to lead a life of absolute renunciation, although there were certain foodstuffs that they were allowed to eat because it was believed that there were in such foodstuffs particles of light which could be saved by eating and thus assimilating them.[8]

It was thus as a hearer that Augustine was a Manichaean for nine years.[9] It seems that what attracted him in this doctrine was the promise that it made of offering a rational explanation of the universe. The Manichaeans rejected most of the Old Testament, and as Augustine had never been able to accept what he took to be the crassness of the Jewish Scriptures, he found here another reason to follow such an enlightened religion. Finally, Augustine had always had difficulties with the problem of how the goodness and love of God could be reconciled with the existence of evil, and now this problem seemed to be solved by the assertion that there was not a single eternal principle, but two, and that one of these was evil while the other was good.

Just as the great strength of Manichaeism was in the claim to be strictly rational and scientific, its great weakness was in its inability to fulfill that promise. From the very beginning of his Manichaean period Augustine had doubts that his teachers were unable to clear. At first he believed that if he would only take such doubts to one of the truly great teachers of Manichaeism, they would be resolved. Meanwhile, he combined his teaching and his Manichaean studies with astrological speculations on which he laid his trust until he found an undeniable proof that astrology was false.[10] When finally he was able to meet one of the most famous Manichaean teachers—Faustus of Milevis—the meeting was such a disappointment that Augustine lost his faith in Manichaeism.

---

8 Puech, *Le Manichéisme*, pp. 90-91, points out that this is the doctrine of "salvation by the belly" that Augustine mocked after abandoning Manichaeism.

9 *Conf.* 3.11.

10 *Ibid.*, 4.3. See: L. C. Ferrari, "Astronomy and Augustine's Break with the Manichees," *RevEtAug* 19 (1973), 263-76.

And for nearly the whole of those nine years during which, with unstable mind, I had been their follower, I had been looking forward with but too great eagerness for the arrival of this same Faustus. For the other members of the sect whom I had chanced to light upon, when unable to answer the questions I raised, always bade me look forward to his coming, when, by discoursing with him, these, and greater difficulties if I had them, would be most easily and amply cleared away. When at last he did come, I found him to be a man of pleasant speech, who spoke of the very same things as they themselves did, although more fluently, and in better language. But of what profit to me was the elegance of my cup-bearer, since he offered me not the more precious draught for which I thirsted? My ears were already satiated with similar things; neither did they appear to me more conclusive, because better expressed; nor true, because oratorical; nor the spirit necessarily wise, because the face was comely and the language eloquent.[11]

Disappointed with Manichaeism as well as with the bad behavior of his Carthaginian students, Augustine decided to move to Rome. There he continued in contact with the Manichees, although he no longer believed their doctrines and was rather inclined to accept the skepticism of the Academy.

For I was half inclined to believe that those philosophers whom they call "Academics" were more sagacious than the rest, in that they held that we ought to doubt everything, and ruled that man had not the power of comprehending any truth.[12]

But Rome was not a much more convenient place for furthering his career as a teacher of rhetoric, for his students found devious ways to avoid paying his fees. He therefore decided to try his luck in Milan, where there was a vacancy for a teacher of rhetoric. It was at Milan that Augustine became a Neoplatonist and later, through the influence of Bishop Ambrose and his teacher Simplician, a Christian.

---

[11] *Ibid.*, 5.6 (trans. Pilkington, pp. 67-68).
[12] *Ibid.*, 5.10 (trans. Pilkington, p. 74).

Neoplatonism

By reading the works of those whom he called "Platonists"—probably Plotinus, Porphyry, and other Neoplatonists—Augustine was not only brought out of his skepticism, but was carried over the two main hurdles that stood in the way of his intellectual acceptance of the Christian faith—the incorporeal nature of God, and the existence of evil. Manichaeism, with its corporeal understanding of God and with its dualism, had offered simple solutions to these problems, but such solutions had been proved to be insufficient. Now Neoplatonism offered Augustine a means of understanding the incorporeal nature, as well as a way of interpreting the existence of evil without having recourse to dualism. Thus, the way was now open to an acceptance of the Christian faith. In these respects, the influence of Neoplatonism on Augustine's thought was such that, as will be seen later on, he always understood the incorporeal nature of God and the problem of evil in Neoplatonic terms.

His Conversion

Augustine's conversion to Christianity, which took place shortly after his discovery of Neoplatonism, combined rational elements with emotional factors. When Augustine arrived at Milan, the bishop of that city was Ambrose, a man of great intellectual gifts and an inflexible sense of duty. Augustine went to hear his preaching, not in order to listen to what he said, but rather to study the manner in which he said it. He thus went to Ambrose not as an anguished soul in search of truth, but as a professional who goes to another in order to judge him and perhaps to learn something of his technique. However, he soon felt that he was listening not only to the manner in which Ambrose spoke, but also to that which he was saying, especially since the allegorical interpretations of the Old Testament which Ambrose put forth came to solve many of the difficulties that had previously stood in the way of Augustine's faith.[13]

---

[13] *Ibid.*, 5.14.

However, this new vision of the meaning of the Christian faith was not sufficient to make Augustine accept it. The Christianity that he had known in his home was ascetic, and so were the moral views of the Neoplatonist philosophers whom he had learned to admire. For these reasons, he thought that if he came to accept the Christian faith this must imply a life of self-denial for which he was not ready. Intellectually, the decision had been made; but his will still refused to follow his mind. His prayer was: "Grant me chastity and continence, but not yet."

Finally, Augustine was led to shame, despair, and conversion by the story of two cases in which others had shown more courage than he. The first was that of Marius Victorinus, whom Augustine greatly admired as the Latin translator of several Neoplatonic works, and who, at a recent date and after a long period of doubt, had made a public confession of his Christian faith. The other case was the story of two men who, upon reading of the *Life of Saint Anthony,* decided to abandon the world and devote their lives to the service of God. This story so touched Augustine's heart that, despairing of his ability to take the final step, he fled to a garden and threw himself down under a fig tree while he cried:

> How long, how long? To-morrow, and to-morrow? Why not now? Why is there not this hour an end to my uncleanness?
>
> I was saying these things and weeping in the most bitter contrition of my heart, when lo, I heard the voice as of a boy or girl, I know not which, coming from a neighbouring house, chanting, and oft repeating, "Take up and read; take up and read." . . . I grasped, opened, and in silence read that paragraph on which my eyes first fell,—"Not in rioting and drunkenness, not in chambering and wantonness, not in strife and envying; but put ye on the Lord Jesus Christ, and make not provision for the flesh, to fulfill the lusts thereof." No further would I read, nor did I need; for instantly, as the sentence ended,—by a light, as it were, of security into my heart,—all the gloom of doubt vanished away.[14]

---

[14] *Ibid.,* 8.12 (trans. Pilkington, pp. 140-41).

What was the exact nature of Augustine's conversion? This is a question that scholars have been debating since the end of the nineteenth century.[15] The question is whether the conversion that took place in the garden of Milan really led Augustine to the Christian faith held by the church and by his own mother, or led him rather to that type of life and of belief which was set forth by the Neoplatonist philosophers. As has already been said, this is the main point at which the historical truthfulness of the *Confessions* has been questioned. There are good reasons for such doubts, for while the *Confessions* give the impression that Augustine was converted to the Christian faith in the garden of Milan, the works that he wrote immediately after that experience have more a Neoplatonist than a Christian flavor. After conversion, Augustine withdrew to Cassiciacum, in the outskirts of Milan, together with a small group of those who were willing to follow him in a life of self-denial and meditation. There he held with his companions a series of conversations from which sprang the "Dialogues of Cassiciacum"—*Against the Academics, On the Happy Life, On Order, Soliloquies,* and *On the Immortality of the Soul.* In these works, Augustine's interest seems to be more in philosophical contemplation than in the study of the doctrines of the church. Furthermore, it is in these writings that the influence of Neoplatonism upon Augustine's thought is most clearly seen. One may then ask, Is it not possible that the conversion that took place in the garden was actually philosophical in nature, and that Augustine became a Christian only at a later date? Such has been the conclusion of some scholars.

---

[15] The early stages of the controversy are summarized by Charles Boyer, *Christianisme et Néo-platonisme dans la formation de Saint Augustin* (Rome: Officium libri catholici, 1953). Other studies deserving attention are: Karl Adam, *Die geistige Entwicklung des heiligen Augustinus* (Augsburg: Haas und Grabherr, 1931); Pierre Paul Courcelle, *Recherches sur les Confessions de Saint Augustin* (Paris: E. de Boccard, 1950); Romano Guardini, *Die Bekehrung des Aurelius Augustinus* (Munich: Kösel, 1950); S. B. Femiano, *Reflessioni critiche sulla conversione di S. Agostino* (Naples: Istituto editoriale del Mezzogiorno, 1951); A. Sizoo, "Augustinus' bekeerings-verhall als narratio," *Ant,* 4 (1954), 240-57; G. Mathon, "Quand faut-il placer le retour d'Augustin à la foi catholique?" *RevETAug,* 1 (1955), 107-27; C. Vaca, "La experiencia religiosa en San Agustín," *RevEsp* 14 (1955), 185-204; F. Bolgiani, *La conversione di S. Agostino a l'VIIIº libro delle "Confessioni"* (Torino: Università, 1956); V. Capanaga, "San Agustín en nuestro tiempo: Problemas sobre la conversión," *Aug,* 1 (1956), 33-48. See also, on the events in the garden in Milan, the series of articles by Cayré and Courcelle published in *AnnTh,* 1951. On the wider question of Augustine's progress, see A. W. Matthews, *The Develoment of St. Augustine from Neoplatonism to Christianity, 386-391 A.D.* (Washington: University Press of America, 1980).

Others have defended the traditional interpretation, which emphasizes the finality of Augustine's conversion. Perhaps the best interpretation of the event is that since his early youth Augustine knew the main Christian doctrines, most of which he had never really doubted, so that the function of his Neoplatonist readings, of Ambrose's sermons, and of his discussions with Simplician, was simply to set aside the doubts that stood in the way of his full acceptance of the Christian faith. However, during his years of search, Augustine had developed a Neoplatonist understanding of the nature of truth and of the life of the true philosopher, which determined the way in which he understood the Christian life as a combination of the self-denial that Jesus advocated and what the Neoplatonists called "the philosophical life." Thus, what took place in the garden was not that Augustine decided to accept one or another of the doctrines of Christianity, but was rather his discovery of a power that enabled him to overcome all the difficulties that he had found standing in the way of a life of contemplation. This was what his mother had been praying for. This was all that he needed to become a Christian. Intellectually he was a Christian even before the events in the garden; from that moment on, he would lead the life that he thought was expected of a Christian—and in so doing he would progressively develop a theology that would be less and less Neoplatonic and more and more characteristically Christian.

After his conversion and the brief retreat at Cassiciacum, Augustine, his son, and a friend returned to Milan, where they were baptized by Ambrose.[16] Then they left for Tagaste with Augustine's mother, but she died at the Port of Ostia[17] shortly

---

[16] The legend according to which Augustine and Ambrose were inspired to sing the *Te Deum* on this occasion is entirely groundless. Furthermore, Ambrose seems to have had no idea of the great gifts of his new convert.

[17] Before his mother's death, Augustine enjoyed moments of deep spiritual communion with her. His narration of one of these moments, the so-called vision of Ostia (*Conf.* 9.10), has been a source of controversy among modern scholars, for it has traditionally been interpreted as the account of a mystical experience, and this interpretation has been questioned by some, notably E. Hendrikx, *Augustins Verhältnis zuur Mystik: Eine patristische Untersuchung* (Würzburg: Rita-Verlag, 1936). The importance of the debate lies in the fact that this is the only text in Augustine's voluminous writings in which he seems to claim a mystical experience. For further bibliography, see J. Heitz, "Une question ouverte: La mystique de saint Augustin," *RHPhRel*, 45 (1965), 315-34; V. Zangara, "La visione di Ostia: Storia dell'indagine e della controversia," *RStLet*, 15 (1979), 63-82.

after leaving Rome. Augustine and his party then spent several months in Rome,[18] and finally made their way back to Africa. In Tagaste, Augustine sold the properties that he had inherited from his parents, gave to the poor most of the money that he received from them, and decided to lead a serene and retired life together with his son and some friends, combining some of the discipline of a monastery with study, meditation, and discussion.[19]

In A.D. 391 he visited the city of Hippo with the hope of convincing a friend to join the monastic community at Tagaste. During that visit, Valerius, the Bishop of Hippo, placed him in a position where he could not avoid being ordained a priest. Thus began Augustine's direct involvement in the life of the church, although he did not abandon his earlier monastic inclinations, but rather developed at Hippo a similar community to that which he had organized at Tagaste.[20] Four years later, he was made a bishop through the insistence of Valerius.[21] This—and Valerius' subsequent death—placed upon him all the responsibilities of the episcopate: preaching, administering the sacraments, judging between various parties in disagreement, the practice and management of charity, the administration of the funds and properties of the church, pastoral counseling and care, etc. However, what led him to produce a number of works of great significance for the development of Christian theology was a series of controversies in which he became involved—mainly with the Manichees, the Donatists, and the Pelagians.

---

[18] It was at this time that Augustine wrote his two books *On the Customs of the Catholic Church* and *On the Customs of the Manichees*, as well as his treatise *On the Quantity of the Soul*. He also began to write *On Free Will*, although he did not finish this work until a later date.

[19] It was during this period that he wrote *On the Teacher*, which was based on a dialogue that he had with his son shortly before the latter's death. At this time he also wrote *On Genesis against the Manichees*, and *On the true religion*.

[20] While being a priest, he wrote numerous works, among them *On the Advantage of Believing*—addressed to a friend whom he had led to Manichaeism—and his *Debate with Fortunatus*—which tells of a two-day discussion with a Manichaean teacher. It was also at this time that he completed his treatise *On Free Will*.

[21] Augustine was opposed to his own consecration both because he feared it would further interrupt his life of meditation and because he did not believe that there should be two bishops in the same church. Although he was not aware of it, the Council of Nicea had declared that there should not be two bishops in a single church. But when those who were trying to convince him that he should be consecrated showed that there had been other cases in which churches had had more than one bishop, he agreed to be made a bishop to serve jointly with Valerius.

The Donatist Controversy

Augustine's life after his conversion may be divided into three periods, as suggested by Bonner:

> Very roughly speaking, Augustine's career as a Christian writer can be divided into three periods. In the first, he was mainly concerned with attacking and refuting the Manichees. During the second, he was preoccupied with the Donatist schismatics; while in the third, he was concerned with the Pelagians.[22]

Most of the works which have been mentioned up to now deal either with the comtemplative life or with the refutation of the Manichees. The latter was Augustine's main concern until A.D. 405, when he wrote his treatise *On the Nature of the Good*. After that he became engrossed in the Donatist controversy—although his first work dealing with Donatism dates from A.D. 394.

The origins of Donatism[23] are to be found in the persecution of Diocletian, which took place in A.D. 303–305. The imperial edicts ordering Christians to deliver all copies of Scripture to the magistrates placed believers in a difficult situation. From ancient times, most Christian teachers had repudiated every action that could incite the authorities to greater rigor, and therefore they almost unanimously counseled flight in time of persecution, although they also insisted that, if worse came to worst, every Christian should be ready to give up life rather than faith. What, then, should be done by those bishops, readers, and Christians in general who were asked to surrender the Scriptures? Should they refuse, even if in so doing they were provoking the wrath of those in authority? Was the act of giving up the sacred writings an act of apostasy? Or was it simply an act of prudence, which could be justified as a means of avoiding suffering for the church at large? There was no agreement regarding these questions; there could not have been, because of the sudden and urgent manner in which they were posed. Some church leaders turned

---

[22] Bonner, *St. Augustine*, p. 133.
[23] For this exposition I am greatly indebted to W. H. C. Frend: *The Donatist Church: A Movement of Protest in Roman North Africa* (Oxford: Clarendon Press, 1956).

in not only the Scriptures, but also the vases and other church artifacts; others refused to surrender anything and were imprisoned, tortured, and even killed; others sought intermediate solutions such as flight, hiding, turning in only part of the manuscripts in their possession, or even giving the magistrate copies not of the Christian Scriptures, but of some heretical book.

After the persecution, questions were raised about the authority of those bishops who had given up the Scriptures—often called the *traditores*—and even more of those other bishops who had been consecrated by them. Some claimed that in surrendering the Scriptures such bishops had completely lost their authority, and that they should therefore be deposed and replaced by others. According to this view, those other bishops who had been consecrated by the fallen *traditores* were not validly consecrated. Over against this position, most North African Christian leaders believed that the validity of a bishop's episcopal acts depended not on his personal purity, but rather on his own office and consecration as a bishop. Therefore, although those who had fallen during the persecution should be subjected to penance, their ministrations—including their actions consecrating other bishops—were still valid. In truth, the controversy had many social, racial, and political overtones, and the question of the steadfastness of the bishops was not always paramount. This explains the otherwise unexplainable fact that several leaders of the rigorist party—later to be called "Donatist" after Bishop Donatus—were actually *traditores*. In any case, the schism grew to alarming proportions. Constantine, and a long series of emperors after him, legislated against Donatism; but neither conciliatory nor violent measures succeeded in healing the breach. An extremist group of Donatists—the *circumcelliones*—turned to robbery and plunder. Augustine and several other bishops attempted to end the schism by various means. But in spite of their efforts Donatism continued in existence at least until the sixth century, and probably even as late as the invasion of North Africa by the forces of Islam.

But our main concern here is not the development and final disappearance of Donatism, but rather its doctrines and the manner in which their refutation shaped Augustine's theology and, through him, that of the Middle Ages. Three basic issues are significant on this score: the nature of the church, the relationship between church and state, and the sacraments.

Donatist ecclesiology insisted on the empirical holiness of the church. Every one of its members must be holy here and now—and quite often this holiness was measured not so much in terms of the practice of love, as in terms of one's attitude during the past persecution. One who is not holy has no place in the church. And, as Cyprian taught that the sacraments were not valid outside the church, all the religious ministrations of the *traditores*, who no longer belonged to the true chruch, were invalid.[24]

It was over against this position that Augustine developed his distinction between the visible church and the invisible, which will be discussed further on.

The question of the relationship between church and state was posed by the violence of the *circumcelliones,* and later by the barbarian invasions. At first, Augustine believed that one should not employ force to attempt to persuade others on spiritual matters. This meant that, even in the case of the Donatists, all that the Catholic bishops could do was to refute their doctrine, and thus attempt to persuade them to return to the communion of the greater church. But as a matter of fact the Donatists themselves were making use of force in order to keep their own members from returning to the church, and used that force in such a way that Augustine finally was led to sanction the intervention of the state to counterbalance the physical force the Donatists used. Thus the violent steps that the empire took against the Donatists were supported from the first by most African bishops, and eventually also by the Bishop of Hippo.[25]

This situation, as well as the invasions of the barbarians, led Augustine to develop the theory of the just war, for which he drew from Cicero as well as from Ambrose and others. According to Augustine, a war is just if it is carried on with a just

---

[24] G. G. Willis, *Saint Augustine and the Donatist Controversy* (London: S.P.C.K., 1950), pp. 117-18.
[25] See *Ep.* 93.5.

purpose—that is, the establishment of peace—if it is led by the proper authorities, and if, even in the midst of killing, the motive of love still subsists.[26]

As to the sacraments, the Donatists appealed to Cyprian's authority in order to claim that they could be valid only within the church, but they went further in affirming that only those who led a holy life were capable of administering valid sacraments. Naturally, also in this case holiness was measured in terms of one's attitude before persecution rather than in terms of love. In any case, what was at stake here was the validity of a sacrament. It was in order to solve this question that Augustine introduced the distinction between valid and regular sacraments. Only those sacraments are regular which are administered within the church and according to its ordinance. But the validity of a sacrament, as will be seen further on, does not wholly depend on its regularity.[27]

Pelagianism

Finally, the last great controversy that contributed to shape Augustine's theology was that which he held against Pelagianism. This controversy is probably the most significant, for it gave him the occasion to formulate his doctrines of grace and predestination, which would have enormous consequences in the future.

Pelagius—from whom Pelagianism draws its name—was a native of the British Isles.[28] Although he is frequently referred to as a monk, it is by no means certain that he was one.[29] Nor is the date of his birth known. What is known is that in A.D. 405, while at

---

[26] Roland H. Bainton, *Christian Attitudes Toward War and Peace* (Apex ed.; Nashville: Abingdon Press, 1960), pp. 91-93; Virgilio Giogianni, *Il concetto del diritto e dello stato in S. Agostino* (Padua: CEDAM, 1951), pp. 145-63.

[27] Besides our discussion of Augustine's doctrine of sacraments further on, the reader may consult Willis, *Saint Augustine, pp. 154-68*. Augustine's main works against Donatism are *On the Unity of the Church, On Baptism Against the Donatists*, and *Against Gaudentius*.

[28] The most significant studies that I know on Pelagius and his theology are: Georges de Plinval, *Pélage: ses écrits sa vie et sa réforme* (Lausanne: Payot, 1943); John Ferguson, *Pelagius* (Cambridge: W. Heffer & Sons, 1956); Torgny Bohlin, *Die Theologie des Pelagius und ihre Genesis* (Uppsala: Lundequist, 1957); S. Prete, *Pelagio e il pelagianismo* (Brescia: Morcelliana, 1961); G. Bonner, *Augustinian and Modern Research on Pelagianism* (Villanova: Augustinian Institute, 1972).

[29] See de Plinval, *Pélage*, pp. 102-3.

Rome, he had his first encounter with Augustine's theology, against which he reacted violently because it made everything dependent on God's grace and seemed to leave no place for human effort and participation. "Give what thou commandest, and command what thou wilt," Augustine had said in his *Confessions*,[30] and Pelagius had no place for such quietism.[31] After this episode, Pelagius disappears from the records until he is found four years later, on the eve of the fall of Rome, on his way to Africa with his disciple, friend, and apostle, Coelestius. He then left Africa for the East, without having had the occasion to meet Augustine. But Coelestius, who was less moderate than his teacher, remained behind to be the main opponent of Augustine in the Pelagian controversy.

In Palestine, Pelagius was able to muster the support of some bishops. But he found a formidable opponent in the fiery Jerome—whom we shall not have occasion to study in this history, but who is without any doubt one of the most remarkable personalities of the fourth and fifth centuries—who thundered from his retreat in Bethlehem, and rained fire and brimstone upon the head of Pelagius. Jerome was joined by Orosius—to whom reference will be made further on—and Pelagius' situation became untenable. Finally, after a long series of African synods that condemned the doctrine of Pelagius, and several oriental synods in which he managed to avoid being condemned, the matter came to Rome, where Bishop Innocent supported the position of the African bishops in condemning Pelagius. His successor Zosimus for a while supported Pelagius and Coelestius, but later changed his mind and condemned them. After that time, Pelagianism constantly lost ground in the West as well as in the East and was finally condemned in A.D. 431 by the Council of Ephesus, as has already been mentioned in the first volume of this *History*.[32]

The doctrines of Pelagius are known directly through several works of his which have survived—a few under his own name,

---

[30] *Conf.* 10.29.
[31] See Augustine, *On the Gift of Perseverance*, 20.
[32] P. 356.

others under the names of orthodox authors, and others, finally, in fragments quoted by his opponents. His main surviving works are his *Exposition of the Pauline Epistles,*[33] and his *Book of Faith,* addressed to Pope Innocent in an attempt to gain his support.[34]

Pelagius' theology seems to be a reaction against the moral determinism of the Manichees.[35] The latter claimed that good and evil were based on the very nature of eternal principles, and therefore that the evil nature could not do any good, nor the good any evil. It was against these claims that Augustine wrote his treatise *On Free Will.* It was also against it that Pelagius opened his theological campaign. Thus, the difference between Augustine and Pelagius was that the former was not willing to relinquish the absolute need for grace, even while defending freedom, whereas the latter believed that Augustine's doctrine of grace was a threat to human freedom and responsibility.

From a practical point of view, Pelagius was interested in leaving no place for the excuses of those who impute their own sin to the weakness of human nature. Against such persons, Pelagius affirmed that God has made us free, and that this freedom is such that through it we are capable of doing good. The power not to sin—*posse non peccare*—is in human nature since its very creation, and neither the sin of Adam nor the Devil himself can destroy it. Adam's sin is in no way the sin of humanity, for it would be absurd and unjust to condemn all for the sin of one. Nor does the sin of Adam destroy the freedom that all his descendants have not to sin. It is true that the Evil One is powerful, but he is not so powerful that he cannot be resisted. The flesh is also powerful, and it struggles against the spirit; but God has given us the power to overcome it. As a proof of this stand the men and women who, according to the Old Testament, led lives of perfect holiness. Thus, we each sin for ourselves out

---

[33] A work that has been preserved under the names of several ancient Christian writers. Erasmus published it and attributed it to Jerome. This is the edition to be found in PL, 30:645-902. There is no doubt that its true author is Pelagius.

[34] Often attributed to Jerome or to Augustine. Printed in *PL,* 48:488-91. The entire list of works that can reasonably be attributed to Pelagius may be seen in de Plinval, *Pélage,* pp. 44-45.

[35] Such is the thesis of Bohlin, *Die Theologie des Pelagius und ihre Genesis.* Against this view see G. de Plinval, "Points de vue récents sur la theologie de Pélage, *RScRel,* 46 (1958), 227-37. On this point we tend to agree with Bohlin's general thesis, although not with his working hypothesis that Pelagius takes the young Augustine as his point of departure (p. 56).

of our own free will, and therefore children who die before being baptized are not lost, for the guilt of Adam is not upon their shoulders.

Does this mean that grace is not necessary for salvation? Certainly not, for Pelagius claimed that there is an "original grace" or "grace of creation" which is given to all. This "grace," however, is not a special action of God, and de Plinval is right in asserting that "it is in a way confused with the grace to which we owe existence and intelligence."[36] Paradoxically, it is "natural grace."

Besides this grace of creation Pelagius affirmed that there is a "grace of revelation" or "grace of teaching," which consists in that revelation by which God shows the way that we are to follow. It is not that revelation offers us a special power to obey God, for to affirm such a thing would imply that, apart from revelation, we are incapable of doing good.

There is, finally, the "grace of pardon" or "grace of the remission of sin." This is the grace that God grants to those who—of their own free will—repent and make an effort to act correctly and to repair the evil that they have done. Once again, this grace does not influence human will, but is limited to the forgiveness of sins.

As to baptism, Pelagius claimed that infants are innocent and therefore do not need it. Furthermore, baptism does not give birth to a free will where there was formerly a will under the bondage of sin. It only breaks the custom of sinning and calls believers to a new life that they can build through the use of their own freedom.

Finally, according to Pelagius, the predestination to which Paul refers is not a sovereign decree of God in virtue of which people are saved or condemned, but is rather God's foreknowledge of what will be future human decisions. "To predestine is the same as to foreknow."[37]

As to Coelestius, the most famous of Pelagius' disciples and Augustine's main opponent, his doctrines are simply a clarifica-

---

[36] *Pélage*, p. 237.
[37] *Ad Rom. exp.* 8. 29: "Praedestinare est idem quod praescire" (quoted by Ferguson, *Pelagius*, p. 138).

tion and exaggeration of those of his teacher. Augustine summarized them in the following nine points:[38]

1. That Adam was created mortal, for he would have died no matter whether he had sinned or not.
2. That Adam's sin injured him only, and not all of humankind.
3. That the Law, as well as the gospel, leads to the Kingdom.
4. That there were some before the time of Christ who lived without sin.
5. That recently born infants are in the same state as was Adam before his fall.
6. That the whole of humankind does not die in the death or fall of Adam, nor does it resurrect in the resurrection of Christ.
7. That, if we will, we can live without sin.
8. That unbaptized infants attain unto eternal life.
9. That the rich who are baptized will have no merit, nor will they inherit the Kingdom of God, if they do not renounce their possessions.

It was against these doctrines of Pelagius and Coelestius that Augustine wrote some of his most significant works, among which the following must be mentioned: *On the Spirit and the Letter, On Nature and Grace, On Original Sin.*[39] He also wrote several works against Julian of Eclanum, a second-generation Pelagian, and in these he further developed his doctrine of original sin, grace, and predestination.

Augustine's views on these matters soon evoked opposition, not only from those who were properly Pelagians, but also from others who were not willing to go as far as Augustine, and who have been given the rather inaccurate title of "semi-Pelagians." Since it would be impossible to understand the semi-Pelagian controversy without a previous exposition of Augustine's views on grace and predestination, that controversy will be postponed for the following chapter. Let it suffice to say here that opposition to Augustine's views centered in southern France,

---

[38] *De pecc. orig.* 11.
[39] These and others are listed by Portalié, *Guide to St. Augustine*, pp. 54-56.

and that its leader was John Cassian. Although most of this controversy took place after Augustine's death, he did write two treatises responding to the objections of the so-called semi-Pelagians: *On the Predestination of the Saints,* and *On the Gift of Perseverance.*

Besides the treatises written in connection with these controversies, four other works of Augustine merit special attention: *The Enchiridion,* the *Treatise on the Holy Trinity, The City of God,* and the *Retractations.*

The *Enchiridion,* written at the request of a friend who wished to have a handbook on the Christian faith, is a commentary on the Creed, the Lord's Prayer, and the Decalogue. It is the best short introduction to Augustine's theology.

The *Treatise on the Holy Trinity,* which took Augustine sixteen years to write, has been discussed in the first volume of this *History,*[40] while dealing with the development of trinitarian doctrine.

The City of God was inspired by the fall of Rome, and by the claims of some pagans that this catastrophe was due to the fact that Rome had forsaken her ancient gods in order to follow the Christian God. As an answer to such claims, Augustine developed his philosophy of history.

Finally, the *Retractations* were written toward the end of Augustine's life, when he reread each of his earlier writings, pointing out that on which he had changed his mind, as well as that which did not seem sufficiently clear. They are a most valuable document for establishing the chronology of Augustine's works, as well as for understanding his attitude toward theological inquiry.

Theory of Knowledge

We must now turn to the theology that Augustine developed as a result of his spiritual pilgrimage and of the various controversies in which he was involved. The best starting point for this task seems to be his theory of knowledge.

---

[40] Pp. 328-34.

With respect to knowledge, there were two problems with which Augustine was deeply concerned: whether it is possible and, if so, how it is acquired.

The question of the possibility of knowledge had been posed by the skeptical academics, whose position had once been a temptation to Augustine. It was for this reason that, almost immediately after his conversion, he wrote a treatise *Against the Academics*. Here he refutes the arguments of the skeptics showing that, even though all that our senses perceive be a mere appearance, we are at least certain that we perceive.[41] Furthermore, mathematical and purely rational truths apply even to the appearances themselves.[42] Finally, the doubt itself of the skeptics is their own refutation, for any who doubt know at least that they doubt.[43] Therefore, doubt is unacceptable as a general and absolute principle, and knowledge must be possible.

However, it does not suffice to refute those who deny the possibility of knowledge, for it is necessary to explain how knowledge is acquired. This question was much more difficult for Augustine since he was interested not in mere "scientia," or knowledge of sensible and perishable things, but rather in "sapientia," that is, the knowledge of eternal and immutable realities. Led by his readings of the Platonists, Augustine accepted the doctrine of an intelligible world in which eternal realities are to be found—except that Augustine saw these realities not as existing above the Creator, as Plato would, but rather as the eternal ideas in the divine mind. How then can these ideas be communicated to the human mind? The classical Platonic solution was to explain knowledge as a memory that the soul has of a previous existence. Augustine, however, could not accept this solution, for he was not willing to accept the theory of the pre-existence of souls.[44] Another

---

[41] *Contra acad.* 3. 11: "I do not see how an academic can refute one who says: I know that this seems white to me; I know that this pleases my ear; I know that I like this odor; I know that this feels sweet to my taste; I know that I feel this to be cold."

[42] *Ibid.*: "But that three times three are nine, and the square of intelligible numbers, is necessarily true, even if all of mankind is snoring."

[43] *De vera rel.* 39: "And if you do not understand what I say, and doubt it, then see if you are not certain that you are in doubt."

[44] In *On Free Will*, 1.12, the matter of the possible pre-existence of souls is left open. Later, in *On the Soul and Its Origin*, he rejects the idea that human souls are in this world because they have sinned in an earlier existence.

possibility would be to explain knowledge as an innate gift that God gives to souls at the moment of their creation. Perhaps Augustine was inclined to that solution for a period.[45] But his final and characteristic doctrine is that of illumination.

> And hence that noble philosopher Plato endeavored to persuade us that the souls of men lived even before they bare these bodies; and that hence those things which are learnt are rather remembered, as having been known already, than taken into knowledge as things new . . . . But we ought rather to believe, that the intellectual mind is so formed in its nature as to see those things, which by the disposition of the Creator are subjoined to things intelligible in a natural order, by a sort of incorporeal light of an unique kind; as the eye of the flesh sees things adjacent to itself in this bodily light, of which light is made to be receptive, and adapted to it.[46]

This is to say that, although the human mind is incapable of knowing eternal truths, be it by its own powers or through the data of the senses, it receives that knowledge by a direct illumination from God. This does not mean that the mind sees the eternal truths in the divine essence,[47] nor does it mean that God simply illumines those truths so that the mind may see them.[48] It is rather that God the Word places in the human mind the knowledge of ideas that exist eternally in God.[49]

This theory of illumination was characteristic of later Augustinian theology, and it is therefore necessary to point out one of the difficulties which it creates. This difficulty has to do with the Neoplatonic origin of the theory itself, and with the tension that is created when, instead of the Neoplatonic doctrine of emanations, one holds the doctrine of creation out of nothing. Plotinus taught that the soul, having its origin in an emanation of

---

[45] See *Soliloq.* 2. 19; *De quant. an.* 20.

[46] *De Trim.* 12. 15. 24 (*NPNF*, First Series, 3:164).

[47] Augustine has been interpreted in this manner by philosophers such as Malebranche, who claimed his authority in favor of the ontologist theory. However, Augustine himself denies the possibility of contemplating the essence of God.

[48] An interpretation found in F. Copleston, *A History of Philosophy*, II (Westminister, Md.: The Newman Press, 1957), 62-67.

[49] See Portalié, *Guide to St. Augustine*, pp. 110-14.

the divine essence, is itself divine. Thus, there is no difficulty in supposing that the soul can somehow share in the eternal ideas. But when one supposes, as did Augustine, that the soul is a creature, and that knowledge must be grounded on the ideas that exist eternally in the mind of God, the question arises how the created soul can possess a divine truth.[50]

God

Augustine's understanding of truth led him directly to the existence of God. Although he did on occasion appeal to other arguments, Augustine usually dwelt on the proof of the existence of God on the basis of the existence of truth.[51] According to this argument, our human mind perceives immutable truths that we can neither change nor doubt, and whose existence leads us to the certainty that there must be a perfect truth, one that neither our mind nor all the minds in the universe can have created. This absolute truth, or rather, the foundation of all truth, is God.[52]

Obviously, this proof of the existence of God is valid only within the platonic presupposition on which it is grounded.[53] In this argument, it is necessary to move from the ideal to the real, a step that can be taken only within a philosophical framework that, like Platonism, holds the objective reality of the ideal world.

[50] É. Gilson, *The Christian Philosophy of St. Augustine* (New York: Random House, 1960), pp. 105-11. Cf. T. Alesanco, "Metafísica y gnoseología del mundo inteligible según San Agustín: En torno a la teoría agustiniana de la iluminación," *Aug*, 13 (1968), 9-36.

[51] The best study of this subject is that of F. Cayré, *Dieu présent dans la vie de l'esprit* (Bruges: Desclée de Brouwer, 1951). According to Cayré, Augustine's proofs of the existence of God have seven main points of departure: universal consensus, the order of the world, the beauty of the world, the degrees of perfection in beings, the mutability of creatures, the longing of the human soul for beauty, and above all, the need to posit a perfect truth that exists above the human mind. Previously, the proof of the divine existence on the basis of the various degrees of perfection in creatures had been studied by Charles Boyer, "La preuve de Dieu augustinienne," *ArchPh*, 7 (1930), 357-95, and by M. Bordoy Torrents, "Antecedentes del argumento henológico en las obras de San Agustín," *CD*, 153 (1941), 257-70. Another article by Boyer, "L'existenza di Dio secondo S. Agostino," *RFilNSc*, 46 (1954), 321-31, discusses Augustine's arguments starting from the need for a superior truth, and from the need for a source of all happiness. In the works of Augustine himself, the best text for an introduction to his argument starting from truth is *De lib. arb.* 2.1-15.

[52] *De lib. arb.* 2.15.

[53] Such is the thesis of J. Hessen, *Augustinus Metaphysik der Erkenntnis* (Berlin: F. Dümmler, 1931) and of B. Kaelin, "St. Augustin und die Erkenntnis der Existenz Gottes," *DivThom*, 14 (1936), 331-52. This is the crucial difference between Augustine and Thomas on this point, as is shown by J. Barion, *Plotin und Augustinus: Untersuchungen zum Gottesproblem* (Berlin: Junker und Dünnhaupt, 1935).

But one should also add that Augustine's purpose is not to "prove" the existence of God in the strict sense, but rather to show that, limited and contingent beings that we are, we fall into absurdity if we do not affirm the existence above ourselves of an infinite and necessary reality.[54] The existence of God is thus an inescapable and manifest reality.[55]

This God is eternal, transcendent, infinite, and perfect. As the supreme light, it is through God that all knowledge takes place. As the supreme good, God is the goal toward which the human will must strive. However, of all that can be said about God, that which most attracts Augustine is that God is triune, which will not be discussed here because logical necessity has led us to discuss it in the first volume of this *History*.[56]

Creation

This triune God is the creator of all that exists. God has made the universe *out of nothing,* and not out of the divine substance or out of an eternal matter. If God had made the universe out of the divine substance, the result would be divine, and would not be a true creation.[57] But, on the other hand, God did not make the world out of the so-called amorphous matter that some philosophers claimed existed from all eternity. That matter itself is created by God out of nothing. Scripture refers to this matter when it says that the earth was "without form and void." Yet, God did not make matter first and form later, but rather created them simultaneously.[58]

In creating the world, God knew beforehand all that was to be made. This was not merely because God foresaw all of creation, but also because all things have existed eternally in the divine

---

[54] See F. Casado, "El ser (Dios) y el ser-no-ser (criatura) en la metafísica agustiniana," *CD,* 170 (1957), 5-18.

[55] See Portalié, *Guide to St. Augustine,* p. 125.

[56] Pp. 328-34.

[57] *Conf.* 13.7 (trans. Pilkington, p. 232): "For Thou didst create heaven and earth, not out of Thyself, for then they would be equal to Thine Only-begotten, and thereby even to Thee; and in no wise would it be right that anything should be equal to Thee which was not of Thee . . . . therefore, out of nothing didst Thou create heaven and earth."

[58] *De Gen. ad litt.* 1. 15: "Amorphous matter is not prior in time to things formed. Both the matter of which things were made, and the things that were made, were created at the same time."

mind. This is Augustine's "exemplarism," whose roots are to be found in Plotinus, but which is, however, very different from the doctrine of that philosopher—a difference that shows that Augustine was aware of the distance between Christianity and pagan philosophy. According to Plotinus, the exemplary ideas were the cause of the origin of the world as an emanation from the One. According to the Christian bishop these ideas are found in the Word—the second person of the Trinity—and they result in the origin of creatures only through a free decision on the part of God.[59]

As to the order of creation, Augustine asked himself whether all things were made at once (Ecclesiasticus 18:1) or were created rather in successive stages (Genesis 1).[60] In order to solve this problem, he introduced the idea of "seminal (or causal) reasons," taken, although with great variations, from the Stoic and Neoplatonic tradition.[61] These seminal reasons are the principles of development which God created since the first day of creation, but which would only mature later, when each would produce the first member—or members—of a species, which would then reproduce by its own natural means. Therefore, God made all things on the very first day, but they were not manifested in the various species until a later time, as Genesis says.[62] In any case, the six days of creation are not to be taken literally, for at the beginning there was no sun or other heavenly bodies that could serve to determine the days and the nights. As to the exact meaning of such days, Augustine offered several symbolic interpretations, which we cannot discuss here.[63]

---

[59] O. Perler, Der Nus bei Plotin und das Verbum bei Augustinus als vorbildliche Ursache der Welt: Vergleichende Untersuchung (Fribourg: Studia Friburgensia, 1931), passim.

[60] Copleston, History, 2:76-77.

[61] On the origin of this theory, see F.J. Thonnard, "Razones seminales y formas substaciales," Sap, 6 (1951), 47-57. On the general scope of this doctrine, see J. M. Brady, "St. Augustine's Theory of Seminal Reasons," NSch, 38 (1964), 141-58.

[62] In spite of several modern attempts to claim an affinity between this doctrine and the theory of evolution, there is a great distance between them. Augustine taught not that some species had evolved out of others, but that God created each species as it is now, through seminal reasons. See A. Coccia, La Creazione simultanea secondo S. Agostino (Rome: Tipografia delle Mantellate, 1948); J. de Blic, "Le processus de la création d'après S. Augustin," in Mélanges offerts au R.P. Ferdinand Cavallera (Toulouse: Institut Catholique, 1948), pp. 179-89.

[63] See Portalié, Guide to St. Augustine, p. 142.

Time

The doctrine of creation leads directly to the question of the nature of time,[64] as Augustine himself pointed out in his *Confessions*.[65] This is not a purely metaphysical question, but rather an existential issue, for it is in time that the Eternal comes to us.[66] "For him it was a matter of the relationship between eternity and time, of the possibility of a beginning of time, of the possibility of creation."[67]

The problem posed is, first, that of time itself, and, second, that of the relationship between time and creation. As to the first, Augustine affirmed that time is a "distention" of the soul according to its various faculties. The past as mere past no longer exists, but is still given to us now in that "present of the past" which is *memory*. The future does not yet exist, but is given to us in that "present of the future" which is *expectation*. Only the present is offered directly to *vision*. All other times are known to us as they are *present* in our soul—the past as memory, and the future as expectation.

As to the relationship between time and creation, the issue is whether God created time or not. Augustine believed that only the first of these alternatives is feasible, for otherwise it would be necessary to declare that not only God, but time also, is eternal.

> For whence could innumerable ages pass by which Thou didst not make, since Thou are the Author and Creator of all ages? Or what times should those be which were not made by Thee? Or how should they pass by if they had not been? Since, therefore, Thou art the Creator of all times, if any time was before Thou madest heaven and earth, why is it said that

---

[64] There is a good bibliography on the subject in R. Flórez, *Las dos dimensiones del hombre augustiniano* (Madrid: Ediciones Religión y Cultura, 1958), p. 122, n. 1. The most significant entry in that bibliography is J. Guitton, *Le temps et l'éternité chez Plotin et saint Augustin* (Paris: Bovin, 1933). The following titles should be added to that bibliography: W. Verwiebe, *Welt und Zeit bei Augustin* (Leipzig: F. Meiner, 1933); J. Chaix-Ruy *Saint Augustin: Temps et histoire* (Paris: Études augustiniennes, 1956); J. MacQuinn, *The Concept of Time in St. Augustine* (Washington: Catholic University, 1969).

[65] *Conf.* 11. 12.

[66] According to J. Chaix-Ruy, "Le problème de temps dans les Confessions et dans la Cité de Dieu," GM, 9 (1954), 431-40, Augustine poses the question of time psychologically in the *Confessions* and ontologically in the *City of God*.

[67] Flórez, *Dimensiones*, p. 124.

Thou didst refrain from working? For that very time Thou madest, nor could times pass by before Thou madest times.[68]

Evil

Another question that the doctrine of creation poses is that of evil.[69] This issue was especially significant for Augustine because the doctrine of evil which the Manichees proposed was wholly unacceptable to him. They affirmed an absolute dualism in which two equally eternal principles—Light and Darkness—struggled with each other. Augustine rejected this theory because it contradicted Christian monotheism, as well as because it was irrational. In fact, Manichaean dualism attributes evils to the principle of good—such as that of being subject to the attacks of evil—and good to the principle of evil—such as that of existing and being powerful. Any absolute dualism—that is to say, any dualism that takes as its starting point the existence of two eternally antagonistic principles, will necessarily fall into absurdity. Therefore, it is necessary to affirm that all that exists comes from God.

> All life both great and small, all power great and small, all safety great and small, all memory great and small, all virtue great and small, all intellect great and small, all tranquillity great and small, all plenty great and small, all sensation great and small, all light great and small, all suavity great and small, all measure great and small, all beauty great and small, all peace great and small, and whatever other like things may occur, especially such as are found throughout all things, whether spiritual or corporeal, every measure, every form, every order both great and small, are from the Lord God.[70]

What then can be said of evil? Evil is not a nature; it is not "something"; it is not a creature. Evil is only a negation of good.

---

[68] *Conf.* 11. 13 (trans. Pilkington, p. 214).
[69] V. Capanaga, "En torno a la filosofía agustiniana: Teología de la acción: El mal en el mundo," *RelCult*, 19 (1932), 5-17; R. Jolivet, "Le problème du mal chez saint Augustín," *ArchPh*, 7 (1930), 253-356; S. Alvarez Turienzo, "Entre maniqueos y pelagianos: Iniciación al problema del mal en san Augustín," *CD*, 166 (1954), 87-125; A. Escher di Stefano, *Il manicheismo in S. Agostino* (Padua: A. Milani, 1960).
[70] *De nat. boni* 13 (*NPNF*, First Series, 4:353).

All that exists is good, for there is a certain "measure, beauty and order"—*modus, species et ordo*—in everything.[71] Those things which are "better" are such only because they enjoy these attributes to a greater degree. Those which we call "worse" are such only because they do not enjoy the same degree of goodness. But they are all truly good, for all have been created by God and all have at least the good of existence. A monkey, for instance, is not "beautiful," relatively speaking, for we compare its beauty to that of other beings who have a greater degree of it. But in the exact and correct sense, a monkey is indeed beautiful, even if it be only with that beauty which is proper to its own kind of creature.[72] Every nature, by the mere fact of being a nature, is good.

In spite of this, evil is not a fiction of the intellect, but is an undeniable and inescapable reality. Evil is not a nature, but is rather the corruption of nature. As a thing, as a substance, evil does not exist; but it does exist as a lack of goodness. At this point, Augustine followed the lead of Neoplatonism, for which evil consisted not in another reality besides the One, but simply in withdrawing from the One.

Free Will

Whence does evil spring? It springs from the free will of certain creatures to whom God has given a rational nature. Among these creatures are the angels, some of whom have fallen and are now called demons. And among them is also the human creature, who has been given free will and has used it for evil.

Here again, Augustine felt compelled to refute the Manichees, who claimed that the good that there is in us will always act rightly, while the evil will always do evil. Augustine, on the other hand, claimed that there is no such thing as a naturally evil being. All being is created by God and is good. Evil is a corruption of the good, and its origin must be attributed to a being that is good in itself, but that is capable of doing evil. Only thus can one claim

[71] *Ibid.*, 3.
[72] *Ibid.*

that God is the creator of all things, but is not the author of evil.[73] Therefore, Augustine taught that God gave free will to Adam and to the angels. This free will is good, for it comes from God and is one of the characteristics of a truly rational being. But it is an "intermediate" good,[74] for it can decide to do what is good as well as that which is evil. However, let it be stated clearly, free will is what makes us truly human and is in no way evil in itself, but is rather a good gift of God which is capable of turning to evil.

> If man is good, and if he would not be able to act rightly except by willing to do so, he ought to have free will because without it he would not be able to act rightly. Because he also sins through having free will, we are not to believe that God gave it to him for that purpose. It is, therefore, a sufficient reason why he ought to have been given it, that without it man could not live aright.[75]

What then makes the will move away from the good? No matter how irrational this may seem, there is only one possible answer: the will itself. The nature of the will is such that one has to say that it itself, and not some extraneous agent or factor, originates its own decisions.

> But what cause of willing can there be which is prior to willing? Either it is a will, in which case we have not got beyond the root of evil will. Or it is not a will, and in that case there is no sin in it. Either, then, will is itself the first cause of sin, or the first cause is without sin. Now sin is rightly imputed only to that which sins, nor is it rightly imputed unless it sins voluntarily.[76]

Original Sin and Fallen Human Nature

One must point out, however, that what has been said about the will is strictly true only before the fall,[77] for that occurrence in such a way affected the totality of Adam's descent that it is no longer possible to speak of a total freedom of the will. It is

---

[73] *De lib. arb.* 1. 2.
[74] *Ibid.,* 2. 19.
[75] *Ibid.,* 2. 1 (*LCC*, 6:135).
[76] *Ibid.,* 3. 17 (LCC, 6:200).
[77] *Ibid.,* 3. 18.

important to note this point because many interpreters of Augustine—even as early as the fourth century—have claimed that he contradicted himself by asserting free will when combating the Manichees, and denying it when opposing the Pelagians.[78]

Augustine accepted and developed the understanding of original sin as an inheritance that Adam bequeathed to his descendants. Such an interpretation of the text which claims that "in Adam all die" is certainly not the only one that has appeared in the history of Christian thought; but it is the one that, from Tertullian on,[79] became more and more common in Latin theology. This was due in a large measure to Augustine's support of it.

Before the fall, Adam enjoyed several gifts, among which was that free will we have described which gave him the power not to sin (*posse non peccare*) as well as the power to sin (*posse peccare*). Adam did not have the complete gift of perseverance, that is, of being unable to sin (*non posse peccare*), but he did have the gift of being able to persevere in the good, the power not to sin.[80]

But the fall came to change matters. Adam's sin was his pride and unbelief, which led him to make an evil use of the good tree that God had planted in the garden.[81] As a consequence of that sin Adam lost the possibility of living forever, his special knowledge, and his power not to sin. After the fall, he was still free, but he had lost the gift of grace which enabled him not to sin and was free only to sin.

By reason of the inheritance of Adam, all human beings are by nature in the same situation as their first forefather. Following a tradition that begins with Tertullian, Augustine affirms that

---

[78] It would be impossible to give here even a brief summary of the various ways in which the relationship between free will and predestination in Augustine's theology has been interpreted. In the following books and articles, however, the main lines of interpretation may be found: E. Tummers, "Augustinus en de vrije wil," *Studiën*, 113 (1930), 339-52; G. Capone-Braga, *La concezione agostiniana della libertà* (Padua: A. Draghi, 1931) G. Vranken, *Der göttliche Konkurs zum freien Willensakt des Menschen beim hl. Augustinus* (Rome: Herder, 1943); J. Ball, "Libre arbitre et liberté dans S. Augustin," *AnnTb*, 6 (1945), 368-82; E. Bailleux, "La liberté augustinienne et la grace," *MSR*, 19 (1963), 30-48; M. Huftier, "Libre arbitre, liberté et péché chez saint Augustin," *RThAM*, 33 (1966), 187-281.

[79] See Vol. I of this *History*, p. 183.

[80] *De correp. et grat.* 12.

[81] *De Gen. ad litt.* 11.5; *De nat. boni* 35.

original sin is transmitted as an inheritance to all the descendants of Adam.[82] But this then poses new difficulties, for the bishop of Hippo was not willing to accept the Stoic materialism that was implied by Tertullian's doctrine,[83] and that had led that earlier Carthaginian theologian to speak of the transmission of the soul—and therefore of sin—as similar to the manner in which the physical characteristics of the parents are transmitted to their children. For this reason, Augustine was inclined to reject "traducianism"—the doctrine that the soul is transmitted from parents to children—and to uphold "creationism"—the doctrine that God directly creates a soul for each individual. On the other hand, the difficulties that creationism posed for an understanding of original sin led Augustine back to traducianism. On this point, he remained hesitant throughout his life.[84]

The result of original sin, which envelops us in such a way that we are a "mass of damnation," is that we are subject to death, ignorance, and concupiscence.[85] The latter is not to be simply identified with sexual desires, although these, in their actual form, are the clearest example of the lordship of concupiscence over human nature. Concupiscence is that power which leads us from the contemplation of the supreme God to the contemplation of inferior and transitory realities. The sexual act has upon it the seal of concupiscence because fallen man is incapable of performing it without turning his gaze from the creator to the creature.[86] Strictly speaking, concupiscence is not sin, although it may be called such because it springs from original sin and is at the root of every actual sin.[87]

---

[82] *Ench.* 35.

[83] *De Gen. ad litt.* 10.25.

[84] The list of pertinent texts may be found in Portalié, *Guide to St. Augustine*, pp. 150-51. See also M. F. Sciacca, "L'origine dell'anima seconde Saint'Agostino," *GM*, 9 (1954), 542-50. This article tries to develop an intermediate position to explain the seeming hesitation of Augustine. C. Riva, "Creazioniste e traducionista, S. Agostino?" *RRosm*, 50 (1956), 1-5, rightly rejects Sciacca's thesis. See also G. J. P. O'Daly, "Augustine on the Origin of Souls," in H. D. Blume and F. Mann, eds., *Platonismus und Christentum: Festschrift für Heinrich Dörries* (Münster: Aschendorff, 1983), pp. 184-91.

[85] *Ench.* 24-25. Ignorance and concupiscence are the common lot of fallen humans and demons, but death does not rule over the latter.

[86] *De grat. Christi et pecc. orig.* 2.34. That in this passage Augustine does not take into account the physiological differences between men and women is an indication of the degree to which he considers the male normative.

[87] *De div. quaest. ad Simpl.* 1. 1. 10.

In summary, fallen human nature is free only to sin. "Thus, we always enjoy a free will; but this will is not always good."[88] This does not mean that freedom has lost its meaning, as though we were only able to choose a particular sinful alternative. On the contrary, we have true freedom to choose between several alternatives, although, given our condition as sinners subject to concupiscence, and as members of this "mass of damnation," all the alternatives that are really open to us are sin. The option not to sin does not exist. This is what is meant by saying that fallen human nature has freedom to sin (*posse peccare*) but does not have freedom not to sin (*nonposse non peccare*).

Grace and Predestination

If all that we can do is sinful, how are we to take the step that will lead us from our present state to that of the redeemed, especially if one takes into account the fact that such a step cannot be called sin? The answer is inescapable: by ourselves, we cannot take such a step. This was the focal point of Augustine's polemic against the Pelagians, as well as of his doctrines on grace and predestination.[89]

Augustine's starting point on this matter is that we can do no true good without the help of grace. Adam could do good because he had that help; but he lost it through his sin and thus became a subject of evil. All his descendants come into the world under the bondage of sin and are therefore incapable of doing true good. Our will is twisted in such a way that it is free only to sin. Therefore, in order to enable us to take the step that will lead us from our present state to that of salvation it is necessary that grace act in us. Only through that grace is conversion possible. Without it, we cannot and will not approach God. Furthermore, it is grace that, after conversion, continues enabling the Christian to do good works.

---

[88] *De grat. et lib. arb.* 15.
[89] Bibliographical material on this subject is abundant. Two works, however, merit special mention: G. Nygren, *Das Prädestinationsproblem in der Theologie Augustins* (Göttingen: Vandenhoeck & Ruprecht, 1956), and J. Chêne, *Théologie de saint Augustin: Grâce et prédestination* (Le Puy: Mappus, 1962).

He operates, therefore, without us, in order that we may will; but when we will, and so will that we may act, He co-operates with us. We can, however, ourselves do nothing to effect good works of piety without Him either working that we may will, or co-working when we will.[90]

Grace is irresistible. It is inconceivable for the will to reject that grace which is given to it, for grace acts in the will, leading it to will the good. This does not mean that Augustine has forgotten or forsaken his defense of free will, for grace does not oppose freedom. Grace does not force us to make a decision against our own will. It is rather that God, through grace, boosts the will, strengthens and stimulates it, so that the will itself, without any coercion, will desire the good. We do not save ourselves, nor are we saved against our will. "Neither the grace of God alone, nor he alone, but the grace of God with him."[91] Grace moves the will, but only through a "soft-violence" that acts in such a way that the will agrees with it.[92]

On the other hand, the fact that one has received the first grace—which, as will be shown later on, comes with baptism—does not mean that one has already achieved the final crown. It is necessary to remain faithful unto death, and this is possible only through the gift of perseverance, which is also a result of grace and does not depend on human merits.[93] Thus, salvation is from beginning to end a work of grace.

This immediately poses the question of predestination.[94] If salvation is only possible through grace, and if that grace does not depend on any merit on the part of the one who receives it, it follows that it is God, through sovereign freedom and action, who decides who is to receive that unmerited gift. The Augustinian doctrine of predestination springs not from speculative considerations regarding the divine omniscience or

---

[90] *De grat. et lib. arb.* 17 (*NPNF*, First Series, 5:458).
[91] *Ibid.*, 5.
[92] *Sermo* 131.
[93] *De dono persev.* 1.
[94] In truth, Augustine's doctrine of predestination stems not only from logical necessity out of his doctrine of grace, but also and foremost from the experience of his conversion and from biblical exegesis. Thus, the logical order followed in this exposition should not give the impression that Augustine was an abstract thinker who was more interested in logical rigor than in existential truth.

omnipotence, but rather from soteriological and existential considerations, in attempting to affirm that human salvation is the unmerited result of God's love.

According to Augustine, the predestination of some to salvation is an undeniable fact, although it is at the same time an inescapable mystery. This predestination is such that the number of the elect is fixed; no matter how much the church grows, the number of those who are to enter the kingdom will always remain the same.[95] On the other hand, God does not predestine any to sin or to damnation. The elect are pulled out of this "mass of damnation" which is humanity through a sovereign act of God, who has predestined them for salvation. Those who are condemned simply continue existing within this "mass" not because God had decreed that it will be so, but by reason of their own sins. Thus, the doctrine of Augustine is not an attempt to conciliate the divine omniscience with human freedom, but an attempt to testify to the absolute primacy of God in human salvation.

The Augustinian system of grace and predestination has led to long controversies—of which the first began during Augustine's lifetime, as will be seen in the following chapter. It is not possible to discuss here each of these controversies, which will be discussed in their proper places within this *History*. One must point out, however, that the Protestant Reformers of the sixteenth century thought that the bishop of Hippo was a forerunner of their doctrine. In this they were partly right and partly wrong. There is no doubt that Augustine's emphasis on the priority of divine action in human salvation, and a great deal of his doctrine of predestination, agree with the theology of the Reformers. It is also true that Augustine stressed the priority of faith over works.[96] On the other hand, however, Augustine differed from the Reformers inasmuch as he did believe that merit had an important and necessary place in salvation. Although grace is not given according to merits, it does operate in us in such a way that we are enabled to perform good works whose merits will lead us to our final salvation.[97]

---

[95] *Sermones* 111, 251; *De correp. et grat.* 13.

[96] *De grat. et lib. arb.* 7.

[97] *Ibid.*, 2.

Finally, one must point out that Augustine understood grace as a divine power or fluid that is infused into us. For him, grace is no longer an attitude on God's part, but rather the manner in which God acts in us. This understanding of grace would have two important consequences in the development of medieval theology. First the question is posed of the relationship between grace and the Holy Spirit, for grace conceived as a divine power in us seems to take over some of the functions that were traditionally ascribed to the Holy Spirit. Second, and partly as an attempt to solve some of the problems posed by Augustine's doctrine of grace and predestination, a system of grace was developed in which various types of grace were distinguished and classified, thus introducing a rigidity that was not present in Augustine's theology.

The Church

Divine grace comes to each of us through Jesus Christ, in the communion of the church, through the sacraments. Augustine's influence in the development of Western Christology has already been discussed in the first volume of this *History*.[98] Therefore, we must now turn to his ecclesiology, and then to his doctrine regarding sacraments.

We have already pointed out that Augustine's ecclesiology[99] took shape over against the Donatist schism. Slightly earlier, Bishop Optatus of Milevis had written *Seven Books on the Donatist Schism*, where he not only attacked the history and practices of Donatists, but also devoted a large section of his second book to expounding the nature of the true Catholic Church. To this end, Optatus developed two main arguments that showed that the true church was that which the Donatists rejected: the argument of the diffusion of the church throughout all the earth,[100] and that of the apostolic succession, which the Bishop of Rome has received from St. Peter, "the head of all apostles."[101]

---

[98] P. 337.
[99] The best study that I know on the subject is that of F. Hofmann, *Der Kirchenbegriff des hl. Augustinus in seiner Entwicklung* (Munich: M. Hueber, 1933).
[100] *De schis. Donat.* 2. 1.
[101] *Ibid.*, 2. 1-4.

Basically, Augustine followed Optatus and, to a certain extent, Cyprian. He saw the catholicity of the church as consisting fundamentally in its presence throughout all the earth.[102] Unity is the bond of love which ties all those who belong to this single body of Christ; where there is no love, there is no unity; but it is also true that where there is no unity there is no love and therefore no church.[103] The apostolicity of the church is based on the apostolic succession of bishops, epitomized in Rome, where it is possible to point to an uninterrupted succession beginning with Peter, "a type of the entire church."[104] As to holiness, Augustine agrees with Cyprian that it is impossible in this life to separate the wheat from the tares. The church is holy, not because all its members lead a life free of sin, but because it will be perfected in holiness at the end of time. Meanwhile, it is a "mixed body" in which tares grow amidst the good grain, so that not even the elect are totally free of sin.[105]

This leads us to the distinction between the church visible and the church invisible. Some interpreters of Augustine have stressed this distinction to such a point that they lose sight of the importance that he gave to the institutional, hierarchical, and visible church.[106] When Augustine speaks of the church he usually refers to this earthly institution or mixed body. God gathers in this body those who are to be saved. Through its sacraments, the elect are nourished in the faith. But in spite of all this it is still true that this earthly church does not coincide exactly with the body of the elect—with the heavenly church of the consummation. There is still chaff in it, and there are still a number of the elect who have not been led to it. Hence the idea of an "invisible church," which helps to understand Augustinian ecclesiology, but which must not be exaggerated if one is properly to understand that ecclesiology.

---

[102] *De unitate eccl.* 3. (A work of doubtful authorship, although certainly Augustinian in its theology.)
[103] *Ibid.*, 4.
[104] *Ep.* 53. 1.
[105] *Sermo* 88. 19.
[106] The importance of the visible, priestly organization for Augustine is clearly shown by D. Zahringer, *Das kirchliche Priestertum nach dem heiligen Augustinus* (Paderborn: F. Schöningh, 1931).

The Sacraments

Augustine's sacramental theory is characterized by the fluidity that appeared in earlier theologians, and that would not disappear before the classifications and distinctions of the scholastics. Augustine did not hesitate to apply the title of "sacrament" to a variety of rites and practices, although he was inclined to use that same term, in a more precise sense, to refer specifically to baptism and the eucharist.[107] It is these two sacraments which will be discussed here, although under this heading several other practices of the church could have been included—some that later received the official title of "sacrament" and some that never did.

Augustine was led to discuss baptism within the double context of Donatism and Pelagianism. The Pelagians believed that infants had no need of baptism, for they had no sin. However, they could be baptized as a "help" to overcome the works of the flesh.[108] The Donatists claimed that only within their church was baptism valid, and based this claim on the authority of Cyprian.[109]

Once again at this point Augustine could draw from Optatus, who in his *Seven Books on the Donatist Schism* had posed the question of the validity of baptism outside the communion of the church, as well as the vital question of the validity of that sacrament when administered by an unworthy person. As to the last question, Optatus affirmed that the sacrament has validity in itself, in spite of the possible unworthiness of the person offering it. In baptism there is the intervention of the Divine Trinity, of the recipient, and of the person administering it. The first two are necessary, but the validity of the rite cannot be said to depend on the third, "for it is God that washes and not man."[110] But on the other hand, the validity of the sacrament does depend on the community in which it takes place, for when it is offered among the schismatics it works not for salvation, but for

---

[107] C. Couturier, "*Sacramentum* et *mysterium* dans l'oeuvre de saint Augustin," in H. Rondet *et al.*, *Études augustiniennes* (Paris: F. Aubier, 1953), pp. 161-332.

[108] De Plinval, *Pélage*, p. 241.

[109] See Vol. I of this *History*, pp. 247-48.

[110] *De schis. Donat.* 5. 4.

condemnation.[111] In any case, the repetition of baptism would deny the uniqueness of the faith, of Christ, and of God.[112]

Augustine agreed with Optatus regarding the validity of the sacrament even in spite of the moral defects of the person administering it.[113] This was necessary to refute the argument of the Donatists, who claimed that, since only they had remained steadfast in persecution, only they had the true sacraments. But, because of his irenic spirit and of his pastoral interest in attracting rather than overwhelming the Donatists, Augustine was ready to depart from Optatus in granting a certain validity to sacraments celebrated among the schismatics. The schismatics do have the sacrament, but do not benefit from it in justice and love.[114] This is why heretics and schismatics returning to the church are not to be rebaptized, but only to submit to the imposition of hands so that they may receive the bond of unity which they did not have because of the irregular nature of their baptism. Thus, Augustine distinguished between the validity and the regularity of the sacrament.

Augustine's eucharistic doctrine has been variously interpreted. These various interpretations are often due to attempts to read Augustine through the lens of later definitions and controversies;[115] but some are also due to the various manners in which Augustine referred to the presence of Christ in the eucharist.[116] There is no doubt that there is a certain ambiguity in his thought at this point. But this ambiguity cannot be solved by an easy attempt at conciliation on the basis of a particular modern understanding of the eucharist. One must rather say that two opposed tendencies are struggling in Augustine: the

---

[111] *Ibid.*, 5. 3.

[112] *Ibid.*: "If you give another baptism, you give another faith; if you give another faith, you give another Christ; if you give another Christ, you give another God."

[113] *Sermo* 99.13.

[114] See Willis, *Saint Augustine*, pp. 154-60; J. P. Keleher, *Saint Augustine's Notion of Schism in the Donatist Controversy* (Mundelein, Illinois: Saint Mary of the Lake Seminary, 1961); E. Lamirande, *La situation ecclésiologique des Donatistes d'après saint Augustin* (Ottawa: Éditions de l'Université, 1972).

[115] A. von Harnack, *HD*, 5:159, illustrates the spiritualist interpretation; the opposite is true of Portalié, *Guide to St. Augustine*, pp. 247-60. A more balanced view may be found in K. Adam, "Zur Eucharistielehre des hl. Augustinus," *TQ*, 112 (1931), 490-535. See also: L. J. Van der Lof, "Eucharistie et présence réelle selon S. Augustin," *RevEtAug*, 10 (1964), 295-304.

[116] J. N. D. Kelly, *Early Christian Doctrines*, 2nd ed. (London: A & C. Black, 1960), pp. 447-49, makes this point very well by contrasting various texts from Augustine's works.

eucharistic realism that was becoming more and more general, and the Neoplatonic spiritualism that earlier had led Origen and others to interpret the eucharist in spiritualistic terms. Another possibility would be to say that Augustine believes that the person who partakes of communion really receives the body and the blood of Christ, not in the sense of physically eating them, but rather in the sense that, by eating the elements of bread and wine, one becomes a partaker of the body and blood of Christ.

The Meaning of History

The church that nurtures its believers through the sacraments is not yet in heaven, but struggles and lives as a pilgrim within historical events. The fall of Rome in A.D. 410, which shook the Mediterranean world, led Augustine to think and write on the meaning of history. This is the purpose of his work *The City of God*, whose subtitle is "Against the Pagans." Here Augustine distinguishes between two "cities" or societies, each led by a different impulse.

> Accordingly, two cities have been formed by two loves: the earthly by the love of self, even to the contempt of God; the heavenly by the love of God, even to the contempt of self. The former, in a word, glories in itself, the latter in the Lord. For the one seeks glory from men; but the greatest glory of the other is God, the witness of conscience. The one lifts up its head in its own glory; the other says to its God, "Thou art my glory, and the lifter up of mine head." In the one, the princes and the nations it subdues are ruled by the love of ruling; in the other, the princes and the subjects serve one another in love, the latter obeying, while the former take thought for all. The one delights in its own strength, represented in the persons of its rulers; the other says to its God, "I will love Thee, O Lord, my strength."[117]

Quite obviously, these loves, and the two cities that spring from them, are incompatible. And yet, in the period that goes from the initial fall to the final consummation of history, the

---

[117] *De civ. Dei* 14. 28 (*NPNF*, First Series, 2-282-83).

heavenly city exists upon this earth in such a way that "these two cities are confused and mingled among themselves in this world, until the final judgment separates them."[118] Meanwhile, the city that rebels against God, as well as the one that obeys and loves God, continues its historical course, and the final result will be the condemnation of the first and the salvation of the latter.

What can one say, then, regarding the course of the history of nations? What of the fall of Rome, which some pagans blame on the abandonment of the ancient gods? The answer follows from Augustine's premises: Rome and other empires, as expressions of the earthly city, had to succumb. If they once became great and powerful, this was only because God so willed it. In the case of Rome, God gave her her lordship so that there would be the necessary peace for the propagation of the gospel, but once that historical mission was accomplished Rome fell as a result of her own sin and idolatry. This has been and will always be the destiny of all human empires, until the end of time. Therefore, meaning may be found in history by reflecting upon the manner in which the sin of the earthly city is always visited by God, but it may be found above all in the eternal destiny of the city of God.

Eschatology

Augustine's eschatology is rather traditional, although there are in it some problems of interpretation which are probably due to the fact that the bishop of Hippo did not claim to be as certain of some inscrutable matters as some later Christians have been. His eschatology is always presented within a veil of mystery, so that his views rarely claim to be more than mere human opinions. Thus, for instance, Augustine speaks of a fire in which those who die without being ready to enter the glory of God make expiation for their sins. There is no doubt that he refers here to what is usually called "purgatory." But his references to such a possibility are always vague and hesitant, so that later

---

[118] *Ibid.*, 1. 25. See also: M. F. Sciacca, *Interpretazione del concetto di storia di S. Agostino* (Tolentino: Edizione agostiniane, 1960); D. X. Burt, "St. Augustine's Evaluation of Civil Society," *Augm*, 3 (1963), 87-94; J. Lamotte, "But et adversaires de saint Augustin dans le 'De civitate Dei'," *Auga*, 11 (1961), 434-69.

interpreters have found texts that seem to imply various different views of that purifying fire. The same may be said regarding the vision of God which the redeemed enjoy, regarding the place where the souls of the dead are awaiting the final resurrection, and in general regarding several aspects of Augustinian eschatology.[119] It is the sign of a great theologian to know where the boundaries of mystery lie.

We thus come to the end of our brief introduction to Augustine's theology. That theology was to such an extent responsive to the needs of human existence as well as to the requirements of the human mind that for centuries, and even to this day, Augustine has been, after Paul, the most influential thinker in the history of Christian thought.

---

[119] Although he plays down the hesitation and imprecision of Augustine's eschatology, Portalié, *Guide to St. Augustine,* pp. 290-304, does include several texts that prove this point. See also P. Jay, "Saint Augustin et la doctrine de purgatoire," *RThAM,* 36 (1969), 17-30.

II

Western Theology After Augustine

At the moment of Augustine's death, the Vandal armies were besieging the city of Hippo. Two decades earlier the world had been shaken by the news of the fall of Rome. These were only two symptoms of a radical change in the political, social, economic, and religious configuration of the western Mediterranean. The ancient empire now belonged to the past, and its place was taken by a variety of barbarian kingdoms—although many of these still considered themselves subjects of the Roman Empire.

The new circumstances profoundly affected the life of the church. It was now necessary to undertake the conversion of the pagan invaders. Those among the barbarians who were not pagans were Arians, and thus a theological question that seemed to have been already settled was posed once again. In the midst of the confusion of the times, original thought was not likely to flourish. Theology became a matter of compilation and commentary rather than of reflection and adventure. Thus, it was a time of lesser lights. And yet, these lesser lights were taking the first steps toward what would later be the great achievements of medieval theology.[1]

---

[1] G. Bardy, "Lettrés chrétiens et civilization romaine à l'aube du moyen âge," *AnnTh*, 3 (1942), 424-62.

Controversies over Augustine's Theology: Grace and Predestination

As was to be expected, Augustinian theology did not immediately become generally accepted, but was rather the occasion for long controversies before its authority was generally recognized. The most important of these controversies had to do with two issues: that of grace and predestination, and that of the nature of the human soul.

In the controversy regarding the first of these issues, the opponents of Augustine's doctrines have traditionally been called semi-Pelagians, although such a name is not wholly justified. Indeed, the so-called semi-Pelagians were in truth "semi-Augustinians" who, while rejecting the doctrines of Pelagius and admiring and respecting Augustine, were not willing to follow the bishop of Hippo to the last consequences of this theology.

Questions regarding Augustine's doctrine of grace and predestination were first posed within the circle of his disciples and followers. Among these were some monks of Hadrumentum, and a certain Vitalis.[2] The latter proposed to Augustine a doctrine according to which all good that one does is owed to the grace of God, but the first step toward salvation, that of accepting grace—the *initium fidei*—is only ours, and God does not intervene in it. Augustine responded to this[3] along the same lines that have been expounded in the preceding chapter: grace, to be truly such, must be entirely unmerited. As to the monks of Hadrumentum, their objections were similar to those of Vitalis, and Augustine responded to them in his works *On Grace and Free Will* and *On Correction and Grace*, which will not be discussed here because their contents are those which have been expounded in the preceding chapter.

It was in the south of Gaul, especially in Marseilles, that the spirit of opposition to Augustine's views on grace and

---

[2] E. Amann, "Semi-Pélagiens," *DTC*, 14:1796-1850. This long article has provided the basic structure for my discussion of this subject, although I have departed from its views on some points. See also, on Augustine and Vitalis, L. Moereels; "Sint Augustinus en het Probleem der voorkomende Gnade," *Ons Geloof*, 16 (1930), 193-209, 241-53, 449-61.

[3] *Ep.* 217.

predestination was strongest.[4] We have direct knowledge of that
opposition through two letters sent to Augustine by two of his
defenders, Prosper of Aquitaine and Hilary of Arles.[5] We also
have a number of writings of the leaders of this opposition, such
as John Cassian, Vincent of Lérins, and Faustus of Riez.

John Cassian[6] was a monk who had settled in Marseilles after
having traveled the eastern section of the Empire, where it is said
that he was a disciple of John Chrysostom and that he spent some
time among the Egyptian monks. In Marseilles, he founded two
monasteries, and it was there that he wrote his three main works:
On the Institution of Monasticism, Spiritual Discourses, and *On the
Incarnation of the Lord Against Nestorius.* In these works, Cassian is
clear in condemning Pelagius,[7] but at the same time he avoids the
extremes of Augustine's position, as may be seen in the following
text:

> As soon as he [God] sees in us the beginning of a good will, he
> illumines, stimulates, and urges it towards salvation, giving growth
> to that which he himself planted, or to that which he has seen
> spring *out of our own effort.*[8]

Texts such as this, which were subtly anti-Augustinian,
prevented the full acceptance of Augustine's doctrine not only
when they were written and during the anti-Augustinian
movement, but even much later, when Augustine's authority
was generally recognized but he was interpreted in the light of
such writers as Cassian.[9]

---

[4] J. Chéné, "Les origines de las controverse semi-pélagienne," *AnnThAug,* 13 (1953), 56-109.

[5] Found in Augustine, *Ep.* 225, 226. See J. Chéné, "Le semi-pélagianisme du midi de la Gaule
d'après les lettres de Prosper d'Aquitaine et d'Hiliare à saint Augustin," *RScRel,* 43 (1955), 321-41.

[6] M. Olphe-Gaillard, "Cassian," *DS,* 2:214-76; M. Cappuyns, "Cassien (Jean)," *DHGE,* 2:1319-48;
O. Chadwick, *John Cassian: A Study in Primitive Monasticism* (Cambridge: University Press, 1950);
F. Jalics, *La tradición en Juan Casiano* (Buenos Aires: Pontificia Universidad Santa María, 1966); D. J.
MacQueen, "John Cassian on Grace and Free Will," *RThAM,* 44 (1977), 5-28; C. Tibiletti, "Giovanni
Cassiano: Formazione e dottrina," *Augm,* 17 (1977), 355-80.

[7] *De inc.* 5. 2-3. The connection that Cassian here attempts to establish between Pelagianism and
Nestorius has no other grounds than the fact that they were both condemned by the Council of
Ephesus. See: C. Smits, "Ephese en het Pelagianisme," *StCath,* 7 (1930), 446-56; M. Disdier, "Le
pélagianisme au concile d'Éphese," *EchOr,* 34 (1931), 314-33.

[8] *Coll.* 13. 8.

[9] Unlike Vincent of Lerins, whom we shall presently discuss, John Cassian was read and followed
throughout the Middle Ages, especially in monastic circles. J. C. Guy, *Jean Cassien: Vie et doctrine
spirtuelle* (Paris: P. Lethielleux, 1961), pp. 60-61.

The attack of Vincent of Lerins was much more far-reaching. In his *Commonitorium* he does not directly attack Augustine, but rather comes to the defense of the traditional doctrines over against anonymous "innovators" who are clearly Augustine and his disciples.[10] Although his work was almost unknown during the Middle Ages,[11] it expounds the argument in favor of the normative authority of ecclesiastical doctrine with a clarity not to be found in any other writer.

According to Vincent, his purpose is to "describe those things which have been bequeathed to us by our ancestors and deposited with us, and to do so with the fidelity of a narrator rather than with the presumption of an author."[12] Scripture is the basic source of true doctrine. But, since its meaning is difficult to discover and may be variously interpreted, the Lord has given tradition as a means to determine what is to be believed.

> Furthermore, in this Catholic Church we are to make certain that we uphold that which has been believed always, by all, and in every place (*quod ubique, quod semper, quod ab omnibus*).[13]

Vincent then repeats his argument once again by appealing to concrete examples taken from the history of heresies. Although he does not mention Augustine, it is clear that, if the doctrine of predestination of the African bishop is not that which has been taught always, by all, and in every place, it must be rejected as an innovation that has no place in the faith of the Catholic Church.

Faustus of Riez (or Reji) is the most ardent exponent of the

---

[10] J. Madoz, *El concepto de la tradición en San Vicente de Lerins: Estudio histórico-crítico del "Commonitorio"* (Rome: Gregorian University, 1933), pp. 59-89; W. O'Connor, "Saint Vincent of Lerins and Saint Augustine: Was the *Commonitorium* of Saint Vincent of Lerins Intended as a Polemic Treatise Against Saint Augustine and His Doctrine on Predestination?" *Doctor Communis*, 16 (1963), 123-257.

[11] *Ibid.*, p. 55. Was this due to mere historical circumstance? Or was it perhaps that the Middle Ages understood Augustine more clearly than has been traditionally supposed and that they were therefore aware of the anti-Augustinian tone of the *Commonitorium*? The only ancient record of the use of Vincent is that of Gennadius, another semi-Pelagian: J. Madoz, "El testimonio de Gennadio sobre S. Vicente de Lerins," *EstEcl*, 9 (1932), 484-502).

[12] *Comm.* 1.

[13] *Ibid.*, 2. A good study of the exact meaning of this threefold rule is that of J. Madoz, "El canon de Vicente de Lerins 'Id teneamus quod ubique, quod semper, quod ab omnibus creditum est,' " *Greg*, 13 (1932), 32-74.

anti-Augustinian thesis.[14] In his treatise *On the Grace of God and Free Will*, he defends the doctrine according to which the *initium fidei*—the first step of faith—depends on human freedom.[15] This freedom gives us the natural capacity to turn toward God and to seek until there is a response. "To God, the liberality of reward; and to the human, the devotion of search."[16] Those who claim that human free will is able only to sin, and can do no good, are mistaken.[17] Christ died for all,[18] and this is sufficient basis on which to reject the doctrine of predestination as Augustine understands it, and to affirm that the so-called predestination is no more than God's judgment based on divine foreknowledge of what each will do with freedom.[19] In summary,

> We stand before a "Christianity without mystery"! Such is the final impression which the book of Faustus leaves. Openly taking the part of man, he wants to make everything depend on man in the last analysis. Hence his phobia for all which might seem to be an internal action of God in the deeper reaches of the soul. Grace is confessed, no doubt; but it does not operate in the very core of the will, but rather remains in the periphery.[20]

Against these various attacks,[21] Augustine and his disciples insisted that the *initium fidei* is in God's grace, and that this grace is given according to an eternal predestination. As has already been said, it was against the objections of Cassian that Augustine composed his treatise *On the Predestination of the Saints* and *On the Gift of Perseverance*. However, the champion of Augustinianism against semi-Pelagianism was Prosper of Aquitaine, whose position may be seen in his *Epistle to Refinus on Grace and Free*

---

[14] On which see A. G. Elg, "In Faustum Reiensem adversaria," *Eranos*, 42 (1944), 24-46; C. Tibiletti, "Libero arbitrio e grazia in Fausto di Riez," *Augm*, 19 (1979), 259-85.

[15] J. Chéné, "Que signifiaient 'initium fidei' et 'affectus credulitatis' pour les Semi-pélagiens?" *RScRel*, 35 (1948), 566-88.

[16] *De grat. Dei et lib. arb.* 1.7.

[17] *Ibid.*, 1. 11.

[18] *Ibid.*, 1. 16.

[19] *Ibid.*, 2.2-3.

[20] Amann, "Semi-Pélagiens," 1836.

[21] The three authors who have been discussed are only three examples—albeit the most significant—of a vast number of theologians who rejected one or another aspect of Augustine's teaching on grace and predestination. A fuller discussion may be found in Amann, "Semi-Pélagiens."

Will, in his *Hymn on the Ungrateful*—that is to say, those "without grace"—and in his treatise *On the Vocation of All Peoples,* which is attributed to him by most scholars.[22]

However, Prosper's own defense shows a tendency to mitigate some of Augustine's most extreme doctrines.[23]

Originally faithful (until about 432), under the blows of semi-Pelagian attacks he abandons the restricted salvific will of God and the predestination to hell before the foreknowledge of guilt (432-435); then, influenced by Rome, . . . he separates the cause of free grace from that of unconditional predestination, and goes as far as to compose a work, his *The Vocation of All Peoples,* in favor of universalism.

Thus from the very day after the death of Augustine a selection of some of his teachings was made, and his selection would later be endorsed by the Council of Orange (529). Therefore one can say that at no point of its history . . . has the Church adopted the entire doctrine of the Doctor of Grace.[24]

The synod that gathered at Orange in 529 is usually considered the end of the semi-Pelagian controversy, although there is no doubt that semi-Pelagianism had a following even after that time. Furthermore, the synod itself, while condemning Pelagianism and some of the positions of the semi-Pelagians, did not adopt more than a diluted form of Augustinianism. The Canons of Orange, taken mostly from the works of Augustine and Prosper,[25] are a good example of the manner in which the

---

[22] See *ACW,* 14:6-9.

[23] Such is the thesis of M. Cappuyns, "Le premier représentant de l'augustinisme médiéval: Prosper d' Aquitaine," *RThAM,* 1 (1929) 309-37, who shows Prosper moved progressively away from the more extreme theses of Augustine. This view is rejected by L. Pelland, *Prosperi Aquitani doctrina de praedestinatione et voluntate Dei salvifica: De ejus in augustinismum influxu* (Montreal: Collegium Maximum Immaculatae Conceptionis, 1936). The latter's work, however, is merely an attempt to coordinate Augustine and Prosper through the use of later scholastic distinctions that are quite foreign to the theology of both ancient theologians. See also R. Lorenz, "Das Augustinismus Prospers von Aquitanien," *ZschrKgesch,* 73 (1962), 217-52.

[24] M. Cappuyns, in *BThAM,* 1 (1929-1932), 216.

[25] See M. Cappuyns, "L'origine des 'Capitula' d'Orange, 529," *RThAM,* 6 (1934), 121-42. Fulgentius of Ruspe and Caesarius of Arles should be mentioned along with Prosper for their contribution to the final victory of Augustianism, even in its mitigated form. In passing, one may mention also that Caesarius is often discussed as one of the early authorities for the perputual virginity and perhaps even the immaculate conception of Mary, for he refers to "the Virgin Mary, who was always a virgin, before and after childbirth, and who remained without contamination nor stain of sin" (*Sermo* 249). The classical study of A. Malnory, *Saint Césaire évêque d'Arles (503-543),* originally published in 1894, has been reprinted recently (Geneva: Slatkine Reprints, 1978).

Middle Ages read the works of Augustine—although one should point out that the canons themselves were not known during most of the Middle Ages.

In Orange it was declared that the fall of Adam corrupted the whole of humankind,[26] and that one receives the grace of God not because one asks for it, but vice versa.[27] According to that synod, the first step of faith—*initium fidei*—is not in human nature, but in divine grace.[28] Free will by itself cannot lead one to the grace of baptism,[29] for that very will has been corrupted by sin and can only be restored through that grace.[30] Adam abandoned his original state by his own iniquity; the faithful abandon their state of iniquity by the grace of God.[31] Christian fortitude rests not on the power of our own will, but on the Holy Spirit, which is given to us.[32] Grace is not based on merit,[33] and only through it can we act rightly,[34] for all that we have of ourselves is misery and sin.[35]

On the other hand, this does not mean that anyone has been predestined for evil—a doctrine that the synod declared to be anathema. On the contrary, all those who are baptized may attain unto salvation with the help of Christ.[36]

It would be incorrect to say that the synod of Orange was a victory for semi-Pelagianism. On the contrary, the synod clearly rejected such typical semi-Pelagian doctrines as that of the human *initium fidei*. It is true, however, that the synod was not truly Augustinian in its doctrine.[37] Nothing is said here—although it is in a way implied—of a predestination that takes place not on the basis of a divine foreknowledge of future human

---

[26] Canon 2.
[27] Canon 3.
[28] Canon 5.
[29] Canon 8.
[30] Canon 13.
[31] Canon 15.
[32] Canon 17.
[33] Canon 18.
[34] Canon 20.
[35] Canon 22.
[36] *Pars* 3. *De pradest.*
[37] On this issue, see J. P. Redding, *The Influence of Saint Augustine on the Doctrine of the II Council of Orange Concerning Original Sin* (Washington: Catholic University of America Press, 1939).

attitudes and actions, but on the basis of a sovereign decision of God. Nor is anything said of an irresistible grace. The emphasis is now rather on that grace which is given at baptism. The overwhelming and dynamic experience set forth in the *Confessions* is being transformed into an entire system of grace—a process that was perhaps inevitable, but nonetheless unfortunate.

Controversies over Augustine's Theology: The Nature of the Soul

Partly because of the influence of Neoplatonism, Augustine had affirmed that the soul was incorporeal. In so claiming he was abandoning the North African tradition established by Tertullian, and was thereby introducing what seemed to many an innovation in Christian theology.[38] As was to be expected, opposition to this doctrine soon developed in those circles which were less inclined to accept the tenets of Neoplatonism. Since the semi-Pelagians moved in such circles, it is not surprising to find some of them opposing Augustine, not only on that which had to do with grace and predestination, but also on his understanding of the human soul.

Among the main opponents of Augustine's doctrine of the incorporeity of the soul was Faustus of Riez,[39] whom we have already met in the context of the semi-Pelagian controversy. Appealing to the authority of ancient Christian writers, Faustus affirms that the soul is invisible, but insists that it is corporeal.[40] Only God is incorporeal, and all souls as well as angels have bodies, although these are much more tenuous than our visible bodies. To claim the opposite would be to erase the distinction between creator and creatures, between the God who is present everywhere and fills everything, and the soul, which is limited to a particular place.

---

[38] G. Mathon, "L'anthropologie chrétienne en Occident de saint Augustin à Jean Scot Erigène" (Unpublished thesis, Lille, 1964) Reviewed by its author in *BThAM*, 9 (1962). 1396.

[39] F. Bisogne, *Fausto de Riez e la polemica sull'anima nei primordi della filosofia medievale* (Cava de' Tirreni: E. Coda, 1948).

[40] *Ep.* 3.

The main defender of Augustine's view that the soul was incorporeal was Claudianus Mamertus,[41] who in his treatise *On the Condition of the Soul*, written in response to Faustus,[42] repeatedly appeals to the authority of ancient philosophers in order to show that the soul is incorporeal. Another argument of Claudianus is that of the divine image in the human creature: if God is incorporeal, it is nonsense to believe that a corporeal creature may bear the divine image.[43] Furthermore, all bodies are composed of four elements, and none of these is to be found in the soul.[44]

Some time later Gennadius of Marseilles, a semi-Pelagian whom we have not discussed, revived the arguments of Faustus in the sense that only God is incorporeal.

> Nothing is to be taken as incorporeal except God (that is, the Father, the Son, and the Holy Spirit) who is to be declared truly incorporeal because he is in all places and fills and fulfills everything; and he is invisible to all creatures precisely because he is incorporeal.[45]

After that time, because of the growing influence of Neoplatonism through the works of Augustine, Marius Victorinus, Gregory of Nyssa, and others, the controversy subsided and eventually disappeared.[46] It would briefly flare up again during the Carolingian period, but this last attempt to affirm the corporeal nature of the soul would be definitively smothered by the Latin translation of Pseudo-Dionysius, which greatly strengthened the influence of Neoplatonism on this as well as other points.

---

[41] The best study on this subject is that of E. L. Fortin, *Christianisme et culture philosphique au cinquième siècle: La querrelle de l'âme humaine en Occident* (Paris: Études Augustiniennes, 1959), pp. 75-110. A brief summary may be found in E. Bréhier, *La filosofía en la Edad Media* (Mexico: Tipográfica Editorial Hispano-Americana, 1959), p. 13.

[42] Claudianus affirms that the work that he refuted reached him anonymously. Therefore, he does not seem to have known that it was Faustus that he was refuting.

[43] *De cond. an.* 1. 4.

[44] *Ibid.*, 1. 7-9.

[45] *De eccl. dogmat.* 11.

[46] The last noteworthy echo of the controversy comes from Licinianus of Cartagena, who attempted to refute Gennadius in his *Epistle to Epiphanius*. But for the most part he merely repeats the arguments of Claudianus. The spiritualist views of Licinianus are studied, without special emphasis on the incorporeity of the soul, by J. A. Platero Ramos, *Liciniano de Cartagena y su doctrina espiritualista* (Oña: Colegio Máximo S. J., 1946).

As a final note to this section, one may note that those who were more inclined to come to the defense of human capabilities and participation in the work of salvation—that is, the semi-Pelagians—were at the same time the most stringently opposed to the use of philosophy in the realm of theology. On the other hand, the Augustinians, who emphasized human impotence to deliver ourselves from sin, were at the same time the most willing to make use of philosophy in theological inquiry. This is especially significant because in later centuries—namely the sixteenth and twentieth—there were those who argued that human frailty should be affirmed, not only with reference to salvation, but also in that which has to do with the true knowledge of God, and that therefore the notion of the use of philosophy as a means to know God must be rejected jointly with the notion that one can save oneself.

Orosius and Priscillianism

Toward the end of the fourth century, when Augustine and Ambrose were still alive, a movement arose in Spain which is usually called "Priscillianism," after Priscillian, its supposed founder, who was bishop of Avila. Whether or not Priscillian taught the doctrines that have been attributed to him is still an open question.[47] In any case, he was condemned to death for immorality and witchcraft under the authority of Emperor Maximus. Beyond this, several ancient writers—Orosius, Sulpitius Severus, Jerome, Damasus, Ambrose, etc.—claim that he held a trinitarian doctrine that was similar to Sabellianism, a Manichaean dualism, and some Docetic views.[48]

---

[47] J. A. Davids, *De Orosio et sancto Augustino Priscillianistarum adversaris: Commentatio historica et philologica* (The Hague: A. Govers, 1930); A. d'Alès, *Priscillien et l'Espagne chrétienne à la fin du IVᵉsiècle* (Paris: G. Beauchesne, 1936); J. Pérez de Urbel, "La teología trinitaria en la contienda priscilianista," *RET*, 6 (1946), 589-606; J. M. Ramos y Loscertales, *Priscilliano: Gesta rerum* (Salamanca: Universidad de Salamanca, 1952); C. Torres, "Prisciliano: Doctor itinerante, brillante superficialidad," *RevEstGall*, 27 (1954), 75-89; R. López Caneda, "Prisciliano: Su ideología y su significado en la historia cultural de Galicia," *RevUMad*, 12 (1964), 629-31; J. Madoz, *Segundo decenio de estudios sobre patrística española* (Madrid: FAX, 1961), pp. 65-68; H. Chadwick, *Priscillian of Avila: The Occult and the Charismatic in the Early Church* (Oxford: Clarendon, 1976); P. M. Sáenz de Argadona, *Antropología de Prisciliano* (Santiago de Compostela: Instituto Teológico Compostelano, 1982). His extant works—about whose authorship there is a great deal of debate—may be found in *CSEL*, 18.

[48] Of these, it seems certain that Priscillian held a trinitarian doctrine akin to Sabellianism. The heterodox Christology that has been attributed to him is more doubtful. As to Manichaean dualism, it is almost certain that he did not hold it.

After Priscillian's death, his followers were to be found throughout all of Spain and Southern Gaul. Even as late as A.D. 561, a synod gathered at Braga felt the need to condemn them, although by that time rather absurd doctrines were attributed to Priscillian.[49]

It was as an opponent of Priscillianism that Paul Orosius first became known, for in A.D. 414 he visited Augustine and presented him with a *Commonitorium of Errors of the Priscillianists and Origenists*. However, his main contribution to the history of Christian thought was not in his opposition to Priscillianism, but in the interpretation of history to be found in his seven books, *On History Against the Pagans*, written at the request of Augustine as a supplement to his *City of God*.[50] In his work, Orosius goes over the entire history of humankind, attempting to show that pagan times were no better than the Christian period, but even worse. His general idea of history is similar to that of Augustine, but in his view Christ is to such an extent the goal of all history that even the invasions of the barbarians, which had caused him personal suffering, were to be interpreted as a means that God was providing for the conversion of the invaders:

> If the only purpose for which barbarians were sent within the Roman borders was that throughout the entire East and West the Church of Christ would be filled with Huns, Suevi, Vandals, Burgundians, and many other peoples of believers, let the mercy of God be praised and extolled, for so many nations have attained to the knowledge of truth which would not have been able to do so without this occasion, even if this has taken place through our own destruction.[51]

Boethius and the Question of Universals

Manlius Torcuatus Severinus Boethius lived in Ostrogothic Italy at the end of the fifth century and the beginning of the

---

[49] Text in José Vives, ed., *Concilios visigóticos e hispano-romanos* (Madrid: Consejo Superior de Investigaciones Científicas, 1963), pp. 65-69.
[50] The best study is that of C. Torres, "Los siete libros de la Historia contra los paganos, de Paulo Orosio," *CuadEstGall*, 3 (1948), 23-48. See also H. J. Diesner, "Orosius und Augustinus," *ActHung*, 2 (1963), 89-102; B. Lacroix, *Orose et ses idées* (Paris: J. Vrin, 1965).
[51] *Historia* 7. 41.

sixth.[52] He had an extensive culture that he had acquired not only in Rome, but also in Athens, and he took upon himself the task of acquainting the Latin world with the inheritance of Greek philosophy, especially that of Plato and Aristotle. To this end he translated the great classics, and also wrote commentaries on them. He is best known for his treatise on *The Consolation of Philosophy*, written while he was in prison by order of King Theodoric, before whom he has been accused of conspiring in favor of Byzantium. But he also wrote a number of theological and speculative treatises such as *On the Unity of the Trinity*, *On the Person and the Two Natures of Christ*, and *Brief Exposition of the Christian Faith*.[53]

The significance of Boethius for the history of Christian thought is not that of an original thinker—which he was not.[54] Nor is it mainly that of a compiler and organizer of the legacy of antiquity—which he was.[55] His significance is rather in three points in which his influence was constantly felt throughout the entire Middle Ages.

First, Boethius influenced later theology through his discussion and use of such terms as "person," "substance," "being," and others of great significance for trinitarian doctrine.[56] Of these, the most important for later theology was his definition of "person" as the individual substance of a rational nature—*persona*

---

[52] The best general introduction is H. M. Barrett, *Boethius: Some Aspects of His Times and Work* (Cambridge: The University Press, 1940). See also A. Crocco, *Introduzione a Boezio* (Naples: Liguori, 1975); M. Gibson, ed., *Boethius: His Life, Thought and Influence* (Oxford: Basil Blackwell, 1981).

[53] Although the authorship of this last treatise has been questioned, scholarly opinion tends to attribute it to Boethius. See A. Hamman, *Patrologia cursus completus: Supplementum*, 3:1279; L. M. de Rijk, "On the Chronology of Boethius' Works on Logic," *Viv*, 2 (1964), 125-62. On the *Consolation*, see J. Gruber, *Kommentar zu Boethius De Consolatione Philosophiae* (Berlin: W. de Gruyter, 1978); C. J. Starnes, "Boethius and the Development of Christian Humanism: The Theology of the 'Consolatio,' " in L. Obertello, *Congresso internazionale di studi boeziani* (Rome: Herder, 1981), pp. 27-38.

[54] On the theology of Boethius in general, see G. Chappuis, "la théologie de Boèce," *Congrès d'histoire du christianisme* (Paris: Rieder, 1928), 3:15-40; R. Carton, "Le christianisme et l'augustinisme de Boèce, " *RevPhil*, 30 (1930), 573-659.

[55] On his influence in general, see H. R. Patch, *The Tradition of Boethius: A Study of His Importance in Medieval Culture* (New York: Oxford University Press, 1935).

[56] K. Bruder, *Die philosophischen Elemente in den Opuscula sacra des Boethius* (Leipzig: F. Meiner, 1928); M. Bergeron, "La structure du concept latin de personne," *Études d'histoire litteraire et doctrinale du XIIIᵉ siècle* (Paris: J. Vrin, 1932); V. Schurr, *Die Trinitätslehre des Boethius im Lichte der "skythischen Kontroversen"* (Paderborn: F. Schöningh, 1935); J. Collins, "Progress and Problems in the Reassessment of Boethius," *ModSch*, 23 (1945), 1-23; M. Nédoncelle, "Les variations de Boèce sur la personne," *RScRel*, 29 (1955), 201-38.

est rationabilis naturae individua substantia. Some of the most
outstanding medieval theologians devoted long pages to clarify
the meaning of this definition and its implications for trinitarian
and christological thought.

Second, Boethius was the channel through which the early
centuries of the Middle Ages knew classical philosophy,
especially that which had to do with logic.[57]

Third, it was mainly through Boethius that the Middle Ages
approached the question of universals. In his commentary on
the *Isagoge* of Porphyry, which served as an introduction to the
Categories of Aristotle, Boethius pointed out that Porphyry posed
a problem and then did not discuss it. The question was whether
genera and the species subsist in themselves or only in our
minds. Furthermore, if they do subsist in themselves—that is if
they are real—one would then have to determine whether they
are corporeal or not, and whether they exist in individual things
or apart from them. This is, briefly stated, the problem of
universals, which was to be debated throughout the entire
Middle Ages.

The question posed is whether generic ideas are real or not,
and, if they are real, how they relate to the individuals that are
included in them. For instance, is the idea of "cat," which
includes all cats, real or not? If it is not—that is, if it is only
a name—what is it that makes all cats be such? If, on the
other hand, that idea is real, how are individual cats related
to the generic idea of "cat"? What, then, is the reality of
individuals?

This was one of the main philosophical problems of the
Middle Ages. Those who affirm that universals are real are
called "realists." Those who, on the other hand, affirm that the
universals are mere names, and that reality is to be found only
in individuals, are called "nominalists." But between the
extreme realists and the radical nominalists there was an entire

---

[57] E. Gilson, *History of Christian Philosophy in the Middle Ages* (New York: Random House, 1955),
pp. 97-100.

scale of intermediate positions, as will be seen as this history proceeds.[58]

The question of universals had great significance for theology. For instance, extreme realism can very easily fall into pantheism, but it can also simplify the problem of the transmission of original sin. Or it may give support to an understanding of the church as a celestial reality that is not dependent on humans for its authority. On the other hand, extreme nominalism has difficulties in developing a theory of knowledge, and in explaining the transmission of original sin; and it tends to see the church as the totality of believers, from whom the hierarchy receives its authority. Several examples of the manner in which these various issues were posed will be seen further on in the development of medieval Christian thought.

The position of Boethius himself with regard to universals is typically Platonic. He sees the universals as corresponding to the ideas of Plato. However, in his commentary on the *Isagoge*, which was to serve as an introduction to Aristotle, Boethius expounded the Aristotelian solution, and therefore many medieval philosophers came to believe that he had hesitated on the issue.[59] This seeming vacillation contributed to keeping alive the controversy over universals.

Cassiodore

Flavius Magnus Aurelius Cassiodorus Senator was a contemporary of Boethius, although somewhat younger than he.[60]

---

[58] I have abstained from the usual procedure of devoting an entire chapter to the question of universals for two reasons: the first is that it would interrupt the basically chronological outline that I have decided to follow; the second, and the most important, is that such a chapter would give the impression that the question of universals was the main concern of medieval thinkers. In spite of the impression given by many modern histories, such was not the case. The question of universals, although basic to an understanding of medieval philosophy and theology, usually lies imbedded in other concerns that were foremost in the minds of the various theologians. In any case, there is an excellent summary of the course of the controversy in Copleston, *History*, 2:136-55.

[59] Gilson, *History*, pp. 99-100. See also J. J. E. Gracia, "Boethius and the Problem of Individuation in the 'Commentaries on the Isagoge,' " in Obertello, *Congresso*, pp. 169-82.

[60] A. van de Vyrer, "Cassiodore et son oeuvre," *Speculum*, 6 (1931), 244-92; J. J. van den Besselaar, *Cassiodorus Senator: Leven en werken van een staatsman en monnik uit de zesde eeuw* (Haarlem: J. H. Gottmer, 1950); G. Bardy, "Cassiodore et la fin du monde ancien," *AnnTh*, 6 (1945), 383-425; M. L. W. Laistner, "The Value and Influence of Cassiodorus' *Ecclesiastical History*," *HTR*, 41 (1948), 51-57; R. Sclieben, *Cassiodors Psalmenexegese* (Dissertation revued in *TLztg*, 96, 1971, pp. 794-96).

Cassiodorus held high positions in the court of King Theodoric, where he served as a mediator between the Arian Goths and the conquered Catholics—although this does not mean that he hesitated in his orthodox convictions. Later, with no other apparent reason than his desire to devote his life to study and meditation, he resigned from his position and retired to Vivarium, where he soon became head of a flourishing monastic community. But eventually he resigned also from that position and lived the rest of his days as a mere monk, widely respected for his sanctity as well as for his erudition.

Cassiodore was an encyclopedic spirit rather than an original thinker. Besides several secular works in which he gathered what he considered best in classical culture, he wrote religious treatises. Outstanding among these is *On the Soul,* in which he shows himself to be a disciple of Augustine and of Claudianus Mamertus—although it is interesting to note that the serene and irenic tone of this treatise suggests that the controversy had already passed, and that the position of Augustine had become generally accepted. The commentaries that Cassiodore wrote on Psalms and on some books of the New Testament show him to be an heir of the allegorical exegetical tradition. In his *Tripartite History,* he is content with compiling and organizing data taken from the historical works of Socrates and Theodoret, translated from Greek into Latin by a friend of his. But the work of Cassiodore which was most influential during the middle ages was his two books on *Institutions of Divine and Secular Letters.* This work, which is a summary of the religious and secular knowledge of antiquity, was the model on which medieval education was based, and it was also one of the main channels through which the Middle Ages were able to receive the inheritance of antiquity.

Cassiodore shares with Boethius and with Gregory the Great the glory of having saved from the shipwreck the remains of Greco-Roman culture and literature.

He has been rightly proclaimed as the hero and restorer of science in the sixth century. In his retreat at Vivarium he offered one of the first and most illustrious examples of the conjunction of religious life with the life of the intellect . . . . The libraries and schools of the cloisters which served as shelters for knowledge in the midst of the rising waves of barbarism, are the result of Cassiodore's initiative, a legacy which the abbot of Vivarium has left to the entire monastic order.[61]

Gregory the Great

The most remarkable figure among those who served as a bridge between antiquity and the Middle Ages is without any doubt Pope Gregory, who occupied the see of Rome from 590 to 604, to whom posterity has given the title of "the Great,"[62] and who is traditionally counted among the four great doctors of the church.[63] The significance of Gregory extends to various fields: for the history of liturgy, he is important through his influence on Gregorian chant, as well as on various other aspects of worship; for the history of canon law, he is important for the manner in which his epistles are an indication of the state of development of that law toward the end of the sixth century and the first years of the seventh; for the history of missions, he is significant through his inspiration of the mission of Augustine to England; the history of monasticism has to take note of his influence on medieval ascetic practice; the history of preaching records that his homilies on Ezekiel and on the Gospels were among the most read and imitated in later centuries.

Gregory's significance for the history of Christian thought is not in his originality—which was rather meager—but rather in his influence on medieval theology, and the manner in which he served as a filter through which that theology read the works of Augustine. His thought is Augustinian, at least in its formulas. And yet, when one reads his works after having read those of Augustine, one cannot help but feel that there is a chasm between the two.

---

[61] P. Grodet, "Cassiodore," DTC, 2:1833.

[62] A title that seems to have been first given to him by his biographer John the Deacon, Vita S. Greg. 4. 61. Good introductions to the life and thought of Gregory are: C. Dagens, Saint Grégoire le Grand: Culture et expérience chrétiennes (Paris: Études augustiniennes, 1977); J. Richards, Consul of God: The Life and Times of Gregory the Great (London: Routledge and Kegan Paul, 1980); G. R. Evans, The Thought of Gregory the Great (Cambridge: University Press, 1986).

[63] It was the Venerable Bede, in the eighth century, who first listed Gregory with Ambrose, Jerome, and Augustine.

Almost everything in Gregory has its roots in the teaching of Augustine, and yet scarcely anything is really Augustinian. That which was un-Augustinian in Augustine becomes the vital element of this Semi-augustinian. The fundamental spirit of Augustine has vanished, and superstition gained supremacy. Everything is coarser, more fixed, and ordinary. The controlling motive is not the peace of the heart which finds rest in God; but the fear of uncertainty, which seeks to attain security through the institutions of the church.[64]

This does not mean that Gregory attempted to transform or even mitigate the Augustinian spirit. On the contrary, he believed himself to be a faithful interpreter of the bishop of Hippo—and as such he was read by the Middle Ages. It is that, between Augustine and Gregory, times had changed. The new times were dark—so dark that the bishop of Rome was convinced that he was living in the very last days.[65] Surrounded by pestilence, barbarism, and ignorance, Gregory attempted to keep order, peace, and culture; but he achieved this only at the price of participating in the circumstances of his times. Therefore, it is important not to condemn the man, but rather to understand him within his own context, and to point out the consequences of his work for later theology.

In his doctrines of God, the Trinity, and the person of Jesus Christ, Gregory was perfectly orthodox and traditional. He believed that the first four councils had an authority similar to that of the four Gospels.[66] The same may be said regarding his doctrine of the soul, where he followed Augustine in declaring the soul to be incorporeal as well as in refusing to take a stand for either creationism or traducianism.

In his doctrine of grace and predestination, Gregory abandoned Augustine in affirming that God has predestined to salvation those whom "he calls elect because he knows that they will persevere in faith and in good works."[67] Furthermore, grace is not irresistible,[68] as the bishop of Hippo had claimed.

---

[64] Seeberg, *Text-book*, 2:26.
[65] *Hom. in Evang.* 1. 1. 1.
[66] *Ep.* 1. 25.
[67] *In Ezech. hom.* 1. 9. 8.
[68] *Mor.* 30. 1. 5.

That Gregory's Augustinism was very mitigated, and that it had suffered the influence of authors such as John Cassian, may be clearly seen in the emphasis that the bishop of Rome placed on penance and on satisfaction for sin. We cannot discuss here the development of the practice of penance.[69] Let it suffice to say that Gregory saw contrition, confession, and satisfaction as the fundamental constituents of penance.[70] Absolution merely confirms the forgiveness that God has already granted, although this does not mean that the faithful can ignore the authority of absolution which has been given to their pastors.[71]

Satisfaction for sin does not take place only in this life. Those who die while still taking with them the burden of minor sins will be purified "as by fire" in purgatory[72]—a doctrine that Augustine had suggested, and Gregory affirms.

Mass as a sacrifice—a doctrine that could also be gleaned from some texts of Augustine, although probably forcing their interpretation—is another of Gregory's favorite doctrines.[73] This sacrifice, in which Christ is offered anew, may be beneficial, not only for the living, but even for those souls which are still in purgatory.[74]

Finally, one must say that Gregory is the doctor of miracles and of angels and demons. His *Dialogues* are, in fact, an extremely credulous compilation of prodigies attributed to various saints. Gregory's basic position before such stories of wonderful happenings may be found in another of his works: "Wonderful things are to be believed by faith, and not searched by reason; for if reason could show them before our eyes they would no longer be wonderful."[75] As to angels and demons,[76] what Gregory claimed to know about them was so much and so

---

[69] See below, pp. 137-39.
[70] "*Convertio mentis, confessio oris, et vindicta peccati*" (*I Reg.* 6. 2. 33; *PL*, 79:439). This work of Gregory, generally considered spurious, does, however, seem to be genuine. See P. Verbraken, "Saint Gregoire sur le premier livre des Rois," *RevBénéd*, 66 (1956), 159-217.
[71] *Hom. in Evang.* 2. 26.6.
[72] *Dial.* 4. 39.
[73] *Dial.* 4. 58 (quoted by Seeberg, *Text-book*, 2:25).
[74] As may be seen in the case of the monk Justus, who, according to Gregory, was released from purgatory after masses were said in his favor for thirty days. *Dial.* 4. 55.
[75] *Mor. in Iob* 6. 15.
[76] See the excellent study by L. Kurz, *Gregors des Grossen Lehre von den Engeln* (Rottenburg: A Bader, 1938).

detailed that some later readers reached the conclusion that he
had been personally inspired. The angels are divided into nine
hierarchical orders, each with its specific functions. The
demons—fallen angels—destroy peace and hinder the work of
angels and Christians.

In summary, Gregory is an indication of the manner in which,
in the midst of a period of political and intellectual decline,
Augustine's theology was accommodated to popular faith in two
main ways: by mitigating the most extreme aspects of the
doctrines of grace and predestination, and by making room for
superstitious beliefs and practices.

Other Writers of the Same Period

Benedict of Nursia was a contemporary of Boethius and
Cassiodore. His importance for the later development of the
Christian church was great, for his *Rule* was very influential in
the shaping of Western monasticism. As a great part of medieval
theology was developed and written in monasteries, the
influence of Benedict was always present, although this
influence had to do more with the practical and ascetic ordering
of life than with theology itself. While there will be no section in
the pages that follow in which we shall discuss "monastic
theology" per se, the reader should be aware that most medieval
theology is indeed monastic theology. Therefore, although
Benedict was not one of the most prolific writers of the Christian
Church, his influence in the life and thought of medieval
Christianity is quite marked.[77]

The same may be said about Martin of Braga, who was famous
for his missionary work among the Suevi, although his influence
on later monasticism is very secondary when compared with that
of Benedict.

---

[77] The bibliography on Benedict is enormous. See B. Jaspert, "Regula Magistri—Regula Benedicti:
Bibliographie ihrer Erforschung 1938-1970," *Studia Monastica*, 13 (1971), 129-71; B. Jaspert,
Bibliographie der Regula Benedicti, 1930-1980 (Hildesheim: Gerstenberg, 1983); J. D. Broekaert,
Bibliographie de la Règle de saint Benoît (Rome: Editrice Anselmiana, 1980); S. Campbell, ed.,
International Symposium in Honor of the Fifteenth Centenary of the Birth of Saint Benedict (1980: Rome: Italy)
(Kalamazoo: Cistercian Publications, 1983). For our purposes, a brief review is that of M. C. Kilzer,
"The Place of Saint Benedict in the Western Philosophical Tradition," *American Benedictine Review*,
25 (1974), 174-99.

Finally, Isidore of Seville, a contemporary of Gregory the Great, was very influential through his *Etymologies*. These are a sort of encyclopedia in which Isidore summarizes all the knowledge of his times, from grammar and rhetoric to theology, without leaving out geography, history, and even all sorts of animals and monsters. This manual of universal knowledge was very popular during the Middle Ages, and there is hardly a significant author who does not quote it. Naturally, given the times, Isidore was no more original than Gregory.

> In Scripture, dogma, morality, discipline, and liturgy, Saint Isidore has summarized the knowledge of his times. But what he gives us is not so much his own thought as that of others. He was content with being the echo of tradition, whose witnesses he took care to collect and reproduce.[78]

"Echo of tradition"—that is the work of the authors whom we have studied in this chapter. As every echo, it lacks the timbre of the original voice; its tone is severe and even hollow. But one should not forget that it was mostly through their work that the Middle Ages heard the distant voices of antiquity.[79]

Gregory — Traditionalist
Not really Augustinian.

Medieval ⟶ Monastic theology

---

[78] B. Bareille, "Isidore de Séville," *DTC*, 8:107. On Isidore, see also M. C. Díaz, *Isidoriana* (León: Centro de estudios "San Isidoro," 1961); H. J. Diesner "Kirche, Papsttum und Zeitgeschichte bei Isidore de Séville," *TLztg*, 96 (1971), 81-90; H. J. Diesner, *Isidor von Sevilla und das Westgotische Spanien* (Trier: Spee-Verlag, 1978). The best general work is J. Fontaine, *Isidore de Séville et la culture classique dans l'Espagne wisigothique,* 3 vols. (Paris: Études augustiniennes, 1979-1983).

[79] On the entire subject of the transmission of classical culture during the Middle Ages, see R. R. Bolgar, ed., *Classical Influences on European Culture, A.D. 500-1500* (Cambridge: University Press, 1971); P. Riché, *Education and Culture in the Barbarian West, Sixth through Eighth Centuries* (Columbia: University of South Carolina, 1976).

The author assumes we know a great deal of History. He also assumes we know the theological issues. His attempt in the chapter is to tie it all together. The introduction is poorly written & gives the reader No background

III

Eastern Theology Between the Fourth and the Sixth Ecumenical Councils

The first volume of this history ended with the christological controversy and its culmination in the Council of Chalcedon. In order to give continuity to our narration, we were forced to leave aside the course of Western theology while the East was engaged in the christological controversies. This is in turn led us to begin the present volume with Augustine's theology, which was chronologically prior to the Council of Chalcedon, and to follow its derivations to the first centuries of the Middle Ages. We must now return to the East, which we had left at the end of the previous volume.

Continuation of the Christological Controversies

The *Definition of Faith* of Chalcedon did not put an end to christological controversy in the East. It is true that the West was satisfied with the official sanction given to a formula that was very close to that which could be found in Tertullian and Augustine, as well as in the *Tome* of Leo. It is also true that those most closely connected with the "Robbers' Synod" of Ephesus—Dioscorus and Eutyches—were exiled. But there were many Eastern Christians who felt that the formula which affirmed that there were two natures in Christ was too clearly opposed to the

76

other formula of Cyril—which he had unwittingly taken from an Apollinarian source—"one incarnate nature of God the Word." It was among these Christians that opposition to Chalcedon first arose.

Most of those who were disturbed by the Chalcedonian definition were really opposed not to the doctrine that the Council had held, but to the formula "in two natures." Their position was what Jugie has called "verbal monophysism,"[1] for they were in truth orthodox believers who rejected the doctrines attributed to Eutyches and who confessed that Jesus Christ, while being consubstantial with God, was also consubstantial with us. The main exponent of the views of these "verbal monophysites" was Severus of Antioch, and for this reason they are often called "Severians."[2]

From the christological point of view, the most important work of Severus is *The Lover of Truth*, whose purpose is to refute a selection of quotations from Cyril which had been compiled and published in order to claim support in the works of the dead patriarch for the doctrine of the two natures. As was to be expected, Severus has no difficulty in showing that the doctrine of Cyril, as opposed to that of Nestorius, was that of "one incarnate nature of God the Word."[3]

Severus categorically affirms the true and total humanity of Christ as well as his true and total divinity, but insists that these are united in a single nature. "Christ partook with us of flesh and blood, and was born of the Virgin Mother of God."[4] Also:

He who was eternally consubstantial to him who begat him is the one who voluntarily descended and became consubstantial to this mother. Thus, he became man, being God; he made himself that which he was not, while at the same time remaining that which he

---

[1] M. Jugie, "Monophysisme," *DTC*, 10:2217. This is a good introduction to the issues involved in the controversy. See R. C. Chesnut, *Three Monophysite Theologians: Severus of Antioch, Philoxenus of Mabbeg and Jacob of Sarug* (London: Oxford University Press, 1976); W. A. Wigram, *The Separation of the Monophysites* (New York: AMS Press, 1978); W. H. C. Frend, *The Rise of the Monophysite Movement: Chapters in the History of the Church in the Fifth and Sixth Centuries* (Cambridge: University Press, 1979).
[2] His most significant works have been edited in Syriac, with Latin or French translations, in *CSCO*, 91-94, 101, 102, 133, 134.
[3] *CSCO*, 133:283.
[4] *Ibid.*, 231.

was, without any change. For he did not lose his divinity in his incarnation, and the body did not lose the tangible character of its nature.[5]

The opposition of these verbal monophysites to the Chalcedonian formula was based on the manner in which they understood the word "nature" ($\phi\acute{v}\sigma\iota\varsigma$), which they took to be a synonym of "hypostasis."[6] Therefore, they believed that there was a contradiction and an open door to Nestorianism in a formula such as that of Chalcedon which distinguished between two natures while claiming that they subsisted in a single hypostasis. Also, many of these verbal monophysites were simply conservatives who wanted to retain the "one nature" formula that had been proposed by Cyril—although Cyril himself had been willing to use the formula "of two natures" as long as it was not interpreted in a Nestorian fashion.

In any case, opposition to the Chalcedonian formula grew to such an extent that it threatened the unity of the Empire, and for this reason several emperors intervened in the matter and attempted to solve it by conciliatory formulas or by offering alternatives to the Chalcedonian definition.[8] The net result of those attempts to resolve the theological conflict through the power of the state was that tempers rose to new heights and that what began as a verbal question became in irreparable schism, and at the same time led to rather absurd discussions.

The first emperor who attempted to set aside the Council of Chalcedon in order to attract those who were opposed to the two-nature formula was the usurper Basiliscus, who in A.D. 476 published an *Encyclion*[9] by which he nullified the decisions of Chalcedon and convoked a new council. But his political

---

[5] J. Lebon, *Le monophysisme Severien* (Louvain, 1909), pp. 206-7. Quoted by Jugie, "Monophysisme," 2221.

[6] As the Greek original text of most of these works has been lost, this assertion is based on a conjectural retranslation of the extant Syrica texts, attempting to discover the terminology that was originally used. However, texts such as that which appears in *CSCO* 133.230-31 leave little room for doubt.

[7] Two other theologians of this group, who, however, cannot be discussed here, were Timothy Aelurus and Peter the Fuller. The latter will appear within another context in this chapter.

[8] R. Haacke, "Die kaiserliche Politik in den Auseinander setzungen um Chalkendon," *DKvCh*, 2:95-177.

[9] *PG*, 86:2600-2604.

downfall and the restoration of Emperor Zeno, whom he had deposed, put an end to these projects.

Later Zeno himself tried to heal the theological divisions that weakened the empire. To this end he did not follow the lead proposed by Basiliscus, that is, he did not openly reject the Council of Chalcedon, but rather promulgated an "Edict of Union" or *Henoticon* (A.D. 482),[10] which he had prepared with the collaboration of Patriarch Acacius of Constantinople. As Acacius had given proof of his historical orthodoxy by his staunch opposition to the *Encyclion* of Basiliscus as well as by presiding over a synod that deposed the supposedly monophysite Peter the Fuller,[11] Zeno hoped that his efforts would be well received by the Chalcedonian orthodoxy.

But the efforts of Zeno were no more successful than those of Basiliscus. His *Henoticon* was actually a rather faithful rendering of verbal monophysism, but it did not attempt to show the semantic obstacles that stood between the definition of Chalcedon and its opponents. Rather, it naïvely attempted to return to what had been the situation prior to Chalcedon. Thus, for instance, the emperor claimed that one should not accept any other faith than that which, by divine inspiration, was expounded in Nicea (325) and confirmed in Constantinople (381). Furthermore, he reiterated the twelve famous anathemas of Cyril against the Nestorians. Finally, he anathematized any who dared think otherwise, "be it at Chalcedon, or in any other synod."[12]

Quite probably Zeno and Acacius did not pretend to reject the decisions of Chalcedon, but tried simply to unite Christians of various persuasions by going beyond the Council whose decisions were at issue, to a compromise similar to the "reunion formula" of A.D. 433. But the net result of their action was to

---

[10] *PG*, 86:2620-25.

[11] Peter the Fuller was accused of having "Eutychianized" the *Trisagion* by adding the words "who wert crucified for us." Those who opposed him claimed that this implied the divinity as such had suffered, and therefore accused Peter of "theopaschism." This formula—which became generally used and still is common in some Eastern churches—was used by Peter only as a way of expressing the reality of the incarnation. It is only by virtue of the *communicatio idiomatum* that one can say that the Word was crucified. Therefore, Peter's theopaschism, like his monophysism, was only verbal.

[12] *PG*, 86:2624.

create deeper dissensions, not only regarding the Council of Chalcedon, but also regarding the *Henoticon* itself.

On the one hand, Zeno's edict led to a break between the Roman See and the Eastern Church. Although the *Henoticon* did not openly condemn the Council of Chalcedon, it did tend to diminish its authority and, with it, that of Leo's *Tome*. The two-natures formula was not even mentioned. The way was open for monophysism, as was clearly shown by the haste with which many monophysite theologians signified their support of the edict.[13] Furthermore, the pope claimed that the emperor had no authority to establish himself as a judge in matters of dogma. Therefore, the entire West, led by the pope, simply had to reject the *Henoticon.* Since Acacius persisted in his support of the imperial edict—and also because of frictions related with the succession to the see of Alexandria—Pope Felix excommunicated Acacius and declared him deposed. As the pope had no means to make that deposition a fact, the result was the split between East and West to which Western historians usually refer as the "Schism of Acacius" (484–519).

This schism lasted beyond the death of its main actors, and even of their immediate successors, until the year 519, when communion was finally restored between the two churches through a series of negotiations between Emperor Justin and Pope Hormisdas. As Justin was interested in re-establishing ties with the Western Church, the new formula of reunion was a triumph for Rome, for all her demands were met by Constantinople: the confirmation of the Council of Chalcedon and of Leo's *Tome;* the condemnation of Nestorius, Eutyches, Dioscorus, Acacius, and their followers; and a full pardon for all orthodox church leaders who had been deposed for their refusal to endorse the *Henoticon.*

On the other hand, the divisive influence of the *Henoticon* was also felt among the monophysites themselves.

In Egypt, the fanaticism of multitudes that insisted on the

---

[13] Although in truth these were only verbal monophysites. See Jugie, "Monophysisme," 2221. Most noteworthy among these was the Patriarch of Alexandria, Peter, whom Pope Felix III would not recognize, but who had the support of Acacius.

express condemnation of Chalcedon led them to withdraw from communion with the patriarchs, who were satisfied with the *Henoticon,* and to create a new sect that, lacking a hierarchy, was called "the acephaloi"—or "headless"—and which lasted until the seventeenth century.[14] In opposition to them, the "henoticists" enjoyed the imperial favor and therefore the possession of the most important sees.

Furthermore, the *Henoticon* led to the final separation between the verbal monophysites, or Severians, and the real monophysites. As has already been said, the Christology of Severus was essentially orthodox in spite of his rejection of the Chalcedonian formula, for he affirmed the complete and real humanity of Christ. From this doctrine of Severus it followed that the body of Christ as such was capable of corruption. It was on this point that controversy first arose between Severus and his followers on the one hand, and the true monophysites on the other. The latter, led by Julian of Halicarnassus, claimed that the body of Christ was by nature incorruptible, and that to affirm the contrary was "phthartolatry"—worship of the corruptible. Christ had truly suffered on the cross; but this was not because of a natural corruptibility of his body, but because of a special concession on his part, with a view to redemption.[15] Against them, the Severians held that the incarnation itself, if taken seriously, required the natural corruptibility of the body of Christ, and that to deny such corruptibility was a veiled form of Docetism; for this reason they called Julian and his followers "Aphthartodocetists"—Docetists of incorruptibility. As a reaction to this, some of Julian's followers resorted to pure Eutychianism in proposing that the body of Jesus was not created—for which they were also called "aktistists."[16]

Later on, the Severians themselves were split. Some of them—the "agnosticists"—applied to the human soul of Jesus the same principles that Severus had applied to his body, and

---

14 See S. Vailhe, "Acéphales," *DHGE,* 1:282-88.

15 Such was the view of Leontius of Byzantium, *Contra nest. et eutych.* 2 (*PG,* 86:1333). See also M. Jugie, "Aphthartodocètes," *DHGE,* 3:946.

16 That is, "non-creationists." They were also known as "phantasiasts" and "Gaianites"—after bishop Gaianos.

thus came to the conclusion that Jesus, as a man, was ignorant of certain things—especially, on the basis of his own words, of the day of judgment. On the other hand, some Severians, led by Stephen of Niobe—and therefore called "Niobites"—were moved by events to the position of Julian and his followers, and eventually joined them.[17]

Such was the story of monophysism in the midst of the struggles and discussions that were prompted by the *Henoticon*. However, in order not to give an erroneous idea of the theology of the so-called monophysite churches that have subsisted until the twentieth century, one should point out that all the extreme sects of monophysism disappeared within a brief span, and that the Christology of the present so-called monophysite churches is closer to a verbal than to a real monophysism.

The schism of Acacius had hardly been healed, and the *Henoticon* repealed, when another christological controversy flared up. The issue now was whether or not it was correct to affirm that "one of the Trinity has suffered," and therefore this episode in the history of Christian thought is usually called "theopaschite controversy"—that is, controversy on the passion of God.[18] As the main proponents of theopaschism were monks from Scythia, it is also called "controversy of the Scythian monks." In truth, this controversy was no more than a new encounter between a "divisive" Christology of the Antiochene type and its "unitive" counterpart, which had traditionally been associated with Alexandria. The Scythian monks, concerned over the seeming upsurge of a divisive Christology after the repeal of the *Henoticon*, began using as their slogan and their measure of orthodoxy the phrase "one of the Trinity has suffered." They were thus emphasizing the *communicatio idiomatum* or communication of the properties, which had become one of the main traditional emphases of a unitive Christology. In fact, the Nestorian and theopaschite controversies were similar in that in both what was at issue was the

---

[17] There were also some controversies among the verbal monophysites due to the attempt that some made to apply christological terminology to trinitarian issues. See Jugie, "Monophysisme," 2243-49.

[18] See E. Amann, "Théopaschite (controverse)," *DTC*, 15:505-12.

possibility of attributing to the divine Word the properties of humanity. In the Nestorian controversy, the issue focused on the incarnation, while in the theopaschite controversy it focused on the passion of Christ. But the christological problem was essentially the same.

The Scythian monks had a long tradition on which to base their position, beginning with Ignatius of Antioch, who had spoken of "the passion of my God," and continuing in Peter the Fuller, who had added to the *Trisagion* the phrase "who wert crucified for us."

In any case, at the beginning of the sixth century, while Justin was emperor, and in the midst of the Chalcedonian reaction that followed the end of the Schism of Acacius, this group of monks opened a campaign to make the formula "one of the Trinity has suffered" part of the official doctrine of the Church. They had the support of General Vitalis, who had helped Justin rise to the purple and was therefore very powerful. However, their views were not well received in some circles in Constantinople, where it was feared that their insistence on a particular formula would give rise to new divisions, and would also prove to be the opportunity for a revival of opposition to Chalcedon. They then went to Rome, where they sought the support of Pope Hormisdas. But in spite of the pressure to which he was subjected from Constantinople, the Pope refused to support the Scythian monks.

Thus the question stood until Justin died and was succeeded by Justinian. Justinian's great dream was to rebuild the unity that the Empire had lost. To this end he sent his generals to the North of Africa. To this end he plunged into diplomatic adventures in Italy. To this end he had the body of Roman law compiled and organized. And to this end the unity of the church was absolutely necessary.

It was for this reason that Justinian was vitally interested in finding a solution to the christological issues that divided his empire. He thought that the best way to achieve this would be to make some concessions to those who were opposed to the decisions of Chalcedon, although without going so far as to alienate the defenders of the Chalcedonian formula. As in so many other cases before and after him, the efforts of Justinian, stamped as they were with the seal of imperial power and imposition, served only to make tempers fly and add fuel to the fire of controversy. Furthermore, Empress Theodora, an open supporter of Severian monophysism, led her husband further and further away from Chalcedonian orthodoxy, and the net result was a growing tension between the civil and ecclesiastical authorities.

At first, Justinian was harsh with the monophysites. But he soon became aware that this policy was not wise and decided to call a meeting between the defenders of Chalcedon and their adversaries, in order to attempt to settle their differences. This meeting, known as the "Contradictory Conference," only served to revive the theopaschite issue and to lead to the "controversy of the Three Chapters."

The theopaschite issue was revived at the Contradictory Conference because the opponents of the Council of Chalcedon insisted on the acceptance of the formula "one of the Trinity has suffered." Justinian believed that those who were opposed to this formula were excessively intolerant, and therefore made use of his authority to have the pope—at that time John II—support it. Thus that unitive Christology which had been traditionally associated with the name of Alexandria gave a rude blow to the opposite Antiochene tendency, which, now a minority, was struggling to set forth the complete reality of the man whom the Word had assumed.

An even stronger blow was to follow. This was the Controversy of the Three Chapters and its culmination in the Fifth Ecumenical Council. The title of "Three Chapters" was developed during the controversy itself as a short way of referring jointly to the work—and sometimes the persons themselves—of Theodore of Mopsuestia, Theodoret of Cyrus, and Ibas of Edessa, who, as has been said in our previous volume, were the principal teachers of Antiochene Christology. To a certain extent, the Controversy of the Three Chapters was the outcome of the Contradictory Conference, where it became clear that the so-called monophysites—most of them in reality only verbal monophysites—were opposed not so much to the

Council of Chalcedon as to the Christology to be found in the works of the Antiochene theologians which had served as a background for the decisions of that Council.[19] Hence seems to have sprung Justinian's notion that a compromise could be achieved by condemning, not the Council of Chalcedon itself, which would retain its authority, but rather the works of the three great Antiochene theologians, brought together under the Three Chapters. In two edicts, Justinian condemned the Three Chapters. In this he had the support of the most outstanding theologian of his time, Leontius of Byzantium, whom we shall study later. Furthermore, the imperial arm was heavy, and one after another the patriarchs of Constantinople, Alexandria, and Antioch added their signatures to the imperial edict, although each of them under pressure and with serious doubts as to the step that he was taking.

The reaction of the West was not slow in coming. There, the condemnation of the Three Chapters seemed a mere prelude to the open rejection of the Council of Chalcedon. But Pope Vigilius, who owed his papal tiara to the support of Theodora and of Justinian's general Belisarius, did not have the strength to resist Justinian's will.[20] Taken to Constantinople by order of the emperor, Vigilius, after some hesitation, finally condemned the Three Chapters in his *Iudicatum,* issued in A.D. 548. This provoked such a reaction among Western bishops, especially those of North Africa, that several of the Eastern hierarchs who had previously signed the edict now dared withdraw their support. The pope himself withdrew his *Iudicatum,* and suggested to Justinian that the best way to achieve the union sought was to call a synod of Western bishops, and there to have the Three Chapters condemned. But the opposition in the West was such that Justinian finally abandoned the project of gathering the Western bishops in a synod, and instead

---

[19] Regarding the importance of the "Three Chapters" in the earlier stages of the christological controversies see H. M. Diepen, *Les Trois Chapitres au Concile de Chalcédoine: Une étude de la christologie de l'Anatolie ancienne* (Oosterhout, Pays-Bas: Éd. de Saint-Michel, 1958).

[20] The deplorable pontificate of Vigilius is succinctly narrated by E. Amann, "Vigile," *DTC,* 15:2994-3005. His participation on the Controversy of the Three Chapters is discussed by the same author, "Trois-Chapitres (affaire des)," *DTC,* 15:1868-924, especially 1888-911.

AD 55 1

reasserted the condemnation of the Three Chapters (A.D. 551). In this new edict, basing his positions on the theology of Leontius of Byzantium, Justinian condemned the Nestorians as well as the monophysites. By "Nestorians" he meant not only those who claimed that Mary was not *theotokos*, but also any who dared affirm that the Word had assumed "a man," as if the man could subsist or pre-exist apart from the Word. Among these Nestorians, Justinian included, besides Nestorius himself, Theodore, Theodoret, and Ibas—that is, the famous Three Chapters. As to the monophysites who were condemned by the edict of 551, they were only the true and extreme monophysites, that is, those who confused the divinity and the humanity of Christ in such a way that the latter was eclipsed. In short, Antiochene Christology was condemned in all its forms, while Alexandrine Christology was rejected only in its most extreme form.

The opposition to Justinian's new edict was such that finally he decided to call a general council, expecting it to add its ecclesiastical sanction to his civil authority. This council gathered at Constantinople in May of the year 553, and Justinian made sure that all the bishops attending were in favor of the condemnation of the Three Chapters, or at least were likely to assent to the imperial will.[21]

Meanwhile, Vigilius regained his composure and refused to accept the decision of the civil authority on a matter that was purely theological. After studying the issues involved he published his *Constitutum* on May 14, 553,[22] while the Council was gathered at Constantinople—where the pope also was, since the emperor had made him come to this capital. The *Constitutum* is a very careful document in which Vigilius studies the various issues involved in the Three Chapters. In the case of Theodore of Mopsuestia, Vigilius is willing to condemn certain views that seem to have been taken from his works; but he will not condemn, and even forbids anyone to condemn, a bishop who died in the communion of the church, for, in the words of

---

[21] Haacke, "Die kaiserliche Politik," pp. 170-171.
[22] *Mansi*, 9.61-106; 69:67-114.

Cyril—whom the monophysites took as the great defender of orthodoxy—"It is a grave crime to insult the dead." As to Theodoret of Cyrus, the second of the authors involved in the Three Chapters, he is not to be condemned, for at Chalcedon he anathematized Nestorius, and the bishops there gathered declared him to be orthodox. Anyone who condemns Theodoret thereby condemns the Council that absolved him. In spite of this, there are certain views that have been attributed to the dead bishop of Cyrus that should be condemned—and Vigilius does declare them to be anathema, although without affirming that they do in fact come from the pen of Theodoret. Finally, the letter of Ibas of Edessa which is included in the Three Chapters was read and accepted by the Fathers at Chalcedon, and therefore one cannot condemn it without rejecting that Council. Therefore, Vigilius concludes that the discussion of the orthodoxy of the Three Chapters is to cease, and all must submit to the authority of the Roman See as it is expressed in the present *Constitutum*, which annuls all that may have been said at any previous time in an opposite sense, including the *Iudicatum* itself, which the pope had given in A.D. 548.

While Vigilius was preparing and publishing his *Constitutum*, the Council that Justinian had called was meeting in Constantinople. This Council is usually called the Fifth Ecumenical Council. It was clear from the beginning that the Council would condemn the Three Chapters and follow the general lines of Justinian's policies. With reference to the Three Chapters, the decision of the Council was as follows: Theodore of Mopsuestia was condemned, jointly with his teachings; Theodoret was not condemned as a person, but his teachings were rejected; the Epistle of Ibas was declared to be heretical, although means were found not to belie the Council of Chalcedon.[23] The Council also followed Justinian's directions in condemning Origen, who was reputed to be the source of many heretical notions.

For more than half a year, Vigilius refused to accept the decisions of the Council. But finally, under great pressure from

---

[23] This was done through a subterfuge, claiming that the letter of Ibas which was read at Chalcedon was another.

the emperor, he issued a second *Iudicatum*[24] in which, while
trying to safeguard his own integrity, he nevertheless surren-
dered to the wishes of the emperor.[25] This provoked a virulent
reaction in the West, to the point that several schisms developed
which took years to heal.[26]

The next and last episode of the christological controversies
during the period that we are now studying took place in the
seventh century. This was the "monothelite" controversy and its
prelude, "monergism." In this new debate, as previously,
political considerations played an important role. The Byzantine
Empire was at war with Persia, and during the conflict the depth
of discontent among the Byzantine subjects in Syria and Eygpt
had been clearly visible. As it was precisely in these two regions
that Severian monophysism had developed some strength, it
seemed urgent to make a new effort to win over the allegiance of
the monophysites. Such seems to have been the motivation of
Patriarch Sergius of Constantinople, who was the main
proponent of monergism and, later, of monothelism.[27]

As a means of rapprochement between the Chalcedonians
and the Severian monophysites, Sergius proposed the formula
"one energy"—μία ἐνεργεία—which he tried to associate with
the formula "two natures." That is, he accepted Chalcedonian
Christology, but was attempting to win over the Severians by
proposing a stronger means of affirming the unity of Christ than
the mere "hypostasis" of Chalcedon. This one energy was
understood in the sense that, as there was in Christ a single
hypostasis to which all the activities of the Savior were to be
referred, there must have been also a single principle of activity,
that of the Word, which served his humanity as well as his
divinity. Hence, the more precise formula "a single hypostatic

---

[24] *Mansi,* 9:457-88.

[25] Vigilius here made use of the same subterfuge to which the Council had recourse, claiming that a
different letter was read at Chalcedon. Theodore is condemned outright, while in the case of
Theodoret only his doctrines, and not his person, are to be condemned, for he recanted at Chalcedon.

[26] See Amann, "Trois-Chapitres," 1911-24. When Pelagius succeeded Vigilius, Rome once again
reversed its position, for even at the time when he was still a deacon Pelagius had been a staunch
defender of the Three Chapters, as may be seen in his treatise *In defensione Trium Capitulorum.*

[27] Not often mentioned, but perhaps earlier than Sergius, is Theodore of Pharan. See W. Elert, *Der
Ausgang der altkirchlichen Christologie: Eine Untersuchung über Theodor von Pharan und seine Zeit als
Einführung in die alte Dogmengeschichte* (Berlin: Lutherisches Verlagshaus, 1957).

energy."[28] The proposal put forth by Sergius was well received by Emperor Heraclius, who was concerned about the need to reconcile the various theological factions within his empire, and who must have been pleased to hear that the new Patriarch of Alexandria had been able to achieve the reconciliation of the orthodox and the monophysites in his city through the use of the monergistic formula.

There was, however, a great deal of opposition to monergism among the supporters of Chalcedon. Speaking for this opposition, Sophronius of Jerusalem[29] attacked monergism with such ardor and penetration that Sergius decided to withdraw his proposal, and in A.D. 634 prohibited the use of the formula "one energy," as well as of its opposite, "two energies."

Instead of monergism, Sergius then proposed monothelism, that is, the doctrine that there is in Christ a single will. There has been a great deal of discussion regarding the exact meaning of this formula, and its imprecision and seeming variation have led one scholar to refer to monothelism as "the chameleon heresy."[30] In any case, Sergius was able to enlist Pope Honorius among the supporters of his new formula, and in A.D. 638 Emperor Heraclius promulgated the *Ecthesis* of Sergius, in which he once again prohibited any discussion regarding the unity or duality of "energy" in Jesus Christ, and at the same time affirmed that there was in the Savior a "single will"—a single *thelema*, and hence the name monothelism.

Opposition to the new formula was not slow in coming. Maximus of Chrysopolis, known as "the Confessor," whom we shall study further on in this chapter, claimed that both the "energy" or principle of activity and the will pertain to the nature—φύσις—and not to the person or hypostasis. Therefore, one must confess that there are in the Savior, not "a single hypostatic energy" or "a single hypostatic will," but rather "two natural energies and two natural wills." The opposition to monothelism soon counted an impressive number of bishops

---

[28] M. Jugie, "Monothélisme," *DTC*, 10:2317.

[29] *Ep. syn. ad Serg.*

[30] Jugie, "Monothélisme," 2307.

and even popes, and eventually Constans II prohibited all discussion of the matter.[31]

Shortly after the edict of Constans, the political situation changed in such a way that the Byzantine emperors lost all interest in gaining the support of the monophysites. The direct cause of this change was the Arabs, who in conquering Syria and Egypt took from the Byzantine Empire the regions where the opposition to the Council of Chalcedon had been most widespread. As a result, the emperors became more prone to affirm Chalcedonian orthodoxy, which was centered in the territory that they still held.

The issue was finally settled in the council that gathered in Constantinople in the year 681, usually called the Sixth Ecumenical Council.[32] There monothelism and its defenders were condemned, and so were Sergius and Honorius—a fact that centuries later would be brought up in the context of the discussion of papal infallibility.[33] On the positive side, the Council declared itself in favor of the doctrine of "two natural wills" in the Lord, that is, one will pertaining to each of the two natures proclaimed at Chalcedon.

Thus ended a long process of dogmatic development and clarification which had begun at least three centuries earlier. The result was the rejection of all extreme positions, the categorical assertion that Jesus Christ was totally and truly human as well as divine, and yet the claim that these two natures were closely bound together in a single hypostasis. In this process, the historical, loving Jesus of the New Testament was left aside, and the Savior had become an object of speculation and controversy; he was now described in terms totally alien to the vocabulary of the New Testament—"hypostasis," "nature," "energy," etc.; he had become a static object of discussion rather than the Lord of believers and of history. But one might ask whether any other road was open to the church once believers began applying their best intellectual faculties to the greatest

[31] *Mansi*, 10:777-78.
[32] *Ibid.*, 11:190-922.
[33] See G. Kreuzer, *Die Honoriusfrage im Mittelalter und in der Neuzeit* (Stuttgart: A. Hiersemann, 1975).

mystery of the Christian faith. The way that was followed through the six councils we have discussed did somehow manage to reject every simplistic attempt to rationalize the faith, and did point to the inscrutable mystery of the incarnation.

Philosophy and Theology

The Christian East, much more than the West, was the heir of Greek philosophy. The mere fact that the East still spoke basically the same language as the ancient philosophers would suffice to explain why it was that, when the West had no contact with Plato and Aristotle except through their interpreters, in the East they were still being studied. Furthermore, until the time of the Arab invasions, toward the end of the period that we are now studying, the East was relatively free of invasions and great disturbances. The Academy in Athens was able to continue functioning until it was closed by an imperial edict in the year 529. Alexandria continued cultivating letters just as it had done in the times of Clement and Origen. Antioch and Gaza vied with it for intellectual supremacy, and at the same time the recently born Constantinople was approaching their stature.

Within such a lively intellectual context, it is not surprising that the question of the relationship between philosophy and theology was repeatedly posed. This took place in three main ways during the period that we are now studying:

In the first place, the problem was posed of the truth of certain Christian dogmas and their compatibility or lack of it with philosophical thought. The questions that were discussed within this context were, as before, the doctrines of creation and of the resurrection of the body. The most outstanding thinkers in this respect were the "three Gazans"—Aeneas of Gaza, Zacharias of Mytilene, and Procopius of Gaza—and the Alexandrine philosopher John Philoponus.

In the second place, the question was asked of the relationship between Neoplatonic mysticism and the Christian life and doctrine. It is within this context that we shall study the thought of Pseudo-Dionysius in our next section.

Finally, the question was asked of the manner in which Greek philosophy in general, and more specifically its terminology, were to be used to solve theological issues, especially in the field of Christology. Under this heading we shall study, in separate sections, Leontius of Byzantium and Maximus the Confessor.

The questions of creation and redemption are posed in the works of Zacharias of Mytilene and his brother Procopius of Gaza, as well as in those of their common friend Aeneas of Gaza, and of the Alexandrine John Philoponus.[34] They believed that the Christian doctrine of creation was opposed to the classical teaching of the eternity of the world. In his dialogue *Theophrastus*, Aeneas affirms that the entire sensible world, including even the heavenly bodies, is created and mortal.[35] Procopius refutes the doctrine of the eternity of the world by affirming that mutable matter cannot be eternal.[36] Zacharias writes an entire dialogue—the *Ammonius*—in order to refute the eternity of the world. He argues that, although God is eternally creator, this does not require creation to be eternal, just as a doctor may continue being such even without a patient.[37] The same subject is discussed in a similar manner by John Philoponus in his treatises *On the Creation of the World* and *On the Eternity of the World*.

On the other hand, the question of the relationship between the resurrection of the body and the immortality of the soul is discussed by Aeneas in his *Theophrastus*. Here it is affirmed that the soul, although a creature, is immortal. Its free will is the clearest indication of that immortality, and it is able to lead humanity toward divinization. The body, which is now mortal, will rise again on the final day to be permanently united with its soul, and will then be immortal. On this point Aeneas differed from John Philoponus, who denied the resurrection of the body,[38] and was attacked for this view by several theologians.

---

[34] In this brief section I have followed B. Tatakis, *Filosofía Bizantina* (Buenos Aires: Sudamericana, 1952), pp. 33-60.

[35] *PG*, 85:961.

[36] *PG*, 87:29.

[37] *PG*, 85:1068.

[38] In his lost work *On the resurrection*. See Photius, *Bib*. 31-32.

Pseudo-Dionysius

The most influential Eastern theologian during the period that we are now studying was without any doubt the one who published his works under the pseudonym of Dionysius the Areopagite. For centuries his writings were believed to have come from the hand of Paul's disciple, and this gave them an authority second only to that of the New Testament. As these works present an entire world view that is basically Neoplatonic, they greatly contributed to the influence of Neoplatonism on Christian theology.

It is impossible to know who the false Dionysius was, although it seems reasonable to suggest that he lived toward the end of the fifth century, possibly near or in Syria. His works are *On the Celestial Hierarchy, On the Ecclesiastical Hierarchy, On the Divine Names, Mystical Theology,* and ten *Epistles.*

In a typically Neoplatonic fashion, Pseudo-Dionysius conceives of the world as a hierarchical structure in which all things come from God and lead to God, although each in a different degree, according to its position in the hierarchical order.[39] God is the One in the absolute sense; God totally transcends every category of human thought; God is even beyond essence. God "is" not, but rather all that is derives its being from the divine. God is unknowable as such, although all beings reveal and lead to God.

Beginning from this ineffable One, all the intellects—our author seems to be almost exclusively interested in the intellectual world—are ordered hierarchically.

In heaven, the angelic intellects are divided into three hierarchies, each with three degrees, so that there are nine hierarchical choirs. The first level comprises the seraphim, the cherubim, and the thrones, in that order. They are followed by dominions, virtues, and powers. Finally, the lower hierarchy comprises principalities, archangels, and angels. It is through

---

[39] R. Roques, *L'univers dionysien: Structure hierarchique du monde selon le Pseudo-Denys* (Paris: Aubier, 1954); J. Vanneste, *Le mystère de Dieu: Essai sur la structure rationelle de la doctrine mystique de Pseudo-Denys l'Aréopagite* (Bruges: Desclée de Brouwer, 1959); B. Brons, *Gott und die Seienden: Untersuchungen zum Verhältnis von Neuplatonischer Metaphysik und christlicher Tradition bei Dionysius Areopagita* (Göttingen: Vandenhoeck und Ruprecht, 1976).

this hierarchy that God pours light upon the earth and rules the peoples. Each nation has an angel through which divine providence acts upon it. Complex as it may seem, this hierarchy is not a barrier standing between God and the various beings, but is rather a channel through which the lower beings—including humans—receive the divine gifts.

Here on earth, before the advent of Christ, the legal hierarchy ruled. This hierarchy was established by Moses, and its function was—as is that of every other hierarchy in this system—to lead to God. But the false Dionysius does not spell out the details of this hierarchy, which in any case has been supplanted by the ecclesiastical hierarchy.

The ecclesiastical hierarchy is formed by two basic orders, each divided in three degrees.[40] The first of these is the priestly order, with its tripartite hierarchy composed of bishops, priests, and deacons. The other order is formed by the laity, and they too are divided in three degrees—the monks, the faithful people, and those who do not participate at the altar with the people, that is, the catechumens, energumens, and penitents. Here our author abandons for a moment his speculative principles in order more adequately to describe the reality of the church. According to the strict hierarchical principle, each degree of being communicates with God through the order that is immediately superior to it. This is not always so in the ecclesiastical hierarchy. For instance, the bishop confirms the faithful, not through the priests and deacons, but directly.

The purpose of the entire hierarchical structure of the universe is the deification of all intellects, who may come to God through the higher orders. It is at this point that Pseudo-Diony-sius introduces the doctrine of the three ways, which would be very influential in later mysticism. These three ways or three mystical stages are the purgative or cathartic, in which the soul is rid of its impurity; the illuminative, where the soul receives the divine light; and the unitive, in which the soul is united with God in an ecstatic vision—a vision that, because of the absolute

---

[40] D. Rutledge, *Cosmic Theology: The Ecclesiastical Hierarchy of pseudo-Denys: An Introduction* (London: Routledge and Kegan Paul, 1964).

transcendence of God, is not "comprehensive," but rather "intuitive."[41] While following these three ways, the soul is aided by the various hierarchies. This they do through the sacraments, although the notion of sacrament found here is very extensive, and includes not only such things as baptism, the eucharist and ordination, but actually the entire process by which all hierarchies reflect the One from whom they come.

If this were the totality of the thought of Pseudo-Dionysius, it would be difficult to call him a Christian. But Christ does have a role to play in the total activity and structure of the hierarchies.[42] The Word, one of the hypostases of the Trinity,[43] has become incarnate, so that in that hypostasis the two "natures" or "essences" of divinity and humanity converge.[44] However, one does not find in these writings the assertion that these two natures subsist in the incarnate Word. On the contrary, the impression is given that the humanity has been absorbed into the divinity in such a way that after the incarnation one can no longer speak of a human nature in the Savior. In a typically Alexandrine fashion, the communication of the properties— *communicatio idiomatum*—is carried to an extreme. The monergist formula "one theandric energy" is employed.[45] For these reasons, Pseudo-Dionysius has been accused of monophysism. These accusations are false if they are meant to imply that he completely denies the existence of a human nature in Christ. But if they mean simply that his Christology is closer to that of the verbal monophysites, or even to a real but moderate monophysism, one cannot but concede that such suspicions are grounded.

Christ is the head of the celestial hierarchy as well as of the ecclesiastical. As God, Christ is the source of being and of illumination for the entire celestial hierarchy, and he is also its object of knowledge. By his incarnation, he is the head of the ecclesiastical hierarchy, not only as source of all being and

---

[41] W. Völker, *Kontemplation and Ekstase bei pseudo-Dionysius Areopagita* (Wiesbaden: Steiner, 1958), pp. 197-210.

[42] P. Chevallier, *Jésus-Christ dans les oeuvres du pseudo-Denys* (Paris: Plon, 1951).

[43] His trinitarian doctrine, which cannot be discussed here, is summarized in *De div. nom.* 2.

[44] See the brief christological statement in *Ecc. hier.* 3.

[45] J. Marić, "Pseudo-Dionysii Areopagite formula christologica celeberrina theandrica," *BogSmotra*, 20 (1932), 105-73.

illumination and as object of all contemplation, but also as the direct founder of that hierarchy. Thus, the incarnate Word appears repeatedly in the pages of Pseudo-Dionysius. But one might ask whether this Word which communicates with humankind only through hierarchical orders is not very different from the Jesus who lived as one among us.

Whatever the answer may be to that question, the fact is that Pseudo-Dionysius had a widespread influence. Originally written in Greek, his works were translated into Syriac in the sixth century, into Armenian in the eighth, and into Latin in the ninth. Since that time, and throughout the Middle Ages, the West would quote him as a faithful interpreter of the Pauline message.

Leontius of Byzantium

The most outstanding theologian of Justinian's reign was the monk Leontius of Byzantium,[46] who took part in the "Contradictory Conference" on behalf of the Chalcedonian party, and was perhaps one of the Scythian monks who gave rise to the theopaschite controversy.[47] If we leave aside several dubious writings as well as others that are clearly spurious, three works have survived under the name of Leontius: his three books *Against the Nestorians and the Eutychians,* his *Thirty Chapters Against Severus,* and his *Solutions to the Arguments of Severus.*

At the beginning of his first book *Against the Nestorians and the Eutychians,* Leontius set out to establish the distinction as well as the relationship between "hypostasis" and "essence" or "nature."[48] He claims that this is of great importance, for the various trinitarian and christological heresies have arisen out of incorrect interpretations of the meaning of these terms. Thus, Nestorianism takes as its starting point the two natures and

---

[46] See the article by V. Grumel, "Léonce de Byzance," *DTC,* 9:400-426; also the excellent monograph by J. P. Junglas, *Leontius von Byzanz: Studien zu seinen Schriften, Quellen und Anschauungen* (Paderborn: F. Schöningh, 1908); and D. B. Evans, *Leontius of Byzantium: An Origenist Christology* (Dumbarton Oaks: Center for Byzantine Studies, 1970).

[47] I say "perhaps," because the name "Leontius" is rather common, and it is impossible to know how many and which of the various men of that name mentioned in the documents are to be identified with the theologian Leonitius of Byzantium.

[48] *PG,* 86:1273.

reaches the conclusion that there are in Christ two hypostases, whereas the Eutychians begin with the single hypostasis of the incarnate Word and deny his duality of natures. By setting forth the true meaning of these two terms of the union that took place in Christ, both heresies will be refuted, and orthodoxy will shine forth.

The main difference between "essence" or "nature" on the one hand, and "hypostasis" on the other is that essence is that which makes a thing belong to a genus, whereas hypostasis is what gives it its individuality. Therefore, every hypostasis has an essence, and every essence requires a hypostasis in order to subsist; but there is a difference between the two, so that the hypostasis always has a nature or essence, whereas the opposite is not always true.

There are three ways in which two realities may be united. In the first place, they may be united by a mere juxtaposition, so that there are two natures as well as two hypostases. This is what the Nestorians call a "moral union." In the second place, two things may be united in such a way that the distinction between their natures is destroyed and a third one appears. This is the doctrine of the Eutychians. Finally, two things may be so united that their distinct natures subsist in a single hypostasis. It is thus that the flame and that which burns are united; the flame has its own nature and that which burns has another, but both subsist in a single hypostasis called fire. Such is also the case in the union of the body and the soul; each of these has its own nature, but as long as they are united, they have a single hypostasis called human being, so that all the operations of the soul and of the body are ascribed to that being. In this third kind of union, each of the two natures could subsist separately by itself; but as long as the union lasts the two subsist in a single hypostasis. This is the kind of union which takes place in Christ, whose human nature subsists in the hypostasis of his divine nature. This may be better understood by distinguishing between hypostasis and "enhypostaton," that is, between a subsistence itself and that which subsists in it. Thus, the hypostasis in Christ is that of the eternal Word, and in it the divine as well as the human nature subsist. It is for this reason that one may say that there is in Christ an "enhypostatic union."

The two natures that come together in this kind of union do not lose their properties. It is on this basis that Leontius opposes Aphthartodocetism, which claims that, because of its union with the divine nature, the flesh of Christ was not capable of suffering or of corruption, except in the specific cases in which he condescended to make it capable of such suffering or corruption. Leontius sees in this view a denial of the true union of two natures, for what would thus take place would be a confusion or mixture of the two, resulting in an intermediate nature, different from the two that came together to form the union—what Latin theology calls a *tertium quid*.

On the other hand, this does not deny the *communicatio idiomatum*. One only has to keep in mind that in that *communicatio* the attributes of one nature are not applied to the other, but rather those of both natures are applied to their common hypostasis. It is thus correct to say that God was born of Mary and that therefore Mary is the Mother of God.[49] In this entire christological development, Leontius uses three main sources: the logic of Aristotle, Platonic anthropology—which had earlier been incorporated into the tradition of the church—and the clarifications of the Cappadocians regarding *ousia* and *hypostasis*. In joining these various elements into a synthesis, he contributed to the final victory of Chalcedonian Christology in the Byzantine Empire.

Maximus the Confessor

The main opponent, first of monergism, and later of monothelism, was Maximus of Chrysopolis, generally known as "the Confessor." Together with Sophronius of Jerusalem and Anastasius Sinaita, Maximus defended the Chalcedonian faith throughout the controversies of the seventh century. He is also well known for his ascetic works, widely used in Eastern monastic circles.

---

[49] In passing, it may be well to point out that Leontius, in his eagerness to safeguard Mary's purity, claims that Jesus was born without physically destroying her virginity. A short time later, the same point would be debated in the West.

From the point of view of the history of Christian thought, Maximus is especially significant for his Christology, which he built on the foundation of Leontius of Byzantium and developed in opposition to monergism and monothelism.[50] Over against monergism, Maximus claims that the "energy" or principle of activity has reference to the nature, and not to the hypostasis. This is true of the Trinity, in which there is only one activity because there is only one essence or nature. The nature determines the principle of activity, although it may also be true that the hypostasis, as the principle of individuality, gives form and particularity to that activity. Therefore, as there are in Christ two natures, there must be in him two principles of activity, and monergism must be rejected.

Maximus argues against monothelism on the basis of the distinction between the "natural will"—that is, the will of the nature—and the "will of the reason." The former is the inclination of the nature toward its own good. The latter is the will that develops on the basis of knowledge, deliberation, and decision. The former is found in every nature, and therefore one must affirm two wills in Christ—the human natural will and the divine natural will. This does not mean, however, that Christ could make contradictory decisions at the same time, for the natural will is always subject to the rational will. Therefore, the two natural wills could never be opposed in a decision, but only in their inclination—as was the case in the Garden of Gethsemane. Christ, although having a natural human will, was incapable of sin, for his rational will would always make every decision on the basis his omniscient reason as the Word of God. Human passions, which are the normal result of the human will, did not move Christ, but were rather moved by the superior rational will.

In summary, during the years between the Council of Chalcedon (A.D. 451) and the Third Council of Constantinople

---

[50] See V. Grumel, "Maxime de Chrysopolis," *DTC*, 10:448-59; L. Thunberg, *Microcosm and Mediator: The Theological Anthropology of Maximus the Confessor* (Lund: C. W. G. Gleerup, 1965); F. Heinzer, *Gottes Sohn als Mensch: Die Struktur des Menschseins Christi bei Maximus Confessor* (Freiburg, Schweiz: Universitätsverlag, 1980); P. Piret, *Le Christ et la Trinité selon Maxime le Confesseur* (Paris: Beauchesne, 1983).

(A.D. 680–681) there was much more original theological activity in the East than in the West. But this theological activity was so technical and so involved in matters of little consequence that here also it would seem that the period of original and creative thought was coming to an end. This will prove to have been the case when, after a new incursion into Western theology, we return to the East, where we shall find the main centers of patristic theology under Moslem rule, the Nestorians and monophysites struggling for survival, the Orthodox Church subjected to imperial power, and theology almost entirely reduced to a mere repetition and discussion of ancient texts and formulas.

The Development of Nestorian Theology

During the period that we are now studying, not all Christians accepted the christological decisions of the councils of Ephesus and Chalcedon. We have already seen that the authority of the Council of Chalcedon was doubted for a long time, even within the confines of the Greek Church. We must now devote a few paragraphs to those who refused to accept the authority of the Council of Ephesus and insisted on the christological formula "two persons." These Christians were forced to settle outside the Roman Empire, but eventually became dominant in the Persian church. This is the reason why that church is usually called "Nestorian," although she herself would not accept such a title. After the discussion of these Christians, a separate section will be devoted to the opposite extreme, that is, to those who refused to accept the formula "in two natures," and were thus led to break the bonds of communion with those Christians who accepted it and required it as a measure of orthodoxy.

The condemnation of Nestorius at Ephesus and the reunion formula of A.D. 433 left no place for the extreme forms of Antiochene Christology. The Council of Chalcedon was seen as a vindication of the moderate Antiochenes. But its later interpretation, culminating in the condemnation of the Three Chapters in A.D. 533, once again gave Alexandrine Christology the upper hand. As a consequence, those who still defended

Antiochene Christology drifted farther and farther from the rest of the church and eventually set up an independent communion which other Christians called "Nestorian," whose main strength was in and around Persia.

Even before the condemnation of Nestorius, Antiochene Christology was common in the Christian outposts in the Western reaches of the Persian Empire. For a while, this budding Persian school of theology centered around Ibas of Edessa, the friend of Nestorius who was condemned in the Three Chapters. Later, when the opposition to Antiochene Christology reached its climax and Emperor Zeno closed the school of Edessa in A.D. 489, the main teachers of this school simply crossed the border and settled at Nisibis, where a theological school was founded by Bishop Barsumas, a former disciple of Ibas. It was mostly through the influence of this school that Antiochene Christology, usually in its extreme form, expanded throughout the Persian Empire, and even beyond its Eastern borders.

This process was aided by political circumstances that led to a growing gap between Persian Christians and those who lived within the Roman Empire. The ancient rivalry between these two great powers led the Persian rulers to doubt the loyalty of subjects who in religious matters seemed to conform to the traditional enemy of Persia. Therefore, they were pleased to see the growing theological disagreement between their Christian subjects and the rest of the church. At the same time, many Persian Christians tended to emphasize their disagreements with Roman Christians in order to dispel any doubt as to their loyalty to their government. The growing tensions finally led to an open break when Persian patriarch Babai called two synods (A.D. 498 and 499), which rejected the Christology set forth at Chalcedon and declared Persian Christianity to be independent from the rest of the church.[51]

The first outstanding theologian of this Nestorian church was Narses (or Narsai), who flourished while Babai was patriarch.

---

[51] A. R. Vine, *The Nestorian Churches* (London: Independent Press, 1937), pp. 37-52.

After several years of work under Barsumas at Nisibis, Narses became the head of that school and held that position until his death in A.D. 507. His surviving works are mostly homilies and hymns.[52] These hymns earned for him the title of "Harp of the Holy Spirit," given him by a Nestorian chronicler. The Jacobite monophysites called him "Narses the Leper."

The main christological formula of Narses is "two natures (*kyane*), two hypostases (*knume*), and one appearance or presence (*parsufa*)." The key to the meaning of this formula is in the manner in which one understands the terms "hypostasis" and "parsufa." In various places in this *History*, we have pointed out the ambiguity of the term "hypostasis," and its Syriac equivalent is just as ambiguous. As to "parsufa," it corresponds to the Greek *prosopon* and thus refers to the person as well as to the appearance of that person. The works of Narses leave no doubt regarding this last point: the *parsufa*, which is the term of the union of the two natures and hypostases, corresponds not to our "person" but rather to the presence or appearance of a person. Narses is very careful not to confuse the humanity of Christ with the divinity of the Word. He who was born of Mary was the man Jesus, who was sanctified, no doubt, by virtue of the Word, but who was not united to that Word in such a way that one can say that the Word was born of Mary, or that she is *theotokos*. As sources for these doctrines, Narses repeatedly quotes such Antiochene teachers as Diodore of Tarsus, Theodore of Mopsuestia, and Nestorius.

The other outstanding theologian before the Arab conquest was Babai the Great, who flourished early in the seventh century and—although never a patriarch—practically rules his church until his death in A.D. 628. The most significant of his surviving works are his *Book on the Union* and a brief *Theological Opuscle*.[53]

---

[52] Two ancient chroniclers affirm that Narses also wrote commentaries on several books of the Old Testament. But such commentaries—if they did truly exist—have been lost, and not a single quotation from them has been preserved by other writers. See R. H. Connolly, ed., *The Liturgical Homilies of Narsai* (Cambridge: University Press, 1909; reprint, Kraus, 1967); F. G. McLeod, *Narsai's Metrical Homilies on the Nativity, Epiphany, Passion, Resurrection and Ascension* (Turnhout: Brepols, 1979).

[53] Edited in the original Syriac, with a Latin translation by A. Vaschalde, *CSCO*, 79-80.

The main occasions for his theological labors were his attempts to refute Jacobite monophysism, which had a considerable following among the Syriac-speaking population, and his opposition to the schism of Henana, who attempted to bring Persian Christology closer to that of Chalcedon.

Babai's Christology follows the general lines of the earlier Antiochene teachers, whom he quotes frequently. Like them, he affirms that the Word dwelt in the man "as in a temple."[54] His basic christological formulation, following that of Narses, places the union at the level of the *parsufa*,[55] although in his case it seems likely that this term is to be understood not as a mere appearance or presence, but rather in the same sense in which Nestorius understood the "prosopon of union."[56] Like all Nestorians, he rejects every attempt to understand the union of the two natures in Christ in terms of the hypostatic union of body and soul that takes place in humans.[57] On the other hand, he categorically denies the possibility of speaking of "two sons" as had been done by Diodore of Tarsus,[58] and, although he does not use the phrase "communication of properties," he does assert that on certain occasions there is an "exchange of names" between the two natures of the word incarnate.[59] It is thus clear that, after the Persian church became definitely independent from Greek Christianity, and especially after the Byzantine Empire began waning, the Nestorians no longer felt the constant need to show their disagreements with Greek Orthodox Christianity, and thus slowly came to approach the general views that were expressed at the Council of Chalcedon, although they never abandoned the traditional Antiochene formulas.

Shortly after the death of Babai, the Arab invasion ended Persian independence and opened a new era in the history of the Nestorian church.

---

[54] *Lib. de unione* (CSCO, 79:236, 245).
[55] *Ibid.*, 124.
[56] See this *History*, 1:361-62.
[57] *Opusc.* (CSCO, 79:291-307).
[58] *Lib. de unione* (CSCO, 79:152-60). On Diodore, see *History* 1:339-40.
[59] E. Herman, "Babai le Grand," *DHGE*, 6:12.

The Expansion of Monophysism

Since the various forms that monophysism took have already been discussed, it only remains here to give a brief idea of its expansion during the years prior to the Arab conquest, so that, upon returning to the East later on in this *History*, the reader will not be surprised to find several monophysite churches in different parts of the Eastern world.

Because the doctrine that is usually called "monophysism" is simply the rejection of the decisions of Chalcedon on behalf of extreme Alexandrine Christology, this doctrine was very popular in Alexandria and throughout Egypt. After the condemnation of Dioscorus, many held him to be a martyr to political interests, and this, coupled with the various actions of several emperors against Egyptian dissent, led many to see in monophysism a symbol of opposition to the emperor and to the government of Constantinople. Thus, monophysism became more widespread among the Coptic-speaking native population than among the higher, Greek-speaking classes. After various schisms and other similar signs of tension, the final breach came when the Arab conquest ended Byzantine rule over Egypt. After that time, most Egyptian Christians rejected the formulations of Chalcedon and formed the Coptic Church, while the minority that remained faithful to Chalcedonian authorities was called "Melchite"—that is, "of the emperor." Since Ethiopian Christianity had very close relations with Egypt, the church in Ethiopia also became monophysite.

As was pointed out in the first volume of this *History*, although Antioch was the center of opposition to Alexandrine Christology, there were always in Syria those who insisted on a unitive Christology. Therefore, there was also a measure of opposition to the decisions of the Council of Chalcedon. Jacob Baradaeus, who died in A.D. 578, spread monophysite doctrine throughout Syria, and from there it moved on to Persia. For this reason, the Syrian-speaking monophysite communion is known as the Jacobite Church.

Finally, Armenian Christianity also followed the monophysite line. This was mostly because when the Council of Chalcedon

God created Christ

took place most of Armenia was under Persian rule, and therefore that church was not represented at the Council. This was coupled with other reasons for friction which led to a growing gap between the Armenian church and Chalcedonian Christianity. Finally, in A.D. 491, the head of Christianity in Armenia anathematized Leo's *Tome*, which expressed traditional Latin Christology and was also at the very foundation of the Chalcedonian *Definition*.[60]

The Advance of Islam

The seventh century saw the beginning of one of the most remarkable religious and political phenomena in the entire history of humankind—the birth of Islam. Led by an almost incredible religious fervor, and somehow inspiring the same feelings in the peoples they conquered, a small group of semi-nomad tribes were able to become a powerful state that destroyed and supplanted the Persian Empire, conquered most of the Asian territories of Byzantium—including such cities as Antioch and Jerusalem—invaded Africa, where its armies poured across the entire northern coast, then crossed over the Iberian Peninsula, destroyed the Visigothic kingdom, and finally traversed the Pyrenees and threatened the rising kingdom of the Franks.

This almost unbelievable advance was facilitated by the various political, religious, and social divisions that existed in many of the conquered lands. Thus, monophysism and Nestorianism in Syria, monophysism in Egypt, and the remnants of Donatism in Africa opened the way to Islam, which was seen by many as the arm that God had caused to rise in order to chastise the Byzantine Empire.

In the lands that it conquered, Islam had a devastating impact upon Christianity. In some regions, the churches eventually died out completely. In others, they managed to survive, but in the process became small, conservative enclaves whose greatest

---

[60] K. Sarkissian, *The Council of Chalcedon and the Armenian Church* (London: S.P.C.K.: 1965); L. Frivold, *The Incarnation: A Study of the Doctrine of the Incarnation in the 5th and 6th Centuries* (Oslo: Universitetsforlaget, 1981).

efforts were devoted to preserving the memory of a past now gone.

On the other hand, Islam itself produced a great civilization, partly an heir of those it had conquered, but with its own very distinguishable characteristics. During the Dark Ages of European Christianity, Islamic civilization was without any doubt more advanced and refined than Western Christianity. In the midst of that civilization great thinkers emerged, and some of them—notably Averroës—eventually made their influence felt on Christian theology. But these developments belong in another section of this *History*.

IV

The Carolingian Renaissance

The ephemeral light of the Carolingian empire shone like a spark in the midst of the darkness of the early Middle Ages. The victories of Charles Martel and Pippin, later consolidated and expanded upon by Charlemagne, created in Western Europe a center of relative quiet and stability in which it was possible to devote oneself to study, thought, and literary production. Although Charlemagne was by no means a scholar, he was concerned for the intellectual and spiritual development of his kingdom, and attempted to attract to it the wisest sages of his times.

The main source of such scholars was the British Isles, whose monasteries had become the principle depositories of classical culture after the passing of Gregory the Great and his contemporaries.[1] In these monasteries, the ancient Christian writings were studied not only in Latin, but also in Greek. Their most significant scholar—a century before Charlemagne's times—had been Bede, usually known as "the Venerable," who wrote works on grammar, biblical commentaries, homilies, and poems, as well as his famous *Ecclesiastical History of the English Peoples*. The tradition that Bede and his fellow workers represented was the connecting link between antiquity and the

---

[1] See J. Décarreaux, *Moines et monastères à l'époque de Charlemagne* (Paris: J. Taillandier, 1980).

107

700 → 800 AD

108 A History of Christian Thought

theological and philosophical awakening that took place in the Carolingian empire.

The most outstanding scholar whom Charlemagne attracted to his kingdom was Alcuin of York, who was instrumental in the organization of the entire system of schools within the kingdom, and was involved in the theological debates of his time. Also significant were Theodulf of Orleans, Paulinus of Aquileia, and Agobard of Lyon.

The Carolingian renaissance was relatively ephemeral, as was also the empire that served as its background. Under Charlemagne—late in the eighth century and early in the ninth—the seeds sowed by Charles Martel and Pippin were beginning to sprout, and under Charles the Bald—who died in A.D. 877—the last fruits of the harvest were being gathered. After that time, a new period of intellectual darkness would cover Western Christianity until the eleventh and twelfth centuries brought a new renaissance.

In the field of theology, the Carolingian renaissance did not produce thinkers comparable to those of the patristic era, or to those which the thirteenth century would produce. There is only one system whose wide scope merits special mention—that of John Scotus Erigena, and he was more of a philosopher than a theologian. There was, however, a great deal of theological acitivity during the Carolingian period, although this activity was directed not toward the development of great systems, but rather toward various controversies regarding specific points of Christian doctrine—Christology, predestination, the virginity of Mary, and the eucharist. On the other hand, new contacts were established with the East, and thus two issues arose in which both branches of the church were included—the question of icons, and that of the *Filioque*.

The preceding paragraph provides the outline for the present chapter. We shall first discuss the various controversies that took place in the West during the Carolingian period. We shall then turn to the issue of the *Filoque*, leaving the controversy over the use of icons to be discussed within the framework of Eastern theology, where it is best understood. A separate section will then deal with John Scotus Erigena. Finally, we shall take up two matters that were left aside in our first volume, and that it seems wise to consider at this point—the development of penance, and the hierarchy.

The Christological Issue: Adoptionism

Chronologically, the first of the various controversies which took place during the Carolingian period had to do with Christology, and was centered in Spain, although it eventually involved several theologians from the Frankish kingdom, as well as the papacy. In this dispute, as in so many other ecclesiastical debates, political matters were an important factor. The Christians in Spain were just beginning to reconquer the peninsula from the Moslems. In that war of reconquest, the kingdom of the Franks played an important role, for it was the main power opposing the Moors in the region of the Pyrenees. However, there were also in Spain many "Mozarabs"—Christians living under Moslem rule—who did not wish to be identified with the political ambitions of the Franks. Therefore, they clung to their Mozarabic liturgy, and were not too concerned about keeping their theology in line with that which was predominant in the rest of Western Europe. Thus, it is significant to note that the first proponent of what eventually became known as "adoptionism," Elipandus of Toledo, lived under Moslem rule, claimed certain phrases from the Mozarabic liturgy in support of his position, and seems never to have had to recant. Yet the center of the controversy was not Elipandus, but Bishop Felix of Urgel, whose see was precisely on the border that at that time was disputed between Franks and Moors. Felix recanted repeatedly, always under Frankish pressure. When he returned to his original adoptionist position, he took refuge among the Moors. Finally, when Charlemagne forced him to retract once again, he was not allowed to return to Urgel, where he would have felt the presence and pressure of the Mozarabic environment. These facts indicate the extent to which political factors were involved in this controversy.

The question of adoptionism was posed when Bishop Elipandus of Toledo attempted to refute the Sabellian tendency of a certain Migetius.[2] Leaving aside the details regarding the historical development of the controversy,[3] one can say that Elipandus, in his effort to refute Sabellianism, but without any real need to do so, proposed a Christology in which he distinguished between Christ's filiation to the Father according to his divinity, and his filiation to the Father according to his humanity. The first is proper and natural, whereas the second is one of "adoption" and grace.

Felix, the bishop of Urgel, then defended the proposal of Elipandus. As Felix was a much abler theologian, adoptionism soon became identified with him and was thus called "the heresy of Felix."

The opposition to Elipandus and Felix was formidable, and was led in Spain by Beatus of Liebana, but beyond the Pyrenees counted also such leaders as Alcuin of York, Paulinus of Aquileia, and popes Hadrian I and Leo III, as well as several synods (Frankfort, A.D. 794, and Rome, A.D. 798), and Charlemagne himself. As a result, Felix was forced to recant repeatedly, although he relapsed at least once and was finally prevented from returning to his diocese. He died at Lyon in 818. As to Elipandus, it seems that, being beyond Charlemagne's reach, he retained his see and doctrine till the end of his days.

Why were so many and so distinguished persons involved in this controversy? The purely political interests involved have already been mentioned, and it is not necessary to dwell on them. But there was also a concern among theologians who believed that adoptionism was a new version of Nestorianism.

In an epistle that he wrote to Elipandus, Beatus of Liebana clearly shows that what disturbs him is the tendency that he finds in the bishop of Toledo to divide the person of Christ. Commenting on the confession of Peter and the Lord's reply, Beatus claims that the revelation that comes not through flesh or blood, but rather from the Father who is in heaven, leads one to affirm, "Thou art the Christ, the Son of the Living God,"

---

[2] If Elipandus is to be believed, Migetius claimed that the Father was David, the Son was Jesus, and the Spirit was Paul. *Ep. i ad Mig.* 3.

[3] Such details may be found in E. Amann, *L'époque carolingienne* (Vol. 6 of Fliche and Martin, *Histoire de l'Eglise*, Paris: Bloud et Gay, 1934), pp. 129-52.

whereas the so-called revelation that comes not from the Father, but from flesh and blood, leads one to affirm, "Thou art adopted according to humanity, and Son of the living God according to divinity."[4] There is only one Son of God, and he cannot be divided.

> Who is the Son of God, if not Jesus, who was born of the Virgin Mary? This name was proclaimed to the virgin by the angel who said: "You should call him Jesus, and he shall be great, and will be called 'Son of the Most High.'" But if what you [Elipandus] say were true, the angel would have said: "Jesus will be called adoptive Son of the Most High according to his humanity, and not adoptive according to his divinity."
>
> Also the Son himself would have said: "God so loved the world, that he gave his adoptive Son, so that whosoever believes in him should not perish." And this unity is such that unbelievers could only see a man in him whom they crucified. They crucified him as a man; they crucified the Son of God; they crucified God. My God was crucified for me.[5]

As may be seen, Beatus emphasizes the unity of the Savior and the communication of the properties of his two natures—the *communicatio idiomatum*. Therefore, the distinction that adoptionism establishes between the two manners in which the Savior is the Son of God must be rejected. In brief, we have here a parallel situation to that which existed in earlier centuries when Alexandrine Christology conflicted with that of Antioch. Elipandus and Felix emphasized the distinction between the divinity and the humanity of Christ, as the way of preserving the latter intact. Beatus and the other opponents of adoptionism feared that this doctrine would so divide the person of the Savior that the reality of the incarnation would be lost. This is why they accused the adoptionists of Nestorianism.

Was such an accusation based on fact? The leaders of adoptionism repeatedly rejected it, and insisted on condemning Nestorianism. Their opponents, on the other hand, constantly

---

[4] *Ad Elip. ep.* 1. 3-4.
[5] *Ibid.*, 1. 8.

Nestorianism — Mary gave birth to J.C. the man that God communicates His nature to man. Icarssss have adoptionism would be ...

claimed that adoptionism led to Nestorianism. Probably there was a measure of truth in both claims. The adoptionist theologians were not Nestorians inasmuch as they confessed the *communicatio idiomatum* and affirmed that Mary was the Mother of God. However, in claiming that there were two manners in which Christ was the Son of God, they approached the doctrine of the "two sons" which was typical of some early Antiochene theologians and which eventually led to Nestorianism.

The adoptionist controversy finally ended without major consequences. After the deaths of Elipandus and Felix, there were few who cared to continue discussing the matter.[6]

The Controversy over Predestination

One of the most bitter theological debates of the Carolingian period had to do with the doctrine of predestination. Although most of the great theologians of the period became involved in it—Rabanus Maurus, Ratramnus of Corbie, Servatus Lupus, Prudentius of Troyes, Florus of Lyon, John Scotus Erigena—the origin of the controversy was a prolonged and painful confrontation between the monk Gottschalk (or Gottescalc) of Orbais on the one hand, and the abbot Rabanus Maurus and the archbishop Hincmar of Reims, on the other.

While still a child Gottschalk had been placed in the monastery of Fulda by his father, Count Berno of Saxony. Since he had not consented to this, he later requested leave to abandon the monastery. But the Abbot of Fulda, Rabanus, Maurus, would not allow this, and the only concession granted the unfortunate monk was to be allowed to transfer to the monastery of Corbie and later to that of Orbais. The immediate consequence of these events was a persisting enmity between Rabanus Maurus and Gottschalk.

When, years later, Rabanus heard of the doctrine of his ex-monk regarding predestination, he wrote against him a

---

[6] The last significant author to discuss this matter during the Carolingian period was Agobard of Lyon, who found among the papers of the late Felix proof that the Spanish bishop, who supposedly had abandoned his adoptionist views, had secretly persisted in them. He then addressed to Louis the Pious a treatise *Against the teaching of Felix of Urgel* (PL, 104:29-70).

treatise *On Foreknowledge and Predestination, and on Free Will,* which he followed by a series of concrete actions against Gottschalk. As a result, Gottschalk was imprisoned and sent to Hincmar of Reims, under whose jurisdiction the monastery of Orbais was.[7] Hincmar had him publicly whipped until Gottschalk agreed to cast his own works into the fire. He was then imprisoned in a monastery where the unfortunate monk spent the rest of his days writing against Hincmar and receiving such treatment that eventually his reason abandoned him.

Gottschalk's doctrine of predestination was derived from abundant reading of Augustine, Ambrose, Gregory, Prosper, Fulgentius, and others. One must say in his favor that he certainly had a clearer understanding of Augustine's doctrine of predestination than did his opponents. But one must add that the manner in which he understood and expounded that doctrine was so severe that it became inhuman. His is not the constant hymn of gratitude which the Bishop of Hippo sang in his doctrine of predestination, but rather an obsession that sometimes seems to turn into morbid joy over the condemnation of the reprobate. God has predestined angels and the elect to salvation, and demons and the reprobates to condemnation.[8] In our condition, free will has been so corrupted that it can no longer do good.[9] Christ died not for all, but only for the elect.[10] All this is simply a strict Augustinianism, which, however, loses the tone of Augustine in such cases as that in which Gottschalk rejoices over the certainty that Hincmar is to be counted among the reprobate.[11]

---

[7] Gottschalk was accused not only of heresy, but also of being a wandering monk. He had left his monastery in a pilgrimage to Rome, and seems then to have continued traveling as far as the Balkans and even Bulgaria. In the ninth century, ecclesiastical authorities were attempting to put an end to the wandering habits of many monks. On Hincmar, see the monumental work by J. Devisse, *Hincmar archevêque de Reims, 845-882,* 3 vols. (Geneva: Librairie Droz, 1976). On his relations with Rabanus Maurus, R. Kottje, "Zu den Beziehungen zwischen Hinkmar von Reims und Hrabanus Maurus," in M. Gibson and J. Nelson, eds., *Charles the Bald: Court and Kingdom* (Oxford: B. A. R., 1981), pp. 255-63.

[8] *Conf. brev.* (D. C. Lambot, ed., *Oeuvres théologiques et grammaticales de Godescalc d'Orbais* [Louvain: Specilegium sacrum Lovaniense, 1945], p. 52).

[9] *De praedest.* 18 (Lambot, p. 253).

[10] *Ibid.* (Lambot, p. 249).

[11] *De trina deit.* (Lambot, pp. 97-98). Two good studies are: K. Vielhaber, *Gottschalk der Sachse* (Bonn: L. Röhrscheid, 1956); L. R. Gustavsson, "Gottschalk Reconsidered: A Study of His Thought as It Bears on His Notion of Predestination" (Unpublished doctoral dissertation, Yale, 1964).

On the other hand, the treatise by Rabanus Maurus shows that he does not understand or does not wish to understand the doctrine of Augustine, even while he claims to be basing his position on the authority of the Bishop of Hippo. Rabanus reduces predestination to divine foreknowledge, by which God knows who is to be saved and who will reject the offer of salvation. According to Rabanus, this is the only way in which one can avoid making God guilty of human sin, and the only way in which one can claim that God will judge justly, for how could God justly condemn that which he had predestined to occur?[12] In short, Rabanus, quite unknowingly, simply expounds the same arguments and views held centuries before by Augustine's opponents.

But it was Hincmar who became Gottschalk's greatest adversary, and who took his opposition to the unhappy monk to such an extreme that he himself was attacked by others who held more moderate views. In fact, Hincmar's zeal was such that soon Gottschalk was pushed to the background, and the Archbishop of Reims became the center of the controversy.

Hincmar's first step in this direction was to compose a brief treatise on predestination. Here he differed from Rabanus in establishing a distinction between foreknowledge and predestination; but he insisted on the participation of the human will in the process of salvation, as well as on the universal will of God that all be saved.[13] Together with his treatise, the Archbishop of Reims wrote to several outstanding theologians requesting their support.

The result of Hincmar's letters to various theologians was not what he expected. Prudentius of Troyes and Servatus Lupus, whose help he requested, openly rejected his doctrine and came out in favor of double predestination, the saving will of God being limited to the elect, and the death of Christ, not for all but for many.[14] The scholarly monk Ratramnus of Corbie, a constant

<hr/>

[12] De praedest.
[13] Amann, L'époque carolingienne, p. 326. The text has been published by Gundlach, "Ad reclusos et simplices," ZschrKgesch, 10 (1889), 258-309.
[14] Prudentius, Epistola ad Hincmarum et Pardulum (PL, 115:971-1010). Servatus, De tribus quaestionibus (PL, 119:621-48).

student of Augustine, addressed a treatise *On Predestination* to Charles the Bald, in which he too rejected the views of Hincmar.[15] To make things worse, Rabanus Maurus, who had opened the controversy by accusing Gottschalk, withdrew from it.

The treatise by Ratramnus, composed in two books, follows Augustinian doctrine to the letter and is strengthened by abundant quotations, not only from Augustine but also from Gregory, Prosper, Fulgentius, and others. According to Ratramnus the whole of humanity is nothing but a mass of perdition. Through sin, humankind has so been subjected to evil and corruption that even our greatest efforts do not suffice to free us from this condition. It is from within this mass of perdition that God, out of great love, has chosen some for salvation and has granted them that grace without which any good action is impossible. The others, God has predestined to damnation. Yet, this does not mean that God predestines to sin, but rather that God predestines some to the condemnation that flows from the sin in which all are already involved.

The unexpected turn of events led Hincmar to seek support from another source, and to this end he approached John Scotus Erigena. Erigena was more at home in matters of logic and philosophy than in doctrinal issues. This may be seen in the treatise *On Predestination*, which he wrote on Hincmar's request, and where, although he frequently appeals to Scripture and to some of the ancient Christian writers, it is clear that in the last analysis all must be judged by the tribunal of reason. In fact, Erigena practically affirms this in the first chapter, where he tries to show that philosophical reasoning is relevant for theology, and concludes that "true philosophy is true religion, and vice-versa, true religion is true philosophy."[16] This approach determines the nature of many of his arguments, which are little more than mere logical exercises. Thus, for instance, he attempts to prove from the absolute simplicity of

---

[15]Ratramnus had earlier written a letter "To my friend"—that is, to Gottschalk—but this letter has been lost.

[16] *De praedest.* 1 (PL, 122:358). Cf. M. Cristiani, "La notion de loi dans le 'De praedestinatione' de Jean Scot," *StMed*, III, 17 (1976), 81-114.

God that double predestination is impossible, and the outcome is a very interesting but not very convincing argument.[17] Although his sincere purpose in publishing his treatise seems to have been to support Hincmar against Gottschalk and Ratramnus, Erigena's rationalism led him to put forth views that could not be accepted by most of his contemporaries, so that his contribution to the debate only served to widen the gap. Such was the case with his remarks regarding Hell, which he quite unnecessarily introduced in the last chapter of his treatise, Hincmar realized his mistake in appealing to Erigena's help, and did not accept the doctrine of the "nineteen chapters"—as he called Erigena's work. Actually, Erigena himself, probably realizing that he would have done better not to get involved in this controversy, decided not to discuss the issue of predestination any further.

However, Erigena's treatise drew such attention that the controversy now shifted to his views, and to Hincmar's doctrine and actions. Prudentius of Troyes wrote a long work *On Predestination Against John Scotus,* in which he categorically rejected the notion that philosophical methods serve to solve theological problems. On the contrary, the reference point of any theological discussion must be the authority of Scripture, as well as the declaration of the councils and the writings of the ancient church. Prudentius then proceeded to refute each of Erigena's arguments by appealing to the authority of Augustine and others. Regarding predestination, he shows that the focal point is Augustine's doctrine of the "mass of damnation," and that the predestination of the elect, as well as that of the reprobate, follows from that doctrine. His position is therefore very similar to that of Gottschalk, although he never openly supported the unfortunate monk, probably in order to avoid friction with the powerful Archbishop of Reims.

Another strong reaction to Erigena's treatise came from Florus of Lyon, who wrote a *Book of the Church of Lyon Against the Erroneous Definitions of John Scotus.*[18] Here he took basically the

---

[17] *Ibid.,* 2 (PL, 122:360).
[18] *PL,* 119:101-250. Although written in the name of the church of Lyon, it is almost certain that its actual author was Florus. It seems clear that the then archbishop of Lyon, Amolo, did not write it, for his attitude was much more conciliatory than this treatise.

same theological position of Prudentius, affirming the doctrines of the mass of damnation and double predestination. But he went further and raised a number of questions regarding the justice of Hincmar's actions against Gottschalk. If in truth the doctrines of Gottschalk were a threat to the peace of the church and to the souls of the faithful, Hincmar should have brought the issue before a national synod.

This work by Florus, written in the name of the very ancient church of Lyon, forced Hincmar to change his strategy. Being defeated in the field of theological debate, he made use of the support of Charles the Bald. After a council in which Hincmar's opinions were not discussed for fear that they might be rejected, the King called together a group of bishops on whose actions he could depend, and these bishops composed the *Four Chapters of Quierzy*, in which Hincmar's position was categorically affirmed as the only correct one.

From then on, the controversy became a confrontation between the two powerful sees of Reims and Lyon. A long series of synods and treatises took one or the other side in the controversy, until A.D. 860 when a council gathered at Thuzey and, presided over jointly by Charles the Bald and Lothair II, proclaimed an intermediate and ambiguous position that did not solve the issue, but whose general acceptance shows that both sides were tired of the fruitless debate.

As to Gottschalk, in spite of several attempts to gain Rome's intervention on his behalf—especially during a period of tension between Hincmar and Pope Nicholas I—he simply was forced to continue living in monastic imprisonment until his death.

The Controversy over the Virginity of Mary

This brief controversy began when Ratramnus of Corbie, whom we have met already in the controversy over predestination, received word that a doctrine had become common in Germany according to which Jesus had not been born of Mary in the natural way, but had sprung out of the virginal womb in a mysterious and miraculous manner. Ratramnus claimed that such a doctrine was a new ruse of the Evil One, who is constantly attempting to poison the faith of the believers. Such an understanding of the events of Christmas—"not to be born, but to break forth"—would certainly lead to Docetism.[19]

Over against these doctrines, whose teachers are unknown to us, Ratramnus claimed that Jesus was born of Mary in the natural manner, and that this in no way contaminated the Savior, nor did it destroy the virginity of his mother. There is nothing wrong with the claim that the Savior was born "per vulvam," for the book of Genesis clearly affirms that all that God has made is good. This is why Adam and Eve were naked and not ashamed. Since we are fallen creatures, there is no doubt that there is in us an evil law of the flesh which leads us to be ashamed. But in the case of the Savior the purifying action of the Spirit included not only his conception but also his birth.[20] One should note, however, that this does not mean that Ratramnus denied the perpetual virginity of Mary. On the contrary, she was a virgin "before the birth, in the birth, and after the birth." This is to be believed, for "it would not make sense to think that the birth through which all things corrupt were restored would corrupt those things which were uncorrupted."[21] Therefore, Jesus was born "by the natural door," although without violating its virginal integrity; and if it is difficult to believe such a thing, it would be even harder to believe that Jesus was born in some other manner without thereby wounding his mother.[22]

As was to be expected, this work by Ratramnus scandalized and preoccupied those pious spirits who had never posed such issues with such clarity. A number of nuns asked Paschasius Radbertus, ex-abbot of Corbie, to clarify the matter. In his response, a two-book treatise On the Virgin Birth, he rejected the position of Ratramnus. Radbertus pointed out that what was being discussed was not the perpetual virginity of Mary—which Ratramnus would affirm—but the manner in which that virginity remained such in the birth of Jesus. His refutation went

---

[19] *De eo quod Chr. de Virg. natus est* 1.
[20] *Ibid.,* 3.
[21] *Ibid.,* 2 (*PL,* 121:84).
[22] It seems that some in Germany held that Jesus had sprung from Mary's side, others, that he had come out of a kidney, and so on.

directly to Ratramnus' core argument: it is true that all things created are good, but the book of Genesis itself clearly affirms that childbirth as it is known to us is the result of human sin. Therefore, one errs in attempting to compare childbirth in the case of Mary with the common case of other women.[23] Actually, Jesus "came to us even while the womb was closed, just as he came to his disciples even while the doors were closed."[24] That is to say, the birth was indeed miraculous, and one can say no more.

This seems to have been the end of the controversy. Sometime later Hincmar of Reims affirmed in passing that Jesus had not been born of Mary in the same manner in which other children are born.[25] But the question was not discussed any further.

The Eucharistic Controversy

This controversy arose[26] when Charles the Bald posed to Ratramnus a double question regarding the eucharist: first, whether the presence of the body and blood of Christ in the eucharist is such that it can be seen only with the eyes of faith—*in mysterio*—or, on the contrary, is real—*in veritate*—in such a manner that what the eyes of the flesh see is actually the body and blood of Christ; and, second, whether the body of Christ which is present in the eucharist is the same that "was born of Mary, suffered, died, and was buried and ascended to the heavens to the right hand of the Father."[27] The king's question had come out of his reading of a treatise presented to him by Paschasius Radbertus, *On the Body and the Blood of the Lord.*[28] Here Paschasius offered an interpretation of the presence of Christ in the eucharist in realistic terms. After the consecration, the elements of the sacrament are

---

[23] *De partu Virg.* 1 (*PL*, 120:1368-69). The most significant texts have been gathered by S. Bonano, "The Divine Maternity and the Eucharistic Body in the Doctrine of Paschasius Radbertus," *EphemMar*, 1 (1951), 379-94. See also J. M. Canal, "La virginidad de María según Ratramno y Radberto, monjes de Corbie," *Marianum*, 30 (1968), 53-160; R. Maloy, "A Correction in the Text of a Recent Edition of Paschasius Radbertus' 'De partu sanctae Mariae,' " *Marianum*, 33 (1971), 224-25.

[24] *De partu Virg.* 1.

[25] *De div. Lot. et Tet.* 12.

[26] That is, apart from the earlier treatise by Amalarius, which does not seem to have created a great deal of controversy. See S. Simonis, "Doctrina eucharistica Amalarii Metensis," *Ant*, 8 (1933), 3-48.

[27] Ratramnus, *De corp et sang. Dom.* 5 (ed. J. N. B. van den Brink [Amsterdam: Noord-Hollandse Uitgevers Mij., 1954], p. 34).

[28] See J. van Opdenbosch, "De eucharistieleer de Nederlanden ten tijde der Karlingers," *OgE* (1944), 1:7-34; 2:9-38 (1945); 1:7-92.

nothing but the flesh and the blood of Christ, the same flesh that was born of the Virgin Mary, which suffered and arose from the dead.[29] This body and blood are normally seen only by the eyes of faith; but sometimes a special concession is made to those who fervently love the Lord, and they are able to see their true color as flesh and blood.[30] Paschasius also understands communion as a repetition of the sacrifice of Christ, so that when it is celebrated, the Savior suffers and dies again.[31]

There is no doubt that Paschasius Radbertus was expressing the feelings of many pious souls in his time. But his views were unsavory to the best theologians among his contemporaries, who had been formed in the spiritualist tradition of Augustine. One of these theologians was Ratramnus.

The treatise by Ratramnus bears the same title as that of Paschasius, *On the Body and the Blood of the Lord.*[32] Here Ratramnus answers the two questions posed by the King, and he does so in such a manner that his treatise has been much discussed in later times.[33] To the first question, he answers that Christ is not present "in truth," but only "figuratively."[34] This does not mean, however, that he denies the real presence of the body of Christ in communion. For him, the difference between that which exists "in truth" and that which exists "figuratively" is that the former can be perceived "externally," through the corporeal senses, whereas that which exists figuratively can only be seen through the eyes of faith. That which exists in truth is not more real than that which exists figuratively, although "truth" is more directly related with the object of knowledge, for a "figure" is a veiled manifestation of

---

[29] Paschasius, *De corp. et sang. Dom.* 1. 2.

[30] The entire Chapter 14 is a long series of miraculous narratives to prove this point.

[31] *De corp. et sang. Dom.* 9. 1.

[32] See note 26, above. On his doctrine, see: J. F. Fahey, *The Eucharistic Teaching of Ratramn of Corbie* (Mundelein, Illinois: Saint Mary of the Lake Seminary, 1952); A. Béraudy, *L'enseignement eucharistique de Ratramne, moine de Corbie an IXeme siècle, dans le De Corpore et sanguine domini* (Lyon, doctoral thesis, 1953); A. Béraudy, "Les catégories de pensée de Ratramne dans son enseignement eucharistique," in *Volume du XIIIᵉ centenaire, Corbie, abbaye royale* (Lille: Facultés catholiques, 1963), pp. 157-80.

[33] During the eleventh century this treatise—then attributed to John Scotus Erigena—played an important role in the controversy between Berengar and Lanfranc. Centuries later, it was used by some Protestants as support for their eucharistic doctrines. As a result, it was included in the *Index* of forbidden books. Finally, in the nineteenth century, more objective study of the treatise was begun.

[34] Ratramnus, *De corp. et sang. Dom.* 49 (ed. van den Brink, p. 46).

Eucharist

Actual — *Spiritual* — *Remembrance*

a reality that is present behind it.[35] Therefore, Christ is truly in the sacrament, although not in such a way that he may be visible to the eyes of the body. This is in fact what King Charles was asking, probably because of the miraculous narratives that he had found in the treatise by Paschasius Radbertus.

To the second question posed by the King, Ratramnus answers that the body of Christ which is present in the eucharist is not the same body of Christ which was born of Mary and hung from the cross, for the latter, which is presently at the right hand of the Father, is visible, and in the eucharist the body of Christ is not seen. The presence of that body in the eucharist is only spiritual, and it is spiritually that the believer partakes in it. This does not mean that Ratramnus understands communion as a mere act of remembrance. On the contrary, Christ is truly present in the elements, but in a spiritual manner, not accessible to the senses of the flesh.[36]

The treatise by Ratramnus did not move Paschasius Radbertus, who persisted in his position, and at the same time clarified it in order to avoid some of the extremes which could follow from it. In commenting on the Gospel of Matthew, when he comes to the words of instituion of the sacrament, he attacks those who affirm that in the sacrament there is "the power of the flesh and not the flesh; the power of the blood, and not the blood; the figure and not the truth; the shadow and not the body."[37] These people stand corrected by the Lord himself, who said: "This is my body," and who refuted those who claim that the eucharistic body is not the same that hung from the cross by completing the description of that which he was offering to his disciples, "This is my body, which is given for you"—that is, the same body, and not another.[38] On this point Paschasius Radbertus remained firm, as may be seen by the fact that some years later, when a monk who had been partially convinced by the treatise of Ratramnus asked Paschasius for more clarification on the matter, he simply repeated the same

---

[35] There is a very good study of the meaning of these and other related terms in Béraudy, *L'enseignement*, pp. 43-95.

[36] See *L'enseignement*, pp. 176-227, from whose conclusions I have departed.

[37] *In Matt. Evang.* 9. 26. (*PL*, 120:890).

[38] *Ibid.*

arguments and added a long list of quotations from the "Fathers."[39]

Gottschalk intervened in the debate from his forced retreat in the monastery of Hautvilliers.[40] In a brief treatise loaded with quotations and ideas taken from Augustine, he opposed the identification of the eucharistic body with the historic body of Christ, and even more the manner in which Paschasius Radbertus referred to communion as a sacrifice in which Christ suffered anew. What there is in the eucharist is a mysterious presence that cannot be defined in the precise terms that Radbertus attempts to use, but whose core is a "power of the Word" active in the believer.

Rabanus Maurus—the same who accused Gottschalk before Hincmar—also intervened in the controversy, although now on the side of Gottschalk and Ratramnus and against Paschasius Radbertus. The work that he wrote to this effect has been lost.[41] John Scotus Erigena took a position similar to that of Ratramnus, Gottschalk, and—probably—Rabanus Maurus.[42] Erigena, however, did not actively participate in the debate, but was rather marginal to it.[43]

In spite of such widespread opposition, the realistic interpretation of Christ's presence in the eucharist would eventually become the most commonly held view. Late in the ninth century, Bishop Haymo of Halberstadt wrote a very brief treatise in which he spoke of a *substantial* transformation of the bread and the wine into the flesh and blood of Christ.[44]

---

[39] *Ep. ad Frudegardum* (PL, 120:1351-66).

[40] That is, if one accepts the view of G. Morin, "Gottschalk retrouvé," *RevBened*, 43 (1931), 303-12, that the *Dicta cuiusdam sapientis de corpore et sanguine Domini*, published in *PL*, 92:1510-18, are Gottschalk's work.

[41] If, in fact, G. Morin (see note 39) is right. Some have attributed the *Dicta* to Rabanus, identifying it with his lost work on the eucharist.

[42] *Exp. super Ierarch. cael.* 1.

[43] Here again, there is some doubt as to the historical facts. Some medieval authors refer to a book by Scotus on the eucharist. Such a book, however, does not seem to have existed, and what probably gave rise to such references was the erroneous attribution to Scotus Erigena of a treatise by another author—most likely, Ratramnus. See M. Cappuyns, *Jean Scot Erigène: Sa vie, son oeuvre, sa pensée* (Bruxelles: Éditions "Culture et Civilisation," 1964), pp. 88-91.

[44] The question of the authorship of Haymo's works is very complex. Several of the works which have been attributed traditionally to Haymo of Halberstadt probably come from the pen of his contemporary Haymo of Auxerre. In any case, the important point here is that someone in the ninth century—be it Haymo of Halberstadt or his homonym of Auxerre—held the views set forth in this text. One must add, however, that there is also the possibility that this treatise is the work of an eleventh-century writer—perhaps Haymo of Hirschau or Haymo of Telleia—although the only argument for this view is the seeming anachronism of the eucharistic doctrine set forth in the treatise.

It is an evil madness that there be in the minds of the faithful any doubt that the substance of the bread and the wine which are placed upon the altar become the body and blood of Christ through the priestly mystery and the action of grace, God doing this through his divine grace and secret power. We therefore believe and faithfully confess and hold that this substance of the bread and the wine is substantially turned into another substance, that is, into flesh and blood, by the operation of a divine power, as has already been said. For it is not impossible for the omnipotence of the divine reason to transform created natures into whatever it will, as it was not impossible for it to create them out of nothing when they did not exist, according to its will. For if it can make something out of nothing, it is not impossible for it to make something out of something. Therefore, the invisible priest, through his secret power, transforms his visible creatures into the substance of his flesh and blood. But although the nature of the substances has completely been turned into the body and blood of Christ, in the miracle of partaking, the taste and appearance of this body and blood remain those of bread and wine.[45]

This text includes all the fundamental elements of the later doctrine of transubstantiation, although expressed in terms that are not exactly those which would later become commonly accepted.

Controversies Regarding the Soul

Among the many controversies that took place during the Carolingian period, two had to do with the soul—one with its incorporeity, and the other with its individuality.

The question of the incorporeity of the soul was posed on several occasions during the Carolingian renaissance,[46] but it was in the middle of the ninth century, during the reign of Charles the Bald, that a brief but open controversy took place regarding this point. The two parties in this theological debate were Ratramnus of Corbie and an anonymous writer from Reims who

---

[45] Haymo, *De corp. et sang. Dom.* (*PL*, 118:815-16).

[46] During Charlemagne's reign, Alcuin wrote a treatise on the subject (*PL*, 101:639-47), and under Lothair I, Rabanus Maurus did likewise (*PL*, 110:1110-20).

may well have been Archbishop Hincmar.[47] It was at the request of a civil official that Ratramnus wrote a treatise on this subject in which he declared that the soul was incorporeal and was not therefore circumscribed to the body.[48] After reading this treatise, the king addressed a series of questions regarding the soul to a wise man from Reims (Hincmar?), who responded with a brief opuscle[49] in which he refuted the claim of Ratramnus. On the contrary, the soul is tied to the body. This does not mean, however, that it is limited to it, for through its knowledge the soul goes beyond the boundaries of the body. Such was the end of this brief debate which had no greater significance than to show that the Augustinian doctrine of the incorporeity of the soul was debated once more.

The question of the individuality of the soul was much more important, for on it depended the possibility of an individual, conscious life after death. A certain Macarius, of whom all that is known is that he was Irish,[50] held the theory of a universal soul, of which individual souls partake. Inspired by Macarius, a monk from Beauvais composed a treatise defending this view. Odo, the Bishop of Beauvais, asked Ratramnus to refute this monk. The wise man from Corbie simply wrote a very brief answer in which he claimed that the opinions of this "puffed up young man" merited no attention. The anonymous young monk, in view of Ratramnus' answer, insisted on his position, and set forth arguments in which he tried to refute his opponent's views. Ratramnus then answered with a "small book." Finally, in view of a new answer and refutation from the young man, Ratramnus decided to write a *Treatise on the Soul to Odo of Beauvais*. All these writings have been lost, except for the latter, which has been discovered and published at a relatively recent date.[51] It is through this treatise that we know the course of the controversy,

---

[47] See Cappuyns, *Jean Scot Erigène*, p. 93 n. 1.
[48] A. Wilmart, "L'opuscule inédit de Ratramne sur la nature de l'âme," *RevBened*, 43 (1931), 207-23.
[49] *De div. et mult. an. rat.* (*PL*, 125:933-40).
[50] On the basis of his Irish origin and some of his views, some scholars have thought that this Macarius may have been John Scotus Erigena. It is more likely that he was a disciple of Erigena.
[51] D. C. Lambot, ed., *Ratramne de Corbie: Liber de anima ad Odonem Bellovacensem* (Namur: Godenne, 1952).

the opinions of Ratramnus' opponent, and his own position.[52]
The historical basis of the controversy was found in a rather
difficult text of Augustine in which the Bishop of Hippo
discussed the question of the number of souls and reached no
clear conclusion. Macarius and his anonymous disciple in
Beauvais used this text as a basis from which to prove that the
soul is at once one and multiple. Interpreting Augustine within
the framework of a Neoplatonic realism, they claimed that there
was a universal soul, and that our individual souls exist only by
participation in that universal soul. The issue was then that of
the result of philosophical realism when applied to the question
of the number of souls, and can thus be interpreted as one more
chapter in the long debate regarding universals.

The refutation by Ratramnus, although claiming to be
formally based on the text from Augustine, was really grounded
on the position of Ratramnus regarding universals, and on his
interest to safeguard human individuality. Ratramnus did not
conceive of universals as real entities in the same sense in which
particular things are real. Universals are concepts and are real
only as such, so that the reality of individuals is not simply to be
placed on the universals. It is from this position that Ratramnus
interprets Augustine. Therefore, when Augustine speaks of the
soul in the singular, he does not refer to a universal soul that
exists above and beyond particular souls, but refers rather to the
concept of the soul—a real concept, but not any more real than
the individual souls, nor metaphysically prior to them.

Other Controversies in the Carolingian West

Issues regarding the Trinity could not but be debated in a
period of such intense theological activity as the Carolingian
renaissance. In a certain sense, adoptionism, which we have
already discussed, was one of these issues. So was the question of
the *Filioque*, which will be discussed further on.

Another such trinitarian controversy took place between

---

[52] This treatise has been carefully studied by P. Delhaye, *Une controverse sur l'âme au IX* siècle* (Namur: Centre d'études médiévales, 1950).

Gottschalk and Hincmar regarding the formula *trina deitas*. This formula was found in an ancient hymn, and Hincmar had it deleted on the grounds that it was Arian: divinity is one, and to affirm the opposite would be to establish between the various persons of the Trinity that exaggerated distinction which was typical of Arianism. Gottschalk and Ratramnus responded to this with a series of patristic texts to prove the orthodoxy of the deleted phrase, and accused Hincmar of Sabellianism: to deny that the divinity is triune is to be guilty of the confusion between the divine persons which was typical of Sabellianism. Finding himself involved in a controversy that was beyond his intellectual capabilities, Hincmar responded with a double thrust: while writing a large treatise *On the Divinity Being One, and Not Triune*, he used his political power to gain the support of a synod that was meeting in Aachen (A.D. 853). As far as we know that was the end of the controversy, although some time later a number of followers of Hincmar were still opposing the formula *trina deitas*. In any case, Hincmar did not succeed in having the phrase deleted from the liturgy.

During the reign of Louis the Pious there was a debate between Fredegisus of Tours and Agobard of Lyon regarding the style of Scripture. Agobard claimed that the apostles and other sacred writers used simple language, and sometimes even incorrect grammar, in order to reach their readers. Such a notion was repugnant to Fredegisus, who came out in defense of the apostles. Agobard responded with a brief *Book against Fredegisus* in which he insisted that the authority of Scripture was not in the grammatical infallibility that Fredegisus was defending, and claimed that the apostles, as well as the patriarchs, judges, and kings of the Old Testament, were humble people who would never have claimed such infallibility. Furthermore, if the grammar of Scripture is not always correct from the human point of view, the reason for this is that the purpose of the sacred writings is to descend to where we are, and not simply to speak to us in such an elevated language that it cannot reach us.[53]

---

[53] *Lib adv. Fred.* 7.

Finally, during the Carolingian period there was a debate on the manner in which the redeemed would see God.[54] During the first half of the ninth century, under the reign of Louis the Pious, a certain Candidus, who had been consulted on the matter, responded that only pure spirits can see God, who is invisible to bodies as well as to impure spirits.[55] Some time later, Gottschalk circulated another consultation on the same subject and offered his own opinion, which was that the resurrected body will be made spiritual in such a way that its eyes will be able to see God.[56] Servatus Lupus counseled him to be more cautious before those mysteries which God has not willed to reveal to us in this life, and suggested that in any case the beatific vision would take place through the eyes of the mind.[57] Hincmar did not let this opportunity to attack Gottschalk go by and therefore raised the issue on several occasions.[58] John Scotus Erigena followed his own philosophical positions and thereby led the discussion to another level by denying the possibility that a creature may see God's substance, be it with bodily eyes or with those of the mind. As to resurrected bodies, Scotus claimed that they would be purely spiritual, and therefore it would be spiritually that we would enjoy the beatific vision—a vision that in any case could never reach the inaccessible glory of God, but only the divine image.[59]

As was to be expected, this controversy reached no definite conclusion. But it serves to illustrate the manner in which idle speculation on inscrutable matters flourished during the Carolingian renaissance.[60]

The *Filioque*

The Nicene-Constantinopolitan Creed, in referring to the Holy Spirit, simply says "who proceeds from the Father." This is

---

[54] M. Cappuyns, "Note sure le problème de la vision béatifique au IXe siècle," *RThAM*, 1 (1929), 98-107.

[55] *PL*, 106:103-8.

[56] *Ep. ad Ratramnum.*

[57] *Ep. xxx, Ad Gotteschalcum mon.*

[58] Cappuyns, "Note," n. 13, 25, 26.

[59] *Ibid.*, pp. 105-6.

[60] Cappuyns also points out that this controversy illustrates the manner in which Augustine fascinated the Carolingian mind (*ibid.*, pp. 106-7). In fact, what was debated was the manner in which various views expressed by Augustine at various times were to be coordinated.

not to be understood as a denial that the Holy Spirit may also proceed from the Son, for this issue was not being debated in the fourth century, and the bishops who met in Constantinople had no need to define the procession of the Holy Spirit. Furthermore, the East as well as the West had traditionally believed that the Son had a role in that procession, although the most common formula in the West was to say that the Holy Spirit proceeded "from the Father and the Son," while in the East it was that the Spirit proceeded "from the Father through the Son."

In the West, some began interpolating in the creed the formula "and from the Son"—*Filioque*—in order to affirm this dual procession of the Holy Spirit, thus saying, "who proceeds from the Father and the Son."[61] Although the origins of this interpolation are obscure, it seems that it first became common in Spain,[62] and that it then passed to Gaul and the rest of the Western church. During Charlemagne's reign, when relations between the Franks and the Byzantines were tense, the *Filioque* issue was the source—and also the excuse—of long controversies. In the *Caroline Books* (A.D. 794), it is claimed that the very ancient Eastern formula that the Spirit proceeds "from the Father through the Son" is not orthodox.[63] In the palace chapel at Aachen it was customary to sing the creed with the addition of the *Filioque*. The controversy erupted when some Latin monks from Jerusalem visited the royal chapel and then returned to the Holy City with the new version of the creed—or when, in order to incite the debate, some Byzantines claimed that the Latins had returned with a modified version of the Creed. As was to be expected, they were staunchly resisted by Eastern Christians, who accused them of being heretics and innovators. In a synod held in Aachen in A.D. 809, the Frankish bishops declared that the Greek formula was heretical, and that it was necessary to confess that the Holy Spirit proceeds "from the Father and the son

---

61 Only a very brief outline of the course of the controversy may be given here. There is an excellent account in Amann, *L'époque carolingienne*, pp. 173-84.

62 Several ancient Spanish councils affirmed the double procession of the Spirit. So did Ildefonsus of Toledo: *De virg. perp. S. Mariae* (*PL*, 96:104).

63 Charlemagne himself showed an interest in the issue. See W. von den Steinen, "Karl der Grosse und die *Libri Carolini*," *Neues Archiv*, 49 (1932), 207-80.

(Filioque)." In taking this action, they claimed the support of several "Latin Fathers." Later, a number of Carolingian theologians wrote on the subject, defending the Western position—Alcuin of York,[64] Theodulf of Orleans,[65] Ratramnus of Corbie,[66] and Aeneas of Paris.[67] At that juncture Pope Leo III avoided what seemed to be an inevitable break with the East by refusing to accept any interpolation in the creed. He thus avoided a direct confrontation between Rome and Constantinople. But his action did not suffice to prevent the entire Latin church from including the *Filioque* clause in the creed. As early as A.D. 867, during the schism of Photius, the *Filioque* became one of the main factors separating the East from the West. It has remained a stumbling block for Christian unity ever since.

Two different kinds of issues were involved in this controversy.[68] On the one hand, the orthodoxy of the interpolation itself was questioned. On the other, what was debated was the right of later councils, or other ecclesiastical authorities, to change or interpolate the ancient creed that was believed to have been produced at Nicea and Constantinople. Very few theologians were able to distinguish between these two matters—Pope Leo III being the most remarkable exception. Because of their confusion, most Western theologians spent their efforts attempting to show the orthodoxy and need of the doctrine involved in the *Filioque,* while most Eastern theologians spent their efforts attempting to show that the creed could not be interpolated. Thus, minor differences were underscored, and the position of one's opponents was turned into a mere caricature.

There was, however, a certain theological issue at stake. This was the difference between the manner in which Eastern theologians had traditionally understood the relationships between the persons in the Trinity, and the manner in which

---

[64] *De proc. Spiritus Sancti (PL,* 101:63-84).
[65] *De Spiritu Sancto (PL,* 105:239-76). This is a mere collection of patristic texts.
[66] *Contra Graec. opposita (PL,* 121:225-346).
[67] *Lib adv. Graecos (PL,* 121:685-762).
[68] U. Küry, "Die Bedeutung des Filioque-Streites für den Gottesbegriff der abendlaendischen und der morgenlaendischen Kirche," *IntkZtschr,* 33 (1943), 1-19.

they were understood by those of the West—the East following in the footsteps of the Cappadocians, and the West in those of Augustine.

Eastern theology took as its point of departure the need to affirm the single origin of the Trinity. There can only be one source of God's being, and that source must be the Father. Still can one not say that the Holy Spirit also proceeds from the Son? Certainly not in the sense in which the Spirit proceeds from the Father, for the Father is the ultimate source of his being, and the Son is not. Hence, the formula, "from the Father, through the Son." On the other hand, Western theologians saw the Holy Spirit as the love that binds the Father and the Son. Since this is a mutual love, one must say that the Spirit proceeds "from the Father and the Son." This does not mean that there are two ultimate sources of being, for the Son is not his own source, but is begotten by the Father.

In any case, the issue was never settled, and through the centuries stood in the way of any rapprochement between the two branches of the Christian church.

One by-product of this controversy was the renewed use of the Old Roman Symbol by the pope and others in the West who wished to avoid conflict by using a creed other than the Nicene. Partly as a result of this policy, eventually the Old Roman Symbol—now known as the Apostle's Creed—became the most common creed of the West.

John Scotus Erigena

The most remarkable figure of the Carolingian renaissance was John Scotus Erigena. A native of Ireland,[69] Erigena came to the Frankish kingdom during the first half of the ninth century.[70] He settled in the Court of Charles the Bald, where he

---

[69] Hence his names "Scotus" and "Erigena"—or "Eriugena." Ireland was called Scotia and Erin as well as Hibernia. However, the pleonastic title of "Scotus Erigena" has been generally applied to him since the seventeenth century. M. Dal Pra, *Scoto Eriugena* (Milan: Bocca, 1951), p. 10. Besides the work of Cappuyns cited above (n. 43), the following are useful: J. J. O'Meara and L. Bieler, eds., *The Mind of Erigena: Papers of a Colloquium* (Dublin: Irish University Press, 1973); C. Allegro, *Giovanni Scoto Eriugena*, 2 vols. (Rome: Città Nuova Editrice, 1974, 1976). On the influence of earlier thinkers on Erigena, W. Beierwalters, ed., *Eriugena: Studien zu seinen Quellen* (Heidelberg: C. Winter, 1980).

[70] His reasons for leaving Ireland are unknown. He may have fled before the Danish invasion, or he may have been summoned to his court by Charles the Bald. In any case, the Irish at that time were notorious wanderers. Cappuyns, *Erigène*, pp. 56-58.

enjoyed great prestige. As has already been said, Hincmar asked him to intervene in the controversy on predestination. His participation in that controversy is a good illustration of his situation within his own times: respected by all for his erudition, he was, however, regarded with suspicion because of his love of Greek philosophy, which he often followed to positions that were not entirely orthodox. For these reasons, he had no followers, although he was used by many as a source of information and ideas for their own theological endeavors. He was quoted with relative frequency during the three succeeding centuries, although often those who quoted him cautioned the reader about his theology. Early in the thirteenth century, his main work, *On the Division of Nature,* was condemned on the grounds that it seemed to support the heresy of Amalric of Bena. However, his influence continued to be felt through the common use of his translation of Pseudo-Dionysius.

A great deal of Erigena's literary work consisted in translating the writings of ealier Eastern theologians. This was especially valuable because of the oblivion and the disuse into which the Greek language had fallen in the West. Besides the works of Pseudo-Dionysius, Erigena translated Maximus the Confessor, Gregory of Nyssa, and probably Epiphanius. Also, his most significant original writings have survived.[71]

Erigena stands in the tradition of Clement of Alexandria, Origen, and Pseudo-Dionysius. His is a philosophy of high speculative flights in which dialectics and the art of precise definition are foremost, and in which everything is included in a vast vision of God and the universe.

According to Erigena, nature includes all that is as well as all that is not.[72] "Non-being" may be understood in various ways. In the first place, all that which is beyond the capacity of the mind and the senses is not. In this sense, essences are not, for we can only comprehend and perceive accidents, but never the essence

---

[71] Most of them are included in *PL,* 122:441-1022. Cf. I. P. Sheldon-Williams, "A List of the Works Doubtfully or Wrongly Attributed to Johannes Scottus Erigena," *JEH,* 15 (1964), 76-98. There is a summary of his system in J. E. Manieres, "Les articulations majeures dans le système de Jean Scot Erigène," *MSR,* 20 (1963), 20-38.

[72] *De div. nat.* 1. 2.

that is behind them. In the second place, everything that is above each element in nature is not as far as that particular element is concerned, for it is unable to know that which stands above it. Therefore, something may be from the point of view of a superior member of the universal hierarchy, and not be from the point of view of an inferior member. In the third place, that which exists only in potency is not. Fourth, that which is subject to time and space, and therefore can change and move, is not. Finally, humans as sinners, inasmuch as we have become separated from God, are not.[73] These various modes of non-being are different, and something may be in a particular sense and not be in another.

On the other hand, nature may be divided in four: nature that creates and is not created, nature that is created and creates, nature that is created and does not create, and nature that neither creates nor is created.[74] The first and last divisions correspond to a single reality—God. The difference between these two is only in our intellect, for the first is God considered as the source of all things and the fourth is God as the end of all things. The second division includes the primordial causes of all things. The third includes all things subject to temporal existence. Erigena's work *On the Division of Nature* follows this outline, devoting a book to each of the first three divisions, and two to the fourth. This will also be our outline in discussing his thought.

God, the creating nature that is not created, is above and beyond all the limitations of our mind. Therefore, we can speak of God only in a paradoxical manner, at once affirming and denying each of our statements—a doctrine that John Scotus takes from Pseudo-Dionysius. The affirmation always must be taken figuratively, and the negation literally. Thus, for instance, God is essence; yet, God is not essence, but much more. This polarity may be summarized by saying that God is super-essence—an affirmation that includes a negation within itself.[75]

In the strict sense, it is impossible to know God. All that the Scriptures affirm regarding God's love, mercy, wrath, etc., must

---

[73] *Ibid.*, 1. 3-7.
[74] *Ibid.*, 1. 1.
[75] *Ibid.*, 1. 14.

be understood not literally, but only metaphorically, according to the dictum of Paul, "I give ye milk, and not meat." Scriptures have been given for the simpleminded, and this is the reason why they use this metaphorical language. In truth, God is unknowable, not only to creatures but even to God. Knowledge implies definition, and definition implies limitation. As God has no limitations, God cannot be known. Therefore, God does not know God. Yet, this divine ignorance is not similar to ours, but is rather a super-ignorance that is well above the highest knowledge.[76]

The basic attribute that one can predicate of the Divine is that God is triune. Here Erigina simply follows orthodox doctrine as it had been defined earlier. As to the *Filioque*, Scotus does not openly oppose its inclusion in the creed,[77] although he does feel inclined to affirm that the Spirit proceeds *from* the Father *through* the Son.[78]

This uncreated but creating nature is the source of the primordial causes, which in turn are the created and creating nature. These primordial causes are eternal—as is indeed the entire creation. Creation is eternal because otherwise it would be accidental to God, and there are no accidents in God. In other words, the eternity and immutability of God require that creation be eternal.[79] God is prior to creation, not in the order of time—for God is not in time—but in the order of being. God is the source of the being of creation.

The triune nature of God is manifest in the entire creation, for every creature shows that God is, that God is wise, and that God lives.[80] The Father is the source of the being of all things, the Son is the Wisdom in whom all things were made, and the Spirit is the source of the universal order.[81]

God has made all things—including the primordial causes— out of nothing. This "nothing" is not the absolute denial of

---

[76] *Ibid.*, 1. 28.
[77] In *ibid.*, 2. 33, he is ironical about it.
[78] *Ibid.*, 2. 31.
[79] *Ibid.*, 3. 8.
[80] *Ibid.*, 1. 13.
[81] *Ibid.*, 2. 21.

being, total vacuum, but is rather God, who is not, and who therefore can be called "nothing." Thus, *creatio ex nihilo* becomes *creatio ex Deo.*[82] The primordial causes, which are the first term of creation and the second great division of nature, are to be found in the Word, where the Father has placed them from all eternity.[83] Following the path that had been opened earlier by other Christians of Neoplatonic tendencies, Scotus claims that the primordial causes that exist in the Word are the prototypes of all temporal creatures. They are eternal, whereas individual creatures pass away. It is because of their existence that one must say that creation is eternal. The eternity of creation is to be found in the primordial causes and therefore in the Word, where the Holy Spirit takes these causes and distributes them in individual historical creatures.[84]

The third division of nature, that which is created and does not create, springs from this action of the Trinity on the primordial causes. This level of creation appeared not in stages, but all at once; and Genesis presents it in a progressive way only to state clearly what otherwise would seem confused, just as we express in consecutive orderly words what are actually instantaneous thoughts.[85]

This third level of nature is what we usually call "creation," that is, that which exists within time and space. Material things are in truth combinations of immaterial qualities. Pure formless matter is not—in the sense that it cannot be known. In short, corporeal beings are formed by constellations of incorporeal beings.[86] This is the origin of the four elements—fire, air, water, and earth. All bodies are formed by various combinations of the properties of these four elements. Besides these, this third level of nature includes spirits, which proceed directly from the primordial causes.

All these creatures which do not create manifest the uncreated and creating nature, God. Therefore, Erigena calls them

---

[82] *Ibid.,* 3. 5, 19.
[83] *Ibid.,* 2. 2.
[84] *Ibid.,* 2. 30.
[85] *Ibid.,* 3. 31.
[86] *Ibid.,* 1. 58.

"theophanies." Of these, he naturally devotes most attention to humans.[87]

Strictly speaking, the human substance is not to be found in individuals, but rather in the idea of the human as it exists in the mind of the Creator.[88] The initial purpose of creation did not include corruptible beings, but descended only to the lowest spiritual being, the human, who was designed to have only a spiritual body.[89] Through Adam's fall, corruption has entered the universe. As the will of all humankind was in Adam, it is not unjust for us to be punished for his sin.[90] This sin consisted in turning his gaze to himself rather than to the Creator, and took place simultaneously with creation,[91] so that the universe has been corrupt from the very moment of its inception.[92] The human body as we know it is part of this fallen creation.[93] The same is true of the existence of two distinct sexes within humankind.[94]

The image of God in humans is manifold, but is to be found above all in the soul. The soul exists throughout the body, just as God is in all things; and it is not limited to a particular member, just as God is not limited to any one thing. The soul knows that it exists, but does not know its own essence—and, as has already been shown, the same may be said of God. The soul, finally, reflects the divine Trinity in that, while being simple, it is also intellect, reason, and inner sense[95]—a theme that Erigena takes and adapts from Augustine and Pseudo-Dionysius. But, as the entire creation reflects the Creator, the image of God can also be found in the human body, for it is, lives, and feels, and these three are a shadow of the Trinity.[96]

---

[87] In his commentary on the *Celestial Hierarchy* of Pseudo-Dionysius, Erigena does discuss the angels in great detail. However, his views cannot be summarized here for lack of space, and in any case are hardly original. On his understanding of theophanies, see T. Gregory, "Nota sulla dottrina delle 'teofanie' in Giovanni Scoto Eriugena," *StMed*, III, 4 (1963), 75-91.

[88] *De div. nat.* 4. 7.

[89] *Ibid.*, 2. 23.

[90] *De praedest.* 16. 3.

[91] *De div. nat.* 4. 15.

[92] Cappuyns, *Erigène*, pp. 358-59.

[93] *De div. nat.* 2. 25.

[94] *Ibid.*, 2. 26.

[95] *Ibid.*, 4. 11.

[96] *Ibid.*, 4. 16.

The fourth division of nature is that which neither creates nor is created. As has already been said, this fourth division is the same as the first, although we are now dealing with God, not as the source of all things, but rather as the end to which all things are moving. The entire creation is being led back to the Creator in a great process of final restoration—the ancient Greek doctrine of *apokatastasis*. This restoration began with the resurrection of Christ, in which the consequences of sin were destroyed. Thus, for instance, in the resurrected Christ there was no distinction of sexes, and the only reason he came to his disciples in a masculine form was that otherwise they would not have known him.[97]

After a series of stages, all will return to God. Although this implies the disappearance of corruptible bodies, even those things which now exist in such bodies will return to God; for their existence is spiritual, and they will therefore be restored.[98] Each thing will be taken up into another higher than it, until all things return to God and God becomes "all in all."

Thus the vast cycle of Erigena's philosophy is completed. The reasons he was regarded with awe by many are clear. The reasons he was also regarded askance should be equally clear, and were mainly three.

The first point on which there was doubt regarding Erigena's doctrine was that which had to do with the relationship between God and creatures. Although Erigena repeatedly tried to show how he differed from pantheism, his philosophy cannot avoid leaving the impression that there is a single reality: God. This God creates not other realities, but only various manifestations of the divine being. In other words, there is not a clear distinction in Erigena's thought between creation and emanation. This was the reason why centuries later Amalric of Bena thought that he could find a basis for his doctrines in the treatise *On the Division of Nature*.

Second, the person of Christ has a very secondary role in Erigena's speculations. It is true that he places the primordial

---

[97] *Ibid.*, 2. 10.
[98] *Ibid.*, 5. 25.

causes in the Word, but it is difficult to see what relationship there is between that Word and the historical Jesus. It is also true that his christological formulas are perfectly orthodox; but the manner in which he discusses the person of Jesus does suggest a tendency to Docetism—as, for instance, his remarks regarding the sex of the resurrected Lord.

Finally, Erigena understood the torments of hell as a metaphor and claimed that they would consist in the sufferings of an evil conscience.[99] In his time, such a position was unacceptable to most.

For these reasons, Erigena's influence in the Middle Ages was not what could have been expected, given the vast reaches of his thought. Furthermore, the Dark Ages that followed the death of his protector, Charles the Bald, resulted in an atmosphere in which it was impossible to follow the high flights of his speculation. Therefore, those who claim that he was the founder of scholasticism are simply exaggerating. His importance is to be seen rather as an individual thinker and in the impressive vastness of his system; and his influence on the future lay mostly in his having introduced earlier Eastern theology into the medieval West.[100]

The Development of Private Penance

In the first volume of this *History,* we repeatedly saw that post-baptismal sins posed a serious problem to the nascent church. What was to be done about them? They certainly could not be ignored. Nor could baptism be repeated as a means to cleanse the believer of sin. As a result, some postponed baptism until they had reached a mature age, after the sins of their youth. Thus Constantine—like many others—was baptized on his deathbed. But this practice distorted the original meaning of baptism as a rite of initiation and incorporation into the body of Christ. Another alternative was the "second baptism" of

---

[99] *Ibid.,* 5. 29.
[100] P. O. Kristeller, "The Historical Position of Johannes Scottus Erigena," in J. J. O'Meara and B. Naumann, eds., *Latin Script and Letters A.D. 400-900* (Leiden: Brill, 1976), pp. 156-64; P. Lucenti, *Platonismo medievale: Contributi per la storia dell'eriugenismo,* 2nd. ed. (Florence: La Nouva Italia, 1980).

martyrdom. But this was possible only in periods of persecution. Finally, a third way to cleanse post-baptismal sins was through repentance and penance. This was the origin of the penitential system of the Church.

Although during the patristic period there were several debates as to which sins could be forgiven and how,[101] there were two points of general agreement: penance was to be public, and it was not to be repeated. By the fourth century, there was also a general agreement that all sins could be forgiven through penance.[102]

Penance was public, not in the sense that a public confession of sin was required, but in that the sinner was publicly excommunicated and publicly reconciled with the church. The confession itself could be done in secret, usually before the bishop. The sinner then became a penitent, wearing a distinctive garb and sitting in a special section in church. When they were reconciled—usually after a long period of penance, although this varied from place to place—sinners knew that, if ever they would sin again, they could not have recourse to a second penance. Naturally, this rigor applied only to grave sins. The believer could be cleansed from minor sins through the practice of daily penance—fasting, praying, and helping the needy.

This system of penance, however, did not suffice to solve the problems posed by post-baptismal sins. It did indeed alleviate the situation by giving the sinner a second opportunity. But the fact that it could not be repeated soon resulted in practices similar to those which had developed earlier regarding baptism—penance tended to be postponed in order to insure one's salvation, and thus became connected with the deathbed. Another development was that seclusion in a monastery became acceptable as an act of penance—which in turn gave rise, during the Merovingian period, to the practice of forcibly secluding in monasteries those who had sinned and even those who had displeased the authorities.

Meanwhile, the Celtic church had developed its own distinctive and independent form of penance. Here, penance

---

[101] I: 231-32, 235.
[102] Council of Nicea, canon 13.

could be repeated as often as necessary. As a result, it was used not only in the case of grave sins, but also in connection with lesser ones. Also, the formal and solemn excommunication by the bishop was replaced by a private, still formal but less solemn, action by a priest. Thus, penance was brought out of the realm of the exceptional into the usual, and what had been reserved for the deathbed became a frequent practice more connected with daily life.[103]

Late in the sixth century, the Celtic practice was still frowned upon by ecclesiastical authorities on the Continent.[104] But during the seventh and eighth centuries Celtic missionary-wanderers introduced the practice, first in Gaul and Spain[105] and then throughout the Latin church. Thus the modern practice of penance had attained its main characteristics by the time of the Carolingian renaissance.[106]

The Growth of Papal Power

At the end of our first volume, when dealing with the complex events that led to the Council of Chalcedon, we saw that the pope was powerless to oppose the will of the emperor. Indeed, at the so-called Robbers' Synod of A.D. 449, Leo's *Tome* was not even read, since it did not agree with imperial policies. When the Council of Chalcedon finally met, it could do so only because the new emperor willed it.

This situation changed rapidly in the West. The center of the Empire was now at Constantinople, which claimed to be the new Rome not only politically but also ecclesiastically. As a reaction, the ecclesiastical authorities in Rome claimed that the ecclesiastical primacy of Rome—which had developed *de facto* out of the political primacy of that city—was based *de jure* on the Lord's words to Peter, whose vicar the pope was. This tension was quite

---

[103] K. Rahner, "Penance," *SM*, 4:395.

[104] Council III of Toledo (A.D. 589), canon 11.

[105] S. González, "Tres maneras de penitencia: La disciplina penitencial de la Iglesia española desde el siglo V al siglo VIII," *RET*, 1 (1940-41), 985-1019.

[106] B. Poschmann, "Das christliche Altertum und die kirchliche Privatbusse," *ZkT*, 64 (1930), 214-52; T. van Eupen, "De praktijk ven de boete in de Middeleeuwen," *TvT*, 2 (1962), 351-74; 3 (1963), 12-44.

understandable, for the emperors at Constantinople—often deeply religious themselves—conceived of their task as divinely given to them. They were anointed by God to rule the universe. Therefore, they were above ecclesiastical authorities—a fact that they repeatedly proved in their dealings with the patriarchs of Constantinople—whom they were called to protect. In turn, church authorities were to sanction the power and actions of the ruler. But in the West the situation was quite different. There, leaders such as Ambrose had insisted that the emperor is a member of the church and is not above it.[107] After the reign of Theodosius—who had to bow before the authority of the church on more than one occasion—the West was notably lacking in able and forceful rulers. The barbarian invasions created a chaos in which the only relatively stable institution was the church. The West thus became the center of resistance to imperial claims, while the East took the opposite tack. One result of this situation was the growing gap between East and West. Another result was the development of the theory of papal supremacy.

Although we cannot here follow all the details of the development of that theory, there are three episodes that may serve to illustrate that development: the clash of Gelasius with imperial authority, the claims and practice of Gregory the Great, and the coronation of Charlemagne.

As a secretary to Pope Felix III, Gelasius had probably drafted some of the letters in which Felix refused to accept the claims of the patriarch of Constantinople—supported by the throne—to universal authority.[108] When he himself was elected pope, he neglected to communicate that fact to his Constantinopolitan colleague, and was therefore reprimanded by both patriarch and emperor. However, the open clash came when Zeno promulgated his Henoticon.[109] At issue here was not only the christological doctrine of Chalcedon, but also the right of the

---

[107] *Ep.* 21. 36.

[108] W. Ullman, *The Growth of Papal Government in the Middles Ages: A Study in the Ideological Relation of Clerical to Lay Power* (London: Methuen & Co., 1955), p. 15. See also H. Fuhrmann, "Innovations théoriques et pratiques relatives au rôle du primat de Rome: Du haut moyen âge à la réforme grégorienne," *Concilium*, 64 (1971), 47-52.

[109] See above, pp. 79-82.

emperor to intervene and decide on doctrinal matters. This latter point seems to have been at least as important for Gelasius as the doctrinal issue. According to Gelasius, the emperor is indeed appointed by God, but this does not mean that he is above the church. He has been anointed to do the will of God, but he cannot judge what that will is. Therefore, his task is not to teach the church, but rather to learn from it.[110] His is the power; but the *authority* belongs to those whom God has appointed, that is, Peter and his successor.[111] Christ is king and priest of all, and his kingly functions are administered by the emperor, whereas his priestly authority he has given to Peter and his successors. But, as the purpose of life in this world is to prepare us for life beyond, Peter's vicar has a higher function.[112]

Gregory the Great clashed with Constantinople because he refused to acknowledge the right that the patriarch of that city claimed to be called "Ecumenical Patriarch." In fact, such a title was a direct contradiction of the claim of the papcy that it had universal primacy over the church. Although that primacy had never been exerted in the East, and Gregory was indeed shrewd enough to realize that it could not be so as long as Constantinople was the center of political power there, he also seems to have realized that such claims could not go undisputed if the authority of Rome over the Western church was to be held. Therefore, he protested that his Constantinopolitan colleague had no right to call himself Ecumenical Patriarch.[113]

However, it was not so much as a theologian, but as a practical administrator, that Gregory contributed to the growth of papal power. At a time when the ancient order of the *pax romana* had collapsed, and threatened to pull down with it every remnant of civilization, Gregory moved the church into the vacuum that was created and turned her into the heir and preserver of the values

---

[110] *Ep.* 10.9. A concrete application of these principles may be seen in O. Bertolini, "La dottrina gelasiana dei due poteri nella polemica per la successione nel regno de Lorena (869-870)," in *Mélanges Eugène Tisserant*, Vol. IV (Vatican City: Bibliotheca Apostolica Vaticana, 1964), pp. 35-58.

[111] *Ep.* 12. 2.

[112] *Tract.* 4. Note that at this time the pope refers to himself as the vicar of Peter, and not of Christ. As will be seen later on, when Innocent III claimed the title of "Vicar of Christ," this implied that he had ultimate authority, not only in the priestly but also in the kingly order. See Ullman, *Papal Government*, p. 26.

[113] *Reg.* 5. 37.

of antiquity, as well as the guardian of order. Thus, while in the East the church and its hierarchy remained subject to the emperor, in the West the Empire disappeared, and the church took over a number of its functions.

This process culminated on Christmas Day, A.D. 800, when Pope Leo III placed the imperial crown on Charlemagne's head. This culmination, however, was also an ominous sign for papal power. Leo himself was present at court because he found it necessary to clear himself from accusations made before the powerful Frankish king. Although the Carolingian Empire was ephemeral, the resurrection of the imperial ideology would eventually lead to grievous conflicts between emperors and popes. As a consequence, the theory of papal authority would be expanded even further.

V

The Dark Age

A famous Roman Catholic historian calls the tenth century "a dark century of lead and iron."[1] These words may be correctly applied not only to the tenth century, but also to the last decades of the ninth and most of the eleventh centuries. After the death of Charles the Bald, the power of the Carolingians rapidly declined. The internecine warfare between the various portions of the ancient Carolingian empire—coupled with the invasions of Normans, Saracens and Hungarians—created a constant state of turmoil. As before, monasteries tried to preserve something of the culture and knowledge of the past. But most of them were not included within the walls of cities and therefore were easily sacked by the invaders, with the resultant destruction of many valuable libraries. The church was incapable of imposing order within this chaos, for she herself was going through difficult times. Popes were created by one or another sovereign and were therefore puppets of political movements. The assassination of a pope was not unheard of, and even dead popes risked being judged and condemned by their successors.[2] In the second half of the tenth century, a young

---

[1] Baronius, quoted in R. García Villoslada, *Historia de la Iglesia Católica*, Vol. 2. *Edad Media. BAC,* 104:131-32.

[2] At what is usually called the "Cadaveric Council" of A.D. 897, the corpse of Pope Formosus was brought before the assembly and there judged and condemned. They then declared his pontificate to be void, and all orders conferred by him were invalidated. Finally, his priestly garments were removed and his fingers cut off. All this because he belonged to a different political party from his successor Stephen VI.

man not yet twenty wore at once the imperial crown and the pontifical tiara, and turned the papacy into a toy not only of his political ambitions but even of his youthful whims.

The advent of the House of Saxony to the imperial throne—with Otto in A.D. 962—brought a measure of peace to politics, but not to the church. Frequently, in spite of the efforts of various emperors, several persons claimed to be the legitimate successor of Peter. Many of these were merely creatures of the emperor or of a particular Roman faction. Under Otto III, when Gerbert of Aurillac occupied the papal throne as Sylvester II (999–1003), there was a brief period of order and an attempt at reformation. But after that brief moment, strife, irregularity, and immorality again surrounded the Holy See.

Conrad II, the first emperor of the House of Franconia (1024–1039), was not able to establish order in Rome. Meanwhile, within the church, a reformist movement had developed, associated originally with the monastic reformation of Cluny and later with the names of Hildebrand, Humbert, Bruno of Toul, and Gerard of Florence. Finally, with the support of Henry III, this party took possession of the Holy See, placing Bruno of Toul on it under the name of Leo IX (1049–1054). From then on, with brief interruptions, a great ecclesiastical reformation developed which culminated during the pontificate of Hildebrand, who took the name Gregory VII (1073–1085). Thus the scene was set for what would be the great renaissance of the twelfth century, to which we shall devote the next chapter.

Yet, in spite of the darkness of the age, theological and literary activity did not entirely die out. It was continued in several monastic centers and cathedral schools, although it was clearly lacking in originality.

In the ninth century, while the Carolingian Empire was dissolving, the most significant of these centers was the monastery of Saint Germain, at Auxerre. It was there that Heiric of Auxerre flourished. He wrote several commentaries on Augustine in which Erigena's influence may be seen, for he follows the scheme for the division of nature which had been developed by the Irish scholar. However, perhaps because of his readings in Boethius, he rejected Erigena's extreme realism and claimed that the reality of things is in their particular substance.[3]

Remigius of Auxerre, a disciple of Heiric, was the foremost thinker of that school. His life illustrates the growing importance of cathedral schools, for in A.D. 893, at the request of the archbishop of Reims, he left the monastery in order to become a teacher in the two schools that had been developed in that city. Later, through a similar call, Remigius moved to Paris. There he had among his disciples Odo, the future leader of the Cluniac reformation. Thus, the career of Remigius shows how the cathedral schools, which received most of their first and best teachers from monasteries, later contributed to the renewal of monastic life. Like his teacher Heiric; Remigius commented on Augustine. His commentary on Boethius, originally attributed to Erigena,[4] set the standard for a long series of similar commentaries. On some points, such as the question of universals, the influence of Erigena is more marked in Remigius than in Heiric; but on others—especially those in which Erigena had followed the Greeks, such as his position regarding the *Filioque*—Remigius departed from Erigena.

The views of Remigius on more traditional theological issues may be found in his commentaries on Genesis and on Psalms.[5] In these he interprets Scripture allegorically, so that such narratives as that of creation refer in a veiled fashion to Christ, to the evangelists, and to the church. Regarding the human creature, Remigius believes that the image of God is in rationality and immortality, while the likeness consisted in the original sanctity and justice. When Adam sinned and fell, he lost the likeness of God, but not the image. Following Erigena, Remigius claims each of us is a microcosmos that reflects the universe, for in the

---

[3] Cf. E. Gilson, *History*, p. 614; E. Jeauneau, "Influences érigéniennes dans une homélie d'Héric d'Auxerre," in J. J. O'Meara and L. Bieler, eds., *The Mind of Erigena* (Dublin: Irish University Press, 1973), pp. 114-24.

[4] Restored to Remigius by M. Cappuyns, "Le plus ancient commentaire des 'Opuscula sacra' et son origine," *RThAM*, 3 (1931), 237-72. On his place within the context of his intellectual times, see C. Leonardi, "Remigio d'Auxerre e l'eredità della scuola carolingia," in *I classici nel Medioevo e nell'Umanesimo*, No. 42 (Genoa: Università, 1975), pp. 271-88.

[5] There are also extant commentaries on the Song of Songs, the twelve minor prophets, and the epistles of Paul, which have been attributed to Remigius but also to Haymo of Halberstadt and to Haymo of Auxerre.

body the soul is present everywhere and is not localized in any one place, just as God is present throughout the world without being limited to any one place.[6]

Theology in the Tenth Century

The most significant theological works of the tenth century are the *Treatise on the Body and the Blood of the Lord,* by Gezo of Tortona, the *Treatise on the Antichrist,* by Adso of Luxeuil (or of Montierender), and the *Commentaries on Saint Paul,* by Atto of Verceil.

Gezo was an abbot who read the treatise of Paschasius Radbertus on the eucharist and was thereby inspired to write on a similar subject. His work is significant not for its originality, but for the lack of it, for it illustrates the measure to which the tenth century was content with repeating the wisdom of the past. Another significant feature is the manner in which Gezo collects and relates the most unbelievable miracles said to have happened in connection with the eucharist.

Adso was one of the most famous scholars of his age, and therefore was called to be a teacher in several cathedral schools. His *Treatise on the Antichrist*—sometimes attributed to Alcuin—was addressed to the widow of Louis IV from Oversea. Here Adso uses the doctrine of the Antichrist, and the claim that many of his ministers are lay people, to call the queen to justice and goodness. But, even should she succumb to the temptation of the Antichrist, the queen may still have the consolation of knowing that in the last times, after the destruction of the Antichrist, the Lord will grant forty days so that those who have yielded to temptation may do penance.[7]

Atto was made Bishop of Verceil in A.D. 924, and later became Grand Chancellor in the court of Lothair II of France. His most

---

6 *In Gen.* 1.37.
7 *PL,* 101:1298. Cf. R. Konrad, *De ortu et tempore Antichristi: Antichristvorstellung und Geschichtsbild des Abtes Adso von Montier-en-Der* (Munich: M. Lassleben Kallmünz, 1964); M. Rangheri, "La 'Epistola ad Gerbergam reginam de ortu et tempore Antichristi' di Adsone di Montier-en-Der e le sue fonti," *StMed,* III, 14 (1973), 677-732; D. Verhelst, "La préhistoire des conceptions d'Adson concernent l'Antichrist," *RThAM,* 40 (1973), 52-103; R. K. Emerson, "Antichrist as Anti-Saint: The Significance of Abbot Adso's 'Libellus de Antichristo,' " *AmBenRev,* 30 (1979), 175-90.

significant works were his *Commentaries on Saint Paul,* which show that even in a period of widespread ignorance and disorder there were still individuals of ample culture who, while unable to show great originality, were capable of keeping alive the exegetical and scholarly traditions of earlier centuries. One should also note that Atto claimed that the presence of Christ in the eucharist was spiritual rather than physical.[8]

There were other signs of intellectual activity during the tenth century which should be noted here in order to show that all was not darkness and conservatism. The nun Hrosvitha dared to compose religious dramas following the model of Terence. The long series of reforming abbots of Cluny must also be mentioned as a sign of hope. Finally, the heretic Willgard of Ravenna is most significant as an indication of the intellectual ferment that seems to have been boiling below the surface. If the chronicles of his time are accurate, Willgard was condemned for revering classical authors—especially Horace, Virgil, and Juvenal—to the point of claiming that they were divinely inspired and even infallible, and claiming for himself the ability to communicate directly with them. After he was condemned and put to death, his followers were to be found in Sardinia and Spain.

The Eleventh Century: Gerbert of Aurillac and Fulbert of Chartres

The eleventh century shows some glimpses of what would be the new life of the twelfth. When the eleventh century opened, the Roman see was occupied by the scholar Gerbert of Aurillac, under the title of Sylvester II. A few years later his disciple Fulbert became Bishop of Chartres, where he started an academic and scholarly tradition that would bear fruit a century later. In the second half of the century, the reformist party finally came to power within the church—an event that led to tension between civil and ecclesiastical authorities. It was also at that time that the eucharistic controversy between Lanfranc of

---

[8] A. J. MacDonald, *Berengar and the Reform of Sacramental Doctrine* (London: Longmans, Green & Co., 1930), p. 245. Cf. S. F. Temple, "Atto of Vercelli: Church, State and Society in the Tenth Century," *Dissertation Abstracts,* 31 (1970-1971), 1715.

Canterbury and Berengar of Tours showed that theological activity was once again becoming a lively and original endeavor. Anselm, Archbishop of Canterbury from 1093 to 1109, properly belongs to the twelfth century, both for his works and for his spirit.

Gerbert was in a sense an heir to the tradition of Remigius of Auxerre,[9] for the monastery of Aurillac had come under the influence of the Cluniac reformation, which in turn was indebted to the teachings of Remigius. Another significant fact that shows the beginning of a new openness is that Gerbert went to Spain, and upon his return brought to Christian Europe some of the science of the Arabs. Most of his scholarly production took place between 972 and 982, while he was teaching at Reims, and a great deal of it shows the influence of his studies in Spain, for he is greatly interested in mathematical questions. His treatise *On the Rational and the Use of Reason* showed his great dialectial ability, and influenced the manner in which the twelfth century posed the question of universals.

The most outstanding of Gerbert's disciples was Fulbert of Chartres,[10] whose fame extended throughout Gaul. Several persons who came in contact with him were later significant in the events of their times. However, his greatest contribution was not in his own theological work, but in turning Chartres into an intellectual center that would become very influential in the twelfth century. His most famous disciple was Berengar of Tours, who did not follow his doctrine, but rather reacted against it, and thus began the most important theological controversy of the eleventh century.

Since the two main themes of the controversy that took place around the doctrine of Berengar were the relationship between faith and reason, and the nature of the presence of Christ in the eucharist, we must pause to discuss these two matters in Fulbert's theology. Fulbert claimed that both faith and reason have been

[9] On his influence on the intellectual life of his times, see U. Lindgren, *Gerbert von Aurillac und das Quadrivium: Untersuchungen zur Bildung im Zeitalter der Ottonen* (Wiesbaden: F. Steiner, 1976).
[10] About his teaching career, there are several points in doubt. See L. C. MacKinney, *Bishop Fulbert and Education at the School of Chartres* (Notre Dame, Ind.: University of Notre Dame Press, 1957), pp. 24-25. See also F. Behrends, *The Letters and Poems of Fulbert of Chartres* (Oxford: Clarendon Press, 1976).

given by God, and that they are therefore good and useful. However, each of them has its own proper objects of knowledge, just as each of the bodily senses has its proper objects of perception. The high mysteries of God are proper objects not of rational knowledge, but rather of faith. Even if the mind wishes to rise to the vision of the divine secrets, its weakness is such that it must err. "The depths of the mysteries of God are not revealed to human intellectual effort [*humanae disputationi*], but to the eyes of faith."[11] These mysteries are necessary for salvation, and are three in number: the Trinity, baptism, and "the two sacraments of life, that is, those which contain the body and blood of the Lord."[12]

The eucharist, like the Trinity and baptism, is a proper object not for reason, but only for faith. "The mystery [of the eucharist] is not terrestrial, but heavenly; it is not given to human comparison, but to admiration; it is not to be debated, but feared; . . . it is not to be judged by the vision of the body, but by the intuition of the spirit."[13] In it, the body of Christ is truly present in the visible elements in such a way that those who partake of them eat that body. If the Word has become flesh, and we truly partake of that flesh in the Lord's Supper, one must confess that Christ is *naturaliter* in us and that therefore we are in God, for the Father is in Christ and Christ truly in us.[14] In referring to the manner in which this takes place, Fulbert does not use the precise language of the doctrine of transubstantiation. He distinguishes not between the substance of the body of Christ and the accidents of the bread and the wine, but rather between the "outer substance," which is the elements, and the "inner substance," which is the body and the blood of the Lord. This inner substance, although very real and although directly connected to the eating and the drinking of the outer substance, does demand an inner disposition in the recipient which involves the "palate of faith," the "gullet of hope," and the "viscera of charity."[15] And if any doubt this doctrine, let them remember

---

[11] *Ep.* 5 (*PL*, 141:196).
[12] *Ibid.*, (*PL*, 141:197).
[13] *Ibid.*, (*PL*, 141:201).
[14] *Ibid.*, (*PL*, 141:201).
[15] *Ibid.*

that God, who was able to make all creatures out of nothing, can also, and with greater ease, transform those very creatures by giving them a higher worth and infusing *(transfundere)* into them the substance of the body of Christ.[16]

Berengar of Tours and Lanfranc of Canterbury: The Eucharistic Controversy

Berengar of Tours, the most famous disciple of Fulbert, took a position very different from that of his teacher. After studying with Fulbert and practicing medicine at Tours for some time, he became a teacher in that city, and eventually his fame grew to such an extent that Tours became one of the principal intellectual centers of France.

Berengar differed from Fulbert and the majority of his contemporaries in that he granted greater authority to reason in matters of faith. According to him, the image of God in humans is in our reason, and one would be most foolish and ungrateful not to make use of it.[17] He therefore became an ardent admirer of Erigena, in whose works Berengar found constant reference to the authority of reason. However, these two understood reason in very different ways, for Erigena believed that reason worked through the presence of eternal and invisible ideas in the mind, whereas Berengar took the senses as his point of departure and applied reason to the data received from them. Therefore, his use of reason was even more perturbing to traditional theological views than that of Erigena, and led Lanfranc to say to him, "You abandon the sacred authorities and take refuge in dialectics."[18] Another consequence of this view of reason and its relationship to sensory experience is that, although Berengar does not seem to have concerned himself directly with the question of universals, he has traditionally been classified among the nominalists—and it is true that his eucharistic doctrine and his insistence on the value of sensory data would very well agree with a nominalist position.

---

[16] *Ibid.* (*PL*, 141:204).
[17] *De sac. coena* (ed. Vischer, Berlin, 1834), pp. 100-101.
[18] *De corp. et sang, dom.* 7.

What led Berengar to the eucharistic controversy was, first, his admiration of Erigena; second, his own rationalistic inclination; and, finally, political and ecclesiastical intrigues that used him as a pawn of ambitions of which he himself was ignorant. The controversy began as a debate regarding the orthodoxy of the treatise of Ratramnus, *On the Body and the Blood of the Lord*, which, as has already been said, was then attributed to Erigena. Berengar believed that it had been written by that admired Irish scholar, and used it as a basis on which to teach his disciples the doctrine of "John Scotus" regarding the eucharist. When the question was raised of the orthodoxy of that treatise, Berengar came to its defense. After that time, the issue was widely discussed, and the result was that Berengar was repeatedly condemned, often in connection with intrigues whose purpose was to establish the primacy of ecclesiastical over civil authority. On several occasions, faced by the alternative between death and recantation, Berengar chose the latter, but returned to his original doctrine as soon as danger had passed.[19] He died an old man, on a small island outside of Tours, without having definitively abandoned his doctrines.[20]

It is impossible to establish precisely the date on which this eucharistic controversy began. On the one hand, it is certain that the question of the presence of Christ in communion was a general concern at the time—and we have already seen that Fulbert wrote on it. On the other hand, the earliest documents in which the name of Berengar appears joined to the eucharistic question date from around 1048. After that time, the texts become more numerous, so that one may safely say that the eucharistic controversy took place early in the second half of the eleventh century.[21]

---

[19] The most important of the synods which condemned him were those held at Rome in 1059 and 1080. The latter took place during the pontificate of Gregory VII, who until that time had dealt with Berengar with extreme patience and understanding.

[20] The repeated claims that he died in what eventually became orthodox doctrine are not trustworthy.

[21] In this entire section, I have followed the chronology of MacDonald, *Berengar, passim*. See also J. de Montclos, *Lanfranc et Bérenger: La controverse eucharistique du XIᵉ siècle* (Louvain: Spicilegium sacrum Lovaniense, 1971). On the early stages of the controversy, see J. C. Didier, "Aux débuts de la controverse eucharistique de XIᵉ siècle: Hughes de Breteuil, évêque de Langres, et Bérenger de Tours," *MSR* special issue (1977), 82-97.

The document of 1048 is a letter that Hugh, Bishop of Chartres, addressed to Berengar when he received word of the latter's eucharistic opinions.[22] From this epistle it is clear that there were two aspects of the teachings of Berengar which caused grave concern to his contemporaries: his denial that the essence of the bread and wine is transformed, and his claim that the body of Christ is present in the eucharist only "intellectually"—that is, spiritually. Hugh rejected these views and told Berengar that the bread is no longer such—it literally becomes the body of Christ, even though it retains the taste of bread. If this were not so, there would be no real power in this so-called body, and the eucharist would be worthless.[23]

Apart from this letter, there are several other documents born out of the first moments of the controversy.[24] But these do not add much to what had already been said by Hugh or by some earlier writers.

The controversy was widened when, after his condemnation in Rome in 1059, Berengar published a brief treatise in which he insisted on his original doctrines. As this treatise evoked Lanfranc's response *On the Body and the Blood of the Lord Against Berengar,* and as the latter responded in turn with *On the Sacred Supper,* the controversy became a direct confrontation between the two greatest theologians of the time. Although a strictly chronological procedure would require that we deal with each of these three works separately,[25] for the sake of brevity we shall first expound the position of Berengar and then that of Lanfranc.

 There were two points in the eucharistic doctrine of his opponents which Berengar found unacceptable and absurd: the notion that the bread and the wine cease to exist, and the claim that the body of Christ which was born of Mary is physically present on the altar.

Regarding the continued existence of the bread and the wine on the altar, Berengar claims that even his adversaries unwittingly concede it. When they say that the bread and the wine are the body and the flesh of Christ, they are actually saying that the bread and the wine are still something—the body and blood of Christ.[26] Furthermore, if the color and the taste of bread and wine remain even after consecration, this means that their substance must also remain, for accidents cannot be separated from the substances in which they exist.[27]

As to the physical presence of the body of Christ in the eucharist, Berengar affirms that such a doctrine leads to absurd consequences. The body of Christ which was born of Mary is in heaven, and one cannot claim that there is a part of its flesh on the altar, nor that there are vast numbers of bodies of Christ.[28] Jesus Christ was sacrificed once and for all, and communion is a memorial of that sacrifice.[29] In summary, neither is the bread raised to heaven nor does the body of Christ descend to earth; and therefore the bread is still bread and the wine is still wine.[30]

This does not mean, however, that Berengar believes that communion is only a memorial of Christ's sacrifice—some sort of psychological exercise in which the church makes an effort to awaken her own memory of the events of Calvary. On the contrary, he insists that communion is efficacious and that, while the bread and the wine continue existing, they become a "sacrament"—that is, a sign—of the body of the Lord, which is in heaven. Therefore, although not in a strict sense, one can say that the sacrament is the body and the blood of the Lord.[31]

The root of the tensions between Lanfranc and Berengar was in their divergent attitudes regarding authority in the church.[32] Lanfranc accused Berengar of giving too much importance to

---

[26] *PL*, 150:414; *De sac. coena*, p. 279.

[27] *De sac. coena*, p. 171.

[28] *Ibid.*, pp. 198-99, 237.

[29] *Ibid.*, pp. 131, 272-73. Lanfranc had quoted Augustine as holding the opposite view: *PL*, 150:425.

[30] *PL*, 150:439.

[31] *PL*, 150-423, 436; *De sac. coena*, p. 84.

[32] Lanfranc had heard Berengar lecture at Tours. Later, before the controversy erupted, ill feelings had already developed when a letter that Berengar addressed to Lanfranc was received by others before him.

dialectics and not enough to authority—a reason that probably led Berengar to include numerous biblical and patristic references in *On the Sacred Supper*. However, Lanfranc himself was not against the use of dialectical reason, for in his own book he often attempted to refute Berengar through the use of logic.[33] Lanfranc's method was rather to make use of reason and of its formal structure—dialectics—but always within the framework of orthodoxy as this was defined by Scripture and the tradition of the church.[34] Although reason is good, and one ought to use it, that which is given through faith cannot be attained by the intellect, but is only to be believed with humbleness and patience.[35]

As a result, Lanfranc's eucharistic doctrine is radically opposed to Berengar's. The body of Christ is really present in the eucharist. This takes place through a real transformation of the consecrated elements,[36] so that they are no longer bread or wine. If Scripture and the ancients refer to them as bread and wine they use these words only symbolically, for that which is now on the altar is truly a symbol, although not of the body and blood of Christ, but of the bread and the wine formerly there![37]

MacDonald points out two ways in which Lanfranc contradicts himself.[38] The first is when he claims that in communion the material bread nourishes the body while the body of Christ nourishes the soul.[39] How can a bread that does not exist nourish a body? The second appears in the double assertion that the eucharistic body of Christ comes to existence at the moment of consecration, and that this body is the same that was born of Mary.[40] These two opinions are clearly contradictory. What has happened is that Lanfranc has attempted to bring together the eucharistic doctrine of Augustine and that of Paschasius Radbertus.

The eucharistic controversy did not end with the condemnation or even the death of Berengar. Besides several antidialectical

---

[33] See MacDonald, *Berengar*, pp. 291-92.
[34] *De corp, et sang. dom.* 17. For a general introduction to Lanfranc's life and thought, see M. Gibson, *Lanfranc of Bec* (Oxford: Clarendon Press, 1978).
[35] *Ibid.*, 21.
[36] *Ibid.*, 9.
[37] *Ibid.*, 20.
[38] *Berengar*, pp. 294-95.
[39] *De corp. et sang. dom.* 20.
[40] *Ibid.*, 18.

writers who attacked Berengar from strictly conservative positions—such as Peter Damian, Wolfelm of Brauweiler, and Manegold of Lautenbach—there was also Otlo of Saint Emmeran, who once again insisted on the Augustinian views and attained a certain measure of success.[41] Guitmund of Aversa made use of logical reason in order to refute Berengar—and in so doing he made more concessions to reason than Lanfranc had made.[42] His treatise *On the Truth of the Body and the Blood of Christ* takes divine omnipotence as its point of departure in order to refute the arguments of Berengar. The old argument, that the God who created things out of nothing is able to transform that which is already in existence, appears here once again. Guitmund must also be given credit for introducing into eucharistic theology the use of the term "substantial" rather than "essential" in order to refer to the change that, according to him, takes place when the elements are consecrated.[43] His realism is such that he claims that the consecrated bread does not physically nourish the person who eats it. If an unworthy priest attempts to prove the opposite by consecrating a large amount of bread and then showing that it is possible to subsist on it, this would prove nothing, for there are three possibilities that would render the proof worthless. First, it is possible that, given the obvious incredulity of the priest, the elements will not be truly consecrated; second, it is conceivable that the demons will change the body of Christ back into bread, in order to deceive the faithful; or, third, the angels may perform such a change, in order to avoid the profanation of the sacrament.[44]

Although the doctrine of transubstantiation was not defined before A.D. 1251, the actual controversy over the eucharist did not extend beyond the eleventh century. The works that in the twelfth century deal with the eucharist take for granted that the only orthodox doctrine is that which asserts that the bread and the wine are transformed into the body and the blood of Christ.

This eucharistic controversy which took place during the eleventh century is significant on two scores. In the first place, it

---

[41] MacDonald, *Berengar*, pp. 331-40.
[42] *Ibid.*, 341.
[43] *Ibid.*, 344.
[44] *De corp. et. sang. dom.* 2.

led directly to the eventual formulation of the doctrine of transubstantiation, for it greatly clarified the issues involved. Second, it serves to show the manner in which the second half of the eleventh century was preparing the way for the renaissance of the twelfth. The eucharistic question was one particular form of the greater issue of the use of reason in theology. Berengar seemed to place it above authority, Peter Damian rejected it, Lanfranc and Guitmund tried to join it to the chariot of authority, but no one could ignore it. In the twelfth century this question of the use of reason—and, quite naturally, that of the nature of reason—would be foremost in theological debate.

On the other hand, the fact that the eucharistic controversy occupies such an extensive portion of this chapter should not lead the reader to believe that this was the only subject with which theology dealt at the time. The growing tension with the Eastern wing of the church led such authors as Cardinal Humbert to write treatises against the Greeks. The issue of ecclesiastical investitures involved the work of several theologians.[45] It was also during this century that the sect of the Cathari began to appear in southern France and in other regions of Western Europe.[46] Late in the century, shortly before the death of Berengar, a converted Jew by the name of Samuel the Moroccan wrote in Arabic a *Book on the Past Coming of the Messiah* in which he attempted to prove, mostly on the basis of Old Testament texts, that Jesus was the Messiah, that the Jews sinned in not receiving him as such, and that it is for this sin that they have been dispersed throughout the world. The last chapter of this work is especially interesting in that here the author adduces the authority of the *Koran* in favor of Jesus.[47] A surprising example of Christian-Jewish-Moslem contact, less than a decade before Pope Urban II, under the motto of "God wills it," would pour upon the Holy Land the ambitions and fanaticism of Western Europe!

---

[45] For reasons of clarity, these two matters will be discussed in future chapters. The growing tension between East and West will be included in our next incursion into Eastern theology. The question of investitures will be included in the chapter on the twelfth century.

[46] The Cathari or Albigenses, already present in Europe late in the eleventh century, would not become an important factor until the twelfth and thirteenth centuries. They will be discussed in the following chapter.

[47] Chapter 27 (*PL*, 149:365-68).

VI

2-27-96 ✓

The Renaissance of the Twelfth Century

The twelfth century brought with itself a new era in the history of Christian thought.[1] The theological awakening that had been interrupted when chaos and decadence swept over the Carolingian Empire now bore its fruit, no longer under the shadow of a great empire, but in a church being reformed and claiming for its princes rights and authority above those of secular princes. The new social and economic conditions resulting in the development of commerce and the growth of cities moved the center of theological activity away from monasteries to urban cathedral schools, thus foreshadowing what would be the great universities of the thirteenth century.

The year 1099, the last of the eleventh century, marks also the death of Urban II, the fall of Jerusalem to the arms of the First Crusade, and the death of the Cid of Spain. The century that is introduced by such events is that of early Gothic, of romantic love, of the Latin Kingdom of Jerusalem, of the translators that in Toledo would make the wisdom of the Arabs available to the Latin world, of Richard the Lionhearted, and of Saint Bernard of Clairvaux.

---

[1] M. de Gandillac and E. Jeauneau, *Entretiens sur la Renaissance deu 12ᵉ siècle* (Paris: Mouton, 1968); M. D. Chenu, *Nature, Man and Society in the 12th Century: Essays on New Theological Perspectives in the Latin West* (Chicago: University Press, 1968); R. L. Benson et al., eds., *Renaissance and Renewal in the Twelfth Century* (Oxford: Clarendon, 1982).

157

The Forerunner: Anselm of Canterbury

However, as far as the history of Christian thought is concerned, this century was born not in A.D. 1100, but rather on that day, somewhat earlier, on which Anselm of Bec—who later became Archbishop of Canterbury—took the pen and started his vast theological production.

Anselm was born in the Piedmont, but several years of pilgrimage, coupled with Lanfranc's fame, eventually led him to the monastery of Bec in Normandy. There he became a well-known teacher who drew disciples from distant regions. It was while at Bec that he wrote most of his works: *Monologion, Proslogion, On the Grammarian,* and *Epistle on the Incarnation of the Word.* He was appointed to the see of Canterbury in 1093; but he clashed with the king on several points, especially on the issue of lay investitures, and in 1097 he departed in voluntary exile. It was during the three years of his exile that he wrote *Why God Became Man,* as well as *On Virginal Conception and Original Sin,* and *On the Procession of the Holy Spirit.* He then returned to Canterbury, only to leave for a new exile three years later. Finally, in 1106, after his difficulties with the lay authorities had been settled, he returned to his see, which he occupied until his death in 1109. His main theological work during these last years was *On the Agreement of Foreknowledge, Predestination, and Grace with Free Will.*

Anselm's theological method[2] consists in posing a theological problem and then solving it not on the basis of the authority of Scripture or of the ancients, but through the use of reason. The type of problem which he usually poses is not a mere speculative question, but is rather the erroneous position of a heretic or an unbeliever who must be refuted. He then sets out from the presuppositions that such a heretic or unbeliever would accept,

---

[2] The best study of that method is J. McIntyre, *St. Anselm and His Critics: A Reinterpretation of the Cur Deus homo* (Edinburgh: Oliver & Boyd, 1954). See also: W. Betzendörfer, "Glauben und Wissen bei Anselm von Canterbury," *ZschrKgesch,* 48 (1929), 354-70; A. M. Jacquin, "Les 'rationes necessariae' de Saint Anselme," in *Mélanges Mandonnet,* II (Paris: J. Vrin, 1930), 67-78; B. Geyer, "Zur Deutung von Anselms Cur Deus homo," *ThGl,* 34 (1942), 203-10; G. B. Phelan, *The Wisdom of Saint Anselm* (Latrobe, Pa.: Archabbey Press, 1960); R. Campbell, "Anselm's Theological Method," *SJT,* 32 (1979), 541-62. For general information and bibliography on Anselm, see also the articles on the periodical publication *Analecta Anselmiana,* published in Frankfurt since 1969.

and from such presuppositions attempts to prove orthodox doctrine. At first sight, this method gives the impression that Anselm is simply an extreme rationalist. He does indeed attempt to prove rationally doctrines such as the Trinity and the Incarnation, which most later theologians would insist were beyond the limits of human reason. But it is necessary to keep in mind that Anselm the theologian is always Anselm the believer, so that he already believes what he attempts to prove. The purpose of his work is not therefore to attain unto faith through reason, but simply to show the error of the unbeliever and to enrich and deepen the faith of Anselm himself. This double purpose is clearly expressed in *Why God Became Man:*

> Those who ask [that he write down some of the things they have heard him say] ask this not in order to attain unto faith through reason, but in order to rejoice in the understanding and contemplation of that which they believe, and also in order to be always prepared in as much as possible, to answer all who may ask for the reason of the hope that is in us.[3]

Therefore, the purpose of Anselm's theology is not curiously to probe into divine secrets, but rather to lead faith to its own understanding.

> I do not try, Lord, to attain Your lofty heights, because my understanding is in no way equal to it. But I do desire to understand Your truth a little, that truth that my heart believes and loves. For I do not seek to understand so that I may believe; but I believe so that I may understand. For I believe this also, that "unless I believe, I shall not understand."[4]

Following this methodology, Anselm poses in the *Monologion* the question of the existence of God, and attempts to prove that existence—as well as the divine attributes and the doctrine of the

---

[3] *Cur Deus homo* 1. 1.
[4] *Proslog.* 1 (trans. M. J. Charlesworth, *St. Anselm's Proslogion,* Oxford: Clarendon Press, 1965, p. 115).

Trinity—without appealing to Scripture.[5] His arguments may be condensed into one: if things have different degrees of goodness, being, and value, these—goodness, being, and value—must have a separate existence above and apart from visible things. For instance, in the case of being, one can say that things are because they participate in being, that is, they subsist not in themselves, but in another. That other is being itself. Since being itself cannot be more than one,[6] one must further say that this is the supreme being or highest good.[7]

Anselm himself was unsatisfied with this argument, not because it seemed erroneous to him, but rather because it was too complicated and required several succeeding steps. After a long search for a simpler argument, he believed he had discovered it in what he expounds in the *Prosologion,* which would later be called the "ontological argument." In the *Proslogion,* Anselm tries to discover why Psalm 13 claims that it is the Fool who denies the existence of God—that is to say, why that denial is folly. His conclusion is the following argument, which ought to be carefully read:

> Even the Fool, then, is forced to agree that something-than-which-nothing-greater-can-be-thought exists in the mind, since he understands this when he hears it, and whatever is understood is in the mind. And surely that-than-which-a-greater-cannot-be-thought cannot exist in the mind alone. For if it exists solely in the mind even, it can be thought to exist in reality also, which is greater. If then that-than-which-a-greater-cannot-be-thought exists in the mind alone, this same that-than-which-a-greater-*cannot*-be-thought is that-than-which-a-greater-*can*-be-thought. But this is obviously impossible. Therefore there is absolutely no doubt that something-than-which-a-greater-cannot-be-thought exists both in the mind and in reality.[8]

---

[5] *Monolog.* prologue. Cf. P. Gilbert, *Dire l'ineffable: Lecture du 'Monologion' de S. Anselme* (Paris: Lethielleux, 1984).

[6] The argument to prove this is that several such beings could not be distinguished in any way, for none of them would lack something that the others have. As that which is undistinguishable is one, being itself can only be one.

[7] *Monolog.* 1-14.

[8] *Proslog.* 2 (trans. Charlesworth, p. 117).

Later on in the same treatise, Anselm insists on this argument, now showing that this being which is such that no greater can be conceived is also God the creator.

You exist so truly, Lord my God, that You cannot even be thought not to exist. And this is as it should be, for if some intelligence could think of something better than You, the creature would be above its creator and would judge its creator—and that is completely absurd. In fact, everything else there is, except You alone, can be thought of as not existing.[9]

No one, indeed, understanding what God is can think that God does not exist, even though he may say these words in his heart either without any [objective] signification or with some peculiar signification. For God is that-than-which-nothing-greater-can-be-thought. Whoever really understands this understands clearly that this same being so exists that not even in thought can it not exist. Thus whoever understands that God exists in such a way cannot think of him as not existing.[10]

As was to be expected, this argument was not simply accepted without question. On the contrary, it has given occasion to lively philosophical and theological debate, as well as to various interpretations.[11] Here, however, we can only discuss the manner in which it was received in its time, and how Anselm responded to the objections that were raised. Shortly after the publication of the *Proslogion,* a certain Gaunilo, a monk at Marmoutiers, published a brief *Defense of the Fool,* where he

---

[9] *Ibid.,* 3 (trans. Charlesworth, p. 119).

[10] *Ibid.,* 4 (trans. Charlesworth, p. 121).

[11] Apart from its importance for the history of philosophy, due to the fact that it has been discussed, reinterpreted, and evaluated by men such as Thomas Aquinas, Descartes, Kant, and Hegel, this argument has been the subject of a vast number of recent studies. Among these, see: K. Barth, *Fides quarens intellectum: Anselmus Beweis der Existenz Gottes im Zusammenhang seines theologischen Programms* (Munich: C. Kaiser, 1931); A. Antweiler, "Anselmus von Canterbury, *Monologion* und *Proslogion,*" *Sch,* 8 (1933); 551-60; F. S. Schmitt, "Der ontologische Gottesbeweis Anselms," *ThR,* 32 (1933), 217-23; E. Gilson, "Sens et nature de l'argument de saint Anselme," *AHDLMA,* 9 (1934), 5-51; A. Kolping, *Anselms Proslogion-Beweis der Existenz Gottes im Zusammenhang seines spekulativen Programms fides quarens intellectum* (Bonn: P. Hanstein, 1939); F. Spedalieri, "De intrinseca argumenti S. Anselmi vi et Natura," *Greg,* 39 (1948), 204-12. There is a good summary of recent discussion by A. C. McGill, "Recent Discussions of Anselm's Argument," in *The Many-faced Argument* (New York: Macmillan, 1967). G. R. Evans, *Anselm and Talking about God* (Oxford: Clarendon Press, 1978). After this lengthy note I should add, however, that it is mostly philosophers and theologians who still debate Anselm's argument, for there is general agreement among historians as to the manner in which Anselm himself understood it.

greatly praised Anselm in many things,[12] but at the same time questioned his argument for the existence of God.

The objection that Gaunilo raised was twofold. First, he was not willing to concede that the atheist has in the mind the idea of a being greater than which nothing can be conceived. Second, he objected to the manner in which Anselm moved from the idea of such a being to its existence. On the first point, Gaunilo argued that the idea of "a being above which nothing greater can be conceived" is not really present in the mind of the person who is supposed to have it, that is, of the atheist, who is here called a fool. What the fool understands are the words that come together to form that idea—and in this case even the words themselves are difficult to understand. This being above which nothing else can be conceived cannot itself be understood by the human mind in such a way that it can be analyzed in order to draw conclusions from its essence. When the fool understands the idea of God, this does not mean knowing what God is—which would be absurd—and therefore one cannot draw any conclusions from such an idea in the fool's mind.[13] The second objection raised by Gaunilo is that the existence of a thing cannot be proved from its perfection. Suppose, for instance, that someone has the idea of an island that is the best possible island. Does that mean that such an island must exist, because if it did not it would be less perfect than those which do in fact exist? Certainly not. Such an argument would only be proposed by someone as foolish as the fool who said that there is no God.[14]

Anselm responded to these objections in his *Defense Against Gaunilo*. To the first objection, Anselm responded that the being above which nothing can be conceived can indeed be conceived, as is shown by the faith of Gaunilo himself. Thus, Anselm did not actually face the objection raised by Gaunilo. This objection was not that God cannot be conceived, but rather that the atheist—the fool—conceives of God as an idea formed by bringing together various ideas—that is, the fool understands

---

[12] *Pro insip.* 7.
[13] *Ibid.*, 4.
[14] *Ibid.*, 6.

which ideas come together in the notion of a supreme being, but does not believe that they can properly be enjoined in one.

The second objection raised by Gaunilo refuted that which Anselm had not said. Anselm did not claim that each thing that is conceived as perfect within its species must therefore exist—in this case, the wondrous island of Gaunilo—but that a being that is conceived as absolutely perfect must also be conceived as existent. The island of Gaunilo belongs to a genus whose members may well exist or not. The perfect being does not belong to such a genus. In other words, perfection itself cannot be thought of as nonexistent, for then it would be an imperfect perfection.

Naturally, Anselm's argument is valid only within the framework of certain presuppositions that are not universally accepted. Thus, for instance, it presupposes that existence is a perfection, that perfection can be conceived, and that the structures of reality correspond to the structures of thought. But in spite of this it has been accepted and used in later centuries by many outstanding theologians and philosophers.

This God whose existence Anselm believed he had proved in the *Monologion* and later in the *Proslogion* is absolutely simple, so that the divine attributes are not accidents, but are rather the very essence of God.[15] God is present in every place and time,[16] and is not in any place or time,[17] for all times and places are in God.[18]

This God is also triune.[19] Anselm believed that this could be shown to be true by rational means, in the same manner in which he had proved the existence of God. We cannot dwell here on the arguments that he adduced in the *Monologion*[20] and the *Proslogion*,[21] but a word must be said regarding his *Epistle on the Incarnation of the Word*, which refuted the teachings of Roscelin,

---

[15] *Monolog.* 16-17; *Proslog.* 12.
[16] *Monolog.* 20.
[17] *Ibid.*, 21.
[18] *Ibid.*, 22-24; *Proslog.* 19.
[19] R. Perino, *La dottrina trinitaria di S. Anselmo nel quadro del suo metodo teologico e del suo concetto di Dio* (Rome: Herder, 1952), discusses not only Anselm's arguments, but also his relationship with Augustine and with later theology on this point.
[20] *Monolog.* 29-65.
[21] *Proslog.* 23.

and of his treatise *On the Procession of the Holy Spirit*, in which he defended the *Filioque*.

Roscelin of Compiégne was a staunch defender of the use of dialectics in theological investigation. Although most of his works have been lost, his *Epistle to Abelard* and the various works written against him which have survived give us an approximate idea of his teachings. In spite of what has been said by his various interpreters—in the twelfth century as well as later—Roscelin was not a rationalist in the strict sense. He was willing to subject his thought to the authority of the church—at least, as willing as was Anselm. What led Roscelin to clash with the established authorities was not that he made use of dialectical reason, but rather that he did so within a nominalist framework. He believed that the words that express universal ideas are no more than "the wind of voice," that is, do not refer to realities that exist apart from individual things. Humankind, for instance, does not exist in itself; what exists is individual human beings. This transposed into the field of trinitarian doctrine, resulted in formulas that surprised his contemporaries. According to Roscelin, the only manner in which the Trinity can be understood is on the basis of three substances, for the assumption that there is in God only one substance would necessarily lead one to say that the Father is the Son, and that the Son is the Father. Therefore, the Greek formula, which speaks of three substances, is more adequate than the traditional Latin one.

> The substance of the Father is nothing but the Father, and the substance of the Son is nothing but the Son, just as the city of Rome is Rome and the creature water is water. Thus, as the Father begets the Son the substance of the Father begets the substance of the Son. For there is a begetting substance and another substance which is begotten, and they are different, and always the begetter and the begotten are several, and not a single thing.[22]

This is practically all that can be said with some measure of certainty regarding Roscelin's theology, for the rest has either

---

[22] *Ep. ad Abaelardum (PL,* 178:366).

been lost or twisted beyond recognition by his adversaries. But this suffices to show why he was accused of tritheism. Called to answer before the Council of Soissons in 1092, Roscelin condemned tritheism—which he could easily do without perturbing his conscience, for he did not believe that there were three Gods. However, his insistence on his original doctrine made him subject to continued attacks, among them that of Anselm—which is of interest to us here—and later another from Peter Abelard.

Following the method that has been described above, Anselm attempted to refute Roscelin, not on the basis of Scripture, for his opponent "either does not believe in it or interprets it in a false sense," but "through reason, by the use of which he attempts to defend himself." However, his purpose was not so much to prove the rational truth of traditional trinitarian doctrine as to show the absurdities to which Roscelin's formulas would lead. Anselm seemed to be satisfied that he had shown such absurdities. But when, centuries later, one reads his work, the general impression that one receives is that Roscelin and Anselm never met. The nominalism of the former and the realism of the latter were such that what appeared absurd to the one was quite reasonable for the other, and vice versa.

In his treatise *On the Procession of the Holy Spirit,* Anselm defends the position of the Latin church over against the East.[23] Faithfully following his theological method, Anselm attempts to show through the use of reason that the Holy Spirit proceeds from the Father and the Son. Here, however, he does appeal to Scripture and to orthodox trinitarian doctrine, for these are authorities that his adversaries do accept.

Apart from the so-called ontological argument for the existence of God, the theological contribution of Anselm which has been most studied and discussed is his treatise on *Why God Became Man.*[24] Here he attempts to show the necessity of the

---

[23] Although rather schematic, the best study is that of M. Wilniewczye, *De processione Spiritus Sancti secundum sanctum Anselmum* (Vatican City: Vatican Press, 1957).

[24] There is a good bibliography, and frequent references to earlier studies, in K. Strijd, *Structuur en inhoud van Anselmus' "Cur Deus homo"* (Assen: van Gorcum, 1958). See also M. Corbin, "Nécessité et liberté: Sens et structure de l'argument du 'Cur Deus homo' d'Anselme de Cantorbéry," in C. Kannengiesser and Y. Marchasson, eds., *Humanisme et foi chrétienne* (Paris: Beauchesne, 1976), pp. 599-632.

Incarnation, once again on rational grounds, although taking for granted such theological doctrines as original sin and God's love and justice.

Anselm rejects the theory that the purpose of the Incarnation and passion of Christ was to free us from our enslavement to the Devil, or to pay a debt owed to the Devil. The purpose of the Incarnation is indeed to pay a debt that is due, although not to the Devil, but to God. "Anyone who sins must return to God the honor which has been withdrawn from him, and that is the satisfaction which every sinner owes to God."[25] God could not simply forgive a debt without any satisfaction, for this would be surrendering to disorder.[26] But on the other hand, we are incapable of offering a satisfaction for our sin, for the most that we can offer is acting justly, and that is only our duty. "When you give God something of what you owe him, even if you have not sinned, you cannot consider this as a payment for your debt."[27] Therefore, one must reach the conclusion of Anselm's partner in this dialogue: "I have nothing left with which to offer satisfaction for sin."[28] And this difficulty becomes even greater as one takes into account the following:

> Judge for yourself, whether it is not contrary to God's honor, that man be reconciled with him, in spite of the offense done against him, without first honoring God by defeating the Devil, as he dishonored him by being overcome by the Devil. This victory must be such that . . . through the straits of death he overcomes the Devil without sinning in any way. But he cannot do this, for as a result of the first sin he is conceived and born in sin.[29]

Therefore we, who must offer satisfaction unto God, are incapable of doing so. Only God is capable of offering a satisfaction that will be worthy of the injured divine honor. On the other hand, only a human being can justly offer satisfaction for human sin. In consequence, this satisfaction "which cannot

---

[25] *Cur Deus homo* 1. 11.
[26] *Ibid.*, 1. 12.
[27] *Ibid.*, 1. 20.
[28] *Ibid.*
[29] *Ibid.*, 1. 23.

be given by anyone but God, and ought to be given by no one but man, must be given by a God-man."[30]

This treatise by Anselm was epoch-making. Although they did not follow it at every turn, most later medieval theologians interpreted the work of Christ in the light of this treatise. After them, most Western theologians have followed the same path, although this manner of understanding the work of Christ for humankind is not the most ancient, nor does it appear to be the main thrust of the New Testament.

Anselm was without any doubt the greatest theologian of his time. Although his theological production consisted in a series of monographic works that did not attempt to include the entire scope of Christian doctrine, his success in his application of reason to questions of faith without thereby abandoning orthodox doctrine paved the way for the great scholastics of the thirteenth century. The content of his works greatly contributed to later theological formulations; but their spirit, both daring and subject to authority, made an even greater impact. With Anselm a new era began in the history of Christian thought.

Peter Abelard

In the person of Peter Abelard theological renaissance, ecclesiastical tragedy, and romantic love came together in a uniquely dramatic way.[31] He was born in Brittany in 1079, and from a very early age showed his exceptional intellectual ability. After studying under Roscelin, the famous nominalist, he became a disciple of William of Champeaux, who was then the principal champion of realism. But Abelard did not find either of these two teachers satisfactory, and even claims to have come out victorious in debates with William. On the basis of these victories over his former teacher, he set up his own independent

---

[30] *Ibid.*, 2. 7.

[31] The outline of his career presented here has been taken from his *Historia calamitatum*. On the value of this work as a source for Abelard's life, see D. Visser, "Reality and Rhetoric in Abelard's 'Story of My Calamities,' " in *Proceedings of the Patristic, Medieval and Renaissance Conference*, 3 (1978), 143-55; C. S. Jaeger, "The Prologue to the 'Historia Calamitatum' and the 'Authenticity Question.' " *Euphorion*, 74 (1980), 1-15. On Abelard in general, see: *Peter Abelard: Proceedings of the International Conference, Louvain, May 10-13, 1971* (Louvain: University Press, 1974); R. Thomas, ed., *Petrus Abaelardus (1079-1142): Person, Werk und Wirkung* (Trier: Paulinus-Verlag, 1980).

lectures with which he attempted to rival those of William. But what he claims was a systematic persecution on the part of William's friends led him to move from city to city until he reached Laon, where he sat at the lectures of the then famous Anselm—who is not to be confused with Anselm of Canterbury. Abelard found him to be eloquent but void of wisdom, and therefore decided to organize his own school, in which he began delivering lectures on Ezekiel. According to Abelard, Anselm did not take such impertinence with grace, but rather persecuted his upstart rival and thereby increased the latter's fame.

From Laon, Abelard moved to Paris, where he became well-known as a teacher of philosophy and theology. It was there that he met Heloise, whom he secretly married and who gave him a son. But this romance ended in tragedy when some relatives of the young woman, believing he had marred the honor of the family, broke into his room and emasculated him. Heloise then became a nun, and Abelard took the habit in the monastery of Saint Denis. That, however, was not the end of the events that Abelard would later call his calamities. He soon fell out of favor with the authorities in the monastery when he claimed—and rightly so—that its founder could not have been Dionysius the disciple of Paul. His trinitarian doctrines, developed in opposition to Roscelin, were no better received than those of his opponent, and in 1121 a synod gathered at Soissons forced him to cast into the flames his own treatise *On the Divine Unity and Trinity*. Broken in body and soul, he then decided to retire to a deserted place.

But even in his retreat he was followed by his renown, his disciples, and his enemies. Soon a community developed around him, and he then founded a school that he dedicated to the Paraclete. He was also followed there by Heloise, who founded a convent with the help of her former lover. Soon these new successes aroused his enemies to action. Bernard of Clairvaux, a famous mystic and preacher and a man of great influence throughout Europe, was scandalized when he heard of Abelard's teachings, and especially of the manner in which he applied reason to matters of faith. As a result, Abelard was called to a synod in 1141 which did not allow him to defend himself, but simply condemned several propositions drawn from his works.

Abelard decided to appeal to the pope, but when he was preparing the case that he would present to Innocent II he learned that the Holy Father—perhaps through Bernard's intervention—had confirmed his condemnation.

Finally, Abelard retired to Cluny, where he was well received and treated by Peter the Venerable. He then composed a *Profession of Faith*, which showed his complete orthodoxy. Upon his death, Heloise made the request, which was granted, that his remains be placed at the Paraclete, near the convent in which she spent the rest of her days.

Abelard was a prolific and original writer. In the field of philosophy, his most important work is *Dialectics*. His *Know Thyself* or *Ethics* suggested a view of original sin which was radically different from that commonly held. His *Dialogue Between a Philosopher, a Jew, and a Christian* is an interesting apology. His *Exposition of the Hexameron* and his *Commentary on Romans* show that he was an able and scholarly exegete. But his most important works are *Introduction to Theology, Christian Theology,* and *Sic et non*—Yes and no.

Abelard's doctrine regarding universals is a good starting point to discuss his thought.[32] His views on this matter were developed in opposition to his two teachers, William of Champeaux and Roscelin. As has already been said, William was the champion of realism. According to him, universals exist before particular things, and are totally present in each of them. This position led to two difficulties. First, one would have to affirm the ubiquity of universals. Second, one would be led to predicate opposites of a single universal; for "animal," for instance, is rational in "human" and irrational in "horse." In order to avoid these and other consequences—which may well have been suggested by his disciple Abelard—William withdrew from his original position and claimed that the essences to be found in various individuals of the same genus are not the same essence, although they are "not

---

[32] On the general lines of Abelard's theology, see D. Hayden, "Notes on the Aristotelian Dialectic in Theological Method," *Thomist,* 20 (1975), 383-418; L. Grane, *Peter Abelard: Philosophie und Christentum im Mittelalter* (Göttingen: Vandenhoeck und Ruprecht, 1969); A. Crocco, *Antitradizione e metodologia filosofica in Abelardo* (Napoli: M. D'Auria, 1971). On his exegetical method, see E. M. Buytaert, "Abelard's Expositio in Hexaemeron," *Ant,* 43 (1968), 163-94.

different"—that is, they are similar. Thus, for instance, the humanity of Peter is one and that of John is another, but they are similar. This, however, does not solve the problem, for one must now explain how two realities can be similar if they do not have something that is common to both—and thus one is back at the original difficulty of explaining how there can be something common to several individuals.

Abelard's solution, although often taken to be the same as that of Roscelin, was different from it. Abelard said that the universal is "the meaning of the name." His teacher Roscelin had claimed that it was "the emission—or the wind—of the voice." Abelard objected that this latter position would make it impossible to explain how and why it is possible to predicate the universal "animal" of a horse, and not of a stone. If universals were mere sounds, there would be no such things as a correct or an erroneous affirmation. Universals are indeed sounds, but they are meaningful sounds. It is that meaning which concerns the philosopher, and the problem cannot be solved by a mere claim that there is no meaning in universals. The solution is to be found by realizing that universals are not "things"—that is, they cannot subsist in themselves except by an abstraction. They are real in a manner similar to that in which form exists in matter—one can abstract form from matter, but form is never actually given without matter. Similarly, universals can be abstracted from individuals— and one must do so in order to think—but they are never given apart from concrete particular things. Such was Abelard's position on the question of universals, which has been called "conceptualism" and which would be influential in later centuries.[33]

Apart from the question of universals, there are three other matters on which Abelard's contribution deserves special attention: the theological method of *Sic et non*, his doctrine regarding the work of Christ, and his ethics.

The title itself of *Sic et non*—"Yes and no"—reveals the nature of the work. It is a series of one hundred and fifty-eight questions

---

[33] There is a good study of Abelard's theory of universals in Gilson, *History*, pp. 155-60. My own discussion of this subject is greatly indebted to his. See also C. Wenin, "La signification des universaux chez Abélard," *RevPhLouv*, 80 (1982), 414-48.

that are answered affirmatively by some authorities and negatively by others. Abelard limited his task to quoting side by side these seemingly contradictory authorities, and did not attempt to offer a solution of his own. Given the spirit of the times, one can easily understand how such a work, which seemed to cast doubt upon the authority of Scripture and of the ancients, was not well received. However, Abelard's purpose does not seem to have been to deny the authority of the church, or to show that Scripture or some of the "Fathers" had erred. He firmly believed in the authority of the texts that he quoted. His purpose was rather to point out some of the difficulties that existed regarding certain theological issues. Abelard seems to have believed that it was possible to interpret the texts that he quoted in such a way that their inner agreement could be shown. He simply wanted to draw the attention of his readers to the necessity of doing so, as he clearly affirmed in the prologue to this work.[34] Thus, after its original negative reception, this book did indeed have immense consequences for the development of Christian theology, although these consequences had more to do with methodology than with content. Scholastic theologians accepted the challenge of Abelard and followed a method in which, after posing each question, a list of authorities was adduced which seemed to lead to one answer, and then another list in the opposite direction. It was then the theologian's task to offer an answer and solve the difficulties posed by the authorities which seemed to oppose such an answer. This method, which is one of the characteristics of the scholastic period, has some of its roots in Abelard.

Later writers have called Abelard's doctrine regarding the work of Christ "subjective" or "moral," in opposition to Anselm's, which they have called "objective" or "juridical." Although these terms are rather inaccurate and therefore do not do justice to Anselm nor to Abelard, they do serve to point to an undeniable contrast between the views of these two theologians. Abelard rejected both the traditional view that Christ had come to pay a debt to the Devil,

---

[34] This prologue has been very ably analyzed by M. Grabmann, *Die Geschichte der scholastischen Methode* (Freiburg im Breisgau: Herder, 1910-11), 2:200-203. On the method of *Sic et non*, see A. Crocco, "Le cinque regole ermeneutiche del 'Sic et Non,' " *RCHist*, 24 (1979), 452-58.

and Anselm's theory that he had come to pay a debt to God. Over against these views, Abelard developed a theory according to which the work of Christ consists in providing an example and teaching, both verbal and factual, of the love of God. This example is such that it moves us to love God, who in turn forgives us on the basis of that love and of the intercessory prayers of the resurrected Christ.[35]

Abelard's ethical theory revolves not around the act itself, but around its intention. This does not mean that there are no good and evil acts; it means that the guilt of an evil action is in its intention, and that the same is true of the merit of a good action. If a hunter aims at a bird and unwillingly kills someone whom he has not seen, the hunter is not guilty of that action. Furthermore, no one can be guilty of that which one has not done, and therefore it is not guilt that Adam has bequeathed to his descendents, but only the penalty of sin. This penalty includes the corruption of the human will, which leads us to evil. But that corruption in itself is not sin. Sin consists in agreeing to the evil inclination of the mind. Finally, Abelard insisted that sin and its satisfaction are a matter between the sinner and God, and therefore the function of confession cannot be to absolve the sinner, but can only be to give one direction as to the manner in which one is to expiate for sin.[36]

Quite naturally, these daring doctrines resulted in a number of enthusiastic disciples and in an even greater number of inexorable adversaries. Abelard's main opponent was the mystic and preacher Bernard of Clairvaux.[37] Bernard's mysticism,

[35] *Comm. ad Rom.* 2. 3. See R. C. Weingart, *The Logic of Divine Love: A Critical Analysis of the Soteriology of Peter Abelard* (Oxford: Clarendon Press, 1970).

[36] P. L. Williams, *The Moral Philosophy of Peter Abelard* (Latham, Md.: University Press of America, 1980).

[37] Bernard was one of the dominant figures of the twelfth century, and if we have not discussed him in detail it is because of the essentially conservative character of most of his theology, and the need to concentrate our attention on those theologians who were proposing new ideas. Probably the points on which his influence was most widely felt after his time were the new impetus which he gave to the monastic life and his devotion to the humanity of Christ. Indeed, such devotion, of which Bernard was the great teacher, was characteristic of many of the great figures of the thirteenth century—including St. Francis and Bonaventure. Two basic introductions to the life and thought of Bernard are B. S. James, *Saint Bernard of Clairvaux: An Essay in Biography* (New York: Harper, 1957) and G. R. Evans, *The Mind of St. Bernard of Clairvaux* (Oxford: Clarendon Press, 1983). See also G. Díez Ramos, ed., *Obras competas de San Bernardo* 2 vols., *BAC* 110 (1953), 130 (1955). For references to older studies on Bernard, see L. Janavaschek, *Bibliographia bernardina* (Hildesheim: Georg Olms, 1959). For

unlike that of Pseudo-Dionysius, was not Platonist and speculative in character, but rather centered on the humanity of Christ and the sufferings of Mary. It was he who, as abbot of Clairvaux, led the great Cistercian reformation that swept through monasticism in the twelfth century. A friend of popes, vexer of kings, and preacher of the Second Crusade, Bernard was also a hunter of heretics, as may be seen in his actions against Abelard and, somewhat later, Gilbert de la Porrée.

This poet of the sufferings of Christ and the virginity of Mary, this champion who fought a constant battle against Satan and his host, could neither understand nor tolerate the attitude of the daring teacher who seemed to apply dialectical reason to the mysteries of faith, who denied that Christ took flesh in order to free us from the yoke of our own flesh, who said that the guilt of Adam was not also ours, who claimed that if those who crucified Christ did so out of ignorance they had committed no sin, who overthrew the foundations of penance, and who already in 1121 had been condemned for his trinitarian doctrines.[38] In consequence, when the synod of 1141 came to the case of Abelard, Bernard was at hand with a list of errors which he asked his adversary to condemn. The scholar wanted to discuss the list, but the monk demanded a recantation and nothing else. Before such an alternative, Abelard decided to allow himself to be condemned by the synod and appealed to the pope, only to find that the Holy See was also dominated by the shadow of Bernard.

A brief selection of the errors for which Abelard was condemned will show which aspects of his doctrine most perturbed his contemporaries. We have excluded those having to do with trinitarian doctrine, for it was here more than in any other point that he was misinterpreted by his judges, so that the "trinitarian errors of Abelard" may perhaps be errors, but are

---

his relations with Abelard, see E. F. Little, "Relations between St. Bernard and Abelard before 1139," in M. B. Pennington, ed., *Saint Bernard of Clairvaux: Studies Commemorating the Eighth Centenary of His Canonization* (Kalamazoo: Cistercian Publications, 1977), pp. 155-68; J. Verger and J. Jolivet, *Bernard-Abélard, ou le cloître et l'école* (Paris: Fayard-Mame, 1982).

[38] These, and others, are the errors that Bernard listed in his treatise *Against the Errors of Peter Abelard* (*PL*, 182:1053-72).

certainly not his. The following were some of the views that were condemned:

4. That Christ did not take the flesh in order to free us from the yoke of the Devil.
6. That free will of itself suffices to do some good.
9. That we have not received the guilt of Adam, but only the penalty.
10. That those who crucified Christ did not sin, for they did not know what they were doing, and that there is no guilt in that which is done out of ignorance.
12. That the power to bind and unbind was given only to the apostles, and not to their successors.[39]

In summary, the most characteristic propositions of Abelard's theology were condemned.

This, however, did not destroy the influence of the great scholar. On the contrary, there is ample proof that both before and after his condemnation there were authors who continued the tradition of Abelard, although often—especially after 1141—with more moderation.[40]

This "school of Abelard" was increasingly influenced by the school of Saint Victor, and vice versa. Thus a theological method was developed which, making use of biblical and patristic authority, and upon it building rational investigation, managed to remain within the bounds of orthodoxy. This was the result of the junction of the rational and innovating spirit of Abelard's disciples with the traditionalism of Victorine theology. Eventually, this development culminated in a person and a work—Peter Lombard and his *Four Books of Sentences*. However, in order to understand him and his importance one must first say a word regarding the school of Saint Victor.

---

[39] *Mansi*, 21:568-69.
[40] Such was the author of the *Summary of Christian Theology* (*PL*, 178:1695-758), which used to be attributed to Abelard. Another anonymous follower of Abelard wrote the *Sentences* of Florian. Finally, Roland Bandinelli, who later occupied the Holy See under the name of Alexander III, also wrote a collection of *Sentences* in which, though not slavishly following Abelard on every point, he did support him on several controversial issues.

The School of Saint Victor

The founder of this school was William of Champeaux, who taught at Notre Dame in Paris until after his debate with Abelard, when he withdrew to the outskirts of the city, near the chapel of Saint Victor.[41] There he organized a monastic school whose goal was to produce a theology with deep roots in religious life. In 1113, William left Saint Victor in order to become bishop of Châlons-sur-Marne, and later it was he who ordained Bernard of Clairvaux. When he died a few years later, he was respected and admired by almost all that knew him—the main exception being Abelard, who hardly respected or admired anybody but himself.

William, like Abelard, had studied under Roscelin of Compiègne and Anselm of Laon. His reaction to the former was clear: he rejected Roscelin's nominalism and adopted the position of extreme realism. According to him, it is one and the same essence which is totally present in each individual of the same species, and that which constitutes individuality is only the totality of accidents that come together upon that essence in each particular case. Prodded by Abelard, who showed the consequences of this type of extreme realism, William corrected his position by claiming that, although the essences in particular things are not the same, neither are they different—that is, they are similar. This did not solve the question, as has already been shown, but it seems to have been William's definitive position.[42]

In his theology, William followed his teacher Anselm of Laon. Although most of his works have been lost,[43] the fragments that have remained show William to have been a moderate and orthodox thinker, without great speculative flights, but also unafraid to use logical reason in order to analyze and understand the truths of faith.

---

[41] J. Chatillon, "L'école de Saint-Victor: Guillaume, Hughes, Richard et les autres," *Communio*, 6 (1981), 63-76.

[42] See the excellent bibliographical note in Gilson, *History*, p. 626.

[43] Of those published in *PL*, 163, only one appears to be genuine: *De sacramento altaris* (*PL*, 163:1039-40). This particular work is significant because it is one of the last medieval texts in which proof may be found that communion was still offered to believers in both elements. In the second half of the nineteenth century, two other works of William were published: *De essentia et substantia Dei et de tribus eius personis,* and *Sententiae vel quaestiones 47.*

Although William was the founder of the school, the person who most contributed to its fame was his successor, Hugh of Saint Victor.[44] Establishing a trend that would be characteristic of the school of Saint Victor, Hugh insisted that the purpose of the sciences is not to satisfy curiosity, but to lead to the higher life. This may be clearly seen in his Prologue to *On the Sacraments of the Christian Faith*, which affirms that all that we must know revolves around creation and restoration.[45]

Within this scheme—which includes an entire philosophy of history as directed toward the ultimate goal of human life—Hugh claimed that all knowledge is part of the way that leads to the knowledge of God. All sciences are useful and necessary, but their worth is not in themselves but in their contribution to the improvement of the soul in order to make it capable of enjoying eternal beatitude.

Hugh's main theological work, *On the Sacraments of the Christian Faith*, shows the importance of the sacraments for his theology. Sacraments are material elements that "by similitude represent, by institution signify, and by sanctification contain, a certain invisible and spiritual grace." [46] As to their number, Hugh was unclear, for he gave the name of "sacrament" to various rites and even mere formulas;[47] but on the other hand his attention centered only on the following: baptism, confirmation, communion, penance, extreme unction, marriage, and ordination. Therefore, Hugh's work was a step in the process that would eventually limit the number of sacraments to seven—a process that would reach its culmination in Peter Lombard. Communion occupied the center of Hugh's exposition, and he interpreted the presence of Christ in it in very realistic terms:

---

[44] The definitive study is that of H. Baron, *Science et sagesse chez Hughes de Saint-Victor* (Paris: P. Lethielleux, 1957). J. B. Schneyer, "Ergänzungen der Sermones und Miscellanea des Hugo von Sankt Viktor aus verschiedenen Handschriften," *RThAM*, 31 (1964), 260-86; G. Zinn, "Hugh of St. Victor and the Ark of Noah: A New Look," *CH*, 40 (1971), 261-72; R. Goy, *Die Überlieferung der Werke Hugos von St. Victor: Ein Beitrag zur Kommunicationsgeschichte des Mittelalters* (Stuttgart: Hiersemann, 1976); A. M. Piazzoni, "Il 'De unione spiritus et corporis' di Ugo di San Vittore," *StMed*, ser. 3, 21 (1980), 861-88; A. M. Piazzoni, "Ugo di San Vittore 'auctor' delle 'Sententiae de divinitate,' " *StMed*, ser. 3, 23 (1982), 861-955.

[45] *De sacr.* prol. 2-3.

[46] *Ibid.*, 1. 9. 2.

[47] *Ibid.*, 2. 9.

Through the sanctification of the words the true substance of the bread and the true substance of the wine become the body and the blood of Christ, so that only the appearance of the bread and the wine remains, and one substance is transformed into the other.[48]

But, as has already been said, the purpose of all this is to lead the soul to contemplation. Here Hugh introduced the Neoplatonic mysticism of Pseudo-Dionysius, with its ascending steps and its goal of an ineffable beatitude. This is why Hugh has justly been called a mystic. But that title has meant that he has often been unjustly denied that of a theologian. Hugh is at once a mystic and a theologian, and it is precisely this that makes him important for the history of Christian thought. In his work and in that of his successors, the ancient opposition between dialecticians and mystics, which had come to the foreground in such encounters as that between Berengar and Lanfranc, or between Abelard and Bernard, came to an end. This conjunction of mystical piety with the use of reason would be an inspiration for the great scholastics of the thirteenth century.

Richard of Saint Victor, Hugh's successor, was a native of Scotland. He continued Hugh's tradition, joining speculative mysticism with rational theology. According to him, there are three levels of knowledge: *cogitatio, meditatio,* and *contemplatio.* The first pertains to imagination, the second to reason, and the third to the intellect. *Cogitatio* creeps on the ground, and thus entails fruitless effort. *Meditatio* walks, and is a balanced combination of effort and results. *Contemplatio* flies, and in it results are achieved without effort. All three are good, and are so connected that the mind may direct *cogitatio* to *meditatio,* and from the latter move on to the higher level of *contemplatio.*[49] At this last stage, the mind attains unto God, although it does not comprehend the divine essence—which is impossible—but rather contemplates God in a rapture or "excess"—that intuitive form of knowledge in which the soul can receive that which is greater than its own capabilities.[50]

---

[48] *Ibid.,* 2. 8. 9.
[49] *Benj. major* 1. 3-4.
[50] *Ibid.,* 8. 8.

The manner in which Richard used reason in order to penetrate those mysteries which were already known to him by faith may be seen in *On the Trinity*. In this work, written against Gilbert de la Porrée, Richard tried to show the cogency of trinitarian doctrine on the basis of the nature of love. Love requires communication, and hence the plurality of persons.[51]

The later leaders of the school of Saint Victor, Gautier[52] and Godfrey,[53] did not continue the earlier tradition of the school, but rather emphasized the importance of piety and faith and tended to reject attempts to apply reason to the mysteries of faith.

There were, however, some disciples of Abelard who joined the theology of their teacher with the pious and traditional spirit of the school of Saint Victor. It was through them, and not through the direct successors of Hugh and Richard, that that school would exert its influence on the thirteenth century.[54]

Peter Lombard

Peter, known as "Lombard" after his native country, arrived at Paris around the year 1130. There he became closely tied to the school of Saint Victor, although it is not certain that he taught or studied in it. After a few years, he held the chair of theology at Notre Dame—the same that William of Champeaux held before retiring to Saint Victor. In 1148 he attended the synod that met at Reims to consider the teachings of Gilbert de la Porrée. He was consecrated bishop of Paris in 1159, and died a year thereafter. His *Four Books of Sentences*, usually known simply as *Sentences*, were the culmination of the theological activity of the twelfth century and its main legacy to the thirteenth.

The *Sentences* are not exceptionally original. Actually, Peter Lombard took much of the form and contents from an

---

[51] Here Richard defined "person" on the basis of the incommunicability of existence. This theme would later be picked up by Alexander of Hales.

[52] *Contra quatuor labyrinthos Franciae* (*PL*, 199:1129-72). The four whom he here attacks are Abelard, Peter Lombard, Peter of Poitiers, and Gilbert de la Porrée.

[53] Fragments in *PL*, 196:1417-22. The epistles of later abbots and a prior of Saint Victor (*PL*, 196:1379-418), and the liturgical verses of Adam of Saint Victor (*PL*, 196:1423-534) are of scant value for the history of Christian thought, although they are not lacking in interest for the history of monastic piety and practice.

[54] E. Luscombe, *The School of Peter Abelard: The Influence of Abelard's Thought in the Early Scholastic Period* (Cambridge: University Press, 1969).

anonymous *Summa of Sentences*,[55] as well as from several other authors. Furthermore, even the joining together of the insights of the schools of Abelard and of Saint Victor is not original with Peter Lombard, for the anonymous author of the *Summa of Sentences* had already done this. The significance of Peter Lombard's work is not in its doctrinal originality, but rather in the manner in which he avoided the extreme positions of dialecticians and anti-dialecticians, and also in the great abundance of the material which he offered with reference to each theological issue. His *Sentences*, more than a piece of constructive theology, are compilations of authorities dealing with each subject. Yet Peter Lombard does not stop here, as Abelard had done in his *Sic et non*, but goes on to offer his own opinions. These opinions are usually moderate, and reflect what was common doctrine in his time. In some instances, however, he does depart from commonly held opinion. In still others, he abstains from pronouncing a verdict on issues that do not seem sufficiently clear. At first, this combination of basic orthodoxy with a measure of daring and another of hesitation created misgivings among some of Peter's contemporaries, but later these very reasons led to general acclaim of his *Sentences* as a basic introduction to theological studies. All the great teachers of the thirteenth to the fifteenth centuries—and many others not so great—commented on the *Sentences* of Peter Lombard. From the thirteenth century on, the title of "Teacher of the Sentences" was one of the stages through which professors went in the process of their formation, and therefore we have *Commentaries on the Sentences* by Bonaventure, Thomas, Duns Scotus, and several others, most of them composed during the early years of their authors' theological activity.

Since it would be impossible—and monotonous—to expound here the entire theology of Peter Lombard, which in any case is essentially the common doctrine of the twelfth century, we shall simply give a brief outline of the *Four Books of Sentences* pointing out some of the issues in which the opinions expressed therein gave rise to later discussions.

---

[55] *PL*, 175:41-174. See J. De Ghellinck, *Le mouvement théologique du XIIe siècle* (Bruges: De Tempel, 1948), pp. 197-203.

The first book deals with God one and triune, and here are expounded the doctrines of the Trinity and the divine attributes. On these points Peter Lombard's opinions were sufficiently traditional to give rise to little discussion, except where he affirmed that the numbers "one" and "three," as applied to God, are only used in a relative sense,[56] and also where he affirmed that charity as it exists among humans is the Holy Spirit.[57]

The second book opens with the doctrine of creation, including angelology, and then moves to anthropology, and to the doctrines of grace and sin. The main discussions arising out of this second book had to do with the merits of angels, and will not be discussed here.

The third book deals with Christology, redemption, the virtues and gifts of the Holy Spirit, and the Commandments. It is here that Peter Lombard denies that Jesus Christ, as a man, is "something."[58] This is not, as some have thought, a veiled Docetism. It is rather an attempt to assert the earlier doctrine that the human nature of the Savior is anhypostatic. Another point on which the Master of the Sentences was censored by some later theologians was in affirming of Christ contradictory things—that he died and did not die, that he suffered and did not suffer, etc.[59]

The fourth book deals with the sacraments and eschatology. Several aspects of his sacramental theology were questioned by later theologians,[60] but in spite of this Peter Lombard had a decided influence in the development of sacramental theology, for it was he who most influenced the fixing of the number of sacraments at seven.

Peter Lombard's authority was not immediately established.[61] The most serious objections were raised regarding his so-called

[56] I Sent. dist. 24.
[57] Ibid., 17.
[58] III Sent. dist. 6.
[59] Ibid., 22.
[60] See PL, 192:963-64.
[61] J. de Ghellinck, "Pierre Lombard: luttes author du 'Livre des Sentences'," DTC, 12:2002-17 summarizes the process by which the Sentences gained their position of high respect. I have followed his outline.

christological nihilism, that is, the proposition that "Christ, as a man, is not something." This proposition, in which Peter Lombard was simply following Abelard, could also be found in the *Sentences* of Roland Bandinelli, who at that time occupied the Roman See as Alexander III. But in the year 1177 Alexander himself, who had changed his mind on the issue, condemned the position of Abelard and Peter Lombard. As was to be expected, this undercut the prestige of the *Sentences* of Peter Lombard.[62] Meanwhile, however, the *Sentences* had achieved great victories. In Paris, two successors of Peter Lombard, Peter "the Devourer"—not of food, but of knowledge—and Peter of Poitiers, continued the tradition of the Master of the Sentences; and Peter of Poitiers established the custom of offering courses on the basis of commenting on the text of the Lombard. This custom became generalized throughout France and eventually spread to Germany, England, and Italy. During the thirteenth century, an attempt was made by some followers of Gilbert de la Porrée—among them Joachim of Fiore—to have the *Sentences* condemned. At the Fourth Lateran Council (A.D. 1215), not only did this attempt fail, but the Council went as far as to condemn the trinitarian doctrines of Gilbert and Joachim—and it did so partly by the use of formulas taken from the *Sentences* of Peter Lombard.

Even after the *Summa* of Thomas was published, the *Sentences* of Peter Lombard remained as the main text for theological studies, and it was only in modern times, toward the end of the sixteenth century and early in the seventeenth, that their place was taken by Thomas' work.

Other Theologians and Schools of the Twelfth Century

Early in the twelfth century, extreme realism found a champion in Odo of Tournai (or Cambrai). This theologian, who believed that nominalism, no matter how moderate, was

---

[62] The main theologians who opposed Peter Lombard on this score were John of Cournailles (*PL*, 199:1043-86), Robert of Melun (in his own *Sentences*), Gerhoch of Reichersberg (works scattered in *PL* 193 and 194), and the anonymous author of the *Apologia de Verbo incarnato* (erroneously included among the works of Hugh of Saint Victor in *PL*, 177:295-316).

? Pudron ✓

heresy, used his realism to show how original sin was to be understood.[63] According to him, neither traducianism nor creationism adequately explains the origin of the human soul. Humankind is a single reality, and each individual is no more than a group of accidents which exists in the universal essence of humankind. Since in Adam that entire essence was present, all of it suffered the Fall. Literally, "in Adam we have all sinned."

Realism was also one of the main characteristics of the school of Chartres. Here the influence of Plato was great, and the various teachers tried to interpret the revealed data of faith in the light of reason as understood within the framework of Platonism. These teachers were Bernard of Chartres, Gilbert de la Porrée, Thierry of Chartres, and William of Conches.[64] Their disciples Bernard Sylvester and Clarembaud of Arras should also be counted within this school. The only remaining fragments of Bernard of Chartres show his concern to conciliate the cosmogony of the *Timaeus* with that of Genesis.[65] Gilbert de la Porrée was an able dialectician, highly respected by some of his contemporaries, but also very much attacked by others. He was especially at home in logic and metaphysics. However, the work that made him most famous was his *Commentary on the Book on the Trinity of Boethius*, where he distinguished between the divine essence and attributes, claiming that the latter were not eternal. This proposition, which seemed to deny the absolute simplicity of God, was condemned at Reims in 1168. Gilbert then abandoned it, but some of his disciples never forgave those who had attacked it. Thierry of Chartres, a brother of Bernard, also attempted to join the creation stories of Genesis with the

---

[63] *De pecc, orig.* (*PL*, 160:1071-102).

[64] See H. E. Rodnite, *The Doctrine of the Trinity in Guillaume de Conches' Glosses on Macrobius: Texts and Studies* (Ann Arbor: University Microfilms, 1974); J. H. Newell, *The Dignity of Man in William of Conches and the School of Chartres in the Twelfth Century* (Ann Arbor: University Microfilms, 1978).

[65] Quoted by John of Salisbury, *Metalog.* 2. 17; 4. 35. In the first of these references, John claims that Bernard and his school attempted to conciliate Plato and Aristotle, but that they "were too late." See J. M. Parent, *La doctrine de la création dans l'école de Chartres* (Paris: J. Vrin, 1938). See also E. Jeauneau, "Nani gigantum humeris insidentes: Essai d'interprétation de Bernard de Chartres," *Viv* 5 (1967), 78-99; W. Weatherbee, *Platonism and Poetry in the Twelfth Century: The Literary Influence of the School of Chartres* (Princeton: University Press, 1972); E. Jeauneau, *Lectio philosophorum: Recherches sur l'école de Charters* (Amsterdam: A. A. Hakkert, 1973); H. R. Lemay, "Platonism in the Twelfth-Century School of Chartres," in *Acta: Center of Medieval and Early Renaissance Studies*, 2 (1975) 45-52.

Timaeus.[66] William of Conches followed the same path,[67] and Bernard Sylvester attempted to do the same through verses and allegories.[68] Clarembaud of Arras was a disciple of both Thierry of Chartres and Hugh of Saint Victor. He combined the realism of the school of Chartres with the concern for orthodoxy of the Victorines, and thus attempted to refute the trinitarian doctrine of Gilbert de la Porrée.[69]

John of Salisbury was intimately connected with Chartres and its school. Although a native of England, he studied in France, and among his teachers were Abelard and William of Conches. When he was made bishop of Chartres, he re-established the bonds that had united him to that city since the time when he was a student. Like the great teachers of Chartres, John was a lover of classical letters as well as of an elegant and polished style. But he greatly differed from them in showing great skepticism regarding all that could not be clearly known through the senses, reason, or faith. Among such issues on which it is best not to pronounce a judgment is that of the nature of universals, which cannot be solved because of the limitations of the human intellect. All that can be said of universals is that we come to know them through abstraction out of individual things. But it is impossible to go beyond this epistemological assertion to the ontological nature of universals themselves.[70]

Anselm of Laon, the teacher of Abelard and William of Champeaux, left a collection of *Sentences* which, although not as influential as those of Peter Lombard, were in any case earlier. The exegetical works that have traditionally been attributed to him[71] are probably spurious.

A vast number of treatises on the eucharist were produced throughout all of Latin Europe. There is little originality to be found here, but still these treatises are valuable as witnesses to

---

[66] Gilson, *History*, pp. 145-48.
[67] Parent, *La doctrine de la création*, pp. 137-77.
[68] Gilson, *History*, p. 622.
[69] *Ibid.*, pp. 149-50.
[70] *Ibid.*, pp. 150-53. See also E. Jeauneau, "Jean de Salisbury et la lecture des philosophes," *RevEtAug*, 29 (1983), 145-74.
[71] In *PL*, 162:1187-586. Some of the history of this school may be seen in V. J. Flint, "The 'School of Laon': A Reconsideration," *RThAM*, 43 (1976), 89-110. See also H. Santiago-Otero, "El conocimiento del alma de Cristo según las enseñanzas de Anselmo de Laón y de su escuela," *Sal*, 13 (1966), 61-79.

the general acceptance of the theory of transubstantiation, which had not been defined as dogma but which, however, was generally held to be the only orthodox view.[72] Another question that became foremost in the minds of theologians during the second half of the eleventh century and throughout the twelfth was that of the relationship between civil power and ecclesiastical authority. This became a burning issue when the question of episcopal investitures led to an open conflict between Gregory VII and Henry IV. As the struggle between the empire and the papacy continued throughout the twelfth century, numerous works were composed regarding the authority of the pope and that of the emperor.[73] In the fifth century, Pope Gelasius had affirmed that both powers were given by God, and that each had its proper function, so that neither of the two was to be placed above the other. However, after that time, not only had it been shown that conflicts of power were unavoidable, but also ecclesiastical authority had tended to center on the pope, so that the theory developed according to which all bishops were subject to him. This theory was endorsed in the *Decretals* of Pseudo-Isidore, composed in the middle of the ninth century, seemingly with the double purpose of establishing the independence of the church vis-à-vis the state, and of limiting the power of archbishops by increasing that of the pope. During the tenth century and the first half of the eleventh, because of the chaotic state of the papacy, no great conflicts developed. But toward the end of the eleventh century, when the reformist party took possession of the Roman See, the papacy gained an authority that had to collide with that of civilian rulers—especially emperors. This collision took place over the issue of investitures, but actually it involved other political and religious factors. The right of appointing bishops was important for emperors, for many bishops were also feudal lords on whose loyalty it was necessary to count. From the point of view of the reformist leaders, the appointment of bishops by

---

[72] MacDonald, *Berengar*, pp. 364-409.
[73] We can give here only a very brief summary. See A. J. Carlyle, *A History of Medieval Political Theory*, Vol. 4 (Edinburgh: Blackwood, 1932).

secular power, be it on the basis of a monetary consideration or on the basis of an oath of loyalty, was simony—the selling of ecclesiastical offices—and had to be ended.

Led by his reforming zeal and by the conviction that God was with him, Gregory VII claimed for himself and for the papacy powers as yet unheard of. According to him, the state had been instituted only in order to control human sin. Since the church is eternal, and its purpose is the final salvation of believers, its authority is above that of the state. Therefore the pope, the head of the church, has the right and the authority not only to appoint bishops, but even to depose princes and emperors.

From the time of Gregory there were many theologians who defended, some with more moderation than others, the authority of the pope over the emperor—such were Cardinal Deusdedit, Bernard of Constance, and Honorius of Augsburg. Others, while defending the rights of the church vis-à-vis the state, denied that the pope had the right to depose the emperor—such were Guy of Osnaburg and Guy of Ferrara. Others, finally, took the position that the emperor was the head of both state and church—such was the view of Gregory of Catina.

In the twelfth century, St. Bernard, Hugh of Saint Victor, and John of Salisbury developed the theory according to which the "temporal sword" belongs to the prince, and the "spiritual sword" to the church. The church gives the temporal sword to the prince. It is the church which constitutes the state, and therefore, in the last analysis she has the final authority. At the time when it was developed, when a reforming party was in possession of the papacy, this doctrine gave great power to that party; but later its consequences would be tragic.

While these developments were taking place in the rest of Europe, in the city of Toledo, recently conquered by Christians, an intense activity of translation was taking place.[74] This work

---

[74] R. de Vaux, "La première entrée d'Averroës chez les Latins," *RScPhTh*, 22 (1933), 193-243; H. Bédoret, "Les premières versions tolédanes de philosophie: Oeuvres d'Avicenne," *RnsPh*, 41 (1938), 374-400; D. A. Callus, "Gundissalinus' *De anima* and the Problem of Substantial Form," *NSch*, 13 (1939), 338-55; J. T. Muckle, (ed.), "The Treatise *De anima* of Dominicus Gundissalinus," *MedSt*, 2 (1940), 23-103; M. Alonso, "Notas sobre los traductores toledanos Domingo Gundisalvo y Juan

was begun under the auspices of Bishop Raymund of Toledo by Domingo González and John of Spain, who translated works of Avicenna, al-Ghazzali, and Ibn Gabirol into Latin. They also wrote original works in which Arabic influence was noticeable. This activity brought other translators to Spain, such as Gerard of Cremona, Alfred the Englishman, Daniel de Morley, Robert of Retines, Michael Scotus, and others. They flooded Latin Europe with works of Aristotle, Euclid, Galen, Hippocrates, Avicenna, al-Farabi, and Averroës. The impact of these works was such that the entire edifice of medieval theology shook, and thus a new epoch in the history of Christian thought was begun. But the discussion of such momentous events belongs in another chapter of this *History*.

Heresy and Schism in the Twelfth Century

The twelfth century, as every period of spiritual awakening, witnessed the appearance of a great number of preachers, teachers, and movements which did not fit within the hierarchical and doctrinal framework of the Catholic Church. Some of these movements departed far from what had traditionally been called the Christian faith. Others were only attempts to lead a deeper religious life, without being subject to ecclesiastical authorities who were sometimes unworthy and often indifferent. All these movements except one—that of the Waldensians—led to a similar outcome—condemned by the church and persecuted by authority, they eventually disappeared.[75]

Most of these movements are known only through the testimony of their opponents, and therefore it is difficult to establish the exact nature of their doctrines. This is especially true of a multitude of sects whose main characteristics were the

---

Hispano," *AlAnd,* 8 (1943), 115-88; M. Alonso, "Traducciones del arcediano Domingo Gundisalvo," *AlAnd,* 12 (1947), 295-338; M. Th. d' Alverny, "Notes sur les traductions médiévales d' Avicenne," *AHDLMA,* 19 (1952), 337-58; J. F. Rivera, "Nuevos datos sobre los traductores Gundisalvo y Juan Hispano," *AlAnd* 31 (1966), 267-80.

[75] C. Thouzellier, *Hérésie et hérétiques: Vaudois, Cathares, Patarins, Albigeois* (Rome: Edizioni di Storia e Letteratura, 1969); R. Manselli, *Studi sulle eresie del secolo XII* (Rome: Istituto storico italiano per il Medio Evo, 1975).

absolute poverty required of their members and their great admiration, and even veneration, toward their leaders. It seems that some of these leaders, such as Tanquelm and Eudes of Stella, even claimed they were sons of God.[76] Others, notably Peter Bruys,[77] seem to have denied transubstantiation, infant baptism, and services for the dead. Peter's followers, known as Petrobrussians, continued their existence as a sect even after their teacher was burned at the stake. The second Lateran Council, in 1139, condemned them, but in spite of that they did not disappear for several decades. In Milan a certain Hugo Speroni came through the study of the Bible to conclusions very similar to those which would later be held by Protestants.[78] It is quite probable that several of these movements of imprecise doctrines were condemned more for the manner in which they perturbed the established order than for their theological views.

The most remarkable and lasting of these movements was that of the Waldensians.[79] Peter Waldo was a Lyonese merchant who, upon hearing the legend of Saint Alexis, decided to devote his life to poverty and preaching. He soon gathered a group of followers dedicated to the same ideal. When Archbishop Guichard of Lyon forbade them to preach, Peter and his followers appealed to Rome. There the English theologian Walter Map made use of subtle distinctions that the Waldensians could not understand in order to ridicule them.[80] They were

---

[76] *Mansi*, 21:720. Cf. L. J. M. Philippen, "De hl. Norbertus en de strijd tegen het Tanchelmisme te Antwerpen," *BijGesch*, 25 (1934), 251-88.

[77] See Peter the Venerable, *Tract. contra Petro-brussianos (PL*, 189:723-850).

[78] I. da Milano, *L'eresia di Ugo Speroni nella confutazione del Maestri Vacario* (Vatican: Biblioteca Apostolica Vaticana, 1945). This is an edition and commentary of Vacarius, *Contra multiplices et varios errores*, which attempts to refute the views of Speroni. It seems that Speroni and Vacarius were former friends.

[79] On their origin, see H. Wolter, "Aufbruch und Tragik der apostolischen Laienbewegung im Mittelalter," *GuL*, 30 (1957), 357-69; G. Gonnet, "Waldensia," *RHPhRel, 33* (1953), 202-54. On their history, A. Patschovsky and K. V. Selge, eds., *Quellen zur Geschichte der Waldenser* (Gütersloh: G. Mohn, 1973); J. Gonnet and A. Molnàr, *Les Vaudois au moyen âge* (Turin: Editions Claudiana, 1974); M. Pezet, *L'épopée des Vaudois: Dauphiné, Provence, Languedoc, Piémont, Suisse* (Paris: Seghers, 1976); A. Molnar, *Die Waldenser: Geschichte und europäisches Ausmass einer Ketzerbewegung* (Göttingen: Vandenhoeck und Ruprecht, 1980).

[80] Map himself proudly tells of this episode (G. Gonnet, ed., *Enchiridion fontium Valdensium* [Torre Pellice: Libreria Editrice Claudiana, 1958], pp. 122-23):

"First I asked them some very simple questions about matters on which no one has the right to be ignorant, for I knew that the ass who eats thorns will not eat lettuce:

—Do you believe in God the Father?

—We do—they answered.

then given permission to retain their vows of poverty, but were told not to preach unless they received the authorization of local ecclesiastical authorities. Upon returning to Lyon and finding that the archbishop was still sternly opposed to them and would not allow them to preach, Waldo and his followers decided to disregard his authority and go ahead with what they thought to be their God-given mission. As a consequence, they were condemned by the Council of Verona in 1184. Condemned and persecuted throughout Europe, the Waldensians found a haven in the isolated valleys of the Alps, where followers of the movement are still to be found. During the thirteenth century other similar movements, notably that of the "poor Lombards," joined the Waldensians in their refuge from persecution and brought with them a growing anti-Roman feeling. In the sixteenth century they established contact with Calvinism and adopted that form of Christianity. They thus became the most ancient of Protestant churches. But Waldo himself and his followers did not originally intend to found a new sect, nor were they in basic doctrinal disagreement with the church of their times. The breach came rather through the issue of authority which was posed when the hierarchy of the church did not allow them to preach. Actually, there is a close parallelism between the original impulse of the Waldensians in the twelfth century and that of the Franciscans in the thirteenth, except that the latter were retained within the fold of the organized church.

There were, however, other doctrines of a very different order which were also condemned by the church. These were born not among the laity but among scholars and monks, and

---

—And in the Son?
—We do—they answered.
—And in the Holy Spirit?
—We do—they answered.
—And in the Mother of Christ?
—We do—they repeated.
At this point all cried out loud, making fun of them. The Waldensians then retired in confusion, and rightly so."
Whether the reason for the laughter was that the Waldensians had been led by Map to affirm that Mary was the Mother of Christ, rather than the Mother of God, or it had to do with the more subtle issue of the differences between belief in the Godhead and belief in Mary, is a matter on which modern interpreters are not agreed. But the point here is that the Waldensians were caught in an unworthy trap.

had to do mostly with the relationships between God and the world. Such were the doctrines of Amalric of Bena, David of Dinant, and Joachim of Fiore.

Amalric of Bena (or of Chartres) studied and taught at Paris during the second half of the twelfth century.[81] His doctrine was inspired by the writings of John Scotus Erigena, and it was a pantheistic monism grounded in an absolute realism. If individual beings have their reality not in themselves but only in superior genera, and these genera have their own reality in other more inclusive genera, it follows that the reality of all beings is to be found in that supreme being, or supreme idea, which includes all. Another point on which Amalric's doctrine was regarded askance by his contemporaries, and which he also took from Erigena, was his claim that sexual differences did not exist before the Fall and will disappear in the final restoration. Among his disciples, the most famous was David of Dinant, whose works have been lost,[82] but who seems to have carried his teacher's pantheism farther by claiming that God is the prime matter of the universe.[83] He may well have based these views not only on the teachings of Erigena and of Amalric, but also on his readings of Aristotle. Therefore the Council of Paris that condemned Amalric and David in 1210 also banned the use of Aristotle's books on metaphysics and natural philosophy.[84]

Furthermore, the doctrine of the Amalricians—the followers of Amalric—went beyond a mere philosophical pantheism. When applied to eucharistic doctrine, their pantheism led them to affirm that the divine presence in the elements after the act of consecration is the same as before the act. As God is everything and in everything, the bread, even without any consecration, is divine. On the other hand, the Amalricians seem to have

---

[81] There is an excellent study by G. C. Capelle, *Autour du procès de 1210*, Vol. III, *Amaury de Bène* (Paris: J. Vrin, 1932). See also K. Albert, "Amalrich von Bena und der mittelalterliche Pantheismus," *MiscMed*, 10 (1976), 193-212.

[82] See however, R. de Vaux, "Sur un texte retrouvé de David de Dinant," *RScPhTh*, 22 (1933), 243-45.

[83] Albert the Great, *S. Th. pars* 1, *tract.* 4, *q.* 20, *m.* 2, *quaestio incidens;* Thomas, *S. Th. pars* 1, *q:* 3, *art.* 8.

[84] Although for reasons of clarity I have asserted that David was a disciple of Amalric, the exact relationship between the two is not settled. There are many points of similarity between them, but there are also striking points of contrast. See G. Thery, *Autour du procès de 1210*, Vol. I, *David de Dinant* (Paris: J. Vrin, 1925).

adopted a scheme of history which is difficult to conciliate with their pantheism. According to one of their enemies, they held that "the Father was incarnate in Abraham and other patriarchs of the Old Testament, the Son in Christ and in other Christians, and the Holy Spirit in those who are called spiritual."[85] The Amalricians and David of Dinant were condemned first in Paris in 1210, and later in the Fourth Lateran Council (A.D. 1215). In 1225 Pope Honorius III tried to attack the very roots of Amalricianism by condemning the treatise *On the Division of Nature*, by John Scotus Erigena.

Joachim of Fiore proposed an interpretation of history in many ways similar to that of the Amalricians, although the relationship between the two is by no means clear. A native of Calabria,[86] Joachim was a Cistercian and later founded his own monastery of Saint John of Fiore. There he spent his life in contemplation and the study of the Bible, especially the book of Revelation. When he died in 1202, he was generally believed to be a saint. However, his doctrines would eventually come under general attack by the theologians of the thirteenth century. The Fourth Lateran Council condemned his treatise on the doctrine of the Trinity, in which he opposed the views of Peter Lombard. It is possible that in this lost treatise Joachim defended views similar to those of Gilbert de la Porrée,[87] although this has been denied by some scholars.[88] In any case, that aspect of Joachim's theology which had the most implications for the future was not his trinitarian doctrine, but the manner in which he attempted to relate the three persons of the Trinity with three stages in history. According to him, history unfolds in three stages. The first begins with Adam and ends with Christ; the second goes from Christ to the year 1260; the last will begin in that date and

---

[85] *Contra Amaurianos* 10. This is an anonymous work, possibly by Garnerius of Rochefort.

[86] So many legends were woven around Joachim's life that it is very difficult to discover the truth behind them. See C. Baraut, "Las antiguas biografías de Joaquín de Fiore y sus fuentes," *AnSacTarr*, 26 (1953), 195-232; B. McGinn, "The Abbot and the Doctors: Scholastic Reactions to the Radical Eschatology of Joachim of Flore," *CH*, 40 (1971) 30-47; M. Reeves and B. Hirsch-Reich, eds., *The Figurae of Joachim of Fiore* (Oxford: Clarendon Press, 1972); G. Wendelborn, "Die Hermeneutik des kalabresischen Abtes Joachim von Fiore," *ComSanct*, 17 (1974), 63-91.

[87] P. Fournier, "Joachim de Flore: ses doctrines, son influence," *RQH*, 67 (1900), 489.

[88] A. Crocco, *Gioacchimo de Fiore: La piu singolare ed affascinante figura del Medioevo cristiano* (Napoli: Empireo, 1960), pp. 107-14.

extend to the end of time. The first is the age of the Father; the second is that of the Son; and the third is that of the Spirit. The date 1260 is fixed through an exegetical process that serves to illustrate Joachim's theological method. If between Adam and Jesus there were forty-two generations, it is to be expected that, in order to keep the concordance between both testaments, there will be also forty-two generations between Christ and the beginning of the third age. Although in the Old Testament these generations were not all of equal length, the perfection of the New Testament requires that they all be equal. If one then calculates on the basis of thirty years for each generation, forty-two generations will be 1,260 years. As to how long the third age will last, Joachim does not venture a guess. The three stages succeed one another in such a way that during the last days of one age there appear signs or forerunners of the following. Thus, for instance, Benedict and all the other great leaders in spiritual life were forerunners of the age of the Spirit. When that age does arrive—and it is almost here—it will be the time when spiritual life, monastic renunciation, and perfect charity will flourish.

Thus, Joachim's doctrine is an enthusiastic and idealistic spiritualism that, in view of the evil that reigns in the world, finds refuge in the hope of a new age. One of his interpreters has rightly said that

> the hope of the third age in history, conceived as that of universal transfiguration, is born in Joachim out of a profound spiritual drama, which originates in the contrast between his very high ideals of individual and collective perfection and the opposite reality of events.[89]

Joachim of Fiore was not condemned while he lived. It was only in the thirteenth century, at the Fourth Lateran Council, that his trinitarian doctrine was—rightly or wrongly—brought together with that of Gilbert de la Porrée and jointly condemned with it. Even then, however, nobody seems to have given much

---

[89] *Ibid.*, p. 85.

thought to the implications that his scheme of history had for the life of the church and of society at large. When the "spiritual" Franciscans—among them the Minister General John of Parma—took up this scheme of history and interpreted it in such a way that they, in their opposition to the church and even to the rest of the order, became the representatives of the age of the Spirit, the ecclesiastical authorities—and especially such Franciscan leaders as Bonaventure—had to face the wider implications of Joachimism.

The most significant heresy of the twelfth century was that of the Cathari or Albigenses.[90] The origin of this doctrine is not known,[91] apart from the fact that it derives from Bogomilism, which was brought from the East by the Crusaders and other travelers returning to their homes in Western Europe. In any case, in Latin Europe the movement of the Albigenses is a phenomenon of the twelfth century, although perhaps with some forerunners in the eleventh.[92] In 1179, the Third Lateran Council called for a crusade against them, and in 1181 there was a brief campaign. But it was, in the thirteenth century, under Innocent III, that the great crusade against the Albigenses took place. Here religious fanaticism and political ambition joined to produce acts of great cruelty. It was in opposition to the Albigenses that the Inquisition developed its most characteristic forms. At the same time, Saint Dominic, convinced as he was that

[90] These are their two most common names, although during their time they were given different names in various places. See A. Borst, Die Katharer (Stuttgart: Hiersemann, 1953), pp. 240-53. "Cathari" means "pure," a name that they were given because the Council of Nicea had applied it to the Novatians. They were called "Albigenses" because it was at Albi that they first became numerous. C. Ennesch, Les Cathares dans la cité (Paris: A. et J. Picard, 1969); E. Griffe, Les débuts de l'aventure cathare en Languedoc (1140-1190) (Paris: Tetouzey et Ané, 1969); M. Roquebert, L'épopée cathare, 2 vols. (Toulouse: E. Privat, 1970); E. Griffe, Le Languedoc cathare de 1190 a 1210 (Paris: Letouzey et Ané, 1971); R. Kutzli, Die Bogumilen: Geschichte, Kunst, Kultur (Stuttgart: Urachhaus, 1977); J. Duvernoy, Le catharisme, 2 vols. (Toulouse: E. Privat, 1976, 1979); E. Bozóky, Le livre secret des Cathares: Interrogatio Iohannis (Paris: Beauchesne, 1980). A classical work of the nineteenth century, recently reprinted, is C. Schmidt, Histoire et doctrine des cathares (Bayone: Éditions Harriet, 1983).
[91] Some scholars claim that it is a derivation of Manichaeism, through the Paulicians and Bogomils. Others believe that it derives from Gnosticism, or from Marcionism. A summary of the various views may be found in H. Söderberg, La religion des Catheres: Étude sur le gnosticisme de la basse antiquité et du moyen âge (Uppsala: Almquist & Wiksell, 1948), pp. 11-19. Söderberg's claim that there was an uninterrupted Gnostic tradition that led to Catharism is not convincing.
[92] It is possible that Leuthard of Chalons was a Cathar. In that case, he would be the earliest known follower of that sect (around A.D. 1000). See Rudolf Glaber, Libri V Historiarum sui temporis 2. 2 (PL, 142:643-44).

the best manner to win over the heretics was by persuasion, decided to found the Order of Preachers. Thus the Albigenses, although stamped out before the end of the thirteenth century, were very significant for the history of the church and of humankind.

Catharism—at least in its extreme form[93]—poses the existence of two opposed eternal principles: good and evil. Creation is to be attributed not to God, the principle of good, but to its adversary, the principle of evil.

Spirits belong to the principle of good, but are imprisoned in the matter of this evil world. These imprisoned spirits can be freed from matter only through a series of successive reincarnations until they come to dwell in a "perfect" believer, the last stage of a long pilgrimage. These perfect believers must lead a life of strict asceticism, which is not required of the mere "hearers"—note here the clear parallelism with Manichaeism. One reached that state through the rite of *consolamentum,* in which the perfect imposed their hands upon a hearer. From that moment, the believer led a life of chastity, poverty, and fasting. Often fasting was carried to the point of suicide, and this act of extreme devotion was called *endura.* A profound opposition to everything material was found in most Albigensian rites, and they therefore opposed the use of crosses, images, and other symbols—although they did have a eucharistic ceremony in which they gathered to break bread. This attitude toward matter may be seen also in their Christology, for some seem to have held that Christ was a celestial being who seemed to take a body in order to show us the way to salvation. They were also vegetarians, probably because of their belief in the transmigration of souls, which could be reincarnate in an animal. Their organization seems to have been regional, so that in various areas, around each center of diffusion, there was an independent church with its own bishop and deacons.[94]

---

[93] Söderberg, *La religion,* pp. 44-108, distinguishes between "absolute" and "mitigated" Cathari. Although perhaps not as sharp as he makes it, this distinction may help to understand some of the seeming contradictions in the sources regarding this movement.

[94] Borst, *Die Katharer,* pp. 231-39.

Thus ends our brief review of the Christian West in the twelfth century. The main impression one receives while studying this century is that of great intellectual activity. While the foundations are being laid for the great Gothic cathedrals, the foundations are also being laid for the high steeples of medieval scholasticism.

VII

Eastern Theology
from the Islamic Conquests
to the Fourth Crusade

Before continuing our discussion of Western theological developments by moving on to the thirteenth century, we must once again pause to return to the East which we had left at the time of the Sixth Ecumenical Council and the Islamic conquests. This chapter will discuss the development of Eastern theology from that point to the first years of the thirteenth century, when the Fourth Crusade, in taking Constantinople, put an end to a period in the history of that city and of the empire whose capital it was.

During the period that we are now studying, the main Eastern church was still the Greek Orthodox or Byzantine, which accepted all the ecumenical councils that had taken place earlier and, in spite of repeated interruptions and growing tensions, generally kept bonds of communion with the Roman See and the Western church. During this period the Bulgarian and Russian churches were born as branches of the Byzantine, and, although they eventually became independent, they did not abandon the doctrine of the great councils. Finally, the so-called Nestorian Church, as well as the various bodies that did not accept the Council of Chalcedon and were therefore called mono-

195

physites—the Coptic, Armenian, Jacobite, and Ethiopian churches—continued their existence, although for the most part under Moslem rule. Hence the outline of the present chapter: we shall first study Byzantine theology, we shall then say a few words about the Bulgarian and Russian churches, and finally we shall turn to the Nestorians and monophysites.

Byzantine Theology up to the Restoration of Icons

Under this heading, we shall study not only that theology which developed within the borders of the Byzantine Empire, but also the work of those theologians who, even while living under Moslem rule, kept their bonds of communion with the see of Constantinople. Thus, under this heading is included the totality of "Orthodox" Christianity within the Empire, as well as all those who belonged to the same communion but lived in Moslem lands, and who were usually called "Melchite Christians"—that is, Christians of the emperor. The last name was not totally unjust, for the Byzantine Church was noted for the degree of its subjection to the authority and even to the whims of emperors. It is true that the most outstanding ecclesiastical leaders, such as German of Constantinople, John of Damascus, and Theodore the Studite, were often opposed to imperial policy, and that the same may be said about a vast majority of the monks. But in spite of these centers of resistance there were few patriarchs of Constantinople who were able to oppose the emperor and yet retain their sees. Therefore, in the history of Byzantine theology the political history of the empire plays an important role. Here the contrast with the West is noteworthy, for while the Western empire was disappearing only to be born later, in times of Charlemagne, under the wing and auspices of the church, in the East the empire was moving toward the autocracy that had characterized Eastern monarchies from ancient times, and the church was made an arm of imperial policy. This historical process developing in different directions was one of the reasons for the widening gap between Rome and Constantinople.

The last years of the seventh century and the first of the eighth were sad times for the Byzantine Empire and the Eastern church. The Moslem conquests, the Bulgarian invasions, and a series of incompetent emperors seemed to indicate the coming end of the Empire, whose territories were now reduced to the northeastern corner of the Mediterranean basin, with a few possessions in Sicily and southern Italy. But in A.D. 717, with Leo III, the "Isaurian" Dynasty came to power, and with it the old empire was given new life. Leo III and his successors reorganized their territories in order to make both defense and fiscal administration more effective; they compiled and codified a legal system that was more just and often more merciful than the preceding codes; they favored centers of study, especially the University of Constantinople; they constructed buildings and monuments; they built roads; and they were successful in their wars against the Arabs and the Bulgarians.

As a part of this vast program of restoration, however, Leo III began, and his successors continued, a religious policy that soon involved the entire empire—and even the Latin West—in bitter controversies. This policy was his opposition to religious images, including those of Christ as well as those of Mary, the saints, the figures of the Old Testament, and angels. The reasons that led him to establish this policy, which is usually called "iconoclastic," are not certain. Probably there was not a single reason, but an entire series of them. Constantinople was in constant contact with Jews, Moslems, and monophysites, all of whom were opposed, for different reasons and in various ways, to the use of religious images.[1] It is also possible that Leo III and his successors wanted to break the power of the monks and to confiscate some of their properties,[2] although on the other hand such a purpose would have been more easily achieved through a series of imperial decrees, without involving in the matter a theological issue that could only serve to complicate the situation. Finally, there is no doubt that some of the iconoclastic emperors—Leo III among them—were moved by sincere

---

[1] Caliph Yazid (720-724), prompted by a Jew, had ordered all images within his territories destroyed. To what extent this influenced Leo's policies, however, cannot be determined. A. A. Vasiliev, "The Iconoclastic Edict of Caliph Yazid II, A.D. 721," *DOP*, 9-10 (1956), 23-47.

[2] Although there were some iconoclasts among them, monks were in general among the staunchest supporters of icons.

religious and theological considerations. Leo believed that his iconoclastic campaign was part of his program of imperial restoration. His son and successor, Constantine V, was convinced that the veneration of images and of the relics of saints was idolatry, and that the notion of the intercession of saints and of the Virgin was false. Therefore, one must be skeptical when the defenders of images draw a picture of an entire dynasty of hypocritical and opportunistic emperors.

In any case, the iconoclastic controversy began in A.D. 725,[3] when Leo III ordered the destruction of an image of Christ to which miraculous powers were attributed. From that time on, the iconoclastic campaign gained in impetus. Since Patriarch German of Constantinople was opposed to this policy, the emperor deposed him and had him replaced by his own man, Anastasius. This in turn led to difficulties with Rome, for Gregory II would not acknowledge Anastasius, and shortly thereafter his successor, Gregory III, excommunicated the emperor. In Moslem lands, John of Damascus, generally considered the last of the "Fathers" of the Eastern church, came out in defense of icons. Constantine V followed the policy of his father, and in A.D. 754 called a council that ratified iconoclastic doctrine and pronounced an anathema upon German of Constantinople and John of Damascus. He then opened a persecution against the defenders of images. When Constantine died, his son Leo IV, still a minor, had his mother Irene as regent. She was an ambitious woman who combined a seemingly sincere devotion to icons with an almost total lack of principles in everything else. She had her follower Tarasius appointed patriarch of Constantinople, and then, jointly with the new patriarch and Pope Hadrian I, she convoked a council that

---

[3] It is impossible to discuss here the entire development of Christian iconography. Let it suffice to say that, although ancient Christian writers attacked pagan idols, this does not seem to have resulted in widespread opposition to figurative art among Christians. It is true that most ancient Christian art was symbolic rather than iconographic, dwelling on such themes as the fish and the cross; but there were also pictures of Christ as the good shepherd, and of the last supper. The church at Dura-Europos, the earliest that has been excavated, was decorated with abundant iconography. From the fourth century on, there are a number of passages, both for and against images. But it was the decree of Leo that brought the issue to the foreground. On the course of the controversy, see E. J. Martin, *A History of the Iconoclastic Controversy* (New York: Macmillan, 1930). A collection of sources: H. Hennephof, *Textus Byzantini ad iconoclastiam pertinentes* (Leiden: E. J. Brill, 1968).

eventually gathered at Nicea in A.D. 787. This council, which is usually called the Seventh Ecumenical Council, decreed the restoration of icons. However, in A.D. 815 Leo V once more returned to iconoclastic policy, deposed Patriarch Nicephorus, and began persecuting the defenders of images.[4] His successor Michael II, although more moderate, continued supporting the iconoclasts, while Theodore the Studite came out in defense of icons. Finally, under another woman regent, Theodora, images were definitely restored. The date of that restoration, March 11, 842, came to be a symbol of orthodoxy in the entire Eastern church, which still celebrates it as the "Feast of Orthodoxy."

In order to give an idea of the basic theological positions of those who attacked the use of icons as well as of those who defended it, we shall expound, as an example of the first, the *Definition* of the iconoclastic council of A.D. 754, and, as an example of the latter, some of what may be gleaned from the works of German of Constantinople, John of Damascus, and Theodore the Studite, as well as the decision of the Seventh Ecumenical Council.

As frequently happens in such controversies, the conquering party, that is, that of the defenders of icons, so destroyed the works of its opponents that it is difficult to gain a clear and precise idea of the theology of the iconoclasts. One of the few iconoclastic documents which has survived is the *Definition—Horos*—of the council of A.D. 754, which has been preserved because it was quoted in the acts of the Seventh Ecumenical Council. There one can see that the theological foundation for iconoclasm was found, on the one hand, in the general prohibition of idolatry in Scripture and, on the other, in the doctrine of incarnation. It is not necessary to insist on the first point—let it suffice to say that the *Horos* quoted the prohibition of the Ten Commandments against the worship of images, as well as several other texts in the New Testament. As to the second point, the bishops gathered in A.D. 754 used the Christology of Chalcedon in order to show that one should not

---

[4] P. J. Alexander, *The Patriarch Nicephorus of Constantinople: Ecclesiastical Policy and Image Worship in the Byzantine Empire* (Oxford: Clarendon Press, 1958).

make images of Christ. According to them, the divine nature cannot be circumscribed. Therefore, if one represents the humanity of the Savior in an image it will be necessary to represent it apart from his divinity, and this would immediately lead to that division of the two natures for which Nestorianism was condemned. If, on the other hand, one claims that in representing the humanity of Christ one also represents his divinity, this would imply circumscribing his divinity, and it would lead to the confusion of the two natures for which monophysism was condemned.[5]

The first great champion of images was Patriarch German of Constantinople (A.D. 715–729). Some years earlier, in A.D. 712, German had yielded to imperial pressure and had supported an attempt to resurrect monothelism. It may well have been his repentance for that action that gave him the strength necessary to oppose the iconoclastic policies of Leo III. In any case, he took a strong position in defense of images and therefore lost his patriarchal see. He died around A.D. 733, when he was almost one hundred years old, venerated by one party and hated by the other. The iconoclastic council of A.D. 754 condemned his views and declared him to have been two-faced—a possible reference to his participation in the monothelite revival of 712. In the Seventh Ecumenical Council his three epistles in favor of icons were formally approved by the assembly.[6] In these three epistles, he refutes the argument according to which the veneration of images is forbidden in Exodus 20:4. He does this by distinguishing between that "worship"—*proskynesis*—which is a mere sign of respect and veneration, and true "worship" in the strict sense—*latreîa*—which is due only to God, and which Exodus rightly reserves for the Divine. Images receive only an inferior cult, which is also relative in that its end is not in itself, but in the supreme worship of God.[7]

Although German of Constantinople was significant for his

---

5 *Mansi*, 13:252-53. See P. J. Alexander, "The Iconoclastic Council of St. Sophia," *DOP*, 7 (1953), 78-99; M. V. Anastos, "The Ethical Theory of Images Formulated by the Iconoclasts in 754 and 815," *DOP*, 8 (1954), 151-60.
6 *PG*, 98:156-94.
7 V. Grumel, "L'iconologie de St. Germain," *EchOr*, 21 (1922), 165-75.

early date as well as for his high rank, the true apostle of images, who set the foundations for later iconology, was John of Damascus. Often counted as the last of the "Fathers" of the Eastern church, John of Damascus was a high official in the caliph's government, but he resigned from that position in order to withdraw to a monastery, and later to become a priest at Jerusalem.[8] His arguments in favor of icons are usually Christocentric. Thus, for instance, the commandments against images to be found in the Old Testament are no longer valid, for the coming of Christ has given us the power to grow to the stature of a perfect human being, and in any case in the Old Testament itself it was proper to render a certain form of cult to beings that were not God, as in the cases of Joshua and Daniel, who worshiped the angel of the Lord.[9] But more significantly, God, although invisible by nature, has become visible in the incarnation and has thus let us know that the Divine can be revealed through visible means.[10] This argument, which is at the very center of John's iconology, is summarized in his *Exposition of the Orthodox Faith:*

> But since some find fault with us for worshipping and honouring the image of our Saviour and that of our Lady, and those, too, of the rest of the saints and servants of Christ, let them remember that in the beginning God created man after His own image. On what grounds, then, do we shew reverence to each other unless because we are made after God's image? . . . But besides this who can make an imitation of the invisible, incorporeal, uncircumscribed, formless God? Therefore to give form to the Deity is the height of folly and impiety. And hence it is that in the Old Testament the use of images was not common. But after God in His bowels of pity became in truth man for our salvation, not as He was seen by Abraham in the semblance of a man, nor as He was seen by the prophets, but in being truly man,

---

[8] His main work is *The Source of Knowledge,* written shortly before his death and divided in three parts: *Philosophical Chapters, On Heresy,* and *Exposition of the Orthodox Faith.* He also wrote numerous polemical works against the Moslems, Manichees, Nestorians, and monophysites. As to images, he deals with them in his *Exposition of the Orthodox Faith,* and in his three *Orations Against Those Who Reject the Holy Images.*

[9] *De imag. or.* 1. 8.

[10] *Ibid.* 2. 5.

and after He lived upon the earth and dwelt among men, worked miracles, suffered, was crucified, rose again and was taken back to Heaven, since all these things actually took place and were seen by men, they were written for the remembrance and instruction of us who were not alive at that time in order that though we saw not, we may still, hearing and believing, obtain the blessing of the Lord. But seeing that not every one has a knowledge of letters nor time for reading, the Fathers gave their sanction to depicting these events on images, as being acts of great heroism, in order that they should form a concise memorial of them.[11]

Furthermore, one should take care lest the arguments used against idolatry become arguments against matter itself, which would lead to a Manichaean dualism.[12]

What is the purpose of images? They teach and remind the faithful of the great events of salvation, and move them to do good. Actually, their usefulness is such that John claimed that they are means of grace, for the power of that which they represent is communicated through them to the person who contemplates and venerates them.[13]

Finally, as had been done by German, John also distinguished between several degrees of cult or reverence. The absolute reverence or worship, which is called *latria,* is due only to God, and if one were to render it to a creature one would be practicing idolatry. But mere reverence, showing respect, honor, and veneration, may be properly rendered to religious objects or even to persons in the secular world—an assertion that reflects the practices of Byzantium.[14]

Theodore the Studite became a champion of images early in the ninth century, when Emperor Leo V, the Armenian, returned to the iconoclastic policies of Leo III. Theodore was an inflexible monk whose main cause was the independence of the church over against civil authority, and who therefore had

---

[11] *De fide orth.* 1. 16 (*NPNF,* 2nd series, 9:88).
[12] *De imag. or.* 1. 16.
[13] *Ibid.*
[14] *Ibid.,* 3. 33-40.

already clashed with Constantine VI when the latter set aside his wife in order to marry a relative of Theodore.

Theodore's iconology is based on the earlier works of German of Constantinople and John of Damascus, and on the decisions of the Seventh Ecumenical Council. His main contribution is in the manner in which he defined the relationships between the veneration of the icon and the veneration of that which the icon signifies. According to him, the veneration of the image and that of its prototype are the same, but the veneration of the icon itself is only relative and not directly addressed to it, whereas the veneration of the prototype is directly addressed to it and, in the case of images of Christ, is an absolute worship of the order of *latria*.[15]

In any case, the final definition of the cult due to images is that of the Seventh Ecumenical Council, in A.D. 787. Here one finds the distinction between various degrees of cult combined with an attempt to ground the cult of icons in christological foundations. Thus, the Council advised that images of Christ, the Virgin, the angels, and the saints be made available in various places, in order to call the believers to render them "respect and veneration, although without offering them a true *latria*, which should only be rendered to the Godhead."[16] The concern to relate iconology with Christology may be seen in the list of anathemas, which opens with a general anathema against the iconoclasts, then condemns those who "do not confess that Christ our God is circumscribed according to his humanity," and finally moves to other more specific anathemas against the opponents of icons.[17]

The iconoclastic controversy was not as bitter in the West as it was in the East. In general, popes supported the use of images, and the same may be said of the various Carolingian emperors, although the latter showed a greater concern to avoid idolatry. Since the Latin translation of the acts of the Seventh Ecumenical Council which reached Charlemagne referred to the veneration

---

[15] V. Grumel, "L'iconologie de S. Théodore Studite," *EchOr*, 20 (1921), 257-68.

[16] *Denzinger*, 201.

[17] *Ibid.*, 203.

of images as "adoratio," the king and the entire Frankish church rejected the decision of the Council. The *Caroline Books,* published a few years after the Council, defended the use of images, but condemned their worship. In A.D. 794 a synod gathered at Frankfort condemned both the iconoclastic council of 754 and the Council of Nicea of 787, and affirmed that icons were to be used, but that they were not worthy of worship— *adoratio.*[18] For several decades the Frankish church refused to accept the decrees of the Council of Nicea of A.D. 787, and this in turn placed the various popes in a difficult situation that required a great deal of diplomatic finesse. Slowly and progressively, as Carolingian power declined, the decisions of Nicea became accepted in the West. But in spite of this the Latin church never extended its sacramental theology in order to include images, as was done by the Greek church.[19]

From the Restoration of Images to the Schism of 1054

After the restoration of images, the Byzantine church remained divided into several parties, which, however, can be grouped into three main tendencies. In the first place, there were some convinced iconoclasts who persisted in their position in spite of its official condemnation at Nicea. Their main theologian was John the Grammarian, who continued writing against icons and for some time kept alive the iconoclastic movement. But his cause was lost, and therefore his influence in

---

[18] *Mansi,* 13:909.

[19] The West tended to emphasize more the value of images as educational means, and sometimes also—especially in the south—as works of art. See G. Ladner, "Der Bilderstreit und die Kunst-Lehren der byzantinischen und abendländischen Theologie," *ZschrKgesch,* 50 (1931), 1-23; G. Haendler, *Epochen karolingischer Theologie: Eine Untersuchung über die karolingischen Gutachten zum byzantinischen Bilderstreit* (Berlin: Evangelische Verlangsanstalt, 1958).

Although the controversy regarding the use of images was of such significance that it eclipsed the rest of Eastern theology during this period, one should not leave the impression that there was not a great deal of theological activity addressing other issues. The question of the *Filioque,* which we have discussed in another chapter, was posed during this period. Owing to the political and ecclesiastical circumstances, the relations between ecclesiastical and civil authorities were debated. Another issue was the relationship between the bishops of Constantinople and those of Rome—an issue that would occupy the center of the stage once the iconoclastic controversy was solved. German of Constantinople discussed predestination and free will. John of Damascus composed a lengthy systematic work in which he discussed all the main philosophical and theological questions of earlier centuries. Several other authors wrote against the ancient christological heresies as well as against the beliefs and practices of Moslems and Jews.

the later development of Byzantine theology was slight. In the second place, there were some pious extremists who had been inflamed by the long decades of bitter struggle as well as by the example of leaders such as Theodore the Studite. Most monks, and the lower classes among the laity, belonged to this party. They insisted on an ascetic rigorism, on the cult of images, and on their opposition to philosophy. Finally, the moderate party had the support of some monks and of the more educated among the laity, who would not accept the views of the iconoclasts but did, however, want to avoid a religious rigorism that would hinder the intellectual and political development of Byzantium. One of their leaders was Photius, who eventually became the center of a new controversy.[20]

The beginnings of this new controversy were not strictly dogmatic, but rather political. Because of a palace revolution, power passed from the regent Theodora to her brother Bardas, who then clashed with Patriarch Ignatius, had him deposed, and put Photius in his place. Because Ignatius supported the rigorist party, many among the people and the monks would not accept his deposition. The clergy was divided, for some accepted the accomplished facts while others still considered Ignatius the true patriarch. Since both parties requested the support of Pope Nicholas I, he made arrangements so that the case of Ignatius be tried anew, now in presence of the papal legates. But at this trial it was clear that the imperial court had previously decided to condemn Ignatius. As a result, tension developed between the pope and the Byzantine authorities. On the other hand, the opening of Bulgaria to the Christian faith was a new source of conflict between the ecclesiastical authorities of Rome and those of Constantinople, for both sees wished to have jurisdiction over the new church. Furthermore, Photius himself was an able writer who was resolutely opposed to the introduction of the *Filioque* in the creed. Prompted by the pope, several Western theologians wrote against the trinitarian doctrine of the Eastern church.[21] Photius

---

[20] G. Zananiri, *Histoire de l'église byzantine* (Paris: Nouvelles Éditions Latines, 1954), pp. 175-78.
[21] Among them Aeneas of Paris, *Liber adversus graecos* (PL, 121:685-762), and Ratramnus of Corbie, *Contra graecorum opposita* (PL, 121:225-346).

countered by writing against the claims of the Roman see and by calling a council that declared Nicholas deposed. At that juncture, a new palace revolution resulted in the deposition of Photius and the restoration of Ignatius. After some maneuvering, the pope—now Hadrian II—managed to have a new council gather at Constantinople. This took place in A.D. 869–70, and is usually known as the Eighth Ecumenical Council. There Photius was condemned. But he eventually returned to the Byzantine court and was reconciled with Ignatius. When the latter died, Photius succeeded him without major opposition in the East, and in the West John VIII accepted a compromise by which Rome acknowledged Photius as patriarch, and Constantinople in turn accepted the jurisdiction of Rome over Bulgaria. The policies of John's successors oscillated between a veiled hostility toward Photius and open opposition to him, but imperial favor sustained the patriarch of Constantinople for several years. When he lost that favor, he withdrew from active life and devoted the rest of his years to writing. During that time, his relations with Rome improved, although they were never cordial. In any case, this protacted tension did nothing to improve the relations between East and West, and the writings of Photius against Latin theology and against the claims of the papacy later became a useful instrument for those who held similar views.

This is not the place to discuss the theology of Photius in detail.[22] His views on the Roman primacy, however, do deserve special attention. Of the various works in which he discusses this matter, the most significant is his treatise *Against the Primacy*, addressed "to those who say that Rome is the first see." Here he argues that the Roman primacy is a groundless claim, for Peter was bishop of Antioch before he was bishop of Rome. In any

---

[22] A subject that has been exhaustively treated in the monumental work by J. Hergenröther, *Photius, Patriarch von Konstantinopel: Sein Leben, seine Schriften und das griechisch Schisma*, 3 vols. (Regensburg: Georg Joseph Manz, 1867-69). F. Dvornik, *The Photian schism: History and Legend* (Cambridge: University Press, 1948); F. Dvornik, "The Patriarch Photius and Iconoclasm," *DOP*, 7 (1953), 67-97; R. Haugh, *Photius and the Carolingians: The Trinitarian Controversy* (Belmont, Mass.: Nordland, 1975); Asterios Gerostergios, *St. Photius the Great* (Belmont, Mass.: Institute for Byzantine and Modern Greek Studies, 1980); D. S. White, *Patriarch Photius of Constantinople: His Life, Scholarly Contributions, and Correspondence* (Brookline, Mass.: Holy Cross Orthodox Press, 1982).

case, if the Roman argument for primacy were followed, that authority should belong to Jerusalem, whose church was led not only by Peter, but also and above all by the incarnate Lord himself. Furthermore, the argument for Rome could also be applied in favor of Byzantium, which—according to legend— had Andrew as a bishop a long time before Peter ever visited Rome. As to the argument based on the words of the Lord, "On this rock I will build my church," there is no truth in it, for the rock to which Christ referred was not Peter, but his confession of the divinity of the Lord. To attempt to circumscribe divine grace to a particular region, as is done by Roman authorities, is to follow the error of the Jews. Finally, let the pope remember the words of Jesus: "He who wishes to be first among you, let him become your servant."

After the death of Photius, the next open conflict between Rome and Constantinople took place while Michael Cerularius was patriarch in the latter city. At that time, the movement for reformation led by Hildebrand and Cardinal Humbert was coming to power. Two of the main emphases of this movement were clerical celibacy and the restoration of the prestige of the papacy. As neither of these two points was viewed with sympathy in the East, conflicts were to be expected. Another point at which there was disagreement between the two branches of the church, and which at this time became involved in the discussion, was the use of unleavened bread at communion by the Latin church. Pope Leo IX made the mistake of choosing as one of his legates to Constantinople Cardinal Humbert, an ardent defender of Roman primacy and clerical celibacy. At Constantinople, Humbert got involved in a series of debates which eventually descended to the level of personal insults. In spite of the efforts of Constantine V to reconcile both parties, the end result was that on July 16, 1054, Humbert placed before the high altar of Saint Sophia a sentence of excommunication against Cerularius and all his followers.

This sentence by Cardinal Humbert was a useful instrument in the hands of Cerularius, for in this document the Roman legate made such unbelievable accusations against the patriarch—he was an Arian, a Pneumatomachian, a Donatist, etc.—that the entire Eastern church saw Cerularius as the victim of a vicious attack by Rome. This made it possible for him to call a council in which Eastern Christianity condemned its Western counterpart for having abandoned the true faith in such matters as the *Filioque,* the use of unleavened bread, the warlike costumes of their bishops, shaving their faces, and eating meat on Wednesdays.

As a consequence of that schism, and of its prelude during the time of Photius, the Greek East and the Latin West drifted farther and farther apart. Although there were periods of supposed reconciliation, this was always limited to the high political and eccesiastical authorities, for the people and the lower clergy retained their distrustful and unbending attitudes.

A by-product of this schism was the theory of the "Pentarchy," which was proposed by Patriarch Peter III of Antioch as a means of bringing together the great sees of Rome and Constantinople. According to the Antiochene patriarch, the head of the body of Christ is the Lord himself, and the five patriarchs of Rome, Constantinorple, Alexandria, Antioch, and Jerusalem are like the five bodily senses, so that the opinion of the majority among them should prevail.[23] This theory was not entirely new, for at an earlier date Emperor Leo VI had used it in an attempt to overcome the opposition of the patriarch of Constantinople to his fourth marriage. Cardinal Humbert refuted Peter of Antioch. But the theory of the Pentarchy was used shortly thereafter by Michael Psellus, and by several other Byzantine theologians from the thirteenth century onward. According to another version of this theory, the primacy among the five patriarchs belongs to Constantinople—a view that was held by Nicetas Suidas.[24]

Eastern theological activity during the tenth and eleventh centuries was not limited to polemics with the Latin West. On the contrary, there was a great interest in mystical theology, as well

---

[23] *Ep. sant. episc. Grad.* 21 (*PG*, 120:776).
[24] N. Ladomerszky, *Theologia Orientalis* (Rome: Pontifical University De Propaganda Fide, 1953), pp. 102-10, gives a brief summary of the latter course of this theory. P. O'Connell, *The Ecclesiology of St. Nicephorus (758-858) Patriarch of Constantinople: Pentarchy and Primacy* (Rome: Pontificium Institutum Studiorum Orientalium, 1972).

as some activity in the study of philosophy and of classical antiquity.

The main exponent of mystical theology late in the tenth century and early in the eleventh was Simeon the New Theologian.[25] After abandoning the academic world and retiring to a monastery, Simeon spent the rest of his life writing on the mystical experience. His work is written with great enthusiasm—which does not simplify the task of systematizing his theology. He was convinced that fallen humans could not act freely.[26] All that is left of our lost glory is our aspiration to be free. Therefore, we can be saved not through our works, but only through an illumination from on high. This illumination, which is an actual encounter with the divine light, so transforms us that ever after, even though the vision itself is no longer present, we are new and live in a state of direct communion with God. This state Simeon called "deification." This is not achieved through a process of ascension, as was generally held by Neoplatonic mysticism, nor does it consist in an ecstasy in the strict sense, as if one were lost in God. On the contrary, the believer does not lose self-consciousness before the eternal light—and this was the most debated point of Simeon's theology. Those who claim that it is possible to receive this light without being conscious of it are simply mistaken and have not had the true experience of illumination. Only those who have had this experience can be true theologians, for it is impossible to speak of what one does not know; and it is impossible to know the divine without having received God in a conscious mystical experience.

> I marvel that most men, even without having been born of God and without having become his children, dare to meddle in theology and to speak of God. For this reason my spirit trembles and I lose my senses when I hear some philosophizing on divine and inscrutable subjects, pretending to be theologians, who are being impure, and explaining divine truths without receiving the mind of the Holy Spirit . . . [27]

---

[25] His biography, written by his disciple Nicetas Stethatos (or Pectoratus), has been edited by I. Hausherr and G. Horn, *OrChr*, 12 (1928).

[26] Such is the point of departure of Tatakis' exposition, *Filosofía*, pp. 144-51.

[27] *Tract. theol.* 2 (*SC*, 122:132).

As the result of this emphasis on mystical experience as the only way to salvation and as a requisite for theological work, Simeon later became one of the favorite authors of the "hesychastic" or "Palamite" movement. But the story of that movement belongs in a later chapter.

The study of philosophy and of classical antiquity developed independently from mystical theology, which often saw such studies as a snare of the Adversary in order to lead the faithful away from revealed truth and mystical contemplation. But Byzantine civilization from the tenth to the twelfth centuries showed enough vitality and flexibility to hold within itself the most exalted mystics as well as a vast number of scholars who studied, popularized, and imitated the knowledge of classical antiquity. While some were devoted to mystical contemplation and others supported Cerularius in his debate with Rome, still others were involved in a great renaissance of classical Greek studies centered around Constantinople. Once again, as in ancient times, there were Christians who tried to bring together their faith with the best of classical culture. This intellectual development reached its climax in Michael Psellus and his disciple John Italos, whom we shall study in the next section of this chapter.

Byzantine Theology from 1054 to the Fourth Crusade

While Michael Cerularius and the papal legates debated the points of conflict between the East and the West, at the University of Constantinople a vast task of research and teaching was taking place. There, the most distinguished scholar was Michael Psellus,[28] an encyclopedic spirit who did not hesitate to draw wisdom from any source where it could be found, including not only the "Fathers" of the church and the classical Greek philosophers, but even popular legends and sayings. He believed truth to be one, and as a consequence he thought that wherever truth was to be found it was to be attributed to the same

---

[28] Tatakis, *Filosofía*, pp. 159-201. J. M. Hussey, *Church and Learning in the Byzantine Empire, 867-1185* (Oxford: University Press, 1937), pp. 73-88; E. R. A. Sewter, ed., *The Chronographia of Michael Psellus* (London: Routledge and Kegan Paul, 1953).

ultimate source and could be assimilated into a single body of knowledge. As a result, some accused him of abandoning Christian doctrine in order to follow the teachings of pagans. The basis for this accusation was his opposition to the anti-intellectual mysticism that was flourishing at the time.[29] Furthermore, he was not willing to remain within the narrow limits of orthodox dogmatic theology. But this did not lead him to abandon the Christian faith; on the contrary, he drank from the source of the ancients, where he found a spirit of intellectual adventure very much akin to his own spirit. He always held that Christian doctrine and the study of Scripture were the last tribunal before which every opinion should be judged. Any opinion contrary to Scripture must be declared false, although it could still be studied, not as truth, but as an opinion worthy of being known.

On the other hand, he attacked the body of superstitions that he called "Chaldeism." Divination, astrology, and magic were popular in Byzantium, not only among the ignorant people, but also among many who held high secular and ecclesiastical posts. Such illustrious persons as the head of the School of Law at the University of Constantinople, and even Michael Cerularius, studied the course of the stars and other means of divination, and often attempted to solve their problems through the use of magic. Psellus believed such ideas to be groundless. The heavenly bodies move according to physical laws, and are not rational beings, as Neoplatonism claimed. So-called miracles are not really such. They are simply events that follow laws that we do not understand.

As to classical philosophy, Psellus justifies his use of it in a manner reminiscent of the Christians who in earlier times had also viewed the great philosophical tradition with sympathy— such as Justin, Clement, and Origen. Philosophy is a preparation for the reception of the Gospel, and it therefore comes from God, who is the source of all truth.

In his study of Plato and Aristotle, Psellus had to come to grips with the problem of universals. According to him, the ideas that

---

[29] However, he was not opposed to mysticism in general. He himself was actually quite sympathetic to Neoplatonic mysticism. It was the anti-intellectual attitude of many mystics that he opposed.

exist in the mind of God are eternal, and God has made all
sensible objects following them as a pattern. But the ideas that
exist in our minds, and that we use for thinking, are not strictly
real. They are—as the Latins would say—*post rem.* Thus, genera
and species are real, and individuals are not isolated beings; but
when we bring them together in our mind we must know that,
although we do group them following the pattern of eternal
ideas, the conceptual tools that we use are strictly ours and are
not eternal.

Psellus died in 1092, but his work had developed an interest in
classical antiquity which would continue for centuries. Thus, it is
not an exaggeration to claim for him the distinction of being one
of the forerunners of the Renaissance. After this time, with only
a brief interruption due to the Fourth Crusade, there was a long
succession of scholars who kept alive the study of antiquity, until
the final fall of Constantinople led them to seek refuge in the
West, where they made a significant contribution to the spirit of
the Renaissance. Many of these scholars, such as Michael Italicus
in the twelfth century, clearly held that final authority was to be
found in Scripture and Christian doctrine.[30] But others, such as
John Italos and his disciple Eustratius of Nicea,[31] applied the
methods of rational inquiry to the most exalted questions and
thereby provoked the suspicion of many pious souls. As a result,
an anti-philosophical current developed which lasted for
centuries. John Italos, who succeeded Psellus in his position at
the University of Constantinople, taught such typically Hellenic
doctrines as the transmigration of souls and the eternity of
matter. He also followed the rationalism of Psellus to its final
consequence in denying miracles and affirming that all the
mysteries of faith could be explained through reason. He was
judged, condemned, and incarcerated in a monastery by the
Holy Synod. From that time on, there was a growing tension
between theologians and philosophers. But the latter managed
to continue their work until Constantinople fell before the
Turks.

---

[30] Tatakis, *Filosofía,* pp. 208-9.
[31] *Ibid.,* pp. 201-8. Hussey, *Church and Learning,* pp. 89-102.

Meanwhile strictly theological activity became increasingly concerned with matters of detail and with hairsplitting.[32]

Finally, during this period Bogomilism made its appearance in Byzantium, and there were several trials of Bogomils. But the discussion of this sect properly belongs in the section devoted to Bulgaria.

In summary, Byzantine theology during this period drifted farther from the West[33] and devoted most of its attention to detailed matters of little significance. Insistence upon strict theological orthodoxy became increasingly important in a state that was constantly threatened at its borders as well as in its inner unity, and whose history recorded a long series of internal divisions born out of dogmatic differences. While Psellus was pursuing his philosophical inquiry, the Byzantine state was at the edge of chaos. Shortly thereafter, the emperor had to ask the West for protection from the Turks. At the end of this period, the Fourth Crusade turned Constantinople into a Latin kingdom. In the midst of so many vicissitudes, dogmatic orthodoxy became a bond of union for the Byzantine state, and therefore it was necessary to avoid the conflicts that naturally arose out of theological innovation, and to insist on strict adherence to the doctrine and the text of the ancients. While this rigidity developed in theology, some sought freedom in philosophical studies, which were gaining a measure of independence from theology.

Christian Thought in Bulgaria

After the conversion of King Boris, and especially during the reign of his son Simeon, Bulgaria became mostly Christian. This

---

[32] Thus, for instance, the Antiochene deacon Sotericos Panteugenos opened a debate regarding the validity of the eucharistic formula, "You are the one who offers, and the one who is offered." He claimed that this formula implies a Nestorian distinction between the two natures of the incarnate Word. He also claimed that the eucharistic sacrifice was offered only to the Son, and not to the Father or the Holy Spirit. In 1156 a synod gathered at Constantinople declared that Christ offers himself upon the altar as a sacrifice to the Trinity. Shortly thereafter, during the reign of Alexius Angelus (1195-1203), there was another controversy on whether the elements that one takes in communion are digested as common food. Those who held the affirmative position were called "stercoranists"—from the Latin *stercus*. The final decision was negative: the elements are not digested. In the twelfth century Demetrius of Lampe proposed an interpretation of the text "my Father is greater than I," which many took to be a new version of Arianism. His doctrines were condemned by a synod in 1166, but his followers did not immediately disappear.

[33] The debate with Rome continued unabated. See J. Spiteris, *La critica bizantina del primato romano nel secolo XII* (Rome: Pontificium Institutum Studiorum Orientalium, 1979).

conversion, however, did not happen without a measure of popular resistance. Although such resistance was promptly crushed, it eventually led to the growth of Bogomilism.

Even before the conversion of Bulgaria to Christianity, there were many Manichees in that country. They had been forcibly placed there by Byzantine authorities with the double purpose of being rid of them and of using them as a buffer against the barbarians.[34] Thus, when Boris accepted baptism, and his son Simeon followed this with a policy of forcing Christianity upon his subjects, Manichaeism became the symbol of opposition to these policies. During the reign of Peter, Simeon's successor, there was a religious teacher who took the name of "Bogomil"—"beloved of God"[35]—and created a new sect, many of whose doctrines were taken from Manichaeism.[36] Very little else is known regarding Bogomil himself. But in any case the new sect soon supplanted Manichaeism and became the great rival of orthodox Christianity. From Bulgaria, Bogomilism spread to Constantinople and later to the West, where it was severely persecuted. In Bulgaria itself, it subsisted at least until the seventeenth century. Because of the importance of Bogomilism in that country, most early Bulgarian theology is concerned with its refutation.[37]

Early Russian Theology

The conversion of Russia, somewhat later than that of Bulgaria, opened a vast field of expansion for Eastern Christianity. Eventually, the Russian church would be larger

---

[34] V. N. Sharenkoff, A Study of Manichaeism in Bulgaria, with Special Reference to the Bogomils (New York: Columbia University Press, 1927), pp. 29-32.

[35] Ibid., p. 37.

[36] The main difference seems to have been that Mani was not central for Bogomilism, as he was for Manichaeism. Bogomil himself did not occupy that central place, but was considered to be only the founder of the true religion, probably through a special illumination.

[37] Most significant is a sermon by the priest Kozma (translated by Sharenkoff, Manichaeism in Bulgaria, pp. 66-78). Toward the middle of the eleventh century, Archbishop Leo of Ochrid wrote to another bishop in Apulia regarding the disagreements between Eastern and Western Christians (PG, 120:835-44). This epistle was significant because it was one of the factors that led to the schism of Cerularius. Some years later, at the end of the eleventh century, Archbishop Theophylact wrote On the Royal Institution (PG, 126:257-86), in which he dealt mostly with the duties of the king. He also attempted to mediate between the East and the West, although always remaining faithful to the views of the Eastern church.

than the Byzantine. But even in its very early stages Russian Christianity began to produce significant scholars and theologians such as Cyril of Turov, Clement of Smolensk, and Hilarion of Kiev.

Cyril of Turov was a profoundly mystical preacher about whose life little is known. One of his favorite themes is the folly of the Jews in not believing in the Messiah who had come. He often interpreted the Bible allegorically, and he seemed to know the Old Testament better than the New—which he quoted erroneously.[38]

The only remaining work of Clement of Smolensk is an epistle that he wrote to a priest by the name of Thomas, who accused him of making use of so-called pagan wisdom in his interpretations of the Bible. Clement defended his biblical exegesis, and in passing offered some of his allegorical interpretations. But sometimes he did interpret the Old Testament in very literal terms. He probably was an eclectic writer who simply gathered material from various sources.[39]

There is no doubt that the most distinguished theologian of the early Russian church was Hilarion of Kiev, who was also the first Russian bishop of that city. He joined Cyril of Turov and Clement of Smolensk in interpreting the Bible as a vast allegory, and in his repeated attack on Judaism. But he went beyond this to an interpretation of history when, in his sermon *On Law and Grace,* he placed the recent conversion of Russia within the wider framework of the entire history of salvation. In spite of his tendency to allegorize Scripture, Hilarion believed that this vast scheme of history would end not in a mere spiritual world, but rather in a new world and a final resurrection.[40]

These three men, jointly with the many translations, anthologies, and adaptations of early Christian writers that were produced in the early years of Russian Christianity, were the early signs of what would later be a flourishing theological activity among Russian Christians. However, in 1236, the early

---

[38] G. P. Fedotov, *The Russian Religious Mind: Kievan Christianity* (New York: Harper, 1946), pp. 69-83.
[39] *Ibid.,* pp. 63-69.
[40] *Ibid.,* pp. 84-93.

development of Russian Christianity was interrupted by the invasion of the Mongols, under whose rule we shall find Russian Christianity when we return to Eastern theology.

Nestorian Theology

During the period that we are now studying, the church that the orthodox called "Nestorian" showed more vitality than is usually attributed to it by church historians. Although subjected to Moslem rule, this church expanded beyond the limits of the lands where the name of the Prophet was called, and penetrated into India and China. In Mesopotamia and in Persia, where it was strongest, it continued an active life. In the field of theology it produced abundant literature, and even the fraction of that production which has survived through the centuries has not been properly studied. On the other hand, it is true that most of this theological work is compilation, repetition, and commentary, and very little of it is original.

The first significant theologian whom the Nestorian community produced during the period that we are now studying was Timothy, who headed this communion between 780 and 823.[41] His remaining works are his canons,[42] some epistles,[43] and his *Debate with Mahdi*.[44] Timothy's interlocutor in this probably fictitious dialogue was the Caliph Mahdi who ruled from 775 to 785. In any case, the fact itself that the dialogue was written shows that Nestorian Christians did not simply submit to Moslem rule, but did indeed attempt to convert the followers of the Prophet. It was only centuries later, under the continuous pressure of restrictive laws, that this church became content with being a small island of believers within an ocean of Moslems. Polemics against Moslem doctrine were taken up by several writers. Probably the most remarkable among them was Elijah bar Senaya, of Nisibis, who in the eleventh century wrote, among

---

[41] His life has been studied by H. Labourt, *De Timotheo I Nestorianum Partriarcha et Christianorum Orientalium conditione sub caliphis Abbasidis* (Paris: V. Lecoffre, 1904), pp. 1-14: R. J. Bidawid, *Les lettres du Patriarche Nestorien Timothée I* (Vatican City: Biblioteca Apostolica Vaticana, 1956), pp. 1-5.
[42] Labourt, *De Timotheo*, pp. 50-86.
[43] Bidawid, *Les lettres, passim.*
[44] Edited by A. Mingana, *Timothy's Apology for Christianity* (Cambridge: W. Heffner & Sons, 1928).

other things, a *Book on the Proof of the Truth of the Faith.*[45] Through this and other similar works it is clear that the main objection that the Moslems raised to Christian doctrine was the seeming polytheism implied in belief in the Trinity. As a consequence, Nestorian theologians tended to emphasize the unity of the divine substance over the distinction between the three persons.

There were also numerous biblical commentaries. Most remarkable among them were, in the ninth century, those of Isho'dad of Merv;[46] in the eleventh, the *scholia* of Theodore bar Koni;[47] and, in the twelfth, the *Questions on the Pentateuch,* of Isho bar Nun.[48] This exegetical tradition contrasted with what was common at that time in the rest of the Christian world in that it avoided allegorical interpretations and preferred to follow the literal and historical meaning of the text. Here one sees the influence of the school of Antioch and of its great teacher Theodore of Mopsuestia, whom Nestorians believed to be the great champion of orthodoxy and whom they still called "the Interpreter." In general, most Nestorian exegetes hold the view that allegorical interpretation is "a source of blasphemy and lies," and one of the main reasons why so many Christians have followed "the stupid Origen" into error. The sacred text is to be understood in its clear literal sense, for the narratives of the Old Testament tell of true events. This does not mean that the characters and events of the Old Testament cannot be figures of the New, but they must always retain their historical veracity.

On the other hand, in all these authors one finds the characteristic traits of Antiochene Christology. For them, the *man* whom the Word assumed was a *temple* in which the divinity dwelt through a *voluntary union,* and in that union one must distinguish between the Word and the man. Thus, for instance, Elijah bar Senaya says:

> When we say that "Christ resurrected the dead and accomplished marvelous miracles," we refer to the Word who is the

---

[45] L. Horst, *Des Metropolitan Elias von Nisibis Buch vom Beweis der Wahrheit des Glaubens* (Colmar: E. Barth, 1886).

[46] *CSCO*, 126, 141, 172, 179, 229, 230 (on the Old Testament), and *HorSem*, 5-11 (on the New).

[47] *CSCO*, 55 and 69.

[48] E. G. Clarke (ed.), *The Selected Questions of Ishō Bar Nūn on the Pentateuch* (Leiden: E. J. Brill, 1962).

divine hypostasis. And if we say that "Christ ate, drank, was tired, and died," we refer to the man assumed through Mary.[49]

And, commenting on John 1:14, Isho'dad of Merv affirms:

The Word was in the flesh, that is, dwelt in it, as when someone says "Moses was the dwelling," meaning by that that he was in it, or "Joseph was the prison," meaning that he was in prison. Just as Joseph was not the prison, nor was Moses the dwelling . . . the Word was not the flesh by nature, but rather dwelt in it as in a temple.[50]

Monophysite Theology

Most of those Christians who received the title of "monophysite" after they rejected the decisions of the Council of Chalcedon now lived under moslem rule. These Christians were not united in a single body, but were distributed among the Coptic Church—and its relatively autonomous branch in Ethiopia—the Jacobite Church, and the Armenian Church.

After the Arab conquest of Egypt, the Coptic language was progressively supplanted by Arabic. Therefore, most Coptic theology after the tenth century was written in Arabic. These works, however, were mostly historical chronicles, introductory catechetical works, and attempts to reform the organization of the church.[51] In the twelfth century there was a brief controversy regarding the need for conversion. But in general, one may say that Coptic theology during this period was lacking in depth and originality. The same may be said of the Ethiopian church, whose only original literature dealt with legends of saints.

The Jacobite Church did have a measure of theological

---

[49] Quoted by E. K. Delly, *La théologie d'Élie bar-Sénaya: Étude et traduction de ses entretiens* (Rome: Pont. Univ. De Propaganda Fide, 1957), p. 50.

[50] *HorSem*, 5:212.

[51] The foremost Coptic theologian in the tenth century was Severus Abu'l ibn al'Muqaffa, who wrote several historical works as well as an *Explanation of the Fundamentals of the Christian Faith*. For a list of his works, mostly unpublished, see M. Jugie, *Theologia dogmatica Christianorum Orientalium ab Ecclesia Catholica dissidentium* (Paris: Letouzey et Ané, 1926–35), 5:461, n. 1. In the eleventh and twelfth centuries there was a movement to reform the canons, led by patriarchs Christodulos, Cyril II, Macarius II, and Gabriel ibn Tarik. See G. Graf, *Ein Reformversuch innerhalb der Koptischen Kirche im zwölfen Jahrhundert* (Paderborn: F. Schönigh, 1923); S. ibn al'Mukaffa, *History of the Patriarchs of the Egyptian Church*, Vol. II, Part III (Cairo: Publications de la Société d'Archéologie Copte, 1959).

activity. During the seventh and eighth centuries Jacob of Edessa and George of Arabia wrote on creation, Christology, and the sacraments.[52] Other authors commented on the biblical text and on Pseudo-Dionysius, and there was some thought given to such topics as predestination and the nature of the soul. In the tenth century, Arabic became the main theological language. After that time, Yahya ben Adi, often called al-Mantiqui—the dialectician—made an effort to bring classical philosophy to bear on theological questions.[53] The main thrust of Jacobite theology was polemical, directed against Moslems, Nestorians, and Copts.[54] There was also a brief debate within the Jacobite Church itself regarding the existence of providence, but those that denied it were soon condemned.[55]

The Armenian Church was going through a period of political struggle. Armenia was first subject to Moslem rule, then became semi-independent under the general overseeing of the Byzantine Empire, and finally was invaded by the Turks. Meanwhile, Little Armenia was born in Cilicia as a result of the migration of vast numbers of Armenians. In the midst of such turmoil, it is not surprising that there was not a great deal of theological activity. What little activity there was, was directed against the sects of the Paulicians and the Thondrachians, and toward union with the Byzantine Church.[56]

292 - 303

---

[52] Jugie, *Theologia*, 5:466.

[53] A. Périer, *Yahya ben Adi: Un philosophe arabe chrétien du Xᵉ siècle* (paris: J. Gabalda, 1920), lists his published works (p. 32) as well as his extant manuscripts (pp. 13-31).

[54] Yahya ben Adi wrote *On the Teaching of Jacobites and Nestorians regarding the Incarnation*. In the ninth century Isho bar Sushan wrote two treatises against the Copts, attempting to justify the Jacobite—and Nestorian—custom of preparing the eucharistic bread with flour, water, leaven, salt, and oil (Jugie, *Theologia*, 5:693-94). In the twelfth century, Patriarch Michael of Antioch was involved in another controversy with the Copts—the issue now being the need to confess one's sins before communion.

[55] Their head was John of Harran (or of Mardin). Jugie, *Theologia*, 5:471.

[56] The Paulicians were a sect of Manichaean tendencies, seemingly popular in Armenia. The Thondrachians rejected the cult of Mary and the saints, the authority of the hierarchy, monasticism, and perhaps even the doctrine of incarnation (Jugie, *Theologia*, 5:480-82). The attempts at union with the Byzantines took place under the leadership of Nerses III Glaietzi, but were fruitless. See P. Tekeyan, *Controverses christologiques en Arméno-Cilicie dans la seconde moitié du XIIᵉ siècle* (Rome: Pont. Inst. Orientalium Studiorum, 1939), pp. 14-33. The rest of the book deals with the continuation of such dialogues and their consequences within the Armenian church.

VIII

General Introduction to the Thirteenth Century

1200's

The thirteenth century was the golden period of the Middle Ages. It was the time in which the great steeples of Gothic cathedrals were raised to heaven, and also the time in which, in Innocent III, it almost seemed that heaven had descended to earth in order to rule over princes and emperors. It was the time in which the Inquisition was formally established, when universities developed, when Aristotle invaded the West, and mendicants invaded the world.

Gothic art, with its aspiration to rise to inaccessible heights, serves to point out some characteristics of thirteenth-century theology. In the first place, although the first manifestations of Gothic architecture appeared in abbeys and monasteries, its great masterpieces were cathedrals. This points to the importance that cities gained in the thirteenth century, when they became great centers of manufacturing and commerce. It also points to the fact that, while in the twelfth century it was the monastic schools that played the most important role in theological activity, in the thirteenth that role passed on to the universities, great urban schools that would henceforth eclipse monasteries as centers of learning. Second, the ordered but very complex architecture of the Gothic cathedral was parallel to the great summae of the scholastics and, in a certain manner, to the

220

crowning work of medieval literature, Dante's *Divine Comedy*. In all these constructions, each element has its proper place; but this was achieved not through a schematic simplification of reality, but rather by placing each element of reality as it was conceived—from the lowest depth of hell to the heavenly mansions—in the place proper to it within a great universal framework. The summae included the fall of Satan, the Garden of Eden, the eucharistic mystery, the nature of angels, and thousands of other subjects, and all these are also to be found depicted in stone and glass in the Gothic cathedrals. The cathedral was the theological summa of the ignorant. The scholastic theologian was an architect of thought. Third, the Gothic cathedral was parallel to scholasticism in the thirteenth century by the manner in which the cold resistance of the material was met by the warm mystical aspiration of the builder. "All expression to which Greek architecture attained was attained *through* the stone, *by means of* the stone; all expression to which Gothic architecture attained, was attained—and this is the full significance of the contrast—*in spite* of the stone."[1] The task of the Gothic architect was to make the stone as light as possible. The result envelops the believer in pillars that seem to rise to heaven like so many prayers. But it was necessary to make the weight of the stone rest on the outside arches that make the building physically sound. Therefore, the architectonic exercise consisted in combining the hard reality of stone with mystical aspiration. The scholastic theologian, likewise, produced a work in which all the weight of intellectual rigor can be found; but inside, in the intimate life of these authors, one discovers the same mystical aspiration that inspired the cathedrals. The architect could produce the mystical effect only through the mathematical balance achieved between the interior and the exterior of the cathedral. The theologian could produce the great scholastic edifice only through a balance between intellectual demand and mystical aspiration.

---

[1] W. Worringer, *Form in Gothic* (London: Alec Tiranti, 1964), p. 106.

Innocent III and Papal Authority

When the thirteenth century opened, the Holy See was occupied by Innocent III (1198–1216). Under his leadership the papacy reached the apex of its power. After reforming the curia and strengthening his authority over the papal states, Innocent III undertook the reformation and strengthening of ecclesiastical life throughout Europe. This led him to intervene in several matters in which politics were involved with morality. These interventions ranged from Armenia in the East to Iceland in the West, including an important participation in the matters of the Empire and of several other monarchies, such as those of France, Aragon, Leon, Castille, Portugal, and Poland. In Hungary, he helped to put an end to civil war. In Bohemia, he gave Ottokar the title of King. In England, after a long struggle, he humiliated King John Lackland, who was forced to turn his country into a fief of the papacy. He became regent of Sicily, which was also subject to him as a fief. During his pontificate, the Fourth Crusade, swerved from its original objective by the Venetians, took Constantinople, established in it a Latin Empire, and forced the Byzantine emperors to seek refuge in Nicea. When a Latin patriarch of Constantinople was appointed, the Eastern church was theoretically united to Rome. The pope himself, who at first deplored the excesses of the crusaders in turning upon Christians the swords that had been dedicated to combat Saracens, eventually accepted the accomplished facts and saw in them an action of providence chastising the schismatics and re-establishing the unity of the church. Meanwhile, another crusade directed against the Albigenses was devastating Provence with Innocent's blessing.

Finally, it was Innocent III who, a few months before his death, directed the deliberations of the Fourth Lateran Council, which has been repeatedly mentioned in various contexts in this *History,* for it was there that the doctrines of transubstantiation and of the eucharistic sacrifice were promulgated, the trinitarian doctrine of Joachim of Fiore was condemned, the need to broaden studies was reaffirmed, an end was put to the institution of new monastic orders with their own new rules, it was ordered that all the faithful should confess and partake of communion at least once a year, it was declared that the appointment of ecclesiastical authorities by secular princes was void, regulations were made regarding marriage among kindred, secret marriage was forbidden, the pope was given the exclusive right to introduce new relics, measures were taken against the Jews, a new crusade was called, and several other measures were taken in order to reform and regulate the life of the clergy.[2] If one takes into account the fact that all this—and a great deal more—was done by the Council in only three sessions of one day each, it is clear that its function was not to deliberate on each point, but simply to endorse an entire program of reform conceived by the pope and his curia.

This policy of ecclesiastical reformation and of intervention in the secular government of states was based on Innocent's view of the position that he as pope held. Leaving aside the more common title "Vicar of Peter," Innocent called himself "Vicar of Christ." As the representative of the Savior, he was the pastor of the entire church. Bishops represented Christ not directly, but only through the pope. Therefore, the pope had authority not only to appoint bishops, but also to depose them.[3]

Furthermore, Innocent claimed to have authority over secular rulers. The pope has been established "above peoples and kingdoms," he has received "the authority by which Samuel anointed David," and "by reason and in occasion of sin" he can depose a prince and give his title to another.[4]

As God the creator of the universe established two great lights in the heavens, the greater to preside over the day, and the smaller to preside over night, thus did he also establish two great authorities in the heaven of the universal church . . . The greater, that it might preside above souls as if they were days, and the lesser, that it might preside above bodies as if they were nights. These are the

[2] *Mansi*, 20:981-1068.
[3] *Reges.* 1. 495-96.
[4] *Ibid.* 7. 1.

pontifical authority and royal power. On the other hand, just as the Moon receives its light from the Sun . . . so does the royal power receive the splendor of its dignity from pontifical authority.[5]

The authority of the pope above the empire is not to be doubted. When the empire was involved in civil war, Innocent intervened claiming that "the business of the empire pertains to us in the first and last instances. In the first, because it was moved from Greece by the Roman Church for her defense. In the last, because, as the crown of the kingdom is always received from another, the emperor receives from us the crown of the empire."[6]

Such was the authority that the papacy claimed for itself at the height of its power. This, however, was not a radical innovation, but was rather a consequence of the importance that the papacy had for the reformist party from the end of the eleventh century. When the reformists gained possession of the papacy, their interest in improving religious and ecclesiastical life led them to stress the authority of the pope. Godfrey de la Vendôme seems to have been the first to use the metaphor of the "two swords" to refer to the spiritual and temporal powers.[7] Bernard took this metaphor and claimed that both swords belonged to the church, although she uses one directly and the other through lay government.

You must admonish them more openly; but with the Word, not with iron. Why should you once again draw the sword which you were told to sheathe? This sword, however, if someone denies that it belongs to you, does not seem to me to listen properly to the Word of the Lord, who said thus: *return thy sword to its sheath.* Thus, it is also yours, although it probably ought not to be drawn by your hand, but only by your indication. Otherwise, if it did not belong to you, when the disciple said: *we have here two swords,* the Lord would not have answered: *it is enough,* but *it is too many.* Both swords, that is, the spiritual and the material, belong to the church, and one is

---

[5] *Ibid.* 1. 401. Note once again the distinction between *power* and *authority.*

[6] *Reg. de neg. Romani Imp.* 21. This text has been very carefully analyzed by F. Kempf, *Papstum und Kaisertum bei Innocenz III: Die geistigen und rechtlichen Grundlagen seiner Thronstreitpolitik* (Rome: Gregorian University, 1954), pp. 57-65.

[7] See G. Glez, "Pouvoir du Pape dans l'ordre temporel," *DTC,* 12:267-72.

handled by the church, by the hand of the priest, while the other is
handled by the soldier, but upon the insinuation of the priest and
the command of the king.[8]

   In this text, Bernard was concerned not with temporal
authority in general, but only with the use of physical force in
order to chastise or repress spiritual evil, such as in the case of
heresy and immorality. But the struggle between secular rulers
and ecclesiastical leaders would lead theologians to claim for the
church and her hierarchy an ever-increasing authority. Thomas
Becket and his contemporary John of Salisbury believed that
kings received their authority from the church. Hugh of Saint
Victor made kings subordinate to priests. Against these views,
some moderates, such as Hugh of Fleury, held that the two
powers were independent and the priests, and even the pope,
did not have any other power over kings and princes than that of
admonishing them for their sins. Others, finally, took the
royalist position. Most noteworthy among these was Gregory of
Catina, who claimed that the emperor was the head of the
church as well as of the empire. In the thirteenth century,
through the actions of Innocent III and his successors in political
matters, the theory developed according to which the pope
possesses both swords directly, and he therefore has the
authority to depose kings and emperors. Such were the views of
Simon of Tournai, Lawrence of Spain, John the Teuton, and,
above all, Henry Bartholomew of Susa and his disciple William
Durand.
   This emphasis on papal authority reached its peak in the last
pope of the thirteenth century, Boniface VIII, who in his bull
Unam sanctam, given on November 18, 1302, after affirming the
unity of the church under the pope as the "Vicar of Christ," went
on to quote almost literally the words of Bernard which we have
quoted above, and then said:

> But one sword must be under the other, and temporal authority
> must be subject to spiritual power. . . . Therefore we must clearly
> acknowledge that the spiritual power is superior in dignity and

---

[8] *De cons.* 4. 3. 7.

ability to the earthly one, just as spiritual things precede those
which are temporal. . . . For taking truth as its witness, it behooves
the spiritual authority to institute an earthly one, and to judge it if
it is not good. . . . Therefore, if the earthly power goes wayward,
it shall be judged by the spiritual. But if a lesser spiritual power
abandons the right way, it shall be judged by a higher spiritual
power. However, *if the supreme spiritual authority abandons the right
way, it can only be judged by God, and not by men.* . . . Therefore
anyone who opposes this power resists the command of God. . . .
On the other hand, we declare, affirm, and define that *it is
absolutely necessary for the salvation of all human creatures that they be
subject to the Roman Pontiff.*[9]

It is ironic and significant that the pope who made such claims
brought to an end the long succession of powerful popes which
began with Gregory VII, culminated in Innocent III, and
crumbled with Boniface VIII, who was attacked, not only by the
University of Paris and Philip the Fair, but also by various
factions in Italy itself. Boniface died in 1303, and in 1309 the
papacy was transferred to Avignon, where it would be an easy
tool of French policies.

The Inquisition

The thirteenth century saw the beginning of the Inquisition as
a pontifical institution.[10] From very ancient times it was generally
believed that bishops were responsible for the refutation and
destruction of error. Before the time of Constantine, this could
be done only through theological arguments and excommunication, for bishops had no other coercive powers. After the
Council of Nicea, the emperor exiled those who had been
condemned by that assembly. Shortly thereafter, Priscillian was
killed by the secular authorities through the counsel of a number
of bishops, but to the horror of most. Throughout the entire
Middle Ages, heretics were physically punished, although this

---

[9] *Corp. iur. can. extrav. comm.* 1. 8 Italics are mine.
[10] See E. van der Vekené, *Bibliographie der Inquisition* (Hildesheim: G. Olms, 1963). On the
thirteenth century, see A. C. Shannon, *The Popes and Heresy in the Thirteenth Century* (Villanova, Pa.:
Augustinian Press, 1949), and H. Maisonneuve, *Études sur les origines de l'Inquisition* (Paris: J. Vrin,
1960).

was usually limited to imprisonment or flagellation. However, in the eleventh century, and especially in France and Germany, the burning and hanging of heretics became increasingly common. In such cases, the action was usually taken by the civil courts or by an enraged mob. But in 1231 Gregory IX instituted pontifical inquisition by commissioning "inquisitors of heretical depravity" who were to act as judges with extraordinary powers in order to uproot heresy. Some historians claim that the pope's purpose was to stop the abuses that often took place in the trial of heretics, where civil authorities used accusations of heresy for political or economic ends. It is true that many of the early inquisitors were moderate, and that the pope took drastic measures to restrain those who seemed to be excessively cruel—such as Robert the Bulgarian. The accused were generally condemned to a particular form of penance or to imprisonment. When the ecclesiastical tribunal believed that they should be killed, they were turned over to the "secular arm" with a plea for mercy. But such a plea was purely formal, and capital punishment was practically automatic. In general, most inquisitors were members of the Dominican order, although some of them were Franciscans.

Although at first the Inquisition did not have great impact on the main centers of theological thought, its origin is noted here because it eventually became one of the great factors hindering freedom and originality.

The Growth of Universities

One of the most significant developments for the history of Christian thought in the thirteenth century was the birth and growth of the universities.[11] At first, these institutions were called "general studies," which meant that they included students and professors from various parts of Europe. Later this title came to mean that the graduates of such institutions had the right to teach at any other center—*jus ubique docendi*. The name

---

[11] The classical study is that of H. Rashdall, *The Universities of Europe in the Middle Ages*, 3 vols. (Oxford: Clarendon Press, 1895). See also A. L. Gabriel, *Garlandia: Studies in the History of the Medieval University* (Frankfurt am Main: J. Knecht, 1969).

"university," which originally referred to the association of students and professors, slowly changed its meaning, until it became the title of the institution itself.

The origin of the most ancient modern universities—Paris, Salerno, Bologna, and Oxford—dates from the twelfth century, and is to be found in a combination of factors such as the tradition of the cathedral schools, the growth of cities, the organization of guilds, and the general development of science. Most of these institutions became famous in a particular field of study in which they specialized. Because Paris and Oxford had the best theological faculties, Western theology during the thirteenth century revolved around those two great university centers.

Although requirements varied from place to place, a candidate for theological studies usually became a student at the Arts Faculty when he was sixteen or seventeen years old. He later went on to theological studies, in which he had to spend a long period—about eight years in the thirteenth century, sixteen in the fourteenth, and fifteen in the fifteenth. During these years, the student was first a hearer, then a bachelor who in turn commented on the Bible and the *Sentences* of Peter Lombard, and finally a "formed bachelor," who devoted several years to various academic exercises consisting mostly in formal *disputationes*. He then received his master's degree, which was followed by a doctorate. In order to receive the latter, one had to be at least thirty-five years old—although in very special cases, such as that of Thomas Aquinas, this rule was suspended.

Apart from the commentaries on the Bible and on the *Sentences* which have already been mentioned, the most important academic exercises were the various examinations, usually oral; the *collationes*, sermons of about one hour which the formed bachelors delivered in the afternoons; and the *disputationes*. The latter were the academic exercise par excellence. Depending on the nature of the exercise, the question to be discussed was sometimes chosen in advance, and sometimes chosen at the very beginning of the exercise itself. Those present—including the public—then offered arguments for or against various solutions to the question. Finally, usually in another session, the teacher who was leading the exercise offered his own answer and solved the objections raised in the first session.

As a consequence of this method, the final structure of scholastic writings is usually the same. First, a question is posed; then arguments for the various positions are offered; then the solution is presented; and finally the various arguments that seem to oppose that solution are refuted. Here one may hear an echo of Abelard's *Sic et non.*

Thus, the universities provided not only the atmosphere and the necessary facilities for the great theological flourishing of the thirteenth century, but also the conditions that determined the structure of the scholastic method.

The Mendicant Orders

The thirteenth century saw the birth of a new style of ascetic life which differed from traditional monasticism in that it did not withdraw from the great centers of population in order to devote itself to mystical contemplation, but rather saw the "apostolate" as its basic function, and therefore transformed the ancient patterns of monastic life and adapted them to the task of preaching and teaching. The social and economic conditions of the times, with the growth of cities and the development of commerce, required new forms of ministry. Various heresies—especially that of the Albigenses—had to be refuted through a combination of intellectual ability and holiness of life. New fields were being opened for missions beyond the traditional borders of Christianity. The mendicant orders were the response of Western Christianity to these challenges.

From our point of view, the two most significant orders were the Preachers of Saint Dominic and the Friars Minor of Saint Francis.

Dominic was a canon in Osma when he and his bishop, Diego de Azevedo, were sent by Alfonso VIII on a diplomatic mission. While in southern France, they met some Albigenses, whom they tried to convince of their error. Sometime later Diego and Dominic requested authorization from the pope to go as missionaries to the barbarians, but Innocent III seems to have redirected their interest toward the refutation of the Albigenses. After a period of joint work, Diego returned to his diocese, and Dominic remained in charge of the enterprise. A few years later he decided that a new order was needed which would follow some of the traditional strains of monasticism, but which would be devoted to refuting heresy through intellectual means and through the example of a holy life. In 1215, he requested permission from the pope to organize such an order; but the Fourth Lateran Council, following the suggestion of Innocent III, had decided that no new monastic rules were to be approved. Dominic then discussed the matter with his followers, and they decided to adopt the so-called Rule of Saint Augustine—and therefore were known for a time as "regular canons of Saint Augustine."

From its very origin, this new order insisted on the importance of study for the accomplishment of its task. Monastic life was adapted to the needs of study, preaching, and the care of souls. At first, the Dominicans centered their study and teaching in their own monasteries. But they soon came to occupy chairs at the main universities, especially Paris and Oxford. As early as 1217 there were Dominicans in Paris, and the first monastery of the order in England was founded at Oxford in 1220.[12] In Paris, the Dominicans had their own center of studies. When in 1229 the University disbanded itself, the Dominicans began admitting secular students to the classes of Friar Roland of Cremona. When the University was reorganized, Roland remained as one of its teachers, and thus the Dominicans gained their first theological chair in Paris. Later, John of Saint Giles, who was already a teacher at the University, took the Dominican habit, and now the order had two professors in the University.[13] The Dominicans gained a foothold at Oxford in 1227, when Roger Bacon, who was already a professor in the University, joined the Order. Around 1240, Richard Fishacre, who was already a member of the Order, became a professor of theology, so that from that time on there were usually at least two Dominicans

---

[12] *Ibid.*, 1:347.
[13] *Ibid.*, 1:373.

teaching theology in that University. However, the two outstanding Dominican theologians of the thirteenth century were Albert the Great and Thomas Aquinas, whom we shall study in a later chapter.

The Order of Friars Minor, founded by Francis of Assisi, had a very complicated history of which we can offer only an outline here. The ideal of Francis was an absolute simplicity of life marked by poverty, humility, and the contemplation of Christ. Primitive Franciscanism was very similar to the original Waldensian movement—except that Innocent III had the good sense to see how the Franciscans could fit within the total structure of the church. The early Franciscans were mostly laymen, and they went about in pairs preaching and exhorting others to follow the way of poverty. Francis, who was himself a man of moderate culture, never held study in high esteem. The primitive organization that he devised was flexible to the point that it was almost nonexistent.

However, the very growth of the Order made it necessary to mitigate the rigor of primitive Franciscan life. The *Rule* of 1223 did not allow the Franciscans, as individuals or as an order, to hold property. Francis left behind a *Will* in which he forbade his friars from requesting that the *Rule* be mitigated in any way, especially in that which had to do with poverty. But the phenomenal growth of the order made greater organization necessary, and this in turn posed the question of properties. For years, the Franciscans were divided into two parties—the rigorists and the moderates.[14] In 1230, Gregory IX declared that Francis' *Will* was not binding upon the friars. In 1245, Innocent IV tried to solve the problem by declaring that the goods and lands that the members of the order had to hold for their use were the property of the Holy See. This was clearly a subterfuge. While John of Parma was Minister General of the order (1247–1257), the rigorist party grew, and was also infiltrated by the eschatological ideas of Joachim of Fiore. The year 1260, of great importance in Joachimist expectations, was drawing near,

---

[14] H. Holzapfel, *Handbuch der Geschichte des Franziskaner-Ordens* (Freiburg im Breisgau: Herder, 1909), pp. 21-44.

and some of the strict Franciscans came to identify themselves with what Joachim had called the "church of the Holy Spirit." Naturally, this led them dangerously close to heresy. It was in the midst of this situation that John of Parma was succeeded by Bonaventure (1257–1274), who has been called "the second founder" of the Order. Bonaventure was an able administrator who did much to give the Order what would be its final form. He suppressed the protests of the rigorists by forcibly secluding their leaders in monasteries. In reaction, the rigorists moved further and further away from the order, and Joachimism among them became more marked. After 1274, the "Spirituals"—a name that the rigorist Franciscans took—were openly persecuted, and they finally disappeared early in the fourteenth century.[15]

The establishment of the Friars Minor in the universities was part of this total history of the movement of the Order toward less rigorism. The early Franciscans did not attempt to become teachers in the main centers of theological activity. But the appeal of the Order itself was such that several university professors decided to join it. The first to take this step in Paris was Alexander of Hales, who in 1236 took the Franciscan habit and thus became the first member of his order to hold a chair of theology. He was later succeeded by Jean de la Rochelle, Odo Rigaud, and Bonaventure. In Oxford, the first Franciscan teacher was Adam Marsh, who taught there from 1247 to 1250.[16] In Cambridge, the Order of Saint Francis penetrated around 1230, when the University was still in its formative stage.[17]

The presence of the friars in the various universities soon drew the opposition of the older teachers.[18] A number of professors at Paris, led by William of Saint Amour, took a series of measures against the friars, culminating in their expulsion from the university in 1253. Innocent IV was not firm in his

[15] Ibid., pp. 44-80; D. S. Muzzey, The Spiritual Franciscans (New York: Columbia University Press, 1907); E. Benz, Ecclesia spiritualis: Kirchenidee und Geschichtstheologie der franziskanischen Reformation (Stuttgart: W. Kolhammer, 1934).
[16] A. G. Little, The Grey Friars in Oxford (Oxford: Clarendon Press, 1892), pp. 29-34.
[17] J. R. H. Moorman, The Grey Friars in Cambridge: 1225-1538 (Cambridge: The University Press, 1952), pp. 19-38.
[18] Rashdall, The Universities of Europe in the Middle Ages, pp. 370-97; M. M. Dufeil, Guillaume de Saint-Amour et la polémique universitaire parisienne (Paris: A. et J. Picard, 1972).

support of the mendicant professors, but his successor, Alexander IV, and King Louis of France were their staunch defenders. In 1254, William of Saint Amour published a *Book on the Antichrist and His Ministers*, in which he attacked the spiritual Franciscan Gerardo de Borgo San Donino. But in this work—as well as later in his treatise *On the Dangers of the Latter Times*—he attacked not only the spiritual Franciscans, but the principle of voluntary poverty itself, which was basic for the mendicant orders. He was refuted by Bonaventure and Thomas Aquinas, condemned by Pope Alexander IV, and exiled by the king. His campaign was carried on by Gerard of Abbeville, who drew new refutations from the friars. But the outcome had already been decided, and from that time on the friars were firmly established in the university—except in the Arts Faculty, from which they were excluded.

The Introduction of Aristotle and of Arabic and Jewish Philosophy

While we were studying the twelfth century, we saw that there was a constant controversy regarding the use of dialectical reason in the field of theology. This debate took place when only a small fraction of the philosophy of Aristotle was known. It was to be expected that the problems would be multiplied when the rest of peripatetic philosophy became known, especially since that philosophy was incompatible in many points with the Augustinian Neoplatonism that was the philosophical foundation on which medieval theology had been built.

This basic problem of the incompatibility between Aristotle and what had become traditional philosophy was complicated by other factors. In the first place, many of the works of Aristotle reached the Latin West through a roundabout way, in translations that had gone from Greek to Syriac, then to Arabic, then—verbally—to incipient Spanish, and finally to Latin. Quite obviously, these translations were not always a faithful reflection of the original text, and therefore some scholars, such as Gerard of Cremona and Henry Aristippus, both late in the twelfth century, devoted themselves to the production of direct translations from the Greek text.[19] In the second place, Aristotle made his appearance in medieval Latin Christianity in the company of several Arabic and Jewish philosophers. Although often these philosophers claimed to be no more than expounders of the philosophy of Aristotle, the truth was that they introduced ideas that did not necessarily follow from the peripatetic system.[20]

Al-Kindi,[21] generally known as the "philosopher of the Arabs," wrote in the ninth century a treatise On the Intellect and the Intelligible, which was widely read by Latin theologians in the thirteenth century. He combined a basically Aristotelian outlook with some elements that ultimately came from Plotinus, but that he believed to be genuinely Aristotelian. His views regarding the active intellect, which later Latin philosophers tended to attribute almost exclusively to Averroës, seem to have been rather common among Arabic philosophers. He believed that the active intellect, that is, the intellect that produces intelligible objects and imprints them on the passive intellect, is a single and common spiritual being shared by all people, and not to be confused with their individual souls.[22]

Al-Farabi,[23] late in the ninth century and early in the tenth, defended the compatibility of the various philosophical systems of antiquity, and thus produced an eclectic philosophy in which the logic and some aspects of the metaphysics of Aristotle were combined with mystical tendencies of Neoplatonic origin. He combined Aristotelian psychology with Neoplatonism, and identified the active intellect of Aristotle with one of the "intellects" of the celestial spheres.

Al-Farabi's theory of the unity of the active intellect was adopted by Avicenna (ibn-Sina),[24] through whom it became known throughout the Latin West.[25] On the other hand,

---

[19] F. van Steenberghen, Aristotle in the West: The Origins of Latin Aristotelianism (Louvain: E. Nauwelaerts, 1955), pp. 62-63.
[20] This was due not always to the inventiveness of these philosophers, but also to the fact that some Neoplatonic writings—notably the Liber de causis—were circulating under the name of Aristotle.
[21] A. Fouad El-Ehwany, "Al-Kindi," in M. M. Sharif, ed., A History of Muslim Philosophy (Wiesbaden: O. Harrassowitz, 1963), 1:421-34.
[22] Gilson, History, pp. 183-84.
[23] I. Madkour, "Al-Farabi," in Shariff, History, 1:450-68.
[24] F. Rahman, "Ibn Sina," in Shariff, History, 1:480-506; G. Verbeke, Avicenna, Grundleger einer neuen Metaphysik (Wiesbaden: Westdeutscher Verlag, 1983).
[25] Gilson, History, pp. 187-216.

Avicenna developed the distinction between essence and existence,[26] which al-Farabi had proposed, and thus established a distinction between the necessary being, whose existence belongs to its essence, and contingent beings, whose existence is an accident. This distinction would have made it possible for him to follow orthodox Moslem doctrine, affirming the doctrine of creation and divine occasionalism.[27] But his conception of the necessary being does not allow him to do so, for the actions of this being are so connected with its essence that they are themselves necessary; and therefore created beings, although contingent in themselves, are necessary as effects of the first cause. In consequence, the world is eternally produced by God, and "the entire Avicennian cosmogony is ruled by an emanationist and monist understanding of the creative power of God."[28]

Al-Ghazzali[29] was an orthodox Moslem who wrote a treatise on *The Intentions of Philosophers,* attempting to show the weak points of their reasoning. But the Latin West had only this work of his, without further commentary, and therefore believed that he was a disciple and defender of the very philosophers whom he attempted to refute.[30]

By far the most significant and famous of Arabic philosophers was Averroës (ibn-Rushd),[31] who was born in Cordoba in 1126. His intellectual curiosity led him to study theology, medicine, jurisprudence, and several other subjects. He believed to have found in Aristotle the "supreme truth," although this did not lead him to reject the Koran but only to interpret it "philosophically." He died in 1198, after conflicting with Moslem authorities for whom his views were suspect. His commentaries on the various works of Aristotle soon became so

---

[26] A. M. Goichon, *La distinction de l'essence et de l'existence d'après Ibn Sina* (Paris: Desclée de Brouwer, 1937).

[27] On this point, see M. Fakhry, *Islamic Occasionalism and Its Critique by Averroes and Aquinas* (London: Allen and Unwin, 1958), especially pp. 56-82, which deal with al-Ghazzali.

[28] L. Gardet, *La pensée religieuse d'Avicenne* (Paris: J. Vrin, 1951), p. 68. See also Goichon, *La distinction,* pp. 201-24.

[29] On his true doctrine, see M. Saees Sheikh and A. Khaliq, "Al-Ghazāli," in Shariff, *History,* 1:581-642.

[30] Gilson, *History,* p. 216.

[31] A brief introduction to his philosophy is L. Gauthier, *Ibn Rochd (Averroès)* (Paris: University Press of France, 1948). See also Gilson, *History,* pp. 216-25.

famous that he was generally known as "the Commentator."
There were three main points in the philosophy of Averroës at
which he conflicted with orthodoxy, not only Moslem but also
Christian: the relationship between faith and reason, the
eternity of the world, and the unity of the active intellect.

Concerning the relationship between faith and reason, the
inner thoughts of Averroës are not entirely clear.[32] There is no
doubt that he sets out from a basically aristocratic view.
According to him, there are various levels of intelligence, and
each corresponds to a level of interpretation of reality: faith for
those who are content with rhetoric and authority; theology for
those who wish to have a reasonable understanding; and
philosophy for the privileged intellects that require strict and
undeniable proof. The question is how Averroës solved the
conflicts that would inevitably arise between assertions coming
from one or another of these three levels. "Through reason I
necessarily conclude that the intellect is one; but through faith I
firmly hold the opposite."[33] What does this mean? Does it mean
that there are two levels of truth and that these are mutually
contradictory? Does it mean that the philosopher, out of concern
for the common good, accepts outwardly what is known to be
false? Does it mean that faith corrects a hidden error of reason?
The explicit answer of Averroës to these questions is clear: when
reason leads to a conclusion that is contrary to faith, the
authority of the latter is to prevail. But it is impossible to know
whether Averroës was sincere at this point, or was simply
avoiding the accusation of heterodoxy. In any case, in the
University of Paris during the thirteenth century, the title of
"Averroists" was given to those who defended the independence
of philosophy to follow its own course, even if it were to arrive at
conclusions opposed to the tenets of faith. They were also
accused of holding the "Averroistic" doctrine of "double
truth"—a doctrine that was never held by Averroës or by them.
As to the eternity of the world, Averroës believed that it

---

[32] L. Gauthier, La theorie d'Ibn Rochd (Averroès) sur les rapports de la religion et de la philosophie (Paris: E. Leroux, 1909).
[33] Quoted by E. Gilson, La filosofía en la Edad Media (Madrid: Gredos, 1958), 1:449.

followed necessarily from the nature of God as a prime unmoved mover,[34] as well as from the doctrine of the thirty-eight movers of the celestial spheres, or "pure acts," which he deducts from complicated astronomical arguments. "In order that the motor action of these pure acts may be continual, movement and things moved must also be so. The world, therefore, has certainly always existed, and will continue always to exist. In short, the duration of the world is eternal."[35] Naturally, this theory found strong opposition among Christians, who had come to affirm the doctrine of creation out of nothing as part of Christian orthodoxy.

Finally, Averroës agreed with one of the main traditions of Arabic philosophy in affirming the unity of the active intellect, which implied a denial of individual immortality. According to him, an individual only has a passive intellect pertaining to the body and dying with it. The active intellect illuminates the passive intellect so that it may know the forms of things. This illumination produces the material intellect, which is no more than the temporary individualization of one's active intellect. When one dies, nothing of the personality remains, for the active intellect, the sole survivor, is common to all.[36]

Besides these three points which were very widely debated when his works became generally known, Averroës was also significant in that he lent his support to Aristotelian empiricism over against the traditional Augustinian doctrine of illumination. His view of universals, which was particularly Aristotelian, reinforced the position of the moderate realists, who held that universals are in things and are known through a process of abstraction.

Two Jewish philosophers who had lived among the Arabs were also influential in Western Europe beginning with the thirteenth century: Solomon ibn Gabirol (Avicebron), and Maimonides (Moses ben Maimon). These two philosophers

---

[34] On his forerunners on this point, see M. Worms, *Die Lehre von der Anfanglosigkeit der Welt bei den mittelalterlichen arabischen Philosophen des Orients* (Münster: Aschendorff, 1900).
[35] Gilson, *History*, p. 222.
[36] P. S. Christ, "The Psychology of the Active Intellect in Averroes" (Doctoral dissertation, University of Pennsylvania, 1926).

followed divergent directions that foreshadowed the various directions that the two great Christian theological schools of the thirteenth century would follow.

Ibn Gabirol was born in Malaga, Andalusia. Although he was also viewed as a poet and statesman, the Latin Middle Ages knew him as the author of *The Source of Life*. The scholastics did not seem to have been aware that he was a Jew—some quote him as a Moslem, and others as a Christian. In any case, ibn Gabirol followed the tradition of Philo in bringing together Judaism and Platonic Philosophy, although he did show that he was influenced by Moslem theology.[37] His cosmology was typically Neoplatonic, and the same is true of the manner in which he understood the relationship between celestial spheres, and that between concrete objects and their forms or ideas. But in dealing with the origin of the world ibn Gabirol abandoned Neoplatonism in order to affirm that the world was created through the Will of God, and not through a necessary series of emanations. In his philosophy, this Will of God is roughly equivalent to the Logos of Philo; but this change of name shows that he believed that the divine Will is prior to reason and that the creator is therefore a reasonable will more than a willing reason. The distinction between God and his creatures rests basically on the composite nature of the latter, for all creatures, including souls and angels, consist of form and matter. This theory, generally known as the "hylomorphic composition of intellectual creatures," was one of the points of disagreement between the Augustinians of the thirteenth century—who accepted it—and nascent Thomism. On the other hand, each created individual receives several superimposed forms, which progressively determine it. This theory of the "plurality of forms" was another of the points debated among the scholastics during the thirteenth century.

The philosophy of Maimonides is very different from that of ibn Gabirol, for, although it is also a synthesis of Aristotelianism,

---

[37] M. Wittmann, *Zur Stellung Avencebrol's (Ibn-Gabirol's) im Entwicklungsgang der arabischen Philosophie* (Münster: Aschendorff, 1905), p. 74: "One can no longer speak of a mere borrowing from an ancient system. . . . Even unwittingly, the ancient ideas take on a new form when being transplanted into a new intellectual world. . . . The outer structure of Neoplatonism remains; but most of the contents are changed."

Platonism, and Judaism, in the case of Maimonides, Aristotelianism made a greater contribution than Neoplatonism. For
him, as later for Thomas Aquinas, Aristotle was the philosopher
par excellence. His best known work among Christian scholastics
was his *Guide for the Perplexed,* addressed to those who found it
difficult to conciliate the doctrine of Scripture with the data of
philosophical reasoning. He did not believe that such a conflict
was real, for, although there are revealed truths that reason
cannot prove, these truths are not really opposed to reason, but
are rather above it. One such truth is the doctrine of creation, for
the arguments against it and for the eternity of the world are not
definitive, as some claim. But the opposite, that is, that the world
has been created by God out of nothing, cannot be proved.
Therefore, the doctrine of creation can be accepted through
faith without any decisive rational argument, but also without
doing violence to reason.[38] This position is closely parallel to that
which Thomas Aquinas would later take. The same may be said
of the method through which Maimonides attempted to prove
the existence of God. This method consists in starting with that
which we know of the universe through the senses and from it to
prove the need for a first cause to explain its existence. Thus, for
instance, the many contingent beings require the existence of a
necessary being that is the source of their existence, and
movement requires a prime unmoved mover.

Toward the end of the twelfth century, and especially during
the thirteenth, the translation of the works of these various
writers opened to Western Christianity rich fields hitherto
unknown. Many of these works stimulated the study of the
natural sciences—astronomy, medicine, optics, etc.—in which
the Arab world, as an heir of Greek antiquity, was further
advanced than the Christian world. But a great deal of this
science was united to a philosophy that was different from that
which Christian tradition had used in developing its theology.
Furthermore, that philosophy seemed to lead to conclusions that

---

[38] A. Cohen, *The Teachings of Maimonides* (New York: Ktav Publishing House, 1968), pp. 50-54.

were clearly unorthodox, such as the eternity of the world[39] and the unity of the active intellect. Therefore, philosophers and theologians in the Latin West were forced to make a difficult decision when faced by the new science.

The Arts Faculty of the University of Paris enthusiastically embraced the new science.[40] As a result, a synod gathered at Paris in 1210—the same that condemned Amalric of Bena and David of Dinant—issued a prohibition of the works of Aristotle having to do with "natural philosophy"—that is, everything except his logic and his ethics. In 1215, this prohibition was ratified by the chancellor of the University, Robert of Courçon.[41] However, the philosophy of Aristotle was still studied elsewhere, for the University of Toulouse advertised on the basis of the freedom that existed within it to read the books of Aristotle. In 1231 Gregory IX appointed a commission to examine these books and to determine what errors were to be found in them; but the death of its main member, William of Auxerre, put an end to this project. In 1245, Innocent IV extended to Toulouse the prohibition that for some years had been in existence in Paris. Meanwhile, at Oxford, Robert Grosseteste[42] and several col-

---

[39] F. van Steenberghen, "La controverse sur l'éternité du monde au XIIIᵉ siècle," *Bulletin des Lettres et des Sciences, Acad. Roy. de Belgique*, ser. V, 58 (1972) 267-87; O. Argerami, "La cuestión 'De aeternitate mundi': Posiciones doctrinales," *Sap*, 27 (1972), 313-34; 28 (1973), 99-124, 179-208; O. Argerami, "Ortodoxia y heterodoxia: En torno a la cuestión 'De aeternitate mundi,' " *PatMed*, 3 (1982), 3-19; L. Bianchi, *L'errore di Aristotele: La polemica contro l'eternità del mondo nel XIII secolo* (Florence: Nuova Italia, 1984). On the larger issues of the period, see E. Tresmontant, *La métaphysique du Christianisme et la crise du treizième siècle,"* (Paris: Éditions du Seuil, 1964). On another controversy that has been generally ignored by historians, see B. C. Bazán, "Intellectum speculativum: Averroes, Thomas Aquinas and Siger of Brabant on the Intelligible Object," *JHP*, 19 (1981), 425-46.

[40] At first, Latin scholars knew little or nothing of Averroes. It was in the third decade of the century that Averroes became generally known, and as a result the controversies over the new philosophy increased. See R. A. Gauthier, "Notes sur les débuts (1225-1240) de premier 'averroïsme,' " *RScPhTh*, 66 (1982), 321-74.

[41] E. Bertola, "Le proibizioni di Aristotele del 1210 e del 1215 e il problema dell'anima," *RFilNSc*, 72 (1965), 725-51.

[42] D. A. Callus, *Introduction of Aristotelian Learning to Oxford* (London: H. Milford, 1943); A. C. Crombie, *Robert Grosseteste and the Origins of Experimental Science* (Oxford: Clarendon Press, 1953); F. M. Powicke, *Robert Grosseteste and the Nicomachean Ethics* (H. Milford, 1930); L. Baur, *Die Philosophie des Robert Grosseteste Bischofs von Lincoln* (Münster: Aschendorff, 1917); C. Geiben, "Bibliographia universa Roberti Grosseteste," *CollFran*, 39 (1969), 362-418. To this bibliography should be added K. D. Hill, "Robert Grosseteste and His Work of Greek Translation," in D. Baker, ed., *The Orthodox Churches and the West* (Oxford: B. Blackwell, 1976), pp. 213-22; J. McEvoy, *The Philosophy of Robert Grosseteste* (Oxford: Clarendon, 1982); C. A. Lértora, "Ciencia y método en Roberto Grosseteste," *Hum*, 18 (1977), 153-82. Grosseteste is especially interesting because, while he stimulated the study of the new science and the new philosophy, he was theologically conservative. This shows that in his time the conflict had not been sharply drawn.

leagues translated and commented on the works of Aristotle.[43] It was from England, through the influence of Roger Bacon[44] and Robert Kilwardby[45] just before the middle of the century, that the interest in the "natural books" of Aristotle was again introduced in Paris.[46] These two teachers from Oxford taught at the Arts Faculty of Paris in 1237 and 1247, and there reintroduced the study of the books that had been formerly forbidden. After that time, little attention seems to have been given to the various decrees against Aristotle. At the same time—around 1230—the first versions of Averroës were reaching Paris. The doctrines to be found therein made the issue much more urgent.

Faced by the question of the extent to which the new philosophy was to be accepted and employed in the task of theology, the thirteenth century offered three different answers that roughly correspond to the next three chapters of this History.

In the first place, some theologians retained the traditional philosophical framework, although often incorporating some Aristotelian elements. This position was most common during the first half of the century, when the depth and extent of the conflict between Aristotelianism and traditional philosophy had not become clear. The most outstanding example of this attitude is Bonaventure, who knew and respected Aristotle but did not attempt to adjust his entire metaphysical system to the new philosophy.

Second, some theologians faced the new challenge with more daring. They assimilated Aristotle and at the same time retained a great deal of the traditional Augustinianism, thus producing a coherent synthesis. Such was the direction followed by Albert the Great and Thomas Aquinas.

---

[43] E. Franceschini, "Roberto Grossatesta, vescovo di Lincoln, e le sue traduzione latine," *Atti del Reale Instituto Veneto di Scienze, Lettere ed Arti,* 2 (1933), 1-138.

[44] The bibliography on Bacon is very abundant, for he has been studied because of his interest in experimental science, his small respect for theologians, and his own superstitions. A good introduction may be found in D. C. Lindberg, ed., *Roger Bacon's Philosophy of Nature* (Oxford: Clarendon, 1983).

[45] D. E. Sharp, "The *De ortu scientiarum* of Robert Kilwardby (d. 1279)," *NSch,* 8 (1934), 1-30.

[46] F. van Steenberghen, *The Philosophical Movement in the Thirteenth Century* (Edinburgh: Nelson, 1955), pp. 46-48. See also R. T. Gunther, *Early Science in Oxford,* 4 vols. (Oxford: University Press, 1921-25).

Finally, in the Arts Faculty of Paris a group of teachers claimed independence for philosophy from the requirements of orthodoxy. Very often these teachers followed not only Aristotle, but also his "Commentator" Averroës, and therefore they have been rather inexactly called "Latin Averroists." The main exponent of this position was Siger of Brabant.

The next three chapters will be devoted to the main representatives of each of these positions—although the discussion will not be limited to the manner in which they reacted to the new philosophy.

IX

The Augustinian Tradition in the Thirteenth Century

Throughout the first centuries of the Middle Ages, Augustine was the main teacher of Western theologians. His works were quoted as a source of authority in theological questions. His only rival in this field was Gregory the Great; but this actually strengthened the influence of Augustine, for the work of Gregory was a popularization of Augustinianism. On the other hand, Gregory, who had followed the teachings of Augustine in other matters, had mitigated his views on predestination, grace, and free will. Therefore, medieval theologians saw in Augustine not so much the doctor of grace and predestination as the teacher of contemplation and theological investigation. The few who became aware of the forgotten aspects of the theology of the great bishop of Hippo were rejected in the name of traditional theology, and even in the name of Augustine, as was the case with Gottschalk.

However, although Western theology had been basically Augustinian for centuries, in the thirteenth century there was a special consciousness of this fact. After the early debates, which we have already discussed,[1] there was no basic opposition to the theology and the philosophy of Augustine, for the entire

---

[1] See above, pp. 57-61.

intellectual tradition of the Latin West was dominated by that Neoplatonism of which he had made use and which he had helped to make dominant. In philosophical matters, the differences between Pseudo-Dionysius and Augustine were minor, and early medieval scholars found ways to conciliate them. Although Aristotle was read and studied in the schools, it was mostly his logic that was known, and this could easily be adapted to fit the framework of Augustinian philosophy. But in the thirteenth century a new situation arose: with the introduction of the new philosophy real alternatives to traditional theology were opened. Therefore, those theologians who followed traditional theology took Augustine as their symbol and devoted themselves to producing a consciously Augustinian theology.

In this chapter we shall first summarize the basic characteristics of this theological school, in order then to study two of its main representatives—Alexander of Hales and Bonaventure.

The first point of conflict between the Augustinians and their opponents was the role that should be played in theology by Plato and Aristotle. Naturally, this referred not to the teachings of these philosophers in their original form, but rather to that which thirteenth century scholars believed to be so. Therefore, the Augustinians were defending not simply Plato, but the entire Neoplatonic tradition that was represented in Christian theology by Augustine and Pseudo-Dionysius. Aristotle seemed to them too much a rationalist and too concerned for the knowledge of things of this world. Over against him, the mystical tendencies of Neoplatonism gave that philosophical tradition a religious aura. Was it not true that it was through his reading of the "Platonists" that Augustine was led to the gospel?

As was to be expected, this new form of Platonism was faithful to the manner in which Christian tradition had adapted ancient philosophy to its own needs. Thus, for instance, eternal ideas were held to subsist not in themselves, but rather in the mind of God, so that only God is eternal in the strict sense. On the other hand, this opposition between the supposedly Platonic and the Aristotelian involved two different ways of understanding the function of theology and its relationship with philosophy. Most Augustinians did not believe that there was a clear line of demarcation between revealed and rational truth. After all, had not Augustine taught that all knowledge is a divine illumination? Over against this the Aristotelians distinguished clearly between reason and revelation, and therefore between philosophy and theology.

This leads to another characteristic of Augustinianism: its theory of knowledge, which followed the doctrine of illumination as it had been expounded by Augustine. These theologians would insist that real knowledge is not that which is derived from the bodily senses, but rather that which one has apart from them. Over against this view, those who followed Aristotle and the new philosophy held an epistemology in which the senses had an important function.

As a consequence of this divergence in the theory of knowledge, there was a further difference regarding the proof of the existence of God. The Augustinians followed Anselm in claiming that the bodily senses could not serve as an adequate point of departure from which to prove the existence of God, and that in any case that existence was implicit in the idea itself of God. The followers of the new science offered proofs of the existence of God which started from facts and objects known through the senses—as will be seen in the next chapter when we study the famous "five ways" of Thomas Aquinas.

Most Augustinians placed will above reason, thereby reflecting the experience of Augustine prior to his conversion. What was important for them was not to know the rational truth, but to do that which is good. Therefore their theology often tended to be practical and moral rather than abstract and metaphysical.

As to the soul, the Augustinians insisted that it was independent of the body. The soul by itself, even apart from the body, is a substance. Its principle of individuation is in itself, and not in its union with the body.

Finally, two other characteristics of thirteenth-century Augustinianism are the theory of the multiplicity of substantial forms and the doctrine of the hylomorphic composition of spiritual beings. The former held that the individuation of matter took place through the various "forms"—or "exemplary ideas"—which were superimposed upon it. On the other hand, those who followed the new philosophy held that it was matter that gave individuality to forms. The doctrine of hylomorphism—which came not from Augustine, but rather from ibn Gabirol—held that all created beings, including those of a purely spiritual nature such as the souls and the angels, consisted of both matter and form.

Although these are the fundamental characteristics of a theological trend that became more clearly defined as the thirteenth century progressed, and which eventually developed into what is usually called the Franciscan school, one should point out that this Augustinian tendency was not monolithic, and it did not become a rigid orthodoxy. Therefore, not all the theologians whom we here call "Augustinians" agreed on all these points. Furthermore, they all included in their thought some elements that were Aristotelian in origin.[2] But they did coincide in their unwillingness to change radically the epistemological and metaphysical framework derived from Augustine and the Neoplatonists.

Early in the thirteenth century, before the mendicant orders gained a foothold in the universities, theological teaching in these institutions was usually in the hands of "seculars"—that is, teachers who did not follow a monastic rule. Of these, the most notable was William of Auvergne,[3] although he, like the other

---

[2] Besides the logic, the most common Aristotelian elements were the theory of the hylomorphic composition of beings in general, and the distinction between potency and act.

[3] He was first a professor of theology at the University of Paris, and then became bishop of that city—and is therefore known also as William of Paris. He realized that the best way to refute the new doctrines was to know them. Therefore, he became very much at home in the new philosophy, although he did not generally accept it. The most interesting aspects of his theology are his doctrine of God, his arguments against the eternity of the world and the doctrine of emanation, and his theory of knowledge. As to the first, William affirmed that God is to be distinguished from creatures mainly in that in God essence and existence are the same, and this is not the case with creatures. This point, which he may well have taken from Avicenna, does however coincide with the basic presuppositions of Anselm's ontological argument, and with what has been said above regarding the main characteristics of the Augustinian tendencies that William represents. Regarding the eternity of the world, William refuted through a *reductio ad absurdum* the argument that claims that God, being eternally the same, is eternally creator, and therefore creation must be eternal. He argued that if this argument were true, it would be necessary to conclude that everything is immovable and eternal, for everything is somehow related to God, and that relationship would have to be unchangeable. On the other hand, the word does not spring out of a series of emanations—as Avicenna claimed—but is rather the work of God, made out of nothing, and not by necessity but rather through a free decision of the divine will—and here we have another example of the manner in which these theologians placed will and goodness above nature and reason. His theory of knowledge is typically Augustinian, although often expressed in Aristotelian terms. According to him, God imprints on the soul the knowledge of the first principles not only of logic, but also of morality, and also imprints on it the

secular theologians of the thirteenth century,[4] was eclipsed by the mendicants.

Although eventually their own order would adopt a different position, almost all the Dominican theologians of the thirteenth century—especially in the first half of that century—followed the traditional Augustinian line.[5]

It was, however, the Franciscan theologians of the thirteenth century who became most identified with the traditional line, accepting from the new philosophy only that which seemed compatible with Augustinianism, and holding Plato and the Neoplatonists in higher regard than Aristotle. In general, their theology was imbued with a mysticism in which the influence of Pseudo-Dionysius and the Victorines joined with that of

knowledge of eternal ideas. God is therefore the true "active intellect," in relation to which the soul is a "passive intellect." Through the body and the senses, the soul can *perceive* particular objects; but it can *know* them only through the divine action. On the question of hylomorphism, William accepted the Aristotelian doctrine that things have form and matter, but did not follow the opinion generally held by most Augustinians that this hylomorphic composition is to be extended to purely spiritual beings. On William's opposition to Avicenna, see R. de Vaux, *Notes et textes sur l'avicennisme latin aux confins des XIIe-XIIIe siècles* (Paris: J. Vrin, 1934), pp. 17-43. On his doctrine in general, see Copleston, *History*, 2:218-27; J. H. Bridges, *The Philosophy of William of Auvergne with Respect to Thirteenth Century Christian Aristotelianism* (University microfilms, 1970).

[4] Other secular theologians with views similar to those of William of Auvergne were Robert Courçon (Ch. Dickson, "Le cardinal Robert de Courson: Sa Vie," *AHDLMA*, 9 [1934], 53-142), Stephen Langton (A. M. Landgraf, ed., *Der Sentenzenkommentar des Kardinals Stephan Langton*, Münster: Aschendorff, 1952), Robert Sorbon (after whom the Sorbonne is named: P. Glorieux, "Sorbon, Robert de," *DTC*, 14:2383-85), and William of Auxerre, who seems to have been the first to apply the distinction between matter and form to the sacraments.

[5] The main Dominican teachers in this group were Richard Fishacre, Robert Kilwardby, and Peter of Tarantaise.

Fishacre taught at Oxford during the first half of the thirteenth century, and there he wrote a *Commentary on the Sentences* in which his concern to assimilate into the traditional theology some of the elements of the new philosophy may be seen. His method to achieve this end consisted in interpreting Aristotle—with the help of Avicenna—as if his doctrines coincided with those of Augustine. In so doing he went so far as to attribute to Aristotle the doctrines of seminal reasons and of illumination. R. J. Long, "The Science of Theology according to Richard Fishacre: Edition of the Prologue to His Commentary on the Sentences," *MedSt*, 8 and 9 (1966-1967), 63-87.

Robert Kilwardby also taught at Oxford and eventually became Archbishop of Canterbury. His doctrine was typically Augustinian, for he taught that illumination was the manner in which knowledge was acquired, that seminal reasons were at the source of causality, and that all beings, including those of a purely spiritual nature, were hylomorphic in their composition. (Gilson, *History*, pp. 355-59.) As will be seen further on, he was a staunch opponent not only of extreme Aristotelianism, but also of Thomism, against which he employed both his intellectual gifts and his hierarchical authority.

Peter of Tarantaise, who later sat on the chair of Peter under the title of Innocent V, taught at Paris on two separate occasions. Like Fishacre and Kilwardby he expounded traditional Augustinianism while attempting to assimilate those aspects of the new philosophy which seemed to be compatible with the old. In his time his renown was such that he was generally called "Most Famous Doctor" (J. Forget, "Innocent V," *DTC*, 7:1996-97). His work against the theory of the eternity of the world remains unpublished. See O. Argerami, "Circa Petri de Tarantasia quaestionem 'De aeternitate mundi,' " *PatMed*, 2 (1981), 74-84.

Bernard and Francis. The first Franciscan teacher was Alexander of Hales, who was surrounded by several illustrious disciples. A few years later, with Bonaventure, Franciscan theology reached its high point for the thirteenth century.

Alexander of Hales became a Franciscan in 1236, when he was around fifty years of age, and after he had produced most of his theological works.[6] Therefore, although Alexander was the first teacher of the Franciscan school, his theology was not basically shaped by the Franciscan ideal; on the contrary it was that theology which gave its basic tone to early Franciscan theology.

Alexander was aware of the new tendencies of his times, but was unwilling to follow them. There is no doubt that he knew most of the writings of Aristotle, whom he often quoted in support of a particular philosophical point. But in spite of this he always remained within Augustinian Neoplatonism. The main sources that influenced his theology were Augustine, Anselm, Hugh of Saint Victor, and several other Christian writers. He seemed to view Aristotle as a support for some of the views which he found in his favorite writers.[7]

Alexander did not believe theology to be an activity through which the intellect builds systems of interpretation of God and the universe. It is not a science that studies causes and effects. It is rather a "wisdom" of the "cause of causes," as it is given to human knowledge in its own revelation. The purpose of theology is not to satisfy human curiosity, but rather to "perfect the soul according to the affections, moving it towards the good through the principles of fear and love."[8] Thus, his theology has

---

[6] These works are: Glossa in quator libros Sententiarum Petri Lomardi, 4 vols. (Quaracchi, Florence: Collegium Bonaventurae, 1951-57), Quaestiones disputatae (I have only been able to use those which he wrote before joining the order, published in three volumes [Collegium Bonaventurae, 1960]) and Summa theologica, 5 vols. [Collegium Bonaventura, 1924-48]). There is some doubt as to the authenticity of the fourth book of the Glossa, which in any case is incomplete (see the prolegomena to vol. 4, pp. 44-46). As to the Summa, Roger Bacon, in 1267, said that the Franciscans "attributed to him this great Summa, which weighs more than a horse, and which was not written by him, but by others" (quoted by V. Doucet in his prolegomena to this work, vol. 3, p. ccclviii). This has led many to deny its authenticity. After a detailed study, Doucet concluded that significant portions of the Summa were not written by Alexander, although they may be based on notes taken by his students.

[7] The best general study of his theology is that of Ph. Boehner, Alexander of Hales, Vol. I of his History of the Franciscan School (St. Bonaventure, N. Y.; St. Bonaventure College, 1943-44). On his contribution to sacramental theology, see G. J. Connoly, "Sacramental Character in the Teachings of Alexander of Hales," CollFran, 33 (1963), 5-27.

[8] S. Th. 1, q. 1, cap. 1.

that practical tone which would be characteristic of Franciscan theology in the thirteenth century.[9]

The influence of Alexander upon later theology is difficult to assess. He seems to have been responsible for the practice that eventually became common at the University of Paris and at other centers of dictating courses on the basis of commentaries on the *Sentences* of Peter Lombard. Bonaventure and several other significant Franciscan theologians of the thirteenth century claimed to be his disciples and showed great respect for him. At that time, he was generally known as the "Irrefutable Doctor." However, Bonaventure so eclipsed Alexander that shortly thereafter it could be affirmed that the *Summa* of the latter was rotting in obscure corners of Franciscan libraries. Thus, it seems fair to say that Alexander was the first teacher of the Franciscan school and gave it some of its basic characteristics, but that the main significance of his work was in opening the path to the true founder of that theology, Bonaventure.[10]

John of Fidanza, better known as Bonaventure or as the "Seraphic Doctor," was born at Bagnorea near Viterbo in 1221. After completing his studies at the Arts Faculty of the University of Paris, he became a Franciscan and studied theology under Alexander of Hales and perhaps under Odo Rigaud and John of Parma. In 1248 he opened his teaching career by commenting on the Gospel of Luke. Two years later he commented on the *Sentences* of Peter Lombard, and received his doctorate around 1253. After a career of distinction as a teacher and as a polemist—for he intervened in the controversies regarding the presence of the friars at the University—he was elected Minister General of the Friars Minor by the chapter that met in Rome in 1257. Because of the manner in which he led the Order through a period of great peril for its existence, he is known as its "second founder." In 1270, he once again became involved in the

---

[9] L. Amorós, "La teología como ciencia práctica en la escuela franciscana en los tiempos que preceden a Escoto," *AHDLMA*, 9 (1934), 261-303; M. D. Chenu, *La théologie comme science au XIII* siècle* (Paris: J. Vrin, 1957), pp. 37-41.

[10] Apart from Bonaventure, the most distinguished disciples of Alexander were Jean de la Rochelle and Odo Rigaud. See the bibliographical notes in A. M. Hamelin, *L'école franciscaine de ses débuts jusqu'à l'Occamisme: Pour l'histoire de la théologie morale* (Louvain: Nauwelaerts, 1961).

struggle between the mendicants and their opponents at the
University of Paris. At that time he also intervened in the debate
regarding the value and authority of Aristotle and his
interpreter, Averroës. With this purpose in mind, he began
delivering a series of lectures on creation, but these were
interrupted when he was made a cardinal. He then decided to
resign as Minister General of the Order, and called a general
chapter, which elected his successor. He died two months later,
while attending the Council of Lyon (1274).[11]

Bonaventure's theology is built on three basic pillars. The first
of these is the authority of the church and her tradition, as well as
of the Scriptures. He saw no tension or contradiction between
Scripture and tradition, and he believed that his entire theology
and life had to be measured by that double authority. Second, his
theology is based on a profound piety of the Franciscan type.
The purpose of his theology is not to solve or to discover the
deepest mysteries of God, but rather to enable one to have
communion with God and to contemplate the Divine. Finally, he
built his entire theology within the philosophical framework that
he had received from Augustine, Hugh of Saint Victor, and
Alexander of Hales.

According to Bonaventure, all knowledge comes from an
illumination of the Word. This in turn implies that all the various
sciences are ordered toward the knowledge of God, and that
they therefore culminate in theology.[12] Therefore, although
reason is good because it has been created by God, and although
philosophy is a good and necessary means to acquire certain
types of knowledge, any philosophy that claims to be autonomous and to be an end in itself necessarily errs.[13] Aristotle, for

---

[11] His works include several mystical and ascetic works, a number of sermons and epistles,
commentaries on various books of the Bible, and a number of systematic treatises. Among his
systematic treatises, the most important are his *Commentary on the Sentences;* his *Breviloquium;* and
several academic exercises and lectures on the Trinity, the six days of creation, the Ten
Commandments, the knowledge of Christ, the gifts of the Spirit, and the relationship between
theology and the various disciplines. His most famous work, the *Itinerary of the Mind Towards God,* is a
systematization of the mystical theology prevalent in his time.
[12] This is the thesis of the entire treatise *De reductione artium ad theologiam.*
[13] *In Hex.* 7. Given this view of the function of philosophy in theology, it is incorrect to say that
Bonaventure sought to refute Aristotelian philosophy. In truth, he was not seeking to develop or
defend a philosophical position. Such is the thesis of O. Argerami, "San Buenaventura frente al
aristotelismo," *PatMed,* 2 (1981), 21-36.

instance, taught that the world is eternal and that the active intellect is one, and denied the existence of a heavenly reward and of eternal punishment because he attempted to understand the world apart from the doctrine of creation. Faith needs no proof, for that which is believed is based on an act of the will and not on a rational exercise. As the subject matter of theology is that which is believed,[14] and this depends primarily on the affections of the will,[15] theology is more than a science—it is a wisdom (*sapientia*).

The existence of God is evident to any mind that follows its best lights. The only reason it is necessary to offer proof of God's existence is that our mind, being corrupted by the Fall, can be ignorant of something that is in itself evident.[16] Therefore, although Bonaventure often made use of the various traditional proofs of the existence of God, he usually presented them in a summary form, as in passing, thereby suggesting that such proofs are not really necessary. Among these proofs, he seemed to prefer the ontological argument of Anselm, precisely because in the last analysis it affirms that the existence of God is evident and that true reason cannot deny it. This does not mean, however, that we have a natural knowledge of God:

There are two manners of thinking about any being: that of its existence [*si est*] and that of its essence [*quid est*]. Our intellect is defective in that which has to do with the essence of God, but not with reference to his existence. . . . It is due to that deficiency in our knowledge of the divine essence that our intellect often thinks that God is that which he is not, an idol, and not that which he is, the just God.[17]

This God has the traditional attributes, and it is not necessary to discuss them here. However, one should point out that

---

[14] *Sent. proem., q.* 1.
[15] Bonaventure illustrated this point by distinguishing between a mathematical proposition, and the proposition: "Christ died for us." The latter moves one to love, whereas the former does not. *Ibid., q.* 3.
[16] *Quaest. disp. de myst. Trin.* 1, *art.* 1, *resp.*; Cf. *I Sent., dist.* 3, *pars* 1, *art, unicus, q.* 1. Also, E. Bettoni, *Il problema della conoscibilità di Dio nella Scuola Francescana* (Padua: A. Milani, 1950), pp. 214-50; G. Morra, "L'evidenza di Dio secondo S. Bonaventura," *Bolletino d'informazioni del Centro di Studi bonaventuriani,* 24 (1977), 7-21.
[17] *I Sent., dist.* 8, *pars* 1, *art.* 1, *q.* 2.

Bonaventure paid more attention to trinitarian doctrine than to negative attributes (immutability, infinity, etc.). In the *Breviloquium*, trinitarian doctrine is the starting point for theology. As will be seen further on, the divine Trinity is reflected in its creatures in various degrees, and it is through their contemplation, and ascending through those degrees as if they were steps in a ladder, that the soul attains to the contemplation of God.

God is the creator of the world. This creation took place out of nothing and within time, in spite of everything that may be found in the works of Aristotle or Averroës.[18]

All created beings have matter—not in the sense of physical body, but as indeterminate potentiality—and form. This is true of bodily beings as well as of spiritual ones, such as the soul and the angels. This is the typical Franciscan doctrine of universal hylomorphism.[19] It is in this hylomorphic composition—in this union of matter and form—that the principle of individuation of creatures is to be found.[20]

On the other hand, although creation took place within time, the "exemplary ideas" of created things are eternal in the mind of God.[21] This is a point on which Bonaventure insisted repeatedly. These ideas—although many from the point of view of our reason—are really a single truth, and that truth is the eternal Word of God.[22] This is why Scripture says that all things were made through the Word. And this is also why the Word is the source of all knowledge.

The manner in which the created universe leads to the creator is one of two focuses in Bonaventure's mysticism. The other focus is the contemplation of the humanity of Christ. The created universe leads to God because the Trinity has left its imprint on each of its creatures, and through them one can

---

[18] *In Hex.* 7. 2. According to him, an eternal creation out of nothing is a contradiction (*II Sent., dist. 1, pars 1, art. 1, q.* 2). Here he differs from Thomas, who grants the logical possibility of such creation, although he denies it as a fact.

[19] See L. Veuthey, *Sancti Bonaventurae philosophia christiana* (Rome: Officium Libri Catholici, 1943), pp. 147-52; F. van Steenberghen, "Le mythe d'un monde éternel," *RevPhLouv*, 76 (1978), 157-79; 80 (1982), 486-99.

[20] *Ibid.,* pp. 152-62; L. Amorós, "Vida de San Buenaventura," *BAC*, 6:119-21.

[21] J. M. Bissen, *L'exemplarisme divin selon Saint Bonaventure* (Paris: J. Vrin, 1929); M. Oromí, "Filosofía ejemplarista de San Buenaventura," *BAC*, 19:3-138.

[22] *Quaest. disp. de scientia Christi* 3, *solutio objectorum* 19.

contemplate the source of their being. This is the theme of Bonaventure's most famous work, the *Itinerary of the Mind Towards God*. This aspect of his mysticism is a development of the Augustinian doctrine of the vestiges of the Trinity to be found in its creatures—the *vestigia Trinitatis*—which is here coupled with the hierarchical ordering of all being as a road leading to God, as this may be found in the entire tradition that follows Pseudo-Dionysius. The imprint of the Trinity is not equally clear in all creatures, but is rather given in various degrees—a vestige, an image, and a likeness.[23] All things have being, truth, and goodness. These three—being, truth, and goodness—are vestiges of the Trinity. In rational beings, the image of the Trinity may be seen in that they have memory, intellect, and will. The likeness of the Trinity is to be found only in those rational beings which have faith, hope, and love. Ascending through these various degrees, the soul may achieve ecstasy, where every intellectual effort ceases and the soul contemplates God in perfect peace.

The other focus of Bonaventure's mysticism is the contemplation of the humanity of Christ. Bonaventure's systematic Christology, as it is found in his *Commentary of the Third Book of Sentences* and in his *Breviloquium*, is perfectly orthodox and traditional. From the point of view of the history of doctrine, what is most significant is that Bonaventure denied the immaculate conception of Mary, and claimed that such a denial was "more reasonable" and agreed with "the authority of the saints."[24] This is not surprising, for several of the most distinguished theologians of the thirteenth century—Thomas Aquinas among them—held similar views. In any case, the Jesus of Bonaventure's mysticism is to be discovered in the works that he devoted to the contemplation of the humanity of Christ. Here he looked at the humiliated, wounded, and crucified Christ, and saw him as the object not of scientific investigation, but rather of that contemplation which leads to love and repentance.

---

[23] This is his most usual scheme, although he offers frequent variations of it. In any case, what is important is not the scheme itself, but the world view and the piety of mystical ascension which it entails.

[24] *III Sent., dist.* 3, *pars* 1, *art.* 1, *q.* 2; *Brev.* 3. 7. Mary was indeed sanctified, but only after being conceived in original sin.

A History of Christian Thought

Bonaventure's mysticism therefore cannot be understood correctly in the light of the *Itinerary* alone, but must also be seen in the light of the central role of the historic Jesus in the spirituality of the Seraphic Doctor. Here the influence of Bernard and Francis was foremost, and that influence freed Bonaventure from a merely speculative mysticism such as that of Pseudo-Dionysius.

For the rest, Bonaventure's ecclesiology, as well as his doctrine of the sacraments and his eschatology, were developed first in the academic environment of the University of Paris, and later in the concrete struggle within the Franciscan Order. On these points, Bonaventure was content with repeating what others had said before him.

In summary, Bonaventure followed the traditional line of Alexander of Hales. If anything, his theology was more consciously Augustinian than that of his teacher. This was partly because during the time of Alexander the various issues posed by the new philosophy were still not as clear as they were during the time of Bonaventure. Now it was no longer possible to accept Aristotle as a mere addition to traditional theology. The points of conflict had been clarified, and it was now necessary either to reject most of the new philosophy—especially on those many points where it was not compatible with the Neoplatonic tradition—or to attempt to reconstruct the entire edifice of theology on new foundations. Bonaventure followed the first of these alternatives. Thomas and his school, although not abandoning Augustine and attempting to be faithful to traditional theology, followed the second.[25]

Those Franciscan theologians who lived between Bonaventure and John Duns Scotus generally held views similar to those of the Seraphic Doctor, although the presence of Thomism—which will be discussed in the next chapter—led them either to oppose it more openly or to accept some of its views, although without abandoning the fundamental positions of the Franciscan tradition. Thus, one could distinguish between an "early

---

[25] On the relations between Bonaventure and Thomas themselves, see E. H. Weber, *Dialogue et dissensions entre saint Bonaventure et saint Thomas d'Aquin à Paris (1252-1273)* (Paris: J. Vrin, 1974).

Franciscan School"—Alexander of Hales and Bonaventure, and "intermediate school"—the theologians to whom we now turn; and a "new school"—that which was born in Duns Scotus. The main theologians of the intermediate school were John Peckham,[26] William of La Mare,[27] and Matthew of Aquasparta,[28] in Paris, and Richard of Middleton[29] in Oxford. During the same period, two other Franciscans, Peter of John Olivi[30] and Peter de

---

[26] John Peckham, generally known during his time as the "Ingenious Doctor," pursued his academic career in Paris, Oxford, and Rome, and later became Archbishop of Canterbury. His theology was basically the same as that of the ancient Franciscan school, for he held the existence of God to be self-evident, that knowledge takes place through illumination, that there is matter and form in spiritual beings, and that there are in a human being several forms hierarchically ordered. But Peckham defended these various positions with the zeal of one who knew that they are not generally held. At least on one point—that of the number of substantial forms in humans—he clashed with Thomas. But this did not mean, as some have claimed, that he was an enemy of Thomas. On the contrary, on the personal level he always defended his Dominican colleague, and they struggled side by side against Gerard of Abbeville and his attack on the validity of the vows of poverty. It is true, however, that in 1284, when he was Archbishop of Canterbury, Peckham ratified the anti-Aristotelian decree of his predecessor Kildwardby. A. Teetaert, "Pecham, Jean," DTC, 12:100-140; D. L. Douie, Archbishop Pecham (Oxford: Clarendon Press, 1952).

[27] William of La Mare wrote a Correction to Brother Thomas, in which he attacked 118 Thomist theses. This treatise played an important role in the controversies that developed around the teachings of Thomas, and was frequently refuted by Dominican theologians.

[28] Matthew of Aquasparta has not been sufficiently studied (the Fathers of the Collegium Bonaventurae, Quaracchi, Florence, have been editing his works since 1903), but there is no doubt that he followed the traditional views of the Franciscan school, emphasizing those points at which that tradition differed from Thomism. Thus, for instance, he attempted to refute the view of Thomas that eternal creation was not absurd (E. Longpré, "Thomas d'York et M. d'Aquasparta: Textes inédits sur le problème de la création," AHDLMA, 1 [1926], 269-309). See also P. Mazzarella, La dottrina dell'anima e della conoscenza in Matteo d'Acquasparta (Padua: Editrice Gregoriana, 1969). During the last years of his life he became a cardinal, and his theological production declined.

[29] Richard of Middleton was one of the most distinguished theologians of the intermediate generation between Bonaventure and John Scotus. He went beyond most of his Franciscan colleagues in making use of the new philosophy, perhaps because of the influence of such Oxford teachers as Robert Grosseteste and Roger Bacon. Thus, he highly valued the empirical data of the senses, which he believed were the starting point for knowledge (M. Grabmann, "Zur Erkenntnislehre der älteren Franziskaner Schule," FranzSt, 4, 1917, 105-26). As to the relationship between philosophy and theology, he also departed from the tradition of the earlier Franciscan school, for he believed that philosophy is a separate science from theology, with its own method and proper subject of study. Although philosophy must be subordinate to theology, for there is an absolute certainty in the data of revelation, it can still pronounce true judgments on the conclusions of the philosophers. On the other hand, on such issues as the hylomorphic composition of all created beings, the plurality of substantial forms in humans, the logical impossibility of eternal creation, and the primacy of will, Richard was a faithful exponent of the Augustinian position. D. E. Sharp, Franciscan Philosophy at Oxford in the Thirteenth Century (Oxford: H. Milford, 1930); E. Hocedez, Richard de Middleton: Sa vie, ses oeuvres, sa doctrine (Paris: É. Champion, 1925).

[30] Peter of John Olivi, who lived during the second half of the thirteenth century, was an able theologian very much respected for his erudition. He defended the traditional Franciscan theses. However, this very Franciscanism, followed to an extreme, led him to embrace the views of the "spiritual" Franciscans, to reject even that use of philosophy which was found in Augustine and in the entire medieval tradition, and to adopt several Joachimist theses. In agreement with the ancient Franciscan school, he held the universal hylomorphic composition of all beings and the plurality of forms in humans. However, he joined Richard of Middleton and other contemporary Franciscans in attempting to reinterpret the doctrine of illumination. In order to do this, he claimed that the divine illumination was a natural light placed by God in every intellect. C. Partee, "Peter John Olivi:

Trabibus,[31] had views that differed from those of the rest of the order. Finally, the Catalan mystic Ramon Lull, although never a Franciscan, was akin to this school.[32]

Historical and Doctrinal Study," *FrancSt*, 20 (1960), 215-60; C. Bérubé, "Olivi, critique de Bonaventure et d'Henri de Gand," in R. S. Almagno and C. L. Harkins, eds., *Studies Honoring Ignatius Charles Brady* (Bonaventure, N.Y.: Franciscan Institute, 1976), pp. 57-121.
    [31] Peter de Trabibus held ideas similar to those of Peter of John Olivi, and so little is known of his life that some nineteenth-century scholars thought that the two were the same. P. F. Callaey, "Oliue ou Olivi (Pierre de Jean)," *DTC*, 11:982-91.
    [32] A native of Majorca, which had been in the hands of Moors almost up to that time, Lull grew up among Jews and Moslems. For this reason, when he had a profound religious experience he was very interested in preaching the gospel to unbelievers. He combined mysticism with rationalism. On the one hand, he claimed that his own experience of conversion, and the great vision that he had of the ultimate cohesiveness of the entire universe in a rational system, were illuminations that he received from on high—and he was therefore called the "Illumined Doctor." On the other hand, he believed that reason in such a way pervades the entire universe that one can prove such doctrines as that of the Trinity and the incarnation by simply starting out from monotheism—a doctrine held by Jews, Moslems, and Christians. His mysticism was a combination of Franciscan contemplation with that of the Moslem mystics of his time, and his rationalism can only be called such if one bears in mind that he never doubted the data of revelation, but believed them to be so true that they could be proven through rational means. This is the purpose of his "means of reaching truth"—*ars inveniendi veritatis*—which he expounded in several of his almost three hundred works. For the rest, his theology consists in traditional orthodox doctrine placed within the framework of an eclectic Neoplatonism such as that which was common in the Franciscan school of the thirteenth century. It is for this reason, and because he always was attracted by Franciscanism, that we have included him among Franciscan theologians, although he never belonged to that order.

X

The Dominican School

Over against those whom we have called "Augustinians," who refused to make any more use of the new philosophy than that which could be worked into the old framework, there was another tendency, represented at first by a few Dominican theologians, which held that the philosophy of Aristotle was very valuable and should not be rejected for the sole reason that it was opposed to the philosophical outlook that had served as the background for earlier theological formulations. It should be clear, however, that those who held this position were attempting not to leave aside Christian orthodoxy, but rather to adopt Aristotle and his philosophy as the philosophical tool for a theological understanding of Christianity. If those theologians whom we have discussed in the previous chapters are called Augustinians, this should not be understood to mean that those to whom we now turn were in any way opposed to the great bishop of Hippo. On the contrary, they believed that Augustine was the greatest theologian among the church "Fathers," but they attempted to interpret his theology within the framework of the philosophy of Aristotle. Naturally, the result of such an attempt can only be called Aristotelian or Augustinian in a wide sense. The first stages of this endeavor—which may be seen in the work of Albert the Great—would consist in an eclecticism in which various elements from one and another source are juxta-

posed without a clear organic connection. In its culmination—with Thomas Aquinas—eclecticism would be left behind
in what would be a new synthesis that would no longer be mere
Aristotelianism, or a Neoplatonic Augustinianism with Aristotelian elements, but would be a new system: Thomism.

Albert the Great

Albert, known by posterity as "the Great," had a varied academic career that took him first to various centers of study in
Germany, and later to Paris, where he taught from 1245 to 1248.
He then went to Cologne as director of the new "General Study"
that the Dominicans had founded in that city. The many responsibilities that were his within the Dominican Order as well as within
the ecclesiastical hierarchy repeatedly interrupted his academic
work, but in spite of this he continued a vast literary production.
He died in 1280 in the Dominican convent of Cologne, six years
after the death of his most famous disciple, Thomas Aquinas.[1]

Albert's literary production was enormous, for as his task he
set himself to comment on the entire works of Aristotle and to
leave as a legacy to the Latin world a vast encyclopedia of all the
knowledge of his time. In the field of natural science, his works
opened new horizons, for his observations on astronomy,
zoology, and botany inspired others to study such subjects.[2] His
theological works consisted mainly of several commentaries on
the various books of Scripture, a *Commentary on the Sentences,* the
Summa of Creatures, the *Summa of Theology,* commentaries on
Pseudo-Dionysius, and several minor writings.

As has already been said, his work was more eclectic than
original, and therefore we shall not pause to expound his
theology and to analyze the sources of his various ideas, but will

---

[1] I. Craemer-Ruegenberg, *Albertus Magnus* (Munich: C. H. Beck, 1980); W. P. Ekert, *Leben und Werk des heiligen Albertus Magnus* (Düsseldorf: Patmos Verlag, 1981); A. Zimmermann, ed., *Albert der Grosse: Seine Zeit, sein Werk, seine Wirkung* (Berlin: W. de Gruyter, 1981); F. J. Kovach and R. W. Shahan, *Albert the Great: Commemorative Essays* (Norman, Ok.: University of Oklahoma, 1979). A series of essays, mostly on details of his biography: A. Layer and M. Springer, eds., *Albert von Lauingen 700 Jahre: Albertus Magnus* (Lauingen: 1980).

[2] On his role in the history of science, see A. Nitschke, "Albertus Magnus: Ein Weigbereiter der modernen Wissenschaft," *HistZschr,* 231 (1980), 2-20; J. A. Weisheipl, ed., *Albertus Magnus and the Sciences: Commemorative Essays 1980* (Toronto: Pontifical Institute of Medieval Studies, 1980).

limit our discussion to some points that illustrate his philosophical and theological method.

Albert's most significant contribution to the development of Christian thought was the manner in which he distinguished between philosophy and theology.[3] The latter differs from every other science inasmuch as that which it proves follows from revealed principles, and not from autonomous ones.[4] In the field of philosophy, Albert was a rationalist who claimed that every assertion must stand before the judgment of reason and observation. Any philosopher who attempts to prove that which cannot be proved is a poor philosopher, even if what is said is quite certain on the basis of revealed truth. But in the field of theology Albert insisted on the limits of reason. Thus a process began here which would be manifest first in the Thomist school and which latter would include other thinkers—a clear distinction was made between philosophy and theology, faith and reason. Eventually, such a distinction would lead to a divorce. But in Albert's time it opened wide horizons to Christian thought: natural science was free to follow its own way and use its own means of research without fear of dogmatic error; philosophy and theology were free to develop as parallel disciplines, so that one could be a true philosopher without becoming a rationalist or a heretic in matters of faith.

Albert believed in creation, and affirmed that it took place within time—that is, that the world is not eternal. Yet he confessed that as a philosopher he could not prove this point scientifically, but only with arguments of probability.[5]

His theory of knowledge attempted to conciliate Aristotelian-

---

[3] See C. Feckes, "Wissen, Glauben und Glaubenswissenschaft nach Albert dem Grossen," *ZKT*, 54 (1930), 1-39; M. Cuervo, "La teología como ciencia y la sistematización teológica según S. Alberto Magno," *CienTom*, 46 (1932), 173-99; M. Grabmann, "De theologia ut scientia argumentativa secundum S. Albertum Magnum et S. Thomam Aquinatem," *Ang*, 14 (1937), 39-60; A. Rohner, "De natura theologiae iuxta S. Albertum Magnum," *Ang*, 16 (1939), 3-23; E. Wéber, "La relation de la philosophie et la théologie selon Albert le Grand," *ArchPh*, 43 (1980), 559-88; G. Wieland, "Albert der Grosse und die Entwicklung der mittelalterlichen Philosophie," *ZschrPhForsch*, 34 (1980), 590-607.

[4] *S. Th.*, I, *tract.* i, *q.* 4 (ed. Lyon, 17:12).

[5] A. Zimmermann, "Alberts Kritik an einem Argument für der Anfang der Welt," in Zimmermann, *Albert der Grosse*, pp. 78-88. See, however, J. Hansen, 'Zur Frage der anfangslosen und zeitlichen Schöpfung bei Albert dem Grossen," *Studia Albertina: Festschrift für Bernhard Geyer* (Münster: Aschendorff, 1952), pp. 167-88, who points out that Albert's views on this point changed with time.

ism with Augustinian illumination.[6] We have a passive and an active intellect. Through divine illumination the active intellect abstracts knowledge from sensory data, and then imprints it on the passive intellect.[7]

As to the soul and its principle of individuation, Albert rejected the theory of universal hylomorphism which was held by the Augustinians, and appealed to the distinction that Boethius established between the *quod est*—the essence, the "whatness"—and the *quo est*—the complete existence, the "thatness." The soul becomes an individual being by virtue of the thatness which God gives to a prior whatness.[8]

Albert's theology was rather conservative. Although he was a great advocate of Aristotelianism, his theology still was built within the traditional Augustinian and Neoplatonic framework. That was to be expected, for the mere task of compilation and interpretation which Albert performed was in itself a titanic enterprise. The task of assimilating this vast body of knowledge and of developing a coherent synthesis would be left to his disciple Thomas Aquinas. However, because of his vast erudition, Albert was very much admired by his contemporaries, who attributed to him a great deal of what he had drawn from Aristotle and other ancient writers.[9]

---

[6] On the sources of Albert's theory of knowledge, see: B. Geyer, "De aristotelismo B. Alberti Magni," *Alberto Magno: Atti della Settimana Albertina celebrata in Roma nei giorni 9-14 Nov. 1931* (Rome: F. Pustet, 1932), pp. 63-80; J. Bonné, *Die Erkenntnislehre Alberts des Grossen mit besonderer Berücksichtigung des arabischen Neuplatonismus* (Bonn: R. Stodieck, 1935); L. A. Kennedy, "The Nature of the Human Intellect According to St. Albert the Great," *ModSch*, 37 (1960), 121-37.

[7] On the role of illumination in knowledge, Albert's views were not constant. See G. de Mattos, "L'intellect agent personnel dans les premiers écrits d'Albert le Grand et de Thomas d'Aquin," *RnsPh*, 43 (1940), 145-61.

[8] *S. Th.*, II, tract. i, q. 4, memb. 1, art. 1 (ed. Lyon, 17:37). An excellent study of this subject is that of E. Gilson, "L'âme raisonnable chez Albert le Grand," *AHDLMA*, 14 (1943), 5-72. See also I. Craemer-Ruegenberg, "Albert le Grand et ses démonstrations de l'immortalité de l'ame," *ArchPh*, 43 (1980), 667-73. I have not discussed here the views of Albert regarding the unity of the substantial form in humans, for this is a highly technical question on which scholars are not in agreement. See: J. McWilliams, "St. Albert the Great and Plurality of Forms," *ModSch*, 9 (1932), 43-44; S. Vanni Rovighi, "Alberto Magno e l'unità della forma sostanziale dell'uomo," *Medioevo e Rinascimento: Studi in onore di Bruno Nardi* (Firenze: G. C. Sansoni, 1955), 2:753-78; L. Ducharme, "The Individual Human Being in St. Albert's Earlier Writings," in Kovach and Shahan, *Albert the Great*, pp. 131-60. On hylomorphism, see J. A. Weisheipl, "Albertus Magnus and Universal Hylomorphism," in ibid., pp. 239-60.

[9] Besides Thomas Aquinas, his best known disciples were Hugh and Ulrich of Strasbourg, and Giles of Lessines.

Thomas Aquinas

Thomas Aquinas was the foremost teacher of the Dominican school, and without any doubt one of the greatest theologians of all times. He has been admired through the centuries not only for the prodigious vastness of his production, but also for its quality. The Thomist school, which he founded, has continued an active existence well into the twentieth century. His intellectual gifts were united to a profound spirituality, and this combination earned him the title of "Angelic Doctor," by which he is still known.

Most of the philosophical works of Aquinas are commentaries on Aristotle, on the anonymous follower of Proclus who wrote the *Book on Causes,* and on Boethius. But he also wrote original philosophical works such as *On Being and Essence* and *On the Principles of Nature.*

In the field of theology proper, the three most significant works of Thomas are his *Commentary on the Sentences,* the *Summa contra gentiles,* and the *Summa theologiae.*

Following his teacher Albert, Thomas established a distinction between those truths which can be grasped by reason and those which are beyond it. Philosophy deals only with those truths which reason can attain; but theology, whose proper field is that of revealed truth, is concerned not only with these, but with truth in all its forms.

> The diversification of the sciences is brought about by the diversity of aspects under which things can be known. Both an astronomer and a physical scientist may demonstrate the same conclusion, for instance that the earth is spherical . . . Accordingly there is nothing to stop the same things from being treated by the philosophical sciences when they can be looked at in the light of natural reason and by another science when they are looked at in the light of divine revelation.[10]

Elsewhere, Thomas affirmed that some truths that are accessible to reason have been revealed nevertheless so that

---

[10] *Th.,* I, *q.* 1, *art.* 1 (T. Gilby, ed., *St. Thomas Aquinas: Summa Theologiae* [Cambridge, England: Blackfriars, 1964 ff.], 1:9).

those who are ignorant may know them, and also because the human mind is weak and easily confused, and therefore its conclusions are not absolutely certain.[11]

However, the true articles of faith, which are the exclusive concern of theology, are distinct from these other truths which reason can grasp but have been included in revelation because of the weakness of the human intellect.

> The truths about God which St. Paul says we can know by our natural powers of reasoning—that God exists, for example—are not numbered among the articles of faith, but are presupposed to them. For faith presupposes natural knowledge, just as grace does nature and all perfections that which they perfect. However, there is nothing to stop a man accepting on faith some truth which he personally cannot demonstrate, even if that truth in itself is such that demonstration could make it evident.[12]

Thus philosophy is an autonomous science that can reach the very limits of human reason. However, this science is not infallible, for the human mind is weak and can easily err. Furthermore, as it requires exceptional intellectual gifts, not all can reach its highest conclusions. Theology, on the other hand, studies truths that have been revealed and that cannot be doubted. Some of these truths—the articles of faith in the strict sense—are beyond the reach of reason, although they do not contradict it. These can never be attained by philosophy. There are other truths that theology knows through revelation and that philosophy can reach through reason, but that God in any case has revealed in order to make them available to us with absolute certainty, for they are necessary for salvation.

Reason has a basic function not only in philosophy, but also in theology. It can prove those revealed truths which are not, strictly speaking, articles of faith, but which have been revealed to give them greater certainty. And even in the case of articles of faith, which are therefore beyond its grasp, reason still has a role, for it shows that the highest revealed truths are not incompatible

---

[11] *Summa contra Gent.* 1.4.
[12] *S. Th.*, I, q. 2, art. 2 (ed. Gilby, 2:11).

with truth in general, and it also uses the articles of faith as principles from which to set out on further inquiry.[13]

Since the main concern of this *History*—as well as that of Thomas Aquinas himself—is theological rather than philosophical, our brief exposition of the Thomist system will focus on its theological aspects, following the basic outline of the *Summa Theologiae*. Yet, in order to understand the theology of Aquinas it is necessary to know something of the metaphysics that serves as its background, and especially of the technical meaning of certain terms. Therefore, we now pause for a brief exposition of Thomist metaphysics, in order then to move on to the theology of the Angelic Doctor. Several philosophical questions of great significance for theology, such as the theory of knowledge, the principle of individuation of rational beings, analogy, and others, will be discussed in their proper place within the framework of the theology of Aquinas.

The metaphysics of Thomas is basically Aristotelian, although with several elements that are Neoplatonic in origin. Its starting point is the notion of being, which is the first notion that the mind conceives, and in which all its various ideas come together.[14] This "being" is not an eternal idea that exists apart from individual beings. On the contrary, what metaphysics studies is concrete, individual being. Here Thomas used a series of technical terms that are best understood in pairs.

The first two of these technical terms are *substance* and *accident.* Substance is that which exists in itself and not in another; an accident, on the other hand, exists only in a substance. This does not mean that substance is a necessary being in the absolute sense, existing in and of itself. On the contrary, substance is a contingent being whose essence is not the same as its existence.[15]

---

[13] Even a select bibliography on the relationship between philosophy and theology in Aquinas would take much more space than is here available. I therefore direct the reader to the bibliographical notes in M. C. Wheeler, *Philosophy and the "Summa Theologica" of Saint Thomas Aquinas* (Washington: Catholic University of America Press, 1956).

[14] *De ver.*, q. 1, art. 1. The very brief description of Thomas' metaphysics which I have included in the following paragraphs is intended only to serve as an introduction to his theology, and should be supplemented by some of the dozens of monographs on the subject which have been published during this century. To these should be added the excellent essays by J. F. Wippel, *Metaphysical Themes in Thomas Aquinas* (Washington: Catholic University of America, 1984).

[15] *S. Th.*, I, q. 3, art. 6.

In this substance, which is always concrete and individual, several accidents or qualities exist. These accidents are not related to a particular substance by mere chance, but are often essential characteristics of that substance. In fact, every accident is "essential" with reference to the concrete subject in which it exists, for even if it seems "accidental" it is still related to the essence itself of this individual being.[16] For instance, the substance "man" may be joined to the accident "ugly," and this may seem to be entirely fortuitous, for in order to be a man it is not necessary to be ugly; but it is not so, for substance is always individual and concrete, and we are therefore dealing not with "man" in general, but with "this man," who is ugly, and whose ugliness is part of his individual and concrete being.

The second pair of terms to be discussed here is *nature* and *essence*. The nature of a substance is the manner in which it acts; therefore, nature is substance considered as a center of activity. Essence is that which makes a substance—or an accident—capable of definition. Therefore, in most cases "substance," "nature," and "essence" refer not to different things, but to various aspects of a single reality.

Third, material substances have *matter* and *form*—that is, their composition is hylomorphic. *Prime matter* is that absolute indetermination out of which all things come by being given a form. That matter which exists in individual things is no longer prime matter, for what makes such things individual and definable is precisely that they have a form. Obviously, the term "form" is not used here in the common sense of "shape." The substantial form is that which determines matter in such a way that it becomes a concrete and individual substance. The principle of individuation of material substances is to be found precisely in this joining of matter and form. This, however, is not true of intellectual beings, such as the soul and the angels, which have no matter.

Fourth, Thomas distinguished between *act* and *potency*. This distinction is wider than the previous ones, for it is applied to all

---

16 *Ibid.*, q. 22, art. 4.

finite beings and not only to those which are material.[17] The distinction itself is quite simple: "that which can be, but which is not, exists in potency; that which already is, exists in act."[18] This distinction is used to understand all change, in the sense not only of mutation, but also of movement. If a child can become an adult, that is because he or she is a child in act and an adult in potency. If this book can be moved to another place, that is because it is here in act and at that other place in potency. Therefore, mutation as well as movement consists in the actualization of that which was previously in potency. Absolute perfection must be pure act, for potency implies non-realized being. This is why God is pure act.

Finally, a word must be said regarding the Thomist distinction between *essence* and *existence.* Like the other distinctions discussed here, this was not original with Thomas, who took this particular one, not from Aristotle, but from Arabic philosophy—al-Farabi, Avicenna, and al-Ghazzali. He believed that there is a formal distinction between essence and existence, between the whatness of a thing and its thatness. This does not mean that there are essences apart from concrete existence, or that existence is a mere predicate of essence, but it means rather that existence is the act that makes essence real. While essence is substance inasmuch as it is definable, existence is that very substance inasmuch as it is real.

After expounding these fundamental points of the metaphysics of Thomas, and before moving on to properly theological matters, a word must be said about the position of Thomas regarding universals. In the strict sense, universals "do not subsist in themselves but have their being in individuals";[19] that is, the universal exists *in re*, in the concrete thing. But it is also true that universals exist *ante rem* in the mind of God, not as a separate reality—for God is absolutely simple—but as God's own essence.[20] Finally, universals exist *post rem* in the human mind, as

---

[17] *Summa contra gent.* 2. 25.
[18] *De princ. nat.* (ed. Parma, 16:338).
[19] *Summa contra gent.* 1. 65.
[20] *S. Th.*, I, q. 55, art. 3.

a result of the process of abstraction.[21] Thus, the position of Thomas is a moderate realism.

The Angelic Doctor rejected the thesis of Anselm that the existence of God is self-evident. It is true that in God essence and existence coincide, and that therefore, in itself, God's existence is evident. But "for us, who do not know the divine nature, that existence is not evident."[22] Therefore, one must prove the existence of God, and Thomas offered "five ways" or proofs. Each of these various ways sets out from that which one knows through the bodily senses, and leads to the existence of God.[23]

The first way sets out from the undeniable fact of movement (*ex parte motus*). There are in the world things that move, that is, that go from potency to act. But since nothing can pass from potency to act by itself but must be moved by another, and that other must itself be in act, one reaches the inevitable conclusion that there must be a first being that is the primary origin of all movement, and that itself is not moved by another. Such a being, which may properly be called the prime unmoved mover or pure act, is God.

The second way is that of causality (*ex ratione causae efficientis*). All things in this world have their causes, and some may be the cause of others, but none is its own cause. Thus an order of causes exists, and in this order there must be a first cause, for if a first cause did not exist the others would also be nonexistent. That first cause is God.

The third way sets out from the distinction between the contingent and the necessary (*ex possibili et necessario*). All things

---

[21] *Ibid.*, q. 85, art. 2.

[22] *Ibid.*, q. 2, art. 1.

[23] *Ibid.*, art. 3. Several of these "ways" may also be found in *Summa contra gent.* 1. 13; but there the first way seems to eclipse the others. Due to the great number of works published recently on the five ways of Thomas, the following bibliographical note has been restricted to those which deal with them as a whole, and in such a manner as may be useful to the student who wishes to be introduced to the basic issues involved: E. G. Jay, *The Existence of God: A Commentary on St. Thomas Aquinas' Five Ways of Demonstrating the Existence of God* (London: S.P.C.K., 1948); E. González, *Las cinco vías de Santo Tomás de Aquino* (Huesca: L. Pérez, 1943); R. A. Markus, "A Note on the Meaning of 'via'," *DomSt*, 7 (1954), 239-45; S. Giuliani, "Perchè cinque le 'vie' di S. Tommaso?" *Sapza*, 1 (1948), 153-66; E. Sillem, *Ways of Thinking About God: Thomas Aquinas and Some Recent Problems* (London: Darton, Longman & Todd, 1961); F. van Steenberghen, *Le problème de l'existence de Dieu dans les écrits de S. Thomas d'Aquin* (Louvain: Institut supérieur de Philosophie, 1980); L. Elders, ed., *Quinque sunt viae: Actes du Symposium sur les cinq voies de la 'Somme théologique'* (Vatican: Libreria Editrice Vaticana, 1980).

that we see in this world are contingent. Therefore the fact that they do exist implies that they have received their existence from another being. If that other being is necessary in itself, it is God; if it is necessary because another one has given it its existence, that other one is God; if it is necessary through a series of other beings, there must be a first member of that series, and that is God.

The fourth way sets out from the various degrees of perfection in beings (ex gradibus). Some beings are better than others, and this can only be due to their greater proximity to the highest degree of goodness. Therefore, something must exist which possesses perfection in its supreme degree, and which is the cause for the various degrees of perfection in all other beings. This supremely perfect being is God.

The fifth way sets out from the order of the universe (ex gubernatione rerum), and is the traditional teleological argument. All things in the universe, even those which have no reason, move toward an end that is proper to them, and they could not do that out of themselves or through chance. That which leads them to their end is God.

It should be noted that these five ways are parallel. Each sets out from things as they are known through the senses; each discovers in them some good that is, however, incomplete in the sense that it is not self-sufficient—movement, existence, degree of perfection, order; and each finds in God the final reason for that goodness. This type of argument is partially due to Thomas' Aristotelianism, for he no longer felt compelled, as Anselm did, to find an argument for the existence of God which is totally independent of sensory perception.

God is absolutely simple, for there is in God no body or hylomorphic composition. God is pure act in whom essence and existence are identical;[24] the perfection of all being;[25] and the highest good.[26]

---

[24] S. Th., I, q. 3.
[25] Ibid., q. 4, art. 2.
[26] Ibid., q. 6, art. 2.

One may therefore call things good and existent by reference to this first thing, existent and good by nature, inasmuch as they somehow participate and resemble it, even if distantly and deficiently . . . And in this sense all things are said to be good by divine goodness, which is the pattern, source and goal of all goodness. Nevertheless the resemblance to divine goodness which leads us to call the thing good is inherent in the thing itself, belonging to it as a form and therefore naming it. And so there is one goodness in all things, and yet many.[27]

God—and only God—is infinite.[28] God is omnipresent, not in a pantheistic sense, but as creator and sustainer of all things, as well as by making it possible that there be such things as places.[29] God is also eternal—which led the Angelic Doctor to discuss the difference between time and eternity.

The difference between time and eternity does not consist simply in that time has a beginning and an end while eternity does not. These characteristics are only accidental, for even if the world did not have a beginning or an end this would not make it eternal. The difference is rather in that eternity is the measure of permanent being, whereas time is the measure of movement.[30]

God is one, which can be proved not only from God's simplicity, but also from the divine perfection (if there were more than one, they would be distinguished by one having something that the other did not, and therefore it would be impossible for both to be perfect) and from the unity of the world (if there were several gods the unified order of the world would be impossible).[31] Furthermore, God is one in the highest degree, for absolute simplicity implies that God is not divisible, even in potency.[32]

---

[27] Ibid., art. 4 (ed. Gilby, 2:93).
[28] Ibid., q. 7, art. 1-2.
[29] Ibid., q. 8, art. 2.
[30] Ibid., q. 10, art. 4. There is also the "aeon"—aevum—which is the measure of angelic existence and stands between time and eternity. The aevum has a beginning and no end, but this distinguishes it from both time and eternity only incidentally. Its essential characteristic is in being the measure of angelic existence, which does not have to change but is capable of it. See ibid., art. 5.
[31] Ibid., q. 11, art. 3.
[32] Ibid., art. 4.

Most of what has been said up to this point regarding the nature of God is negative, for infinity, eternity, indivisibility, pure act, and so forth, are negations of imperfection rather than affirmations of attributes. But if theologians had to be limited to these negative affirmations regarding God, theology would be a very narrow discipline. Therefore, Thomas was interested in discussing whether and how it was possible to know the essence of God, as well as how one might speak of God.

As to whether it is possible to know the essence of God, Aquinas declared that such a knowledge is unattainable in this life.[33] But the blessed in heaven will see the essence of God,[34] and it will be in that essence that they will know all other things, by contemplating the ultimate cause.[35] This knowledge will not embrace the totality of the divine essence, or even all the things knowable through that essence, for it is impossible to comprehend God. There will be various levels of knowledge, so that some will know God better than others, but none perfectly. Finally, this knowledge will be attained not through the natural powers of the understanding, but through a divine illumination—*lumen gloriae*.[36]

On the other hand, even in this life we can know and say something regarding God through the use of analogy.[37] When one predicates one term of another, such predication may be equivocal, univocal, or analogous. Equivocal is a term that is applied to more than one object with no reason—or with

---

[33] *Ibid.*, *q. 12, art.* 12.
[34] *Ibid.*, *art.* 1.
[35] *Ibid.*, *art.* 10.
[36] *Ibid.*, *art.* 5.
[37] There have been many studies of Thomas' theory of analogy. One of the main issues is whether he accepted not only an "analogy of proportionality" (Cajetan, *De nom. analog.*), but also an "analogy of attribution" based on the relationship of causality between God and creatures (Suarez, *Disp. metaph.* 18; ed. Vives, 26:13-21). See J. Habbel, *Die Analogie zwischen Gott und Welt nach Thomas von Aquin* (Regensburg: J. Habbel, 1928); G. B. Phelan, *Saint Thomas and Analogy* (Milwaukee: Marquette University Press, 1941); A. Gazzana, "L'analogia in S. Tommaso e nel Gaetano," *Greg*, 24 (1943), 367-83; H. Lyttkens, *The Analogy Between God and the World: An Investigation of Its Background and Interpretation of Its Use by Thomas of Aquino* (Uppsala: Almqvist & Wiksells, 1952); O. A. Varangot, "Analogía de atribución intrínseca en Santo Tomás," *CienFe, 13* (1957), 293-319; O. A. Varangot, "Analogía de atribución intrínseca y análoga del ente según Santo Tomás," *CienFe, 13* (1957), 467-85; O. A. Varangot, "El analogado principal," *CienFe,* 14 (1958), 237-53; B. Montagnes, *La doctrine de l'analogie de l'être d' après saint Thomas d' Aquin* (Louvain: Publications Universitaires, 1963). A collection of the most significant texts may be found in G. P. Klubertanz, *St. Thomas Aquinas on Analogy: A Textual Analysis and Systematic Synthesis* (Chicago: Loyola University Press, 1960).

insufficient reason. The word "canis," for instance, can refer to a dog, a constellation, or a fish. Univocal is a term that is applied to another according to its only proper meaning, as when one says that a dog or a person is "blind." But between these two extremes of equivocal and univocal predication, there is analogy. There are terms that do not express exactly the same thing in various contexts, but that can be used correctly in all of them. Thus, for instance, the word "healthy" would not mean exactly the same in the following expressions: "this animal is healthy," "this medicine is healthy," and "this urine sample is healthy." This form of predication, based in a real similitude but without the identity of that which is univocal, is called "analogy." Analogy may be classified in various ways.[38] But that which concerns us here is that analogy is the basis on which one may speak about God. Since we know God through creatures, and the distance between creator and creature is infinite, "it is impossible to predicate anything univocally of God and creatures."[39] But, on the other hand, there is a relationship of cause and effect between God and creatures. This relationship implies that creatures are somehow similar to the Creator. Therefore, it is possible to apply to God, through analogy, terms that in our current use refer to perfections in creatures—"wise," "good," "powerful," "merciful," etc.

> In this way some words are used neither univocally nor purely equivocally of God and creatures, but analogically, for we cannot speak of God at all except in the language we use of creatures, and so whatever is said both of God and creatures is said in virtue of the order that creatures have to God as to their source and cause in which all the perfections of things pre-exist transcendently.

---

[38] In I Sent., dist. 19, q. 5, art. 2, Aquinas distinguished between three forms of analogy: of intention, but not of being; of being, but not of intention; and of both intention and being. In De ver., q. 2, art. 11, he seems to be discussing the third of these types of analogy while further distinguishing between "analogy of proportion," in which two terms are related by virtue of their relationship to a third—as in the case of "healthy," predicated of a dog and of a medicine by virtue of their relationship to "health"—and "analogy of proportionality," in which proper predication takes place by virtue of relationships proper to each of the two subjects—as when one says that God is like a "lion," not meaning thereby that there is a direct connection between "God" and "lion," but that God acts within a certain sphere of action in a way similar to that of a lion within its own sphere. In other texts, Thomas suggested still other ways of classifying analogy—and this is one of the reasons there are various interpretations of his views on this matter.

[39] S. Th., I, q. 13, art. 5 (ed. Gilby, 3:63).

This way of using words lies somewhere between pure equivocation and simple univocity, for the word is neither used in the same sense, as with univocal usage, nor in totally different senses, as with equivocation. The several senses of a word used analogically signify different relations to some one thing, as "health" in a complexion means a symptom of health in a man, and in a diet means a cause of that health.[40]

This doctrine of analogy is not a mere semantic recourse in order to apply human terms to God, nor is it only a theory regarding the knowledge of God. It goes much farther than this. What is given to us in knowledge really corresponds to being. It is not that God is similar to creatures. It is that in truth creatures are similar to God, since every effect somehow reflects its cause.[41] If it is possible to speak of God in analogical terms, this is because there is an "analogy of being"—*analogia entis*—which is previous to our own discovery of it. Therefore, "in analogous things, the real order is not the same as the conceptual order."[42]

From this use of analogy, Thomas goes on to discuss how and in what sense God is wise, living, willing, loving, and powerful. It is not possible to discuss here the exact meaning of each of these attributes, but only to point out that each of them is interpreted from the starting point of the absolute simplicity of God, so that all are identical among themselves and are indeed identical with God.

Regarding providence and predestination, it must first be affirmed that God's knowledge and power are such that God is able to establish a distinction between certain things that occur of necessity and others that are contingent.

God wills some things to become real necessarily, and others contingently, in order to furnish the full equipment of the universe. Accordingly for some he has designed necessary causes which cannot fail, from which effects result necessarily, and for others defectible and contingent causes from which effects result

---

[40] *Ibid.* (ed. Gilby, 3:65, 67).
[41] *Summa contra gent.* 1.29.
[42] *Ibid.*, 34.

contingently. Hence the ultimate reason why some things happen contingently is not because their proximate causes are contingent, but because God has willed them to happen contingently, and therefore, has prepared contingent causes for them.[43]

However, in spite of this distinction, all that happens is subject to the divine will, which is always fulfilled,[44] not always as a direct "operation" but sometimes also as a mere "permission."[45] God orders certain things to take place, while merely permitting others. Therefore, all is subject to the divine providence, of which predestination is an aspect.

The doctrine of predestination becomes necessary, because apart from the help of God we cannot attain eternal life.[46] Predestination to glory is an election on the part of God which causes good in the elect—whereas in human election we choose according to the good that we see in the choice.[47] Those who are not within the scope of this divine predestination are reprobate through a *permissive* act of God, who does not extend to them the unmerited gift of election. Reprobation, as well as election, is not limited to God's foreknowledge of our future actions. On the contrary, predestination includes the will and thought of God to give one grace and glory, and reprobation includes a permissive decision to allow another to sin, to remain in that sin, and to be punished for it.[48] Finally, Thomas followed Augustine in claiming repeatedly that divine providence and predestination do not contradict free will, for God produces the intended results through the various secondary causes, including human free will.[49]

All that exists, including prime matter, has been created by

---

[43] *S. Th.*, I, q. 19, art. 8 (ed. Gilby, 5:39).

[44] *Ibid.*, art. 6.

[45] *Ibid.*, art. 12.

[46] *Ibid.*, q. 23, art. 1. R. Velasco, "Providencia y predestinación: Estudio positivo de una cuestión disputada en la escuela tomista," *RET*, 21 (1961), 125-51, 249-87.

[47] *Ibid.*, art. 4. This point is significant, for it contradicts the notion, commonly held among Protestants, that the entire medieval tradition was "Pelagian" in that it did not understand the absolutely unmerited nature of predestination as Augustine saw it.

[48] *Ibid.*, art. 3.

[49] *Ibid.*, art. 5; *Summa contra gent.* 3. 88-91.

God.[50] Here Thomas felt compelled to abandon Aristotle,[51] who postulated an eternal matter and who was followed at this point by several teachers in the Arts Faculty of Paris, as will be seen in the next chapter. Thomas claimed that the theory according to which God simply gave form to a pre-existent matter denied the doctrine of creation, for if God acted simply by changing and moving that which originally existed, God is not the universal cause of being.[52] Thomas believed that there were several rational arguments that could be adduced against the theory that matter is eternal, but that none of these arguments was conclusive. As to the time of creation, he refuted those who claimed that they could prove that creation is eternal,[53] although here again he agreed that creation within time could not be rationally proved beyond all doubt, and that it could only be known with certainty because it had been revealed.[54]

God created simultaneously the heavens, matter, time, and angelic nature.[55] It was at this point that Aquinas dealt with the much debated question of whether angels have matter.[56] As has been said already, the hylomorphic composition of intellectual beings—and therefore of angels—was held by the Franciscan school, which on this point had the support of most conservative theologians. Over against this position, Thomas affirmed that it was impossible for a spiritual substance to have any sort of matter, and that therefore every intellectual substance must be wholly immaterial.[57] This put Thomas in a difficult position. He believed that the distinction between various individuals in the

---

[50] S. Th., I, q. 44, art. 1-2; Summa contra gent. 2. 15-16. The background of the insistence of Thomas on this point may be seen in L. H. Kendzierski, "The Doctrine of Eternal Matter and Form," ModSch, 31 (1953-54), 171-83. See also the Spanish translation: J. I. Raranyana, "Santo Tomás: 'De aeternitate mundi contra murmurantes,' " Anuario filosófico, 9 (1976), 399-424.

[51] See R. Jolivet, "Aristote et la notion de création," RScPhTh, 19 (1930), 5-50, 209-25.
[52] Summa contra gent. 2. 16.
[53] S. Th. 1, q. 46, art. 1.
[54] Ibid., art. 2.
[55] Ibid., art. 3.

[56] The best discussions of this issue, in which several characteristics of Thomism are manifest, are: H. van Rooy, "De middeleeuwen over materia en forma bij de engelen," StCath, 5 (1928-29), 108-27; E. Kleineidam, Das Problem der hylemorphen Zusammensetzung der geistigen Substanzen im 13. Jahrhundert, behandelt bis Thomas von Aquin (Liebenthan, private publication, 1930); A. Martínez, "Introducctión al Tratado de los Angeles," BAC, 56:52-60. A closely related study is that of J. Goheen, The Problem of Matter and Form in the "De ente et essentia" of Thomas Aquinas (Cambridge: Harvard University Press, 1940).

[56] S. Th., I, q. 50, art. 2.

same genus came through the union of matter and form. In consequence, all angels would be indistinguishable. His only way out was to claim that each angel was a different species.[58]

Thomas discussed anthropology in great detail. Within this context, what most interests us here is the human nature, the theory of knowledge, and the end of human existence.

A human being is not simply a soul united to a body, but is rather a composite of both soul and body, so that neither of the two by itself is a person.[59] Following the principle that intellectual beings are not hylomorphic, Thomas claimed that the soul has no proper matter.[60] The soul is the form of the body, which serves as the matter of the soul; and it is therefore the human being, and not the soul, that is composed of matter and form[61]—a composition that, as has been previously said, is the principle of individuation of all created beings.[62] The soul that exists in each body is different from other souls, in spite of the contrary opinion of some so-called interpreters of Aristotle.[63] This is one of the main points on which Thomas felt compelled to reject what was at his time the common interpretation of Aristotle, for to affirm the unity of all souls would imply the denial of personal immortality. On the other hand, the soul of each person is a unity[64] in spite of the fact that it does have several

---

[58] Ibid., art. 4.

[59] A brief introduction to the issues involved at this point is S. Vanni-Rovighi, "La concezione tomistica dell'anima umana," Sapza, 10 (1957), 347-59. Somewhat more detailed and technical, and giving some attention to the development of Thomas himself, is A. C. Pegis, St. Thomas and the Problem of the Soul in the Thirteenth Century (Toronto: St. Michael's College, 1934). Also worth mentioning are: V. E. Sleva, The Separated Soul in the Philosophy of St. Thomas (Washington: Catholic University of America Press, 1940); M. E. Anderson, The Human Body in the Philosophy of St. Thomas Aquinas (Catholic University of America Press, 1953); C. S. Zamoyta, The Unity of Man: St. Thomas' Solution to the Body-Soul Problem (Catholic University of America Press, 1956); K. Bernath, Anima forma corporis: Eine Untersuchung über die ontologische Grundlage der Anthropologie des Thomas von Aquin (Bonn: H. Bouvier, 1969). A good study of the historical background of this question is R. Zavalloni, "La métaphysique du composé humain dans la pensée scholastique préthomiste," RevPhLouv, 48 (1950), 5-36. On its ulterior history, see P. Muñiz, "El constitutivo formal de la persona creada en la tradición tomista," CienTom, 68 (1945), 5-89; 70 (1946), 201-93.

[60] S. Th., I. q. 75, art. 5. See E. von Ivanka, "Aristotelische und thomistische Seelenlehre," in Aristote et saint Thomas d'Aquin (Louvain: Publications Universitaires, 1957), pp. 221-28.

[61] S. Th., I. q. 76, art. 1.

[62] This has been variously interpreted by later students of Thomas. See BThAM, vol. 6 (1950-53), no. 621.

[63] S. Th., I. q. 76, art. 2. See J. Mundhenk, Die Seele im System des Thomas von Aquin: Ein Beitrag zur Klärung und Beurteilung der thomistischen Psychologie (Hamburg: F. Meiner, 1980); M. Sánchez Sorondo, "La querella antropológica del siglo XIII: Sigerio y Santo Tomás," Sap., 35 (1980), 325-58.

[64] Ibid., art. 3.

distinct faculties,[65] for it is a single and indivisible form—against the view of the Augustinian tradition.[66]

The theory of knowledge is one of the characteristic points in the doctrine of Thomas.[67] The problem that he had to face was that of conciliating the Aristotelian proposition that nothing could be in the intellect without formerly being in the senses with the long philosophical tradition that claimed that true knowledge could not be limited to individual and transitory objects, but must somehow be knowledge of universal essences.[68] On the one hand, he could accept neither the Platonic doctrine of reminiscence nor Augustinian illumination, for both theories attempted to explain the possibility of knowledge of essences by leaving aside the function of the senses in the cognitive process. On the other hand, the problem could not be solved by going to the opposite extreme—that is, by affirming that only that which is given to the senses can be known, and that therefore knowledge must be limited to particular and material objects and can never attain universal essences.

The solution that Thomas offered consisted in explaining knowledge as a process in which, starting from sensory data, we attain knowledge of essences. Since we are a composite of body and soul, we do not know with the soul alone, nor do we feel with the body alone. On the contrary, the soul plays a role in sensory perception, and in knowledge the bodily senses provide the primary data. The data of the senses are given not as a chaotic multiplicity of sensations, but rather as an image or "phantasm"

[65] Ibid., q. 77, art. 2. These faculties are, according to Aristotle, of five different kinds (ibid., q. 78, art. 1; De anima, 2). See P. Künzle, Das Verhältnis der Seele zu ihren Potenzen: Problemgeschichtliche Untersuchung von Augustin bis und mit Thomas von Aquin (Fribourg: Universitätsverlag, 1956).

[66] On the background of this problem, see D. A. Callus, "The Origins of the Problem of the Unity of Form," Thomist, 24 (1961), 257-85. On Thomas himself, as compared with the fully developed Franciscan school, see B. J. Campbell, The Problem of One or Plural Forms in Man as Found in the Works of St. Thomas Aquinas and John Duns Scotus (Paterson, N. J.: St. Anthony Guild, 1940).

[67] So much has been written on the subject that it is impossible to offer here even a basic bibliography. The following works are mentioned as introductions to the issues involved and to further bibliographical references; B. Gerrity, The Relations Between the Theory of Matter and Form and the Theory of Knowledge in the Philosophy of Saint Thomas Aquinas (Washington: Catholic University of America Press, 1936); J. Santeler, Der Platonismus in der Erkenntnislehre des heligen Thomas von Aquin (Innsbruck: F. Rauch, 1939); A Rebolla, Abstracto y concreto en la filosofía de Santo Tomás: Estructura metafísica de los cuerpos y su conocimiento intelectivo (Burgos: Seminario metropolitano, 1955). The pertinent texts in Thomas have been edited by J. de Vries, De cognitione veritatis textus selecti S. Thomae Aquinatis (Münster: Aschendorff, 1953).

[68] This may be clearly seen in S. Th., I, q. 84, art. 6.

in which the various sensations are related in such a way that they represent a material and concrete object.[69] This image is not the object; but it is not purely subjective, for it faithfully represents a real object. However, such a "phantasm" is not yet true knowledge, for it is the image of a concrete and passing object, whereas true knowledge refers to the essence of things. It is necessary, therefore, that the intellect extract from the phantasm that which corresponds to its essence. It is not that the mind attempts to discover an ulterior reality behind concrete objects, but rather that it distinguishes in the object itself which is present before the senses that which corresponds to its essence. The essential reality of things is to be found not apart from them, but rather in them, and therefore the discovery of essence is an act of abstraction rather than of penetration beyond the sensible.

Abstraction is an activity of the active intellect, which "illuminates" the phantasm and thus discovers that which is essential in it. Although Thomas here used the term of Augustine, his theory is very different from the Augustinian illumination that takes place through divine action. Thomist "illumination" is an act through which the human mind discovers the essence in a phantasm just as light uncovers the colors that are in things. The active intellect discovers in the phantasm the "intelligible species,"[70] which is then imprinted on the passive intellect. The latter produces the "expressed species," or universal and essential concepts. It is thus that we attain knowledge, although one must insist once again that the concept is not the object of knowledge, but rather the instrument through which objects are known. Thus, for instance, the concept "dog" is not knowledge; knowledge is the application of that concept to a particular and concrete individual. Therefore, Thomistic epistemology begins from the concrete and ends at it, but acquires its validity because in that process from concrete to concrete the intellect goes through the essential and universal concepts.

---

[69] *Ibid., art.* 7.
[70] *Ibid., q.* 85, *art.* 1.

Our knowledge of God and of our own souls, at least during this life, also stems from the senses. We know such incorporeal realities not by virtue of a direct illumination, but as a consequence of our knowledge of corporeal realities that witness to the existence of those which are incorporeal. This may be seen in the five ways to prove the existence of God which we have already discussed.

As everything is to be directed according to the end to which it is ordered, the foundation of moral theology is to be found in the ultimate end of human existence. Here Thomas agreed with Aristotle, who affirmed that our end is happiness and that therefore ethics should lead us to that goal. But Thomas believed that happiness is beyond our natural powers, for it consists in the beatific vision, which can only be attained in the future life and through a supernatural aid. "Therefore, the ultimate happiness of man will be in the knowledge of God which the human mind will have beyond this life."[71] On the other hand, although only God can grant such happiness, divine justice demands that we prepare ourselves through acts of merit to receive this unmerited gift.[72]

The starting point for moral theology is the doctrine of law.[73] The origin of every law and of every order is the "eternal law," which is in God as supreme ruler of the universe. From this law follows the "natural law," which is the manner in which creatures participate in the eternal laws. This is especially true of rational creatures, in whom this natural law is so imprinted that it directs them toward moral truth. This natural law is the foundation of universal or general morality, that is, of that morality which is not limited to the particular group of those who know the revealed law of God, or to those who follow a particular set of human rules. Natural law is universal, for it is written in the hearts of all, and its precepts are the first principles of practical reason.

The first principles of natural law are self-evident. But there are other precepts that follow from that law that demand the

---

[71] *Summa contra gent.* 3. 48.
[72] *S. Th.,* I^a II^{ae}, *Q.* 5, *art.* 7.
[73] The so-called Treatise on Law is to be found in *S. Th.,* I^a II^{ae}, *q.* 90-108.

correct use of reason in order to discover them. Thus Thomas could build a great deal of his moral theology on the foundation of natural law, and could claim that his conclusions had universal validity.[74] However, this natural law must be completed by divine law, given by God in a more explicit and detailed way. The high point of divine law is the new law, or gospel law, whose commandments are loving, and which also include "counsels of perfection," which do not have to be followed by all but which do lead to a greater perfection.[75]

The most remarkable trait of Thomas' Christology is the influence of Cyril of Alexandria, almost completely unknown by most Western theologians. Partly because of his study of Cyril, Thomas interpreted the union of the two natures in Christ in terms of an anhypostatic union. The person or hypostasis has its own subsistence, but the two natures do not, and therefore it is in the person of the Word that the human nature of the Savior subsists.[76] By virtue of that union, and because the operations and properties of each nature are to be referred to the hypostasis, the *communicatio idiomatum* takes place, and one can therefore predicate of the Word that which properly belongs to human nature—to have been born of a virgin, to have suffered, and the rest.

Another aspect of Thomas' Christology which was later very much debated was his answer to the question whether God would have become incarnate even if humans had not sinned.[77] Without categorically denying the opposite opinion, the Angelic Doctor said that it seemed more reasonable to say that if humans had not sinned God would not have become incarnate, although one must acknowledge that God is omnipotent and could have decided to do otherwise.

Finally, because of its intimate connection with Christology, this is the proper place to say a word regarding Thomas'

[74] See for instance, *Summa contra gent.* 3. 121-29.
[75] *S. Th.*, I^a II^{ae}, *q.* 108, *art.* 4. These "counsels of perfection" were the basis for the vows of the mendicants, and therefore were very much debated at the University of Paris during the thirteenth century.
[76] *Ibid.*, III, *q.* 2, *art.* 3.
[77] *Ibid.*, *q.* 1, *art.* 3.

Mariology. On the honor due to Mary, the Angelic Doctor taught what has become the general doctrine of the Roman Church.[78] However, his position regarding the immaculate conception of Mary is categorically opposed to what would later become official doctrine of that church.[79] While he showed great respect for the Virgin, who never committed any actual sin[80] and who was always a virgin,[81] he did affirm that Mary inherited original sin, of which she was cleansed by being sanctified *after* her conception and not before. Furthermore, even that sanctification did not free her from the penalty of sin, and she therefore was able to enter paradise only by virtue of the sacrifice of Christ.[82]

The sacraments receive their power from the incarnate Word.[83] A sacrament is a sign of a sacred reality which has power to sanctify.[84] Since we are composed of body and soul and can only reach intelligible things through those which are sensible, in the sacrament intelligible realities are revealed through the sensible.[85] However, this does not mean that we can choose any object as a sacramental sign; we must choose only those which God has chosen and established as such.[86] A sacrament has a matter and a form: those things which are employed in the sacrament are its matter, and the words are its form.[87] The "sacraments of the new law"—that is, those which are valid after the passion of the Lord—have the power to give grace to those who receive them,[88] and they imprint an indelible character in the partaker.[89] This takes place whenever the act takes place with the intention of offering the sacrament,[90] even if the minister is lacking in faith or charity.[91]

---

[78] *Ibid., q.* 24, *art.* 5.
[79] *Ibid., q.* 27, *art.* 2.
[80] *Ibid., art.* 4.
[81] *Ibid., q.* 28, *art.* 3.
[82] *Ibid., q.* 27, *art.* 1.
[83] *Ibid., q.* 60, *proem.*
[84] *Ibid., art.* 2.
[85] *Ibid., art.* 5.
[86] *Ibid.*
[87] *Ibid., art.* 6-7.
[88] *Ibid., q.* 62, *art.* 4.
[89] *Ibid., q.* 63, *art.* 5.
[90] *Ibid., q.* 64, *art.* 8.
[91] *Ibid., art.* 9.

The sacraments are seven. Thomas seemed to accept this number as the traditional doctrine of the church, although it had actually been rather recently, through Peter Lombard's influence, that that number had become fixed.[92]

Thomas was without any doubt the most outstanding theologian of the Middle Ages. This was partly owing to the manner in which—especially in his *Summa Theologiae*—he posed and solved various questions. His work was like a vast gothic cathedral in which the various aspects of the medieval world view were present, from the highest heavenly mansions to the darker corners of hell, and in which all seemed to point upward, being held and moved by a masterful balance.

However, the most important aspect of this theology was not its imposing structure or its detailed discussion, but the manner in which Thomas was able to respond to the challenge of the new philosophy that was invading the Latin West. For centuries theology had followed the inspiration of Augustine and Pseudo-Dionysius—and, through them, of Plato and Plotinus. This philosophical framework, which had proved very useful to early Christians in the effort to oppose idolatry and materialism, was, however, a hindrance when it came to doctrines such as the incarnation and the sacraments, in which material and sensible elements were of capital importance. If the early centuries of the Middle Ages were not greatly interested in the study of nature and its laws, this was partly because of the invasions of the barbarians and the subsequent chaos, but it was also partly because of the otherworldly orientation of a theology built on Neoplatonic principles. Therefore, it is not suprising that the thirteenth century, which saw the development of a new philosophy that insisted on the importance of the senses as the starting point of knowledge, also witnessed an awakening in the study of the natural sciences. It was not mere coincidence that Albert the Great, a convinced Aristotelian, was also a devoted student of the natural sciences.

To this new philosophy, Thomas' contemporaries reacted in

---

[92] *Ibid., q.* 65, *art.* 1.

two basic ways. Some, such as Bonaventure, clearly rejected it and only took from it a few isolated elements that in no way affected the basic structure of traditional theology. Others, such as Siger of Brabant, embraced it enthusiastically and placed it at the very center of their thought, so that they were quite ready to abandon anything in which traditional theology and philosophy seemed to oppose the new philosophy. The former were condemning themselves to remain within the ancient framework, thus losing any positive value that there might be in the new philosophy. The latter lost their contact with the traditional faith of the church, and were thereby reduced to a small group whose influence was soon lost.

Between these two extremes, Albert and Thomas attempted to produce a theology faithful to the tradition of the church and the authority of Scripture, but framed within the new philosophy. Albert took only the first steps in this direction, and his work remained at the level of the eclectical. But Thomas was able to fuse these various elements in a synthesis that was neither Aristotelian nor Augustinian, but "Thomist."

In so doing, Thomas rendered a great service not only to theology, but to the entire Western civilization. Theology gained in that it was able to emphasize more strongly the scriptural principle that the God of Israel and of the church is revealed in the concrete events of history. Western civilization, in regaining the inquisitive spirit of Aristotle regarding the physical world, was able to follow routes of observation and investigation which eventually led to those technological developments which would become the trademarks of that civilization.

Later Development of Thomism

A theological and philosophical doctrine of such wide scope and such originality as that of Thomas is not easily accepted by most persons. On the one hand, Siger of Brabant and his followers accused him of making excessive concessions to traditional theology, and of thereby abandoning the original sense of Aristotelian philosophy. At the other extreme, Augustinian theology accused him of approaching the position of the extreme Aristotelians, and of abandoning fundamental aspects of traditional theology. The first of these two enemies never seriously threatened the survival of Thomism, for Siger and his followers were a small minority even within the Arts Faculty of the University of Paris. But the attacks on the part of more traditional theologians were a more serious threat. During the earlier struggle in favor of the Mendicant Orders against the accusations of William of Saint Amour and Gerard of Abbeville, Franciscans and Dominicans marched arm in arm. This situation was radically changed when Thomism became generally known. The Franciscans, under the leadership of John Peckham, many seculars, and even some Dominicans, began openly attacking the "innovations of Brother Thomas." He would not be intimidated, but rather wrote a small treatise *On the Eternity of the World,* which denied that the world was eternal, but disagreed with traditional theologians by insisting that such eternity was not a rational absurdity.

The struggle reached its climax in 1277, three years after the death of Thomas, when Stephen Tempier, the Bishop of Paris, published and condemned a list of 219 propositions, taken mostly from Siger of Brabant and other teachers in the Arts Faculty, but also from Thomas and his followers.[93] In an action seemingly coordinated with that of his Parisian colleague, Robert Kilwardby, then Archbishop of Canterbury, published and condemned at Oxford another list of thirty propositions in which several Thomist theses were included.[94] The Franciscan William of La Mare published a *Correction of Brother Thomas* in which he virulently attacked the Dominican.[95] In 1282, the

---

[93] J. F. Wippel, "The Condemnations of 1270 and 1277," *JMedRenSt,* 7 (1977), 169-201.
[94] Cf. L. E. Wilshire, "Were the Oxford Condemnations of 1277 Directed against Aquinas?" *NSch,* 48 (1974), 125-32.
[95] R. Creytens, "Autour de la littérature des Correctoirs," *ArchFrHist,* 12 (1942) 313-30. On chronological questions, see F. Pelster, "Einige ergänzende Angaben zum Leben und zu den Schriften des Willhelm de la Mare O. F. M.," *FranzSt,* 37 (1955), 75-80. The text has been edited by Pelster, *Declarationes Magistri Guilemi de la Mare O. F. M. de variis sententiis S. Thomae Aquinatis* (Münster: Aschendorff, 1956); T. Schneider, *Die Einheit des Menschen: Die anthropologische Formel 'anima forma corporis' im sogennanten Korrektorienstreit und bei Petrus Johannis Olivi: Ein Beitrag zur Vorgeschichte des Konzils von Vienne* (Münster: Aschendorff, 1937); L. Hödl, "Anima forma corporis: Philosophisch-theologische Erhebungen zur Grundformel der scholastischen Anthropologie im Korrektorienstreit (1277-1287)," *ThPhil,* 41 (1966), 536-56; M. D. Jordan, "The Controversy of the 'Correctoria' and the Limits of Metaphysics," *Spec.,* 57 (1982), 292-314.

general chapter of the Franciscan order recommended the reading of this work to all its members.[96] Meanwhile, the Dominicans had rallied to the defense of their illustrious theologian. Their general chapters of 1278 and 1279 took measures to make sure that members of the order would not attack Thomas. In 1309, the doctrine of the Angelic Doctor was declared the rule of all teaching and study by Dominicans. Also, during the last years of the thirteenth century, several authors refuted the *Correction* of William of La Mare—often under the suggestive title of *Correction of the Corruptor of Brother Thomas*.[97]

In spite of its condemnation in the two main centers of theological studies, Thomism found several defenders who followed the Angelic Doctor in a number of points but avoided open contradiction of the decrees. Such were, among others, Giles of Rome,[98] Godfrey of Fontaines,[99] and Peter of Auvergne.[100]

Finally, in 1323, John XXII, Pope at Avignon, canonized Thomas, and from that time on his influence increased. The condemnation at Paris was removed in 1324. His commentators and followers multiplied, and even his opponents saw him as the greatest theologian of the thirteenth century. In 1567, Pope Pius V gave him the title of "Universal Doctor of the Church."

---

[96] S. Ramírez, "Introducción general," *BAC*, 19:90.

[97] P. Glorieux, *Les premières polémiques thomistes: I—Le Correctorium corruptori "Quare"* (Kain, Belgium: Biblioteque thomiste, 9, 1927), pp. vii-xix.

[98] His treatise *Errores philosophorum* has been edited by J. Koch, with an English translation by J. O. Riedl (Milwaukee: Marquette University Press, 1944). His *Theoremata de esse et essentia* has been translated by M. V. Murray (Marquette University Press, 1952). Scholars are not agreed on the exact relationship between Giles and Thomas. There are undoubtedly several points of contact between them—such as the real distinction between essence and existence. But the influence of Neoplatonism on Giles is much more evident than on Thomas.

[99] A brief discussion of Godfrey may be found in Gilson, *History*, pp. 424-25, 739-40. More detailed studies are those of V. Heynck, "Die Kontroverse zwischen Gottfried von Fontaines und Bernard von Auvergne O. P. um die Lehre des hl. Thomas von der confessio informis," *FranzSt*, 45 (1963), 1-40, 201-42; and B. Neumann, *Der Mensch und die himmlische Seligkeit nach der Lehre Gottfrieds von Fontaines* (Limburg: Lahn Verlag, 1958); N. F. Gaughan, "Godfrey of Fontaines: An Independent Thinker," *AmEccRev*, 157 (1967), 43-54; J. F. Wippel, *The Metaphysical Thought of Godfrey of Fontaines: A Study in Late Thirteenth-Century Philosophy* (Washington: Catholic University of America, 1981). One of the most significant points in Godfrey's thought is his insistence on the priority of reason over will. On this point he would be refuted by the later Franciscan school under the leadership of John Duns Scotus.

[100] See E. Hocedez, "La théologie de Pierre d'Auvergne," *Greg*, 11 (1930), 526-52; W. Dunphy, "Two Texts of Peter of Auvergne on a Twofold Efficient Cause," *MedSt*, 26 (1964), 287-301.

XI

Extreme Aristotelianism

As has already been said, the central issue that was posed during the thirteenth century was that of the attitude that one was to assume toward the recently discovered philosophy of Aristotle and his Commentator. Some theologians, whom we have called Augustinian and among whom the most noteworthy were Alexander of Hales and Bonaventure, retained the traditional philosophy and theology and accepted from Aristotelianism only that which was clearly compatible with the inheritance of the earlier Middle Ages. Others, whom one might call "moderate Aristotelians," accepted the basic principles of Aristotelianism and made a conscious effort to remain faithful to the traditional teaching of the Church, although placing it within a basically Aristotelian framework. Still others—to whom this chapter is devoted—decided to explore freely the new horizons before them, concentrated on the new philosophy, and engaged in rational investigation, although without necessarily abandoning their Christian faith. The main representative of this group was Siger of Brabant.

Siger of Brabant

Siger[1] was a member of the Arts Faculty at Paris, and instead of continuing his academic career by entering the theological

---

[1] The rather complex problems having to do with the chronology, authorship, and transmission of the text of Siger's works cannot be discussed here. See: F. van Steenberghen, *Siger de Brabant d'après ses*

faculty, as was usual in his time, he decided to continue as an "artist," without ever becoming a theologian. This decision is itself a reflection of the new atmosphere that was beginning to take possession of the universities: philosophy, now enriched by the new traditions, was no longer a mere instrument for theology, but became a field of research in its own right. Siger undertook the exploration of that field with enthusiasm. His main ambition seems to have been to understand Aristotle and, through the application of his principles, to investigate rational truth. Such an enterprise would inevitably lead him to clash with the theologians—and he seems to have been well aware of it, for he had no scruples in placing Augustine and Aristotle against each other as representatives of two different points of view. However, this does not mean, as some have claimed, that he rejected the data of revelation, or that he claimed that philosophical truth could contradict theological truth. On the contrary, he seems always to have remained a sincere Christian, although his task of interpreting Aristotle frequently led him beyond what many considered to be the limits of orthodoxy. Siger and his followers have often been called "Latin Averroists." The origin of such a title, which seems to have originated with Thomas, is to be found in the undeniable fact that Siger followed the teachings of Averroës regarding the unity of the active intellect. But in general Siger grants Averroës no more authority than that which he has as the Commentator of Aristotle, whose interpretations can always be debated. In fact, Siger seems to have received a strong influence from Avicenna and, through the *Book on Causes*, from Proclus and Neoplatonism. But he still believed that the epitome of philosophy was to be found in Aristotle, and that his own task was the restoration and amplification of that philosophy.

---

oeuvres inédites, 2 vols. (Louvain: Institute Supérieur de Philosophie, 1931, 1942); F. van Steenberghen, *Les oeuvres et la doctrine de Siger de Brabant* (Brussels: Palais des Académies, 1938); F. Stermüller, "Neugefundene Quaestionen des Siger von Brabant," *RThAM*, 3 (1931), 158-82; R. A. Gauthier, "Notes sur Siger de Brabant," *RScPhTh*, 67 (1983), 201-32; 68 (1984), 3-49. On the entire movement, see K. Kuksewicz, *De Siger de Brabant à Jacques de Plaisance: La théorie de l'intellect chez les averroïstes latins des XIIIᵉ et XIVᵉ siècles* (Warsaw: Éditions de l'Académie polonaise des sciences, 1968); P. Glorieux, *La faculté des arts et ses membres au XIIIᵉ siècle* (Paris: J. Vrin, 1971); F. van Steenberghen, *Maitre Siger de Brabant* (Louvain: Publications universitaires, 1977). The classical study is P. Mandonnet, *Siger de Brabant et l'averroïsme latin au XIIIᵉ siècle: Étude critique et documents inédits* (reprint, Geneva: Slatkine, 1976).

Siger's philosophy is not profoundly original, but is essentially a
restoration of integral Aristotelianism. For him, Aristotle is the
philosopher par excellence, the genius who founded philosophy.
His philosophical authority has no rival. In the rational field,
Siger never openly contradicts the teaching of Aristotle, whose
solution is always to be preferred above any other. To
philosophize is above all to investigate what Aristotle and the
other philosophers think about a problem.[2]

The title of "Averroist" and his interest in philosophical
investigation apart from theology, are the reasons that the
doctrine of "double truth" has often been attributed to Siger.[3]
This is an anachronism, for no one in the thirteenth century
seems to have held such a view. What is indeed true is that Siger
always insisted on the right of philosophy to follow the route of
rational investigation to its ultimate consequences, even if this
forced one to declare that, in view of the seeming contradiction
between the conclusions of reason and the data of faith, it was
necessary to abandon the former and confess the latter. In
consequence, although in the field of philosophy he was a strict
rationalist, in that of theology he would have been pushed to
fideism. Seemingly, his affirmations were sincere, and he was a
convinced Christian. But in spite of this his dichotomy between
faith and reason threatened to undermine the entire edifice of
scholasticism, which was precisely based on the presupposition—sometimes explicit and sometimes not—that, although
there are truths that reason cannot reach, such truths are not
contrary to reason but are rather above it, so that though reason
may be unable to discover and prove them, it is also unable to
contradict them. Therefore, the first point that made extreme
Aristotelianism unacceptable to the theologians was its insistence
on the independence of philosophy, which should be free to
follow its own way apart from theological considerations.

The second point of conflict between Siger and orthodoxy was

---

[2] Van Steenberghen, *Les oeuvres et la doctrine*, pp. 166-67.
[3] F. Sassen, "Siger de Brabant et la doctrine de la double vérité," *RnsPh*, 33 (1931), 170-79; F. van
Steenberghen, "Une légende tenace: La théorie de la double vérité," *Bulletin des Lettres et des Sciences
morales*, Académie roy. de Belgique, ser. 5, 56 (1970), 179-96.

the question of the eternity of the world. On the basis of the Aristotelian understanding of the prime being as a first unmoved mover, Siger felt compelled by rational necessity to affirm that the effect of an eternal God must also be eternal, and that therefore all the "separate substances" are eternal. The world, time, movement, matter, and the soul must be eternal.[4] Over against this position, Bonaventure claimed that the eternity of the world was absurd; and Thomas, while denying that it was absurd, did claim that reason could offer arguments of probability against it.[5]

Third, Siger believed that the physical movement of the heavenly bodies determined the movement of earthly beings, and that therefore the entire course of history is like a heaven that moves in a cyclical way, repeating itself again and again.[6] As was to be expected, such a doctrine which contradicted free will and implied that the present Christian era was only one of many that would take place before and after it, was wholly unacceptable to the theologians.

Finally,[7] the doctrine that earned for Siger and his followers the title of Latin Averroists was that of the unity of the active intellect.[8] The rational soul—which is to be distinguished from the vegetative-sensitive soul—is one, universal, and eternal. Actually, within the metaphysical framework that Siger had

---

[4] One must add, however, that Siger's respect for orthodoxy led him to hestitate on some of these points. See van Steenberghen, *Les oeuvres et la doctrine*, p. 130. Cf. T. P. Bukowski, "The Eternity of the World according to Siger of Brabant: Probable or Demonstrative?" *RThAM*, 36 (1969), 225-29.

[5] The relevant texts have been translated into English by C. Vollert *et al.*, *St. Thomas Aquinas, Siger of Brabant, St. Bonaventure on the Eternity of the World* (Milwaukee: Marquette University Press, 1964). On others who may have held similar views, see H. Schmieja, *Das Problem der Ewigkeit der Welt in drei anonymen Kommentaren zur Physik des Aristoteles* (Cologne: Universität, 1978).

[6] Van Steenberghen, *Les oeuvres et la doctrine*, pp. 140-42.

[7] He has also been accused of denying divine providence. P. Mandonnet, *Siger de Brabant et l'Averroïsme latin au XIIIᵉ siècle*, 2nd ed. (Louvain: Institute Supérieur de Philosophie, 1911), 1:165-68. Against this view, see van Steenberghen, *Les oeuvres et la doctrine*, p. 128, n. 1, and J. J. Duin, *La doctrine de la providence dans les écrits de Siger de Brabant: Textes et étude* (Institut Supérieur de Philosophie, 1954), p. 458, where Duin concludes that Siger is perfectly orthodox on this point.

[8] Also on this point scholars are not wholly agreed. The question is whether or not Siger held—and held to the end—those opinions which have traditionally been ascribed to him. He probably held that reason would lead one to hold the unity of the active intellect, but that he was willing to subscribe to the higher authority of faith. In any case, the debate cannot be solved until an agreement is reached on the question on the seventh chapter of *De anima intellectiva*. Van Steenberghen, *Les oeuvres et la doctrine*, pp. 150-52, argues that Siger modified his views as a direct result of Thomas' criticism. See also B. C. Bazán, "La unión entre el intelecto separado y los individuos, según Sigerio de Brabante," *PatMed*, 1 (1975), 5-35.

adopted it was impossible for the soul, a wholly immaterial being, to be multiple, for an immaterial form is incapable of individuation.[9] In consequence, there is in each of us, besides a body and a vegetative-sensitive soul, a universal spiritual substance, which is common to all, and which is usually called the intellectual soul. Although in each of us this soul seems to be individual and only ours, the truth is that the soul of all is a single one, and its individuation in each is only apparent and fleeting. The rational soul is united to a person not substantially but only accidentally. When one dies, the rational soul returns to its original unity, which Siger probably identified with God.[10] This position, directly taken from Averroës, was the reason Thomas called him an Averroist,[11] and the crucial point on which theologians based their opposition to Siger and his followers.

Boethius of Dacia

The best known among Siger's followers was Boethius of Dacia,[12] whom some manuscripts of the condemnation of 1277 place next to Siger. Although most of his works have not been published, several treatises have been published at a relatively recent date, among them *On the Highest Good*[13] and *On Eternity of the World*.[14] The first of these deals with the philosophical life as

---

[9] Compare this problem with that posed to Thomas, when he attempted to explain the individuation of angels and was forced to conclude that each angel is a different species. See above, pp. 273-74.
[10] Such is the view of B. Nardi, "Il preteso tomismo di Sigieri di Brabante," *GCFilt,* 17 (1936), 26-35; 18 (1937), 160-64.
[11] Van Steenberghen, *Les oeuvres et la doctrine,* p. 181.
[12] A very brief general introduction may be found in A. Chollet, "Boèce de Dacie," *DTC,* 2:922-24. Some of the basic points of his teachings are discussed in A. Maurer, "Boethius of Dacia and the Double Truth," *MedSt,* 17 (1955), 233-39; F. Sassen, "Boëthius von Dacië en de theorie van de dubbele waarheid," *StCath,* 30 (1955), 262-73; E. Gilson, "Boèce de Dacie et la double vérité," *AHDLMA,* 30 (1955), 81-99; P. Michaud-Quantin, "La double vérité des Averroïstes: Un texte nouveau de Boèce de Dacie," *Theoria,* 22 (1956), 167-84.
[13] M. Grabmann, "Die Opuscula *De Summo Bono de vita philosophi* und *De somniis* des Boetius von Dacien," *AHDLMA,* 6 (1932), 287-317. See also M. Grabmann, *Der lateinische Averroismus des 13. Jahrhurderts und seine Stellung zur christlichen Weltanschauung: Mitteilungen aus ungedruckten Ethikkommentaren* (Munich: Verlag der Bayer, 1931).
[14] G. Sajó, ed., *Tractatus de aeternitate mundi,* revised edition (Berlin: W. de Gruyter, 1964); G. Sajó et al., eds., *Boethii Daci Opera* (Hauniae: G. E. C. Gad, 1969, 1972). Another work by Boethius has been edited by M. Grabmann, "Texte des Martinus von Dacien und Boetius von Dacien zur Frage nach dem Unterschied von *essentia* und *existentia*," in *Miscellanea philosophica R. P. Josepho Gredt . . . oblata* (Rome: Herder, 1938), pp. 7-17. See R. C. Dales, "Maimonides and Boethius of Dacia on the Eternity of the World," *NSch,* 56 (1982), 306-19; H. Roos, "Der Unterschied zwischen Metaphysik und Einzelwissenschaft nach Boetius von Dazien," in P. Wilpert, ed., *Universalismus und Partikularismus im Mittelalter* (Berlin: W. de Gruyter, 1968), 105-20.

the highest good that one can attain. Its content is practically the same as that of the best ethical treatises of pagan antiquity, except that Boethius, following the example set by Siger, claims that, although philosophical life is the supreme good within the framework of this life and of human reason, there is an even higher good in the blessedness that faith promises for the future life. In the second treatise Boethius proposes a long series of arguments both for and against the eternity of the world, and concludes that human reason cannot pronounce a definite judgment on the matter, so that Christian faith is the basis on which one is to affirm that the world is "new," and not eternal. He then goes on to refute the various arguments that he had originally expounded, in a typically scholastic procedure. The final impression given by this treatise is similar to that which the entire work of Siger conveys: that one is here faced by a strict rationalism in philosophical matters which yields to fideism in matters of faith.

The Condemnation of 1277

As was to be expected, the first opposition to the extreme Aristotelianism of Siger and Boethius came from Augustinian theologians. In 1267 and 1268, in his lectures *On the Ten Commandments* and *On the Gifts of the Holy Spirit,* Bonaventure began attacking the Aristotelian theses, and in 1273, while commenting *On the Six Days of Creation,* he defended Augustinian exemplarism. Meanwhile, in 1270, Thomas had composed a treatise *On the Unity of the Intellect* in which he attacked the doctrine of the unity of the active intellect as it had been proposed by Siger, and gave the title of "Averroists" to those who held it. On the other hand, it was at that time that the gap was opening between Thomas himself and the conservative theologians whom we have called Augustinians, so that the intermediate position of Thomas began gaining its clear profile between the two extremes.

In 1270 the Bishop of Paris, Stephen Tempier, condemned a list of thirteen errors of extreme Aristotelianism, dealing mostly with the eternity of the world, the denial of divine providence, the unity of the active intellect, and determinism. In spite of this episcopal action, the debate continued within the University of Paris. As a result, Pope John XXI asked Tempier to study the situation and report to him. Instead of this, the bishop of Paris called a commission that prepared a list of 219 propositions. These propositions Tempier formally condemned in 1277.

As has already been said, this condemnation was not limited to Siger and his followers, but included also some of the views of Thomas. It was not merely an attempt to place the artists under the authority of the theologians within the university structure, but also an intervention on the part of ecclesiastical authority to impose conservative Augustinianism and reject the various ways in which Aristotelianism was being introduced into thirteenth-century thought.[15]

The condemnation of 1277 was unable to hinder the final triumph of Thomas—who in any case was not attacked in person, for he had died three years earlier. But the case of Siger and Boethius was different. Both were forced to abandon France and go to Rome even before they were officially condemned. In Rome they were both imprisoned. Siger was murdered by a madman, and Boethius disappeared from the records of history.

The Survival of Extreme Aristotelianism

In spite of the condemnation of 1277, and of the tragic end of Siger and Boethius, extreme Aristotelianism persisted in Paris as well as in Italy. The new Aristotelians went even further than Siger and Boethius, for they were true Averroists who accepted and defended the entire doctrine of the Commentator, including his claim that faith is inferior to reason and must be subject to it—a position diametrically opposed to that of Siger and Boethius. These Averroists—who did deserve this title— taught the unity of the active intellect, eternal creation, and

---

[15] T. de Andrés Hernansanz, "Un problema de hoy hace setecientos años: En torno a los acontecimientos de París de 1277," *CuadSalFil*, 4 (1977), 5-16; V. Muñoz Delgado, "La lógica en las condenaciones de 1277," *CuadSalFil*, 4 (1977), 17-39; J. Châtillon, *L'exercise du pouvoir doctrinal dans la chrétienté du XIIIᵉ siècle: Le cas d'Étienne Tempier* (Paris: Beauchesne, 1978); R. Hissette, "Étienne Tempier et ses condamnations," *RThAM*, 47 (1980), 231-70.

moral determinism. This tradition seems to have disappeared in Paris after the death of John of Jandum (1328); but in Italy it persisted until the seventeenth century. In Padua during the sixteenth century this Averroistic interpretation of Aristotle conflicted with those who followed the interpretation of Alexander of Aphrodisias, for while the former held that there was a universal active intellect, the "Alexandrists" denied this and interpreted Aristotle in materialistic terms.[16]

---

[16] F. van Steenberghen, "L'averröisme latin," *Philosophica Coimbricensia*, 1 (1969), 1-32. Cf. A. Chollet, "Averroïsme," *DTC*, 1:2628-30 who follows the more traditional interpretation of Siger as a true Averroist.

XII

Eastern Theology
to the Fall of Constantinople

When we last discussed Eastern theology—Chapter VII—we left Constantinople in the hands of the Latin crusaders; Russia under the Mongols; and the ancient sees of Jerusalem, Antioch, and Alexandria—as well as most Nestorians and Monophysites—as subjects of Islam. This situation, which was substantially changed only in the cases of Constantinople and Russia, is the context within which Eastern theology developed during the period that we are now studying. It was a dark period for Eastern Christianity. The Byzantine Church found itself in a situation in which it was not always clear whether its worst enemies were the Turks or the Western Christians. Russia, divided as it was among several principalities, attracted the greed of Western Christians, who invaded the country and established a zone of Roman influence. Eventually Russia would come out of this period as a unified kingdom, but Christian Constantinople would cede its place to Moslem Istanbul.

Byzantine Theology

Byzantine theology during the last two and a half centuries of its existence was dominated by the issue of its relationship with the Latin West. This was mostly because of the political situation,

292

which forced the last Byzantine emperors to perform a difficult balancing act between their more powerful neighbors—the Turks in the East, and the Latin Roman Catholics in the West. This is evident in the political instructions that an emperor left to his son:

> The Turks fear our union with Western Christians above anything else . . . . Therefore when you wish to make them fear you, let them know that you will call a council to reach an understanding with the Latins. Think always about this council; but take care never to call it, for it seems to me that our people are unable to yield to the conditions of peace and concord. . . . Such an assembly would have no other result than to increase our separation and leave us at the mercy of the Turks.[1]

This prediction proved true, for not quite fourteen years after the Council of Florence had solemnly declared the union of the churches, Constantinople was taken and sacked by the Turks.

In a church on which imperial policies had traditionally had a great deal of influence, the matter of union with Rome, politically so important, would necessarily overshadow every other theological concern. For two and a half centuries Byzantine theology was devoted to a bitter controversy between those who favored union and those who opposed it. It was a struggle in many ways similar to the iconoclastic controversy, for here again the emperors often found themselves supporting an unpopular position, and unable to make their wish obeyed by the people, the monks, and the various ecclesiastical dignitaries who were not within Constantinople's sphere of political influence. The main supporters of union with Rome were people such as Patriarch John Veccus, whose theological positions were closely allied with the unionist policies of Emperor Michael VIII Palaeologus.[2] Apart from such people

---

[1] Manuel Palaeologus to his son John VIII, quoted in Zananiri, *Histoire*, p. 242.

[2] Several of his works may be found in PG, 141. For further references to more complete and recent editions, see H. G. Beck, *Kirche und theologische Literatur im byzantinischen Reich* (Munich: C. H. Beck, 1959), p. 683; D. J. Genakoplos, *Emperor Michael Paleologus and the West (1258-1282): A Study in Byzantine-Latin Relations* (Cambridge: Harvard, 1959).

and their immediate followers,[3] the vast majority of the populace, as well as of the theologians, were against union with Rome, and it was not uncommon to find Christians asserting—perhaps remembering the events of the Fourth Crusade—that if the West ever came to rescue of Constantinople it would be in order to destroy rather than to save it.[4]

On the other hand, most of the theologians who opposed union with Rome were no more original than their opponents. Men such as Patriarch German II of Constantinople[5]—who actually resided in Nicea, for Constantinople was still in Latin hands—and Emperor Theodore II Lascaris[6]—also of Nicea—were content for the most part with repeating the old arguments that had been adduced in the time of Photius. Therefore, the issues discussed were basically the same that were at stake at that earlier time—the *Filioque*, the use of leavened or unleavened bread in the eucharist, and the primacy of Rome.

Twice did the ecclesiastical and civil authorities of both East and West achieve the formal union of their churches—at the Council of Lyon in 1274, and at the Council of Ferrara-Florence in 1439. But in both cases public sentiment was so opposed to the decisions of the councils that real union never came about. The attempt at Lyon lost impetus when the Byzantine clergy refused to accept the decisions of the Council, and decidedly failed when Pope Nicholas III responded by demanding more concessions on the part of the Greeks. The decisions of Florence were still being debated when the Turks took Constantinople, but by that time it was clear that this new attempt at union would not succeed. In 1443 the patriarchs of Alexandria, Antioch, and Jerusalem condemned the decisions of the Council, to which they had previously agreed. Shortly thereafter, all the Eastern churches that were not politically subject to Constantinople followed suit.[7]

---

[3] In the case of Veccus, his friends Constantine Melitionites (Beck, *Literatur*, pp. 683-84), and Theoctistus of Adrianopolis (*ibid.*, pp. 684-85).
[4] Quoted in Zananiri, *Histoire*, p. 241.
[5] See Beck, *Literatur*, pp. 667-68.
[6] *Ibid.*, pp. 673-74.
[7] Zananiri, *Histoire*, pp. 246-47; J. Gill, *The Council of Florence* (Cambridge: University Press, 1959); J. Macha, *Ecclesiastical Unification: A Theoretical Framework together with Case Studies from the History of Latin-Byzantine Relations* (Rome: Pontificium Institutum Orientalium Studiorum, 1974).

The one point at which the question of relations with the West took an original turn was the Hesychastic or Palamite controversy, for here Western scholasticism clashed with Eastern mysticism.[8] The origins of the Hesychastic movement—so called because its followers lived in holy silence, ἐν ἡσυχίᾳ—could be traced far back to the early years of Byzantine Christianity, or at least to Simeon the New Theologian.[9] But the actual controversy broke out when some theologians, trained in the Western scholastic tradition, began ridiculing certain ascetic practices that had become popular in Byzantine monasteries.

The person who seems to have introduced the debated practices in Byzantine monasteries was Gregory of Sinai, who visited Mount Athos and several monasteries in Constantinople during the fourteenth century. Gregory's method of attaining ecstasy[10] consisted in sitting with his chin resting on his chest, looking at his navel, and holding his breath as much as possible while constantly repeating "Lord Jesus Christ, have mercy upon me." By doing this for a prolonged period of time, and leading his spirit away from the mind and toward the heart, the mystic achieves ecstasy, experiencing the divine and uncreated light that the disciples saw on Mount Tabor.

These teachings drew the ridicule of Barlaam, a Calabrian monk who was well versed in Aristotelianism and Western scholasticism.[11] He was in favor of union with Rome, and to that effect had proposed the view—which he based on Pseudo-Dionysius—that, since God is unknowable, it is impossible to know whether the Holy Spirit proceeds from the Father alone, or from the Father and the Son—Filioque. Such agnosticism irritated several Byzantine theologians, among them the celebrated Gregory Palamas, who attempted to refute Barlaam. Thus, the opposition to Hesychasm began—and continued—among those who favored union with Rome.

---

[8] There were, however, other issues involved in the Hesychastic controversy. See J. Meyendorff, A Study of Gregory Palamas (London: The Faith Press, 1964), pp. 134-56; G. Palamas, Défense des saints hésychastes, 2 vols., ed. J. Meyendorff (Louvain: Spicilegium Sacrum Lovaniense, 1973).

[9] On Simeon, see earlier, p. 209.

[10] See his treatise De quiet. et duobus orat. modis, PG, 150:1313-30, especially Chapter 2.

[11] See Beck, Literatur, pp. 717-19.

The Hesychastic monks called on Gregory Palamas to defend them against the ridicule cast upon them by Barlaam. Gregory did come to their support, but managed to shift the controversy from the very vulnerable ascetic practices of the Hesychasts to the deeper theological issues involved. Barlaam claimed that there could be no such thing as an uncreated Taborite light, for such light would be very God and would therefore be invisible. Palamas responded by establishing a distinction between the divine essence and the divine operations, which are not created because they are manifestations of the divine substance. If such manifestations of God did not exist, it would be impossible to know God.

The controversy lasted several years. In general, those who were in favor of union with Rome, and who had studied Western scholasticism, sided with Barlaam and his successor in the controversy, Gregory Acindynus,[12] while the "zealots" who were against such union sided with Palamas and the Hesychasts.[13] The situation grew more complex because there was a civil war in which the question of Hesychasm was involved—although only as a minor issue among many. Eventually, in 1351, a council approved the doctrine of the Hesychasts and condemned Barlaam and Acindynus. Palamas has since been regarded as a saint by the Eastern Orthodox Church.

Although the question of union with Rome occupied the center of the stage, the Byzantines still found time to devote themselves to the study of philosophy and the sciences. There was a revival of classical antiquity which was the continuation of the work of Psellus,[14] and which would eventually contribute significantly to the Western Renaissance. This was coupled with interest in the astronomical and mathematical knowledge of the Persians, which in turn gave Byzantine science great impetus.

---

12 His letters have been edited and translated by A. C. Hero (Washington: Dumbarton Oaks, 1983).
13 The one significant exception was Scholarios, who took the monastic name of Gennadius. He was well versed in the theology of Thomas, and translated into Greek portions of the *Summa Theologica*. But in spite of this he was a convinced Palamist and a zealous opponent of union with the West. See Beck, *Literatur*, pp. 760-63; M. Jugie, "Georgios Scholarios et saint Thomas d'Aquin," in *MelMand*, 13:423-40.
14 See above, pp. 210-12.

While Constantinople was dying, her legacy to later civilizations was being completed.[15]

The end did not come unexpectedly. The Byzantines themselves knew that all hope was lost, but did not cease in their bickering. Someone remarked that ten thousand warring Turks would not make as much noise as a hundred Christians debating theological issues.[16] The evening of May 28, 1453, expecting the worst, the populace gathered in the Cathedral of Saint Sophia to prepare for death. This would be the last Christian ceremony to be held in Saint Sophia, for that night the Turks managed to penetrate the city walls. Three days of pillage followed, after which the Sultan entered the ancient city of Constantine and dedicated to the Prophet the shrine where the name of the Savior had been invoked for a thousand years.

The Russian Church

The Mongol conquest left Russia in a state of chaos. Entire cities were destroyed, never to rise again. For centuries, the country was divided into small principalities, all subject to indirect Mongol rule. Slowly, some of these—notably Moscow—gained predominance over the others, thus establishing the political foundations for the Russia of the Tsars. But this took two and a half centuries, that is, the entire period that we are now studying, and that historians call the "Russian Middle Ages."[17]

The impact of this period on the life of the church was twofold—on the one hand, it strengthened it; and on the other, it weakened it. It strengthened its hold upon the Russian people, for whom the church was the most visible bond joining all Russians together. The church became the symbol of Russian nationality. Popular art witnessed to a general deepening of piety. The monastic movement flourished and took on traits that were characteristically Russian. When the nation emerged from

---

[15] Tatakis, *Filosofía,* pp. 219-47, 264-84.
[16] Quoted in Zananiri, *Histoire,* p. 248.
[17] On the origins of this term, see G. P. Fedotov, *The Russian Religious Mind: The Middle Ages* (Cambridge: Harvard University Press, 1966), p. 3. On the general history of the period see A. M. Ammann, *Abriss der ostslawischen Kirchengeschichte* (Vienna: Herder, 1950), pp. 63-147.

its Middle Ages into the epoch of the Tsars, it considered itself
the heir not only of ancient Kievan Russia, but also of the then
defunct Byzantine Empire—of its emperor and its patriarchate,
as well as of its claim to be the "New Rome."

But the Russian Middle Ages also weakened the church. The
beginnings of theological thought which we have discussed in a
previous section[18] never came to fruition. Instead, practically all
the literature that the period has bequeathed us consists of
hagiographic legends filled with miracle narratives and of
chronicles that are very interesting to the historian, but almost
entirely lacking in reflective depth. The decline of letters and
knowledge in general was so great that one of the most famous
monasteries, with one of the best libraries in all of Russia,
possessed only the book of Jeremiah of the Old Testament, and
then included among its manuscripts of the Bible two clearly
apocryphal writings. But this was not all, for Archbishop
Gennadius of Novgorod, in writing to this monastery, includes
among the books of the Bible a collection of excerpts from a
fourth century B.C. Athenian author of comedies![19]

By far the most interesting developments in Russian
theological thought during the "Middle Ages" were the
appearance of two sects—the Strigolniks in the fourteenth
century,[20] and the Judaizers in the fifteenth.[21] The Strigolniks—a
name whose origin is not clear—seem to have begun by
criticizing the clergy for the practice of charging fees for
ordinations and other ecclesiastical services. As a result of their
strong feeling that the clergy was unworthy, they rejected the
sacraments, and emphasized the study of Scripture and personal
piety over the established ecclesiastical practices. This in turn led
them to the practice of confessing their sins to the Earth—a
practice that had a long history in Russian religiosity, even
before the advent of Christianity. Thus a movement that at the

---

18 See above, pp. 214-16.
19 Fedotov, *The Middle Ages*, pp. 32-33.
20 See *ibid.*, pp. 113-48.
21 B. Rarain, "La logique dite des Judaisantes," *RevEtSl*, 19 (1939), 315-29; R. A. Klostermann,
Probleme der Ostkirche: Untersuchungen zum Wesen und zur Geschichte der griechisch-orthodoxen Kirche
(Göteborg: Elanders Boktryckeri Atkiebolag, 1955), pp. 221-22.

outset was a protest on the part of a relatively educated group against the abuses of the clergy ended by returning to ancient pre-Christian forms of religiosity. The origin of the Judaizers is just as obscure as that of the Strigolniks, and it is not altogether certain that the name given to them does justice to their position. Their opponents accuse them of denying the divinity of Christ, the past advent of the Messiah, and the Trinity, as well as of refusing to honor the cross, the icons, and the saints. It is said also that they regarded Saturday rather than Sunday as the day to be set aside for worship. In any case, what seems certain is that the Judaizers studied the Bible and the writings of the saints with a more critical eye than did the orthodox Christians. Thus, it may well be that these two movements were attempts on the part of a relatively cultured minority to renew a church that seemed to them to have fallen into corruption and obscurantism.

Nestorian and Monophysite Theology

During the last centuries of the Middle Ages, Nestorian theology followed a course that was mostly a continuation of what had gone on before.[22] The vast majority of the literary production of the period consisted of translations, devotional poetry, and canonical and liturgical materials. One theologian, however, is worthy of mention, and that is Ebedjesu bar Berika,[23] a poet and scholar,[24] whose *Book of the Pearl on the Truth of Christian Doctrine*[25] is a remarkable piece of systematic theology. This treatise is divided into five sections dealing with God, creation, Christology, the sacraments, and eschatology. In the third section, which is the most significant because of the focal importance of christological questions in the disagreement between Nestorians and other Christans, Ebedjesu expounded a typically Antiochene Christology in which the assumed human being was as a temple in which the divinity dwelt. His favorite

---

[22] See above, pp. 213-16.
[23] F. Nau, "Ebedjésus bar-Berika," *DTC*, 4:1985-86.
[24] He earned the title of poet in his poem *The Paradise*, in which he shows himself to be a master of the poetical style of his time. As a scholar, his most significant work is his *Catalogue of Nestorian Authors and Their Works*.
[25] Ed. Mai, *SVNC*, 10:317-66.

image was that of a pearl on which the sun shone, and in which one could see the very light of the sun, but which was not the sun itself. Another significant point is that, in listing the patriarchs of the Christian church, Ebedjesu declared that the Patriarch of Rome had the place of honor among his colleagues. This may have been an indication that the efforts that Rome was then making to bring all of Christianity under her wing had an impact even on the leading Nestorian theologian.[26]

Monophysite theology was represented in the Coptic Church by works of exegesis,[27] polemics,[28] and brief summaries of Christian faith and practice.[29] But originality was lacking in that ancient church.

The Ethiopian church showed more vitality and originality than its Coptic counterpart, on which it was constitutionally dependent. In the thirteenth century, Ethiopia began emerging from a long period of chaos and internecine struggles. This was accomplished mostly through the establishment of the "Solomonid" dynasty. As some monks had been instrumental in that political change, they were given vast privileges and holdings in lands. This in turn led to a revival of monastic and scholarly life. Yet the net result of this new situation was not a united, dynamic ecclesiastical life, but rather the discussion of trivial and legalistic matters which eventually led to accusations of heresy and bitter struggle. This is not the place to go into details regarding these controversies, which were often embittered by political entanglements. Let it suffice to say that the main points debated were the observance of the Sabbath, the bodily presence of Christ in the eucharist, the sense in

---

[26] Another Nestorian theologian worthy of mention is Patriarch Timothy II, who ruled early in the fourteenth century and left a book *On the Seven Bases of the Ecclesiastical Mysteries*. This work summarized the main points of Nestorian sacramental theology. See W. de Vries, "Timotheus II. (1318-32) über die sieben Gründe der kirchlichen Geheimnisse," *OrChr*, 8 (1942), 40-94.

[27] Notable are those of Jaradj Ibn al'Assal, who in the thirteenth century commented on most of the New Testament. M. Jugie, "Monophysite (Église Copte)," *DTC*, 10:2270.

[28] Fadail Ibn al'Assal, a brother of the former, was an able polemist as well as a compiler of canonical materials. Abul-Barakat Ibn Kabar wrote a *Response to the Moslems and Jews*. E Tisserant, "Kabar, Abul-Barakat Ibn," *DTC*, 8:2295.

[29] Most noteworthy among these is Kabar's *Lamp of the Darkness*, which attempts to summarize all the knowledge that may be significant to a Christian priest, from the doctrine of creation to the building of churches. Tisserant, "Kabar," 2293-94.

which humanity was created "in the image of God," and the cult due to Mary and the cross.[30]

Although the Jacobite church was rent often by schism,[31] the fact that Syria itself was going through a period of renewed political and intellectual life[32] allowed that church to produce one of its most distinguished theologians, Gregory Bar-Hebraeus.[33] The son of a converted Jew—hence the title of Bar-Hebraeus—Gregory studied at Antioch and Tripoli, and eventually was placed in a position of high responsibility within the Jacobite Church. Because this position involved extensive travel, Gregory was able to visit a number of libraries and thus to collect heretofore scattered knowledge. In philosophy, he became a convinced follower of Aristotle, whom he seems to have known mostly through Arabic commentators. In the history of theology, his significance lies both in his work as a compiler and in his insight into christological matters, where he at once offered a new formula[34] and acknowledged that a great deal of the controversy between the various branches of Christianity was more verbal than real.[35] If his word had been heeded, the sad history of Christian divisions over matters of verbal detail could well have been shortened by several centuries.

[30] The controversy on the Sabbath was partially an excuse by which King Amda-Sion crushed the opposition of a number of monks—notably a certain Anorios—who accused him of immorality. Since these monks were very powerful, and their claim that the Christian observance of Sunday had supplanted the Jewish Sabbath was not popular among the masses, the king took this opportunity to crush the monks. See E. Coulbeaux, "Ethiopie (Église de)," *DTC*, 5:939. The bodily presence of Christ in the eucharist was denied on trinitarian grounds by the Michaelites—followers of Za Michael—and for other reasons by the "heresy of Mount Zion"—actually, those who rejected the very realistic eucharistic doctrine of the convent of Mount Zion. The Michaelites also claimed that being made in the "image of God" must be understood allegorically. The cult of Mary and the cross was rejected by the Stephanites, who seem to have flourished early in the fifteenth century, and were physically suppressed before the turn of that century. On these three movements, see C. Santi, "Etiopia," *EncCatt*, 5:690. On still another controversy, see Y. Beyene, *L'unzione di Cristo nella teologia Etiopica: Contributo di ricerca su nuovi documenti etiopici inediti* (Rome: Pontificium Institutum Studiorum Orientalium, 1981).

[31] This was mostly because of political circumstances, for the lands where the Jacobites were most numerous were politically divided. G. de Vries, "Giacobiti," *EncCatt*, 6:315.

[32] See P. Kawerau, *Die Jakobitische Kirche im Zeitalter der Syrischen Renaissance* (Berlin: Akademie Verlag, 1955), especially pp. 49-66.

[33] F. Nau, "Bar Hébraeus, Grégoire Abûlfarge," *DTC*, 2:401-6. His *Candélabre du sanctuaire* may be found in *PO*, 22:4; 24:3; 27:4; 30:2, 4; 31:1.

[34] His original formula was the phrase "double nature"—not in the sense of two natures, but of one nature that is somehow "double"—which he employed in order to acknowledge that, in spite of that unity of the incarnate Lord which the Jacobite tradition had so staunchly defended, there was still a sense in which he was double. See *BibOr*, 2:297.

[35] *BibOr*, 2:291.

The Armenian church, like its Jacobite sister, was increasingly divided by political considerations.[36] While Lesser Armenia—in Asia Minor—moved closer to Rome, the rest of the Armenian communion rejected this new trend. This was the source of constant friction within the Armenian church itself, and the final result, after the Council of Florence attempted to unite all Eastern Christians with Rome, was a long-lasting schism between the patriarchates of Sis, in Lesser Armenia, and Echmiadzin, in the old country.[37] As was to be expected given the circumstances, the leading theologian in the Armenian church during the fourteenth century, Gregory of Datev, devoted a great deal of his energies to refuting the views of those Armenians who had joined the Roman church.[38] This he did in his *Book of Questions*, where he attempted to show the errors of his adversaries by asking a series of questions that could not be properly answered from their presuppositions. Thus, for instance, Gregory asked of those who claimed that there are two natures in Christ: "Which nature in Christ is to be worshipped? If the divine, you worship as a Jew .... If the human nature only [is to be worshiped], you fall under blasphemous man-worship."[39]

In summary, the most outstanding feature of Eastern Christianity during the last three centuries of the Middle Ages was the manner in which the issue of relations with Rome tended to eclipse every other issue, and presented itself in various ways in each of the Eastern communions. Although we have not attempted to survey that story here, the consequences of the Council of Florence throughout the East were basically the same as they were in the Byzantine Church. This was most unfortunate, for under the guise of a quest for unity a divisive element was introduced into the life of churches that were

---

[36] M. Ormanian, *The Church of Armenia*, 2nd ed. (London: A. R. Mowbray, 1955), pp. 50-59, summarizes the events of this period.

[37] L. Petit, "Armenie. Conciles," *DTC*, 1:1930-32.

[38] H. A. Chakmakjian, *Armenian Christology and Evangelization of Islam: A Survey of the Relevance of the Christology of the Armenian Apostolic Church to Armenian Relations with its Muslim Environment* (Leiden: E. J. Brill, 1965), pp. 46-49.

[39] Quoted in *ibid.*, p. 46.

already hard pressed by their own local problems. Thus, it is no wonder that in the sixteenth century, when Western Christianity was torn asunder by momentous theological issues, these debates found a strong echo in the Eastern church. But that story properly belongs in the next volume of this *History*.

XIII

Theology in the Later Middle Ages

The last years of the thirteenth century mark a period of transition from the high point reached by Innocent III, Thomas Aquinas, and Bonaventure, to the low ebb of medieval ecclesiastical life. It has already been stated[1] that Boniface VIII, who made the greatest claims for the papacy, also marked the beginning of the decline of papal power. Both Thomas and Bonaventure died in 1274; John Duns Scotus, the main theologian whom we shall study in this chapter, was born less than a decade earlier. And again, as in the case of Boniface VIII, Scotus may be interpreted as the culmination of the Augustinian school of theology, or as the beginning of a process of decline which would eventually destroy the entire scholastic edifice.

Scotus died in 1308, and the decline of the medieval church was apparent in that one year later the pope established his residence in Avignon, where he was increasingly becoming a tool in the hands of the French crown. For almost three quarters of a century (1309–1378) the papacy stayed at Avignon. In order to cover the expenses of their court at Avignon, the popes established a system of ecclesiastical taxation which made the entire church vulnerable to the charge of simony. The emerging nations of Europe, which were increasingly asserting their nationhood vis-à-vis the idea of a universal Empire,

---

[1] Above, pp. 225-26.

304

were led to question also the idea of a universal ecclesiastical authority, especially since it seemed that such an authority was too much in the hands of the French monarchy—and one must not forget that this was the period of the Hundred Years' War with England. People of reforming zeal such as the radical Franciscans—or Fraticelli—began referring to the "Babylonian Captivity of the Church." The net result of all this was a loss of prestige for the papacy, which seemed to have reached the lowest level possible.

And yet a greater shame was in store for the papacy. In 1378 the pope returned to Rome, and the French cardinals simply elected a pope of their own. This gave rise to the Great Western Schism, which lasted well into the fifteenth century (1378–1417). As a result, all of Western Europe was divided in its allegiance to two—and sometimes three—different popes.

As a way out of this situation, and also as a way to combat heresy and promote reformation, the conciliar movement gained momentum. The proponents of conciliarism were mostly moderate reformers who claimed that a council representing the entire church should have the authority and the power to determine who was the rightful pope, as well as to heal the schism, renew the church, and put an end to heresy. The conciliar movement had one great success inasmuch as the Council of Constance—the same that condemned and burned John Hus—was able to end the papal schism and thus restore a measure of order. But conciliarism itself failed, for the Council of Basel (1431–1449) split when the pope requested that it move to Ferrara. Thus, the final outcome of a movement that had begun in order to heal a division within the church was a schism within that movement itself.

However, the papacy, which was thus restored to its position of supreme rule over all of Western Christianity, would never again reach the heights of power of Innocent III. The popes of the second half of the fifteenth century were imbued with the spirit of the Italian Renaissance. They were earthly princes contending for political power in Italy and beyond. They were as interested in the embellishment of Rome as any other princely Maecenases, and this in turn led them to devote to the arts a

great deal of their financial and human resources. Thus, while
cries for reformation were being heard in Bohemia, the
Netherlands, England, and other parts of Europe, the popes
simply continued accumulating beauty and wealth in their states.
Some participated in warfare almost as a pastime. When the New
World was discovered, Alexander VI was too busy to concern
himself with missions to it, and he and his successors simply
shoved the entire responsibility onto the crowns of Portugal and
Spain. In consequence, the papacy lost its previous role as a
spiritual authority to be respected by all, and as a political
mediator to be heeded by all.

Faced by the general decline of the spiritual authority of the
church, believers sought a solution in various ways. Some, as has
been said already, hoped that a general council—or a series of
them—could set things straight and reform the church. Others
were more inclined simply to leave the church and its problems
aside, and turn to mysticism as a way of finding communion with
God. Finally, a third group—such as Hus, Wycliffe, and
Savonarola—sought a more general renewal and reformation of
the church, even knowing that this course would lead them into
conflict with the established authorities.

From the preceding paragraphs follows the outline for the
rest of the present chapter: we shall study first John Duns
Scotus; then the conciliar movement—and its theological ally,
nominalism; third, late medieval mysticism; and finally the
various attempts at reformation which foreshadowed the great
Reformation of the sixteenth century.

John Duns Scotus

Very little is known of the life of the man in whom the
Augustinian-Franciscan tradition reached its zenith.[2] And the
same is true, in another sense, of his works, in which the textual

---

[2] The uncertainty includes the date of his birth (sometime between 1265 and 1266), as well as
several details of his academic and ecclesiastical career. There are numerous studies of particular
aspects of his life. On the more general questions see: A. G. Little, "Chronological notes on the Life of
Duns Scotus," *EngHistRev*, 47 (1932), 568-82; J. M. Martínez, *Vida breve y criteriología del Doctor Sutil
Juan Duns Escoto* (Santiago de Compostela: El Eco Franciscano, 1957).

problems are many and very complex.[3] This, coupled with his difficult style and his frequent use of subtle distinctions, has resulted in widespread ignorance of his metaphysics and theology, as well as in a general misunderstanding regarding the nature and purpose of his work. Duns Scotus merited indeed the title of "Subtle Doctor" by which he is commonly known. And his distinctions did undermine a great deal of what traditionally had been accepted without question. However, his aim was not simply to criticize and destroy, but rather to offer a new synthesis that would be profoundly Augustinian and Franciscan without thereby ignoring the problems raised by the Aristotelian critics of traditional theology. This he achieved to a great extent, although the difficulties of his style, the contrasting clarity of Thomas Aquinas, the use to which later theologians put his criticism of traditional views, and the general decline of the later Middle Ages, made it impossible for his views to gain the measure of acceptance which Aquinas eventually enjoyed.

In spite of the subtlety of his distinctions, Scotus was basically a Franciscan theologian in that for him theology was a practical discipline.[4] This does not mean that he thought it had to be simple and directly applicable to what we would today call "practical" matters, but rather that the purpose of theology was to lead to the attainment of the end for which humanity had been created.[5]

The first point at which Scotus found it necessary to offer a new alternative that avoided the problems of Thomism as well as those of traditional Augustinianism was the question of the proper object of the human intellect. The traditional Augustinian doctrine of illumination had led the Parisian teacher Henry of Ghent to conclude that God is the proper object of the human intellect. Indeed, if true knowledge consists in the presence of the eternal ideas in our minds, it follows that the proper object of

---

[3] The first volume of the new critical edition currently being published by the Scotist Commission (Vatican City: Vatican Press, 1950 to present) devoted three hundred pages to the matter. A briefer introduction is K. Balic, "Duns Scotus' werken in het licht van de tekstkritiek," *CollFranNeer*, 7 (1946), 5-28. Balic was the director of the Scotist commission.

[4] *Ord., prol., pars* 5, *q.* 1-2 (ed. Scotist Commission, 1:217).

[5] This is the central theme of the excellent introduction to Scotus by B. M. Bonansea, *Man and His Approach to God in John Duns Scotus* (New York: University Press of America, 1983).

the human intellect is none other than God. If, on the other hand, one takes the Aristotelian-Thomist position, one must conclude that the human intellect has as its proper object the essence of material things. Each of these two positions, however, involves difficulties. That of Henry of Ghent would require that we be somehow able to have a direct and intuitive knowledge of God, and that such knowledge be sufficiently clear to make it possible for the mind to contemplate particular, material objects in the divine essence. This is clearly not the case, for our knowledge of God in our present state is by no means direct or primary. On the contrary, we come to know God only after we know a number of physical objects. The position of Thomas, on the other hand, would lead one to deny that the human mind is capable of going beyond material objects. What then of the knowledge of God? One could have recourse to the doctrine of analogy, as did Thomas, but we shall see that Duns Scotus had reason to be dissatisfied with the doctrine of analogy. Therefore, the only alternative left, as Scotus saw the issues involved, was to declare that the primary and proper object of the human intellect is being.

Duns Scotus avoids these difficulties by affirming that the primary and adequate object of the human intellect is neither immaterial being, God, nor material being, ... but *being* simply and without qualification, i.e., being as being (*ens in quantum ens*). Being can be predicated of everything, and nothing can be known that is not a being. Whatever is, by the very fact that it is, is intelligible. It can be the subject of at least one predicate; it exists. For being has the same limits as the intelligible, and only non-being or nothingness is unintelligible to us and to any other intellect.[6]

The fact that this "being" is known to us as such, without any qualification, in turn implies that "being" is predicated univocally of all beings.[7] This was one of the main points at which

---

[6] E. Bettoni, *Duns Scotus: The Basic Principles of His Philosophy* (Washington: Catholic University of America Press, 1961), pp. 32-33.

[7] T. Barth, "Zur 'univocatio entis' bei Johannes Duns Skotus," *WuW*, 21 (1958), 95-108; Bettoni, *Duns Scotus*, pp. 33-39.

Scotism clashed with Thomism—which claimed that "being" was predicated of God and of creatures analogously—and was the subject of long debates involving the followers of these two schools.[8] Scotus himself rejected this theory because it seemed to create more problems than it solved. Indeed, it would make metaphysics, the study of being as being, well nigh impossible, for there would be no one univocal sense in which all things—including God as well as creatures—could be said to be.[9] Furthermore, analogy is impossible without the univocity of being, for if being is predicated of God and of creatures only analogically it follows that the concept of being is double—there is a "being" of God, and a "being" that is properly attributed only to creatures. Such a view would lead to two insurmountable difficulties: first, it would require some third connecting item whose function would be to join the two concepts of being; second, given the Thomist theory of knowledge, it would make it impossible to explain the origin of the concept of being as applied to God, for it could not be simply derived from that other being which is known through material things.[10] Thus Scotus established the theory of the univocal predication of being, which is characteristic of his system.

This doctrine of the univocal predication of being is basic for an understanding of Scotus' proof of the existence of God.[11] Here again he was not quite satisfied with the traditional

---

8 M. Schmaus, *Zur Diskussion über das Problem der Univozität im Umkreis des Johannes Duns Skotus* (Munich: Bayerische Akademie der Wissensschaften, 1957). On his metaphysics, see also: T. Barth, "Die Grundlage der Metaphysik bei Johannes Duns Scotus: Das Sein der Synthese von Gemeinsamkeit und Verschiedenheit," *WuW*, 27 (1964), 211-28; H. Borak, "Metaphysischer Aufbau des Seinsbegriffes bei Duns Scotus," *WuW*, 28 (1965), 39-64.

9 *Op. Oxon.* I, d. 3, q. 3, art. 2, n. 6.

10 *Ibid.*, q. 2, art. 4, n. 8.

11 As there are various interpretations of Scotus on this point, I offer the following bibliography, which includes the main different views: F. P. Fachler, *Der Seinsbegriff in seiner Bedeutung für die Gotteserkenntnis bei Duns Scotus* (Friedberg-Augsburg: K. Baur, 1933); T. Barth, "Die Stellung der univocatio im Verlauf der Gotteserkenntnis nach der Lehre des Duns Skotus," *WuW*, 5 (1938), 235-54; T. Barth, "Zur Grundlegung der Gotteserkenntnis: Problemvergleichende Betrachtung von Thomas über Skotus bis heute," *WuW*, 6 (1939), 245-64; E. Bettoni, "Duns Scoto e l'argomento del moto," *RFilNSc*, 33 (1941), 477-89; A. Epping, "De structuur van Scotus' Godsbewijs," *StCath*, 18 (1942), 86-98; A. Epping, "Scotus en het anselmiaans Godsbewijs," *CollFranNeer*, 7 (1946), 29-60; E. Gilson, *Jean Duns Scot; Introduction à ses positions fondamentales* (Paris: J. Vrin, 1952), pp. 116-215; B. M. Bonansea, "Duns Scotus and St. Anselm's Ontological Argument," in J. K. Ryan, ed., *Studies in Philosophy and the History of Philosophy*, vol. 4 (Washington: Catholic University of America, 1969), pp. 129-41; G. Scheltens, "Der Gottesbeweis des J. Duns Scotus," *WuW*, 27 (1964), 229-45.

Anselmian and Franciscan view that the existence of God is self-evident, nor with the five ways of Thomas. Scotus would agree that the existence of God is self-evident in principle, that is, that a proper understanding of the notion of the Divine would lead one to affirm its existence. But he would insist that such is not the actual case with us, and that therefore the existence of God must be proved. On the other hand, the proofs that Thomas offered are "physical" rather than metaphysical, that is, they claim to prove the existence of God, the necessary being, from the existence of contingent beings. Such arguments are clearly at fault, especially if one takes the concept of being in these two cases to be analogous rather than univocal, for the jump is too great from contingent "beings" in one sense of the term to the necessary "being" in another sense of that term. Thomas based his arguments on the divisions of physical being, mainly that between act and potency, and thus concluded that there must be a being that is pure act. All that this can prove is a being that must necessarily follow from the existence of contingent being, and that is therefore not a necessary being in the strict sense.

Scotus set out to prove the existence of God on the basis of metaphysics, that is, of being itself. Since this being is always predicated univocally, it must be predicated of God in the same sense in which it is predicated of creatures. Therefore, the process by which the existence of God can be proved sets out from the notion of being and follows a path parallel to that of Thomas, that is, from contingent being to necessary being; but the difference is that the Scotist proof is based not on the contingent existence of physical beings, but on the notion of being itself. Thus, Scotus set out by establishing that there are certain characteristics of being which are universally applied to it—what he called the *passiones convertibiles simplices,* such as one, true, good, and beautiful; and others that are given in pairs of which one term must be applied to every being—what he called *passiones disiunctivae,* such as necessary and contingent, infinite and finite, uncreated and created, etc. He then argued from the existence of beings to which the imperfect terms of these pairs are applied to the existence of a being to whom the other terms of the same pairs are applied. Therefore, Scotus' argument for the existence of God combines certain features of the so-called ontological argument of Anselm with others of the Thomist arguments. It is basically an argument *a posteriori*, for Scotus agreed with Thomas that concrete beings must be the starting point. But it does not set out from the contingent existence of beings, for from the existing contingent beings it draws the univocal notion of being, and this then becomes the real starting point of the argument.

The God whose existence is proved by this argumentation has all the traditional attributes—simplicity, immutability, omniscience, etc.[12] However, what has aroused the most discussion within this context is the emphasis that Scotus placed on the divine will—his so-called voluntarism. Following the entire Augustinian tradition, Scotus insisted on the primacy of will over reason. This is true not only of God, but also of humans. God's will—as well as ours—is such that it is the only cause of its own action. This does not mean, however, that the God that Scotus described is a capricious being who acts arbitrarily. In God, who is absolutely simple, reason and will are the same. But from our point of view we must assert the primacy of will over reason in God—or, in other words, the primacy of love over knowledge.[13] Therefore, those who interpret Scotus as claiming that God's freedom is such that God can do anything, no matter how opposed to reason, are simply reading into him the views of later thinkers—although it is true that many of those thinkers took Scotus' voluntarism as their point of departure, which they then exaggerated.[14]

As a corollary of the primacy of will in God, as well as of the divine omnipotence, Scotus claimed that the incarnation was not simply the result of human sin, our need for redemption, and God's foreknowledge of these facts. Rather, Christ was

---

[12] How the various attributes, univocally predicated of God, may be distinct, and yet not deny the absolute simplicity of God, is an interesting problem in Scotus' theology. See Gilson, *Jean Duns Scot*, pp. 243-54.

[13] See W. Hoeres, *La volontà come perfezione pura in Duns Scoto* (Padua: Liviana Editrice, 1976).

[14] Which in turn has led Gilson, *ibid.*, pp. 575-76, to suggest that it would be better to cease speaking of Scotus' "voluntarism."

predestined to be incarnate as the primary object of the divine love. Thus, the incarnation is not simply the focal point in the history of humanity as it has unfolded, but also the focal point of the entire purpose of God, even apart from human sin.[15]

Three other points are especially noteworthy in connection with Scotus' Christology: his view of the hypostatic union, his theory of redemption, and his advocacy of the immaculate conception of Mary. His view of the hypostatic union has been very much discussed,[16] since it seems to go too far in the distinction it establishes within the person of Christ. But one should note that his notion of the "person" in which the two natures are united was very similar to Cyril's understanding of hypostasis,[17] and that the distinction that Scotus established in Christ when he spoke of two *esse* means not that there are two subsistent subjects in the Savior, but merely that there are in him two real essences—the divine and the human—and that each of these must have its own *esse*.[18] It is true, however, that Scotus emphasized the reality of the humanity of Jesus, and of its limitations, in a way that could be interpreted as endangering the union of the human with the divine nature. But in this emphasis on the humanity of Christ he was only following a tradition that had been part of Franciscanism from its very inception.

Scotus' theory of redemption[19] included elements derived

---

[15] On this point, see R. de Courcerault, "Le motif de l'incarnation: Duns Scot et l'école scotiste," *EtFran*, 28 (1912), 186-201, 313-31; K. Balic, "Duns Skotus' Lehre über Christi Prädestination im Lichte der neuesten Forschungen," *WuW*, 3 (1936); E. Hocédez, "La place du Christ dans le plan de la création selon le bienheureux Jean Duns Scot," *FrFran*, 19 (1936), 30-52; J. M. Bissen, "De praedestinatione absoluta Christi secundum D. Scotum: Expositio doctrinalis," *Ant*, 12 (1937), 3-36; E. Parente, "Prédestination absolute et primauté du Christ chez Duns Scot," *Culture*, 7 (1946), 460-84; E. Caggiano, "De mente Ioanni Duns Scoti circa rationem incarnationis," *Ant*, 32 (1957), 311-34. It should be obvious to readers of this *History* that this understanding of the centrality of the incarnation is a fairly common theme in the history of Christian theology, although one often neglected. In various ways, it appears in Irenaeus, Scotus, and Teilhard de Chardin, among others.

[16] L. Seiller, "La notion de personne selon Duns Scot: Ses principales applications en christologie," *FrFran*, 20 (1937), 209-48; P. Migliore, "La teoria scotistica della dipendenza ipostatica in Cristo," *MiscFranc*, 50 (1950), 470-80; J. L. Albizu, "En labor racional en la cristología de Juan Duns Escoto," *VyV*, 24 (1966), 101-68.

[17] *Op. Oxon.* III, *d.* 1, *q.* 1, *n*, 10.

[18] *Rep. Par.* III, *d.* 6, *q.* 1, *n*. 9.

[19] P. Minges, "Beitrag zur Lehre des Duns Scotus über das Werk Christi," *TQ*, 89 (1907), 241-79; T. Fetten, *Johannes Duns Skotus über das Werk des Erlösers* (Bonn: P. Hauptmann, 1913); J. Rivière, "La doctrine de Scot sur la rédemption devant l'histoire et la théologie," *EstFran*, 25 (1933), 271-83.

from the two currents represented by Anselm and Abelard.[20] He was willing to speak of Christ's work both as a great act of love overcoming our estrangement from God, and as an act of satisfaction for the sins of humankind. But in the latter case he rejected Anselm's claim that this satisfaction and the way it was offered were somehow directed by the requirements of rational necessity. God could have forgiven us without any satisfaction whatsoever; if a satisfaction was to be offered, it did not have to be from the God-human; and in any case the merits of Christ, since they are the merits of the human will, are not in themselves infinite. If a satisfaction was required and offered, and if God accepted Christ's merits and granted them an infinite value, this was not because of some intrinsic rational necessity, but simply because of the free will of God, who decided to save us in this manner. Thus we have here one of those instances in which Scotus, though not entirely abandoning traditional views nor claiming that they were in themselves irrational, did undercut the underlying assumption that the events of the history of salvation could be shown to be eminently rational.

The third point of Scotus' Christology that has drawn a great deal of attention is his advocacy of the immaculate conception of Mary.[21] As a result of his views on this point he has been granted the title of "Doctor of the Immaculate Conception."[22] His basic argument is that it was most fitting for Christ to merit salvation for Mary in the most perfect way, that is, by keeping her free from original sin. Thus, Scotus rejected the theory that the Virgin inherited original sin, and was sanctified after her conception—a view held, among others, by Thomas.[23] In 1854,

---

[20] See above, pp. 165-67, 171-72.

[21] V. Mayer, "The Teaching of Ven. John Duns Scotus Concerning the Immaculate Conception of Our Lady," *FrancSt,* 4 (1926), 39-60; K. Balic, "De debito peccati originalis in B. Virgine Maria: Investigationes de doctrina quam tenuit Joannes Duns Scotus," *Ant,* 16 (1941), 205-42, 317-72; K. Balic, "Joannes Duns Scotus et historia Immaculatae Conceptionis," *Ant,* 30 (1955), 349-488; J. F. Bonnefoy, *Le Vénérable Jean Duns Scot, docteur de l'Immaculée Conception: Son milieu, sa doctrine, son influence* (Rome: Herder, 1960). The texts of Scotus and other Franciscan theologians on this subject have been published in *Virgo immaculata* (Rome: Academia Mariana Internationalis, 1957), vol. 7, fasc. 1-3.

[22] M. Brlek, "Legislatio Ordinis Fratrum Minorum de Doctore Immaculatae Conceptionis B. B. Virginis," *Ant,* 29 (1954), 497-522.

[23] See above, p. 279.

Pope Pius IX defined the Immaculate Conception of Mary as official doctrine of the Roman Catholic Church.

According to Scotus, we are a composite of body and soul.[24] The body has its own form, but the soul is the form of a human being. In any case the soul, while separated from the body, though alive, is not in truth a person. In the soul, the will has primacy over the intellect.[25] Thus, Scotus' "voluntarism" may be seen once again in his understanding of human nature. One must note again, however, that this primacy of the will over the intellect does not mean that Scotus argued in favor of irrationality. What he meant was, first, that our greatest perfection is not reason, but freedom; and, second, that the will is free in the sense that it does not necessarily desire what is good. Thomas, for instance, would say that, if we only had a clear understanding of the supreme good, we would necessarily choose that good. Scotus rejected this subordination of will to understanding, and went so far as to say that, in principle, even the blessed in heaven retain their freedom to sin—although in fact they cannot sin.

The immortality of the soul was another of those points at which Scotus felt compelled to reject the confidence of some of his predecessors in the power of the human intellect to prove what are really statements of faith.[26] Pure reason can prove that the soul is the specific form of a human being. But when it comes to the immortality of the soul, all that reason can offer are arguments of probability, which may have a certain power of persuasion and which may even prove that the immortality of the soul is not against the dictates of reason, but which have no final demonstrative authority.[27]

---

[24] The best study I know of this subject is Gilson, *Jean Duns Scot*, pp. 478-510.

[25] J. Carreras, *Ensayo sobre el voluntarismo de J. Duns Scoto* (Gerona: Carreras, 1926); C. Libertini, *Intelletto e volontà in Tommaso e Duns Scoto* (Naples: Perella, 1926); L. de Sesma, "La volonté dans la philosophie de J. Duns Scot," *EstudiosFran*, 21 (1927), 220-49, 572-93; J. Auer, *Die menschliche Willensfreiheit im Lehrsystem des Thomas von Aquin und Johannes Duns Scotus* (Munich: M. Huebner, 1938); E. Chiocchetti, "Il volontarismo di G. Duns Scoto," *StFran*, 37 (1940), 232-39.

[26] A. Cresi, "La posizione di Scoto nella questione dell'immortalità dell'anima," *La Verna*, 11 (1913-14), 49-65; S. Vanni-Rovighi, "L'immortalità dell'anima nel pensiero di Giovanni Duns Scoto," *RFilNSc*, 23 (1931), 78-104.

[27] I have not included a discussion of Scotus' theory of knowledge, for in order to do so it would be necessary to enter into highly technical matters. Let it be said in passing, however, that here again Scotus steered a middle course between the Augustinian doctrine of illumination, as developed by Henry of Ghent, and the Aristotelian-Thomist position. He definitely rejected the theory of illumination, but he insisted that the intellect has an active role in knowledge, and that in this role it is directed by the will. See Gilson, *Jean Duns Scot*, pp. 511-73; Bettoni, *Duns Scotus*, pp. 93-131.

The contribution of Duns Scotus to the development of Christian thought has been evaluated in various ways. For some, he is the critic who began the demolition of the medieval synthesis. For others, he is the culmination of the Franciscan school, the one in whom the intuitions of Bonaventure come to their final fruition. Some emphasize his tortuous argumentation and his love of subtlety, and claim that this in itself is already a mark of decadence. Others insist on the penetration of his intellect, and view his work as a synthesis similar to that of Thomas. Some see in him the beginning of the divorce between faith and reason which would eventually spell the downfall of scholasticism. Others point to his obviously orthodox faith, his submission to the authority of the church, and his advancement of the doctrine of the immaculate conception, as signs of his sincere faith in medieval Christianity.

Both interpretations are partly correct. Scotus was indeed a high point in medieval theology; and he was also, like every high point, the beginning of a descent. He developed the scholastic method, with its subtle distinctions and its love of reason, to its ultimate consequences. But in so doing he was led to question much that previously had been taken for granted. He was no skeptic, no critic of the traditional doctrine of the church, no conscious innovator. There is no doubt that he saw himself as a faithful follower of the Franciscan tradition, coming to grips with the problems raised by the increasing popularity of Aristotle, and by the Thomist alternative to traditional theology. Therefore, on many points, he was more conservative than was Thomas. Copleston is thus right in the following evaluation:

In fine, then, the philosophy [and, we would add, the theology] of Scotus looks backward as well as forward. As a positive and constructive system it belongs to the thirteenth century, the century which witnessed the philosophies of St. Bonaventure and, above all, of St. Thomas; but in its critical aspects and in its voluntaristic elements, associated though the latter are with the Augustinian-Franciscan tradition, it looks forward to the fourteenth century.[28]

---

[28] F. Copleston, *History*, 2:485.

As has been said already, Scotus' voluntarism is not to be
interpreted in the sense that God acts in an arbitrary fashion.
But in many instances Scotus did claim that God is not subject to
our human rationality. Thus, his criticism of Anselm's understanding of redemption was basically that although Anselm's
arguments may seem very reasonable, they are not really such in
the sense of having a rational necessity. In discussing the
immortality of the soul, Scotus again claimed and argued that
the various so-called proofs that could be offered have no more
weight than that of establishing the probability that the soul is
immortal. His attitude was basically the same toward such
traditional attributes of God as omnipresence, omnipotence,
and omniscience, as well as toward creation out of nothing. He
did believe that all these doctrines were true, but he made it clear
that he did so on the basis of authority and not of rational
demonstration. As a noted medievalist has said, "Duns Scotus
had considerably increased the list of those revealed truths
which a Christian should believe, but cannot prove."[29]
    The growth of this list was one of the characteristics of
Western theology during the fourteenth and fifteenth centuries,
and one of the main factors contributing to the disintegration of
the medieval ideal of a harmonious synthesis between faith and
reason. Yet, it is an exaggeration to call his theology "the key to
the dogmatic history of the fourteenth and fifteenth centuries,"[30] for there were many other factors—political, ecclesiastical, economic, cultural—that contributed to set the tone of
theology during the last years of the medieval period.

Nominalism and the Conciliar Movement

Scotus may be said to be the last of the great scholars of the
Middle Ages who did not develop his theology in the light of
urgent political and ecclesiastical problems. He died in 1308,
and in 1309 Clement V fixed his residence in Avignon, thus
opening the period of the "Babylonian Captivity" of the church,

---

[29] E. Gilson, *Reason and Revelation in the Middle Ages* (New York: Scribner's, 1938), p. 85.
[30] R. Seeberg, *Text-book*, 2:162.

and its aftermath, the Great Schism. These and other related problems were the background against which theology developed in the fourteenth and fifteenth centuries. It was a period dominated by the issues of ecclesiastical reform and unity, and therefore its most distinguished scholars devoted a great deal of their attention to questions of ecclesiology—and, more specifically, to the question of the proper means to reform and unite the church. If we here include under one heading the conciliar movement and late medieval nominalism, it is because they were in fact closely interrelated, and the leaders of these two movements were basically the same.

Typical of the age, and its most notable theologian and philosopher, was William of Ockham (c. 1280–1349). Ockham was a nominalist, and one of the foremost actors in the process of driving a wedge between reason and revelation. It was later, among his followers, that this process would be taken to its extreme conclusion. But Ockham himself did not hesitate to make use of his intellectual abilities to undercut the authority of the pope. A Franciscan who supported the Spiritualist branch, Ockham clashed with the pope. He and other leaders among the Spirituals found refuge with Emperor Louis of Bavaria, who found them useful in his own conflicts with the pope. In connection with those struggles, Ockham wrote a number of treatises on the authority of the pope. In these treatises, he argued that the civil authority has been instituted by God just as much as has the ecclesiastical, and thus he contributed to the growth of the theory of an independent state, which would become generalized in the sixteenth century. On more strictly doctrinal matters, Ockham remained orthodox, although repeatedly stating that he believed various doctrines—such as transubstantiation—not because they made sense, but because authority taught them.[31]

---

[31] The best introduction to Ockham's thought is G. Leff, *William of Ockham: The Metamorphosis of Scholastic Discourse* (Manchester: Manchester University Press, 1975). A more basic introduction, with a selection of pertinent texts from Ockham, is A. Coccia, ed., *Guglielmo Ockham: Filosofia, teologia, politica* (Palermo: Andó, 1966). For the connection between his support of the Spiritual Franciscans and his political thought, see M. Damiata, *Guglielmo d'Ockham: Povertà e potere*, 2 vols. (Florence: Studi Francescani, 1978-1979).

Ockham, as well as the vast majority of the theologians of his time, has been called a "nominalist." However, the first thing to be said about the late medieval "nominalists" is that they were such only in a very wide and inexact sense, "for this so-called 'nominalism' never asserted that universals are merely names, or denied that universal concepts convey truthful knowledge of external reality."[32] Perhaps, were it not that the term "nominalism" has been in general use for a long time, it would be better to refer to them as "realistic conceptualists," for they were realists in the sense that they believed that universal concepts were adequate representations of reality, and conceptualists in the sense that they believed that such universals had a real existence, but only as concepts in the mind.[33]

Perhaps the most characteristic note in their theology is the distinction that they established between God's absolute power—*potentia absoluta*—and God's ordered power—*potentia ordinata*. This distinction had been used as early as the eleventh century by those who argued that dialectical reason was incapable of penetrating the mysteries of God.[34] But in the fourteenth and fifteenth centuries it became a constant guiding principle for those who had been trained in an exaggerated version of Scotus' voluntarism. For them, the distinction between the *potentia Dei absoluta* and the *potentia Dei ordinata* was a means of safeguarding the absolute primacy of will over reason in God, and they applied it to the totality of their theology. Scotus had said that God did not have to accept Christ's merits as infinite, but simply wished to do so; the nominalists of the late Middle Ages took this type of theological distinction—which was rather exceptional in Scotus—and made it the rule rather than the exception. Although the more moderate among the

---

[32] G. A. Lindbeck, "Nominalism and the Problem of Meaning as Illustrated by Pierre d'Ailly on Predestination and Justification," *HTR*, 52 (1959), 43. See also P. O. Kristeller, "The Validity of the Term 'Nominalism,' " in C. Trinkaus and H. A. Oberman, eds., *The Pursuit of Holiness in Late Medieval and Renaissance Religion* (Leiden: E. J. Brill, 1974), pp. 65-66. On the movement in general, see H. A. Oberman, "Some notes on the Theology of Nominalism, with Attention to its Relation to the Renaissance," *HTR*, 53 (1960), pp. 47-76.

[33] Ph. Boehner, "The Realistic Conceptualism of William Ockham," in *Collected Articles on Ockham* (St. Bonaventure, N.Y.: The Franciscan Institute, 1958), pp. 156-74.

[34] G. Leff, *Gregory of Rimini: Tradition and Innovation in Thirteenth Century Thought* (Manchester: Manchester University Press, 1961), p. 91.

nominalists made use of this distinction in a way different from that of the more radical, the distinction itself was understood by all to mean that, given the divine omnipotence, God could act otherwise than reason expects or requires, and that therefore it is futile to attempt to prove by arguments of logical necessity what is in fact true only because God has chosen to make it so. When it comes to speaking about how God acts, we can speak only within the context of that ordered power—*potentia ordinata*—which God has ordered out of the divine free will. While such theologians as Gregory of Rimini understood the *potentia absoluta* in such a way that it could not contradict the revealed attributes of God—especially God's loving goodness— the more extreme among the nominalists understood it in terms of an arbitrary power. *De potentia absoluta*, God could even change the basic distinction between good and evil, so that what is now evil would then be good.[35]

This distinction, however, was not a mere logical game. On the contrary, it had important religious and theological implications of which the nominalists were well aware. Thus, for instance, it made it clear that the present order, the means offered for salvation, and even human reason, were such not by necessity but out of God's loving kindness.[36] In the field of theology, it destroyed the union of faith and reason which had been at the heart of the great scholastic systems. What Gilson refers to as "the list of those revealed truths which a Christian should believe, but cannot prove" now grew to such an extent that it encompassed practically the whole of theology, which now had to fall back on revelation and become more of an exposition of revealed truth. If by *potentia absoluta* God can become incarnate, not only in a human being, but also in an ass or a stone,[37] there is no sense in trying to argue for the rationality of the incarnation, and of redemption through the suffering of Christ. Likewise, if

---

[35] Along the same lines, the question was posed of whether God can change the past or deceive humans. See W. J. Courtenay, "John of Mirecourt and Gregory of Rimini on Whether God Can Undo the Past," *RThAM*, 39 (1972), 224-56; 40 (1973), 147-74; T. Gregory, "La tromperie divine," *StMed*, 3d. series, 23 (1982), 517-27.

[36] P. Vignaux, *Justification et prédestination au XIV* *siècle: Duns Scot, Pierre d'Aurriole, Guillaume d'Occam, Grégoire de Rimini* (Paris: Leroux, 1934), pp. 127-30.

[37] Pseudo-Ockham, *Centiloquium*, concl. 7.

God can forgive even the unrepentant sinner,[38] the sacrament of penance can be defended only on the basis of the revealed fact that God has freely decided to connect repentance and penance with forgiveness.[39]

This means that the relationship between merit and salvation is not direct or strictly necessary. God has freely decided to save those who repent of their sins and do good works. In themselves, such works are never sufficient for salvation. But, by *potentia ordinata* God has decided to grant salvation to those who perform good works. Since most of these theologians claimed that God grants grace to those who put forth their best efforts, Luther was partially right in declaring them to be Pelagians. On the other hand, their doctrine that the connection between works and salvation is strictly on the basis of God's sovereign decree, and is therefore a gracious act, may be seen as the background to Luther's insistence on salvation by nothing but a gracious and unmerited act of God's grace.[40]

That there is a heroic tone to this outlook there is no doubt. It is the ultimate confession of God's omnipotence and human finitude. But once one has said this, there is no more that one can say, at least as far as reason is concerned. All that one can do is receive the divine revelation as it has pleased God to grant it to us, and ask no questions—not because asking questions would be a sign of unbelief, but because it would be a sign that one has not really understood the finite and contingent nature of all human reasoning. After such a development in the history of Christian thought, three alternatives were open: an attempt to discover anew the meaning of revelation, a return to the period of the great medieval syntheses, or a search for a new understanding of reason. As the reader of the next volume of this *History* will readily see, various later theologians followed each of these roads.

---

[38] Ockham, *VI Sent.*, *q.* 8.

[39] There is a very perceptive analysis of the significance of the distinction between the two powers of God in H. A. Oberman, *The Harvest of Medieval Theology: Gabriel Biel and Late Medieval Nominalism* (Cambridge: Harvard University Press, 1963), pp. 30-47.

[40] See *ibid.*, pp. 175-78; W. Ernst, *Gott und Mensch am Vorabend der Reformation: Eine Untersuchung zur Moralphilosophie und-theologie bei Gabriel Biel* (Leipzig: St. Benno Verlag, 1972); T. N. Tentler, *Sin and Confession on the Eve of the Reformation* (Princeton: Princeton University, 1977).

We cannot study here in detail the teachings of the late medieval nominalists on each of the traditional themes of Christian theology.[41] Rather, we shall turn our attention to the point at which their teachings were more immediately influential in the life of the church—their conciliarist theories.

Conciliarism should not be completely identified with nominalism, for it had other roots that went far back into the preceding centuries. One of these roots was canon law, which did indeed support papal supremacy, but which from a relatively early date had dealt, at least in theory, with the possibility of a heretical or schismatic pope.[42] Another such root was the criticism of papal authority, and especially of the material riches and corruption of the curia, which was connected with Joachimism and with the Spiritual Franciscans, but which was by no means limited to them.

On the other hand, however, there is a close connection between the late medieval nominalists and the conciliar movement. This was partly because the most outstanding theologians at the time of the Great Schism were nominalists. But it was also due to the inner relationship between nominalism itself and the ecclesiology associated with conciliarism. If one holds—as did these so-called nominalists—that universal concepts are real, not as separately subsistent entities but as concepts

---

[41] The most important points here would be their views on predestination and on the eucharist. The question of single and double predestination was discussed during this age; but much more interesting is the manner in which their own presuppositions led thinkers such as Ockham, Gregory of Rimini, and even the rather conservative Pierre d'Ailly, "to go even beyond what later history knows as double predestination and admit that the reasons for God's decisions are not simply unknown, are not simply mysteries, but are in actual fact non-existent" (Lindbeck, "Nominalism," p. 54). On this, see also Vignaux, *Justification, passim*.

The nominalist doctrine of the eucharist is significant because they questioned transubstantiation and proposed ways of understanding that sacrament which were in many ways akin to what the sixteenth-century Reformers advocated. See Seeberg, *Text-book*, 2:203-5; E. Iserloh, *Gnade und Eucharistie in der philosophischen Theologie des Wilhelm von Ockham: Ihre Bedeutung für die Ursachen der Reformation* (Wiesbaden: Franz Steiner, 1956); R. Damerau, *Die Abendmahlslehre des Nominalismus: Insbesondere die des Gabriel Biel* (Giessen: Wilhelm Schmidt, 1963), pp. 253-58.

[42] On the background for conciliarism in canon law, see B. Tierney, *Foundations of the Conciliar Theory: The Contribution of the Medieval Canonists from Gratian to the Great Schism* (Cambridge: The University Press, 1955). For recent bibliography on the entire movement, see P. de Vooght, "Les résultats de la recherche récente sur le conciliarisme," *Concilium*, 64 (1971), 133-40. On the debate on the relative authority of pope and council, see P. de Vooght, "Les controverses sur les pouvoirs du concile et l'autorité du pape au Concile de Constance," *RevThLouv*, 1 (1970) 45-75; B. Bertagna, *Il problema della "plenitudo potestatis ecclesiasticae" nella dottrina ecclesiologica di Giovanni Gersone (1363-1429)* (Rome: Università Lateranense, 1971).

truly representing individuals, it follows that the reality of the
church is to be found not in some eternal idea, or in the
hierarchy—as if they embodied the idea of the church and then
transmitted ecclesiastical reality to the faithful—but rather in the
believers themselves as a joint body. The faithful do not derive
ecclesiastical reality from the hierarchy. On the contrary, the
body of believers—the *congregatio fidelium*—is the church, and
the pope, bishops, clergy, and laity are its members. As a result,
"the pope ceases to be a dogmatic entity; he is an administrator
of the devotional services of the church."[43] He can err, and if he
does he is to be deposed. This is strongly asserted by Dietrich of
Niem:

> I would go so far as to say that if Peter, to whom the papacy was
> given in the first place before the Passion of Christ, had persisted
> in his denial of Christ, by which he sinned mortally, and had not
> repented, he certainly after the resurrection of Christ would not
> have received the Holy Spirit along with the others, nor remained
> the prince of the apostles.[44]

Thus, a general council of the church has the right to depose a
pope or to determine who is the rightful pope when there is
more than one claimant to the Holy See. On this basis, the
conciliarists—such as Dietrich of Niem, Jean de Gerson, and
Pierre d'Ailly—argued that the best means to end the schism and
reform the church was the convocation of a great general
council.

This did not mean, however, that the leaders of the conciliar
movement believed that a council was infallible. Ockham had
pointed out—and d'Ailly insisted—that one could hardly expect
that Christians who were quite fallible yesterday would become
infallible today simply because they are gathered with other
similarly fallible people. Ockham suggested that it may be that a
council itself, and the pope and the bishops and the theologians,
will err, and that the truth of the Christian faith will be asserted

---

[43] Seeberg, *Text-book*, 2:169.
[44] *De modis uniendi ac ref. eccl.* (*LCC*, 14:155).

by laymen—or even women or children, he added—who read the Bible with a spirit of humility and a correct use of reason.[45] But in spite of this, a council, as the representative of the true church—the *congregatio fidelium*—has a better chance of upholding true doctrine, of reforming the church, and—Pierre d'Ailly would add after the Great Schism—of restoring unity.

Conciliarist ideas were carried to their final consequences in the *Defensor pacis* of Marsilius of Padua (c. 1275–1342)—perhaps in collaboration with John of Jandum. Here, it was declared that the church and its hierarchy should have no jurisdiction. Jesus submitted to the power of the state, and both he and his apostles lived in poverty. Therefore, church leaders should do likewise. As to the state, ultimate authority lies, not with the rulers, but with the people—by which the *Defensor pacis* meant adult males. They have the authority to make the laws, and any authority rulers have is delegated from the people. Quite rightly, the *Defensor pacis* is seen by scholars as a major step toward both the secular state and democracy.[46]

Although such views had their critics,[47] they gained a measure of acceptance and were eventually applied when it became evident that the Great Schism could be healed in no other way than by convening a general council. But when the conciliar views were put to a test they were found wanting. Eventually, as a result of the conciliar movement, Western Christianity was relieved to find itself once again united under a single pope, but was simultaneously perplexed by the opposing claims of two rival councils. Thus, during the latter half of the fifteenth century, the conciliar ideal remained, but the view that the authority of the council was above that of the pope receded into the background. This may be seen in the case of Gabriel Biel, one of the later nominalists, who retained the notion of the church as

---

[45] Ockham, *Dial. de imper. at pontif. potestate*, 3. 1. 3. 13. Compare with Luther at the Leipzig Debate.

[46] G. de Lagarde, *La naissance de l'esprit laïque au déclin de moyen âge*, vol. 3: *Le Defensor pacis*, 2d. ed. (Louvain: E. Nauwelaerts, 1970); E. Lewis, "The 'Positivism' of Marsiglio of Padua, *Spec.*, 38 (1963), 541-82; P. di Vona, *I principi del Defensor pacis* (Naples: Morano, 1974).

[47] M. Martins, "A ética estatal de Frei Alvaro Pais no *Speculum regnum*," *RevPortFil*, 11 (1955), 403-11; *Seminario de estudios internacionales "Alvaro Pelayo"* (Santiago de Compostela: University Press, 1956); L. J. Daly, "Some Political Theory Tracts in the Vatican Barberini Collection," *Ms*, 5 (1961), 28-34, 88-95.

A History of Christian Thought

the body of believers and would even say that in case of conflict the council should override the pope, but who at the same time did not see such conflict as a real possibility, and was himself a defender of papal authority.[48] The papacy was progressively regaining its authority over the Western church, although it would be long before the conciliar ideal would die out.[49]

Late Medieval Mysticism

The fourteenth and fifteenth centuries witnessed a widespread revival of mystical piety. Although this was most evident in the Rhine basin,[50] the Rhineland movement had its counterparts in Britain,[51] Spain,[52] and Italy.[53] On the shores of the Rhine, the great teacher of fourteenth-century mysticism was the Dominican John Eckhart.[54] It is typical of the new mystical tendencies that Eckhart was not an emotional enthusiast, an ignorant firebrand, or a quietistic anchorite. On the contrary, he was a scholar who studied at the University of Paris, a calm spirit who rejected undue emotionalism, and an active participant in the practical and administrative life of the Dominican Order. The same may be said of his disciples John

[48] Oberman, *The Harvest*, pp. 412-22; I. W. Frank, *Der antikonziliaristische Dominikaner Leonard Huntpichler* (Vienna: Österreichischen Akademie der Wissenschaften, 1976).
[49] It was very much alive in the minds of Luther and the early Reformers. See C. T. Johns, *Luthers Konzilsidee in ihrer historischen Bedingtheit und ihrem reformatorischen Neuansatz* (Berlin: Alfred Töpelmann, 1966), especially pp. 127-43; F. Oakley, "Conciliarism in the Sixteenth Century: Jacques Almain Again," *ARG*, 68 (1978), 111-32.
[50] *La mystique rhénane* (Paris: University Press of France, 1963); M. Michelet, trans. and ed., *Le Rhin mystique: De maître Eckhart à Thomas à Kempis* (Paris: A. Fayard, 1960).
[51] D. Knowles, *The English Mystical Tradition* (London: Burns and Oates, 1960), deals with the mystical doctrine of Richard Rolle, Walter Hilton, Augustine Baker, and others.
[52] E. A. Peers, *Studies of the Spanish Mystics*, 3 vols., 2nd ed. (London: S.P.C.K., 1951-60).
[53] I know of no study on Italian mysticism comparable to those mentioned in the three preceding notes. In order to gain a basic understanding of it, however, one may turn, in the fourteenth century, to Catherine of Siena, and in the fifteenth, to Catherine of Genoa. A. Grion, *La dottrina di S. Caterina da Siena* (Brescia: Marcelliana, 1962); U. Bonzi da Genova, *Teologia mistica di S. Caterina da Genova* (Torino: Marietti, 1960); P. Debongnie, *La grande dame du pur amour, sainte Catherine de Gênes, 1447-1510: Vie et doctrine du purgatoire* (Bruges: Desclée De Brouwer, 1960); P. Debongnie, "Sainte Catherine de Gênes: Vie et doctrine d'après des travaux recénts," *RevAscMyst*, 38 (1962), 409-46; 39 (1963), 3-31, 137-51.
[54] R. B. Blakney, *Meister Eckhart: A Modern Translation* (New York: Harper, 1941); J. M. Clark, *Meister Eckhart: An Introduction to the Study of His Works with an Anthology of His Sermons* (Camden, N.J.: Thomas Nelson, 1957). A brief introduction, connecting Eckhart with his predecessors and his times, is J. Ancelet-Hustache, *Maître Eckhart et la mystique rhénane* (Paris: Editions du Seuil, 1956). This last work has been translated into English: *Master Eckhart and the Rhineland Mystics* (Harper, 1957); R. Schürmann, *Meister Eckhart: Mystic and Philosopher* (Bloomington: Indiana University, 1978); A. Klein, *Meister Eckhart: La dottrina mistica della giustificazione* (Milan: Mursia, 1978).

Tauler[55] and Henry Suso,[56] although they were less scholarly than their mentor. Further down the Rhine, in the Low Countries, lived John Ruysbroeck,[57] another well educated mystic who influenced Gerard Groote, the founder of the Brethren of the Common Life.[58] Soon this movement and others like it spread throughout the Rhineland and beyond, promoting a "new devotion"—*devotio moderna*—whose followers led a common life dedicated simultaneously to manual labor and to the cultivation of the inner self, not so much through extreme ascetic practices as through study and meditation, mutual confession of sins, and the imitation of the life of Christ. Perhaps their most typical work—and certainly the most influential—was *The Imitation of Christ,* traditionally attributed to Kempis.[59]

This new wave of mysticism was not consciously directed against the established church, but in fact it often led an existence that was marginal to the life of the organized church. Eckhart was accused of pantheism, and Pope John XXII declared some of his views to be heretical. The practice of mutual confession of sins tended to undercut the sacrament of penance as established within the ecclesiastical organization. Furthermore, the entire sacramental system was undermined by the claim that it was possible to attain to direct communion with God, even apart from such visible aids as the sacraments and the ecclesiastical hierarchy. Sometimes this claim of direct communion with God went so far as to leave little need for the mediating

[55] John Tauler, *Spiritual Conferences* (St. Louis: B. Herder, 1961); I. Weilner, *Johannes Taulers Bekehrungsweg: Die Erfahrungsgrundlagen seiner Mystik* (Regensburg: F. Pustet, 1961); J. A. Bizet, *Jean Tauler de Strasbourg* (Tournai: Descleé, 1968).

[56] Henry Suso, *Little Book of Eternal Wisdom and Little Book of Truth,* trans. J. M. Clark (New York: Harper, n.d.); J. A. Bizet, *Henri Suso et le declin de la scolastique* (Paris: Aubier, n.d.); D. Planzer, *Heinrich Seuses Lehre über das geistliche Leben* (Freiburg im Briesgan: Die Ewige Weisheit, 1960).

[57] John of Ruysbroeck, *The Adornment of the Spiritual Marriage; The Sparkling Stone; The Book of Supreme Truth,* ed. E. Underhill, trans. C. A. Wynschenk (London: John M. Watkins, reprint, 1951); A. Ampe, *De mystieke leer van Ruusbroec over de zieleopgang* (Antwerp: Ruusbroec Genootschap, 1957). This latter work has been summarized twice by its author: *Theologia mystica secundum doctrina Beati Joannis Rusbrochi doctoris admirabilis in compendium redacta* (Ruusbroec Genootshap, 1957), and "La théologie mystique de l'ascension de l'âme selon le Bienheureux Jean de Ruusbroec," *RevAscMyst,* 36 (1960), 188-201, 303-22. P. Verdeyen, *Ruusbroec en zijn mystiek* (Louvain: Davidsfonds, 1981).

[58] E. F. Jacob, "Gerard Groote and the Beginnings of the 'New Devotion' in the Low Countries," *JEH,* 3 (1952), 40-57; T. P. van Zijl, *Gerard Groote, Ascetic and Reformer* (Washington: Catholic University of America, 1963).

[59] J. Huyben and P. Debongnie, *L'auteur ou les auteurs de l'Imitation* (Louvain: Bibliothèque de l'Université, 1957). However, some scholars argue that the *Imitation* is Italian in origin: P. Bonardi and T. Lupo, *L'Imitazione di Cristo e il suo autore,* 2 vols. (Turin: Società Editrice Internazionale, 1964).

role of Christ. As a result, even though the avowed and sincere purpose of most of these mystics was to strengthen and renew the church, their own success in leading an exemplary and often joyful life in the midst of ecclesiastical corruption led many to believe that the church was not so important after all, and that it was possible to lead a good Christian life without the aid of a corrupt hierarchy. From this, it was only a step further to decide—as many Rhineland Christians did in the sixteenth century—that in order to be faithful to the gospel it was necessary to break with the corrupt practices and false doctrines of the established church.

Besides undermining the authority of the church, this type of mysticism contributed to the decline of scholasticism. Although most of its leaders had been trained in the best tradition of the schools, they had become painfully aware of the hairsplitting that was taking place in academic circles, and had come to the conclusion that such endeavors had little to do with the life of faith. Thus, they tended to emphasize the limits of reason and to assert that, although rational knowledge is good, the basic Christian attitude must be one of "learned ignorance"—*docta ignorantia*, as Nicholas of Cusa would call it. Furthermore, their basic philosophical outlook was more akin to Neoplatonism than to Aristotelianism. This was to be expected, for Neoplatonism was a mystical philosophy, and had been the frame of reference of Pseudo-Dionysius and Augustine, both very highly regarded by the Rhineland mystics. They then tended to equate the theology of the schools, and especially the nominalism of people such as Ockham, with Aristotelianism and with "human knowledge," and to reject it in favor of the Christianized Neoplatonism of Pseudo-Dionysius. In so doing, they were undercutting the scholastic tradition that had developed since the thirteenth century. Although several of them were Dominicans, and by this time the Order had declared Thomas to be its official theologian, these mystics were as influential in the final downfall of scholasticism as was their contemporary Ockham.[60]

---

[60] Cf. S. Ozment, "Mysticism, Nominalism, and Dissent," in Trinkaus and Oberman, eds., *The Pursuit of Holiness*, pp. 67-92.

Further Attempts at Reformation

In a way, both the conciliar movement and late medieval mysticism were attempts at reformation. One followed the path of institutional renewal, while the other sought reformation through a deeper spiritual life. We must now turn to a third mode of seeking renewal: through direct, local acts of reformation—practical as well as doctrinal and structural—performed without waiting for the consent of established authority, and often therefore leading to schism and accusations of heresy.

The undercurrent of dissatisfaction with the institutional church which was manifested earlier in such movements as Franciscanism and the Fraticelli continued throughout the Middle Ages. But, while the older movement of protest had been led mostly by people of sincere conviction yet lacking in academic training, in the fourteenth and fifteenth centuries several among the learned raised their voices in protest against much of what had become traditional Christianity. In many of their doctrines, they were forerunners of the great protest of the sixteenth century. Among these precursors of the Reformation, the most noteworthy—although certainly not the only ones— were Wycliffe, Hus, and Savonarola.

John Wycliffe was a native of Yorkshire who spent most of his life at Oxford, first as a student and then as a teacher.[61] During his earlier years, he seems to have devoted most of his attention to philosophical and theological scholarship. But toward the end of his career, and especially after the beginning of the Great Western Schism in 1378, he became increasingly radical in his criticism of the institutional church. At first he had some political support, especially from John of Gaunt, a son of Edward III.[62] But as his views grew more radical, his former political allies found him less useful. After the peasants' revolt of 1381, which he had not encouraged but which many attempted to connect

---

[61] The standard biography of Wycliffe is that of H. B. Workman, *John Wyclif: A Study of the English Medieval Church*, 2 vols. (Oxford: Clarendon Press, 1926). However, this must be corrected at several points, as has been shown by J. H. Dahmus, *The Prosecution of John Wyclif* (New Haven: Yale University Press, 1952).

[62] That Wycliffe's political support was not widespread has been shown by J. H. Dahmus, "John Wyclif and the English Government," *Spec*, 35 (1960), 51-68.

with his views, he found himself increasingly isolated. Having lost the support of his colleagues at Oxford, he withdrew to his parish of Lutterworth, where he remained until his death in 1384. Although his views were repeatedly condemned by the pope and by various English bishops, he himself was allowed to die in relative peace. But later the "poor preachers" whom he had sent out, commonly known as Lollards, were intensely persecuted, and in the fifteenth and sixteenth centuries a number of them were burned at the stake.[63] In 1415, the Council of Constance condemned over two hundred of Wycliffe's propositions, and ordered his remains to be cast out of consecrated ground. This was done in 1428, when his remains were dug out, burned, and then cast into the Swift River.

Wycliffe's doctrines developed through years of bitter struggle and increasing isolation, and therefore a detailed study of his thought must take into account that development. But for the sake of brevity and clarity we must here expound his views in their final form. Likewise, we shall find it necessary to present in a logical order what chronologically developed otherwise. But in so doing we shall not be doing violence to Wycliffe's thought, for he was himself a man of unflinching logic, willing to follow every assertion to its final consequences. His main weakness was precisely his inability to cope with the distance between the logical and the ideal on the one hand, and the political and the real on the other.

Wycliffe was above all a scholar in the medieval tradition, who on the question of universals opted for the realist position.[64] In this he was very much influenced by Augustine and his Neoplatonism,[65] and he therefore preferred Plato's doctrine of

63 J. A. F. Thomson, *The Later Lollards, 1414-1520* (Oxford: The University Press, 1965), pp. 220-38.
64 See J. A. Robson, *Wyclif and the Oxford Schools: The Relation of the "Summa de ente" to Scholastic Debates at Oxford in the Later Fourteenth Century* (Cambridge: The University Press, 1961). S. H. Thomson, "The philosophical basis of Wyclif's theology," *JRel*, 11 (1931), 86-116, attempts to show the intimate connection between Wycliffe's philosophy and his theological views, to the point that many of the latter seem to be required by the former. On the other hand, G. C. Heseltin, "The Myth of Wycliffe," *Thought*, 7 (1933), 108-21, tends to diminish Wycliffe's stature as a thinker and a scholar.
65 On this point, as well as on the doctrine of predestination, Wycliffe seems to have read Augustine through the eyes of Bradwardine, an earlier Oxford theologian who later became Archbishop of Canterbury. J. F. Laun, "Thomas von Bradwardin, der Schüler Augustins und Lehrer Wiclifs," *ZschrKgesch*, 47 (1928), 333-56; J. F. Laun, "Die Prädestination bei Wyclif und Bradwardin," in *Imago Dei* (Giessen: A. Töpelmann, 1932), pp. 63-84; G. Leff, "Thomas Bradwardine's 'De causa Dei,' " *JEH*, 7 (1956), 21-29.

ideas to the Aristotelian views that were current in his time—although, as was common among his contemporaries, he was also profoundly influenced by Aristotelianism. But this realism is not merely something that Wycliffe held because Augustine had done so; on the contrary, it is at the very core of Wycliffe's way of thinking and of being. He could not tolerate the disorderly, the arbitrary, the illogical, which seemed so much a part of later medieval nominalism. To ask such questions as whether God, by virtue of absolute divine power, could have acted in a different way from that in which God did act, is pure nonsense, for that which is not real—real in the mind of God—is simply unthinkable. God did not choose the present world out of a series of possibilities. This world, inasmuch as it is the only one that God has thought and produced, is the only possible one. Likewise, the final moral category is order, for that which makes an act sinful is its lack of harmony with the universal order established by God.

This understanding of reality is reflected in Wycliffe's view of the relationship between reason and revelation. These two cannot contradict each other, for they both lead to the same universal truth. Although it is true that human reason has been weakened by the fall, and that therefore we stand in need of revelation to supplement that which we can know by our own powers, reason is still capable of proving a great deal of Christian truth—including the Trinity and the necessity of the incarnation.

Up to this point, Wycliffe seems to be a conservative rather than a radical. It is when we come to his understanding of revelation that he departs from the accepted views of his time. Although at first he granted that the church and its tradition were to serve as guides in the interpretation of Scripture, he grew increasingly convinced that much of so-called Christian tradition contradicted the Bible.[66] His unflinching love for logic

---

[66] This development is the reason why it is possible, by examining only his earlier works, to conclude that on this point he was in basic agreement with traditional catholic teaching. P. De Vooght, *Les sources de la doctrine chrétienne d'après les théologiens du XIV* siècle et du début du XV* (Bruges: Desclée De Brouwer, 1954), p. 259. This interpretation has been refuted by M. Hurley, *Scriptura sola: Wyclif and His Critics* (Bronx: Fordham University Press, 1960). See W. R. Thomson, *The Latin Works of John Wyclyf: An Annotated Catalogue* (Toronto: Pontifical Institute of Medieval Studies, 1983).

and coherence, as well as his abhorrence of the corruption and division that he saw in the church, eventually led him to affirm that the authority of the Bible must be placed over that of any ecclesiastical tradition or dignitary. The Bible has been given as God's word to a faithful people and not as the monopoly of a corrupt clergy. Hence the need for translating it into English, the language of the people—a project that Wycliffe inspired and his followers brought to reality.

Once one takes this stance regarding the authority of tradition and of ecclesiastical teaching, the rest follows. But before discussing those other aspects of Wycliffe's teachings in which he was at variance with his contemporaries, we must turn to another basic element in his theology—his view of "dominion."

Dominion, or lordship, is one of the central themes of Wycliffe's theology, even before the Great Schism and other events led him to the more radical consequences of his thought. He discussed it mainly in his two treatises *On Divine Lordship*, and *On Civil Lordship*. Divine lordship is the ground for all other lordship, for it is only God that has rightful and necessary dominion over others. Humans, and even angels, can have dominion over other creatures only because God, to whom that dominion properly belongs, bestows or "lends" an infinitesimal part of it to a creature, to be used according to the divine will.[67] It is true that people often use their dominion—both civil and ecclesiastical—in an improper way; but when they do so their power is no longer the evangelical dominion in which one is in fact a servant, but is rather a coercive or "human" dominion.[68] It follows that ecclesiastical authority—whose dominion in any case is limited to the spiritual—loses its dominion when it ceases to use it justly, and the laity no longer owes it any allegiance.[69] Although one would do Wycliffe an injustice by interpreting him as calculating the political consequences of his views—of which he seems to have been constitutionally incapable—there is

---

[67] *De domin. div.* 1. 3. 2.
[68] Wycliffe established a distinction between three kinds of dominion: first, there is natural dominion; second, human dominion, which is by nature coercive; third, evangelical dominion, which is the highest and is a ministry rather than a lordship in the human sense.
[69] *De civ. domin.* 1. 8.

no doubt that such views would inevitably draw the immediate attention and support of many at a time when England was struggling to limit the influence of the church in political affairs, and to stop the flow of English monies to the papal coffers in Avignon. But even this support he would lose as he drew the ultimate conclusions of his theories on the primacy of Scripture and on the nature of dominion.

These consequences were seen most clearly in Wycliffe's ecclesiology and in his understanding of the eucharist. His ecclesiology is based on the Augustinian distinction between the visible and the invisible church. The invisible church is the body of the elect, while the visible church includes some who are elect and some who are reprobate. Although there is no way one can distinguish with absolute certainty between the chosen and the reprobate—indeed, one cannot even know into which category one falls—there are certain indications that permit one to make a relatively accurate guess. These indications are a life of piety and obedience to the will of God. On the basis of such indications, one can be fairly certain that the pope is not only a reprobate, but is the Antichrist himself, and has lost therefore all rightful claim to any sort of dominion over the faithful.[70]

It was in 1380, approximately four years before his death, that Wycliffe attacked the doctrine of transubstantiation.[71] This he felt compelled to do because he could no longer accept the notion that the elements consecrated in the eucharist ceased to be true bread and wine. Such a claim would be tantamount to Docetism, for, just as that early heresy denied the incarnation of God in a true human being, this eucharistic doctrine denies the presence of the Lord in true, physical bread and wine. Therefore, even after the act of consecration, the bread remains bread and the wine remains wine. But in spite of this, the body

---

[70] Although, for the sake of brevity, I have not included here a discussion of Wycliffe's views on merits and their role in salvation, it may be well to point out that he rejected the notion that one can acquire any merit before God *de condigno*—that is, true merit, to which a reward is due—although it is possible for an action to be meritorious *de congruo*—that is, that God may count it as such. Therefore, no one can have more merit than is needed for salvation, there is no such thing as a treasury of merit that the church can apply to the faithful, and the whole penitential system—and especially the practice of selling or otherwise granting indulgences—must be abandoned.

[71] That seems to be the date of his treatise *On the Eucharist*. A year earlier, in *On Apostasy*, he had hinted at his uneasiness with this doctrine, but had not gone into more details.

and blood of Christ are also present in the eucharist. They are present in that they act for the salvation of the faithful; they are present in a spiritual sense, within the souls of the partakers; and they are also present in a sacramental and mysterious sense, for the body of Christ, which remains physically present only in heaven, at the same time makes itself present in a spiritual manner throughout the host, just as the soul is present throughout the body.

It is not difficult to see why Wycliffe's doctrines were considered to be dangerous. His theory of dominion, if carried to its final outcome, would effectively undercut both ecclesiastical and civil authority. His view of the church, his rejection of the penitential system, and his eucharistic doctrine would do away with much that was central to medieval Christianity. Thus, the fact that he put forth such theories was a sign that the Middle Ages were coming to an end; the fact that his theories did not gain widespread acceptance shows that their time had not yet come.

However, Wycliffe's ideas did not die. We have already mentioned that they survived in England long after his death through the preaching of the Lollards, who persisted well into the sixteenth century and whose remnants eventually merged with the English Reformation. They also spread to Bohemia, where they would again emerge, somewhat modified, with Hus and his followers.

John Hus was a preacher in the chapel of the Holy Innocents of Bethlehem, in Prague, and rector of the university of that city. He was deeply influenced by Wycliffe's writings,[72] and sought reformation in ways similar to those of the English scholar. Since at that time there was considerable anti-German sentiment in

---

[72] J. Loserth, Huss und Wiclif: Zur Genesis der hussitischen Lehre (Munich: R. Oldenbourg, 1925), stresses Hus's dependence on Wycliffe. The opposite tack is taken by M. Spinka, John Hus and the Czech Reform (Chicago: University of Chicago Press, 1941), pp. 12-20. On this question, see also J. Kvacala, "Hus und sein Werk," JKGSlav, new series, 8 (1932), 58-82, 121-42. On other movements in Bohemia which may have contributed to Hus and his movement, see S. H. Thomson, "Pre-Hussite Heresy in Bohemia," EngHistRev, 48 (1933), 23-42; J. Macek, Jean Hus et les traditions hussites (Paris: Plon, 1973); A. Molnár, Jean Hus, témoin de la vérité (Paris: Les Bergers et les Mages (1978); A. C. Bronswijk, Hervormers, ketters en revolutionaren: Jan Hus en de Tsjechische kerkreformatie (Kampen: J. H. Kok, 1982). The best short biography is that of M. Spinka, John Hus: A Biography (Princeton: Princeton University Press, 1968).

Bohemia, and Hus became the symbol of that sentiment, political considerations were not entirely alien to the course of this new movement—as indeed they had not been alien to Wycliffe and the final outcome of his movement. After a long struggle that it is impossible to recount here, Hus was summoned to appear before the Council of Constance, and to that end was granted a safe-conduct by Emperor Sigismund. But in spite of that safe-conduct, and partly through the intervention of such otherwise notable reformers as Pierre d'Ailly and Jean de Gerson, Hus was condemned by the Council and burned at the stake. When the news reached Bohemia, Hus became a national hero, and many of his views became a matter of national pride. Although his followers were soon divided, and these divisions even led them to the field of battle, the doctrines of Hus did not disappear. In the middle of the fifteenth century, his followers joined with some Waldensians and formed the Bohemian Brethren, who eventually embraced the ideas of the Protestant Reformation.

Although Hus's doctrines were not exactly the same as those of Wycliffe,[73] it would be fair to say that on the essential points he coincided with his British precursor. As it is impossible here to compare these two in every aspect of their teaching, let it suffice to say that Hus was in general more moderate than Wycliffe, especially in his use of language, that circumstances led him to devote more attention than Wycliffe to the matter of indulgences,[74] and that his position as preacher at the chapel of the Holy Innocents of Bethlehem provided him with the opportunity to translate his doctrinal view into liturgical reforms.[75]

Finally, a word must be said about Girolamo Savonarola, an ardent reformer who combined the Thomistic training of a Dominican with the apocalyptic expectations of a Joachimist.[76] Although not outstanding as a theologian, Savonarola interests

---

[73] See P. De Vooght, *Hussiana* (Louvain: Publication Universitaires, 1960).
[74] See Spinka, *Hus*, pp. 130-64.
[75] E. C. Molnar, "The Liturgical Reforms of John Hus," *Spec*, 41 (1966), 297-303.
[76] D. Weinstein, "Prophecy and Humanism in Late Fifteenth Century Florence: A Study in the Relations Between Savonarola and the Florentine Humanists," *DissAbs*, 17 (1957), 1989. A well written biography is that of R. Ridolfi, *The Life of Girolamo Savonarola* (London: Routledge and Kegan Paul, 1959).

us here as proof that even in Italy, where the Renaissance was taking a turn toward a revival of ancient pagan art and toward an emphasis on aesthetics over religion, there was sufficient concern for religious reform to make possible the repeated "burnings of vanities" which took place in Florence under Savonarola's leadership. If one were to turn to Spain, Poland, or any other section of Latin Christendom, one would find there the same search for renewed spiritual life. It was this search that would eventually lead to the Protestant Reformation of the sixteenth century and to the Catholic movement usually known as the Counter-Reformation.

XIV

Dawn or Dusk?

We have come now to what was clearly the end of an era. Constantinople, the Christian city of Constantine, was no more. It would be renamed Istanbul, and where the name of the Savior was once called now rang the praise of the Prophet. Her claim to be the "New Rome" now was taken up by Moscow, around which a new empire was emerging. In the West, old Rome was not faring much better than her Eastern counterpart. She had lost her former status as the center of the world and was now just one more political factor in a Europe increasingly divided by nationalism. In Spain the various petty kingdoms were united, the Moor was gone, and new horizons were opening far to the West, where there was gold to attract the wordly-mindly and millions of souls to save for those of a more religious inclination. The movable type printing press was just beginning to disseminate written materials at what seemed then an incredible speed. Greek-speaking exiles from Constantinople were re-introducing classical Greek learning in Italy. Scholars such as Lorenzo Valla were questioning the authenticity of documents on which stood a great deal of the medieval conception of the world. Others were discovering the extent to which manuscript transmission had corrupted the genuine texts of Christian antiquity.

The view generally held by many of those involved in these great events was that they were living in the dawn of a new day

when the ignorance and superstition of the last thousand years
would be overcome. It was this widespread notion that the
previous thousand years had stood in the way of genuine human
development that led to the naming of those years as the "Middle
Ages" and of the new emerging age as the "Renaissance"—that
is, the new birth. The highest artistic achievements of the age
now gone were called "Gothic"—that is, barbaric—and archi-
tects, painters and sculptors began striving to recover the spirit
of classical Greco-Roman art.

It would be wrong to assume that the organized church
opposed these developments. The popes themselves vied with
other Italian princes in their efforts to attract the best artists and
scholars to their entourage. Lorenzo Valla, who more than any
other single person undercut the papal claims to temporal
power by proving the spuriousness of the Donation of
Constantine, was himself supported by the pope. Although
there was widespread protest by the monks and by some of the
laity, the papacy had been captured by the spirit of the times.

This is not the place to discuss the thought of the Renaissance.
But we must pause to ask the question of the correctness of the
judgment that it passed on the Middle Ages.

The first point to be made within this context is that whoever
has read this volume with some care will be aware that this was no
uniform period to which one could justly apply a sweeping
evaluation. The early years after the invasions of the Germanic
peoples, as well as the century and half that followed the decline
of the Carolingian empire, were indeed dark. But if there is a
period in the history of Western civilization which one can call
"classic" for the wholeness of its world view, for its originality,
and for the beauty that it created, it certainly is the twelfth and
thirteenth centuries. Therefore, whatever judgment one might
pass on the Middle Ages must be made on the basis of their high
point of achievement, and not on the basis of the dark centuries.

Second, it will be clear that any evaluation of the Middle Ages,
even at their highest point, will reflect the theological
presuppositions on which such an evaluation is made. If one
believes that the purpose of history is to evolve to the point
where humanity comes of age and is emancipated from all that

has traditionally bound it, one will value the Renaissance and the subsequent centuries as the time of emancipation from the religious and political authorities of the Middle Ages. If, on the other hand, one sees the human purpose as basically spiritual and believes that such purpose can only be accomplished within the structure and under the authority of a Christian order, one will value the Middle Ages as the time when religious authority was accepted most widely, when people were most concerned for their eternal destinations, and when doubts regarding crucial religious questions were less prevalent. In either case, one's evaluation of the Middle Ages is a reflection of one's own views.

One can say, however, that if the incarnation is the focal point of the Christian faith, as was said in the first volume of this *History*, then the end of the Middle Ages was to be both welcomed and regretted. It was to be welcomed in that it once again brought awareness of the value of life in all its aspects. While the hieratic style of Byzantine religious art gave the impression that the events connected with the incarnation stood apart from normal human experience, and the languid expression of Western medieval painting seems to imply that in order to be Christian one must be less than human, Michelangelo's figures in the Sistine Chapel make one proud to be a human, and proud to be a member of this race in one of whose members God was incarnate. But on the other hand, the passing of the Middle Ages must be regretted, for never again until the twentieth century—and then for different reasons—would people see themselves as part of God's harmonious creation, existing on this earth amidst animals, plants, clouds and oceans through the sheer mercy of God. The passing of the Middle Ages was also the passing of the human creature as an incomplete being whose goal could be fulfilled only because in the incarnation God made it possible for us to live in harmony with the divine and in harmony with creation, both as a consequence of harmony with God and as a means to attain it. The new human being that emerged at the Renaissance as the ruler of its own life and of all that surrounds it, who does not stand in need of the condescending incarnation of God, would soon become the exploiter and destroyer of its environment.

The Middle Ages were followed by the Protestant and Catholic Reformations as well as by the Renaissance. In a sense, both of these reformations were new departures, but in a sense they were also continuations of the Middle Ages. It was these movements, as we shall see in our next volume, that provided the means for people to proclaim and live anew, in their new circumstances, the basic tenet of the Christian faith—that God was in Christ reconciling the world unto himself.

Appendix

Suggestions for Further Reading

As in the case of the first volume of this *History,* a program of parallel readings is suggested as follows:

I. Augustine (chapter I):
   A. *On the Nature of Good,* 1-20
      1. LCC, 6:326-32
      2. NPNF, 1st series, 4:351-55
      3. W. J. Oates, ed., *Basic Writings of Saint Augustine,* 2 vols. (New York: Random House, 1948), 1:431-38
   B. *Grace and Free Will*
      1. NPNF, 1st series, 5:443-65
      2. Oates, 1:733-74
   C. *The Correction of the Donatists:* NPNF, 1st series, 4:633-51
   D. Although too extensive to be part of this program, the reading of the *Confessions* is also highly recommended. There are many editions in English
II. Western Theology After Augustine (chapter II):
   A. Vincent of Lerins, *Commonitorium:* NPNF, 1st series, 11:131-56
   B. Gregory the Great, *On Pastoral Rule,* Part I, and Part III:1-8
      1. ACW, 11:20-44, 89-106
      2. NPNF, 2d series, 12:1-9, 24-29

3. C. J. Barry, *Readings in Church History*, 3 vols.
   (Westminster, Maryland: Newman Press, 1966),
   1:135-40 (similar selections)
III. Eastern Theology (chapters III, VII, and XII):
   A. Pseudo-Dionysius, *Mystical Theology*
      1. J. D. Jones, trans., *The Divine Names and Mystical
         Theology* (Milwaukee: Marquette University
         Press, 1980), pp. 211-22
      2. C. E. Rolt, trans., *Dionysius the Areopagite on Divine
         Names and Mystical Theology*, reprint (London:
         SPCK, 1957), pp. 191-201
   B. Sixth Ecumenical Council, *Sentence Against the Monoth-
      elites*, and *Definition of Faith*
      1. NPNF, 2d series, 14:342-46
      2. LCC, 3:383-85 (briefer selection)
   C. John of Damascus, *On the Orthodox Faith*, 1:1-10:
      NPNF, 2d series, vol. 9 (part 2), pp. 1-10
   D. Seventh Ecumenical Council, *Decree:* NPNF, 2d series,
      14:549-51
   E. Photius, *Encyclical Letter:* Barry, 1:316-18
IV. The Carolingian Renaissance (chapter IV):
   A. Paschasius Radbertus, *The Lord's Body and Blood:* LCC,
      9:94-108
   B. Ratramnus, *Christ's Body and Blood:* LCC, 9:109-117
V. The Twelfth Century (chapter VI):
   A. Anselm
      1. *Proslogion*
         a. LCC, 10:69-93
         b. M. J. Charlesworth, *St. Anselm's Proslogion* (Ox-
            ford: Clarendon Press, 1965), pp. 111-55
         c. J. Hopkins and H. Richardson, trans., *Anselm's
            Works*, 4 vols. (Toronto: Edwin Mellen Press,
            1974-76), 1:89-112
         d. Barry, 1:357-61 (good selection)
         e. Kerr, pp. 84-85 (brief excerpt)
      2. *Why God Became Man*
         a. LCC, 10:97-183
         b. Hopkins and Richardson, 3:49-137

c. Kerr, pp. 85-94 (good selection of texts summarizing the main argument)
B. Abelard, *Ethics*, selections: LCC, 10:288-97
C. Hugh of Saint Victor, *On the Sacraments*, selections: LCC, 10:300-318
D. Peter Lombard, *Four Books of Sentences*, selections
   1. LCC, 10:334-51
   2. Kerr, pp. 100-101 (different selections)
VI. The Thirteenth Century (chapters VIII-XI):
   A. Bonaventure, *The Journey of the Mind to God*
      1. LCC, 13:132-41
      2. L. S. Cunningham, trans., *The Mind's Journey to God* (Chicago: Franciscan Herald Press, 1979), pp. 23-121
      3. E. Cousins, trans., *Bonaventure* (The Classics of Western Spirituality; New York: Paulist Press, 1978), pp. 51-116
   B. Thomas Aquinas, *Summa Theologica*, Part I, question 1. There are several editions in English. The best is the Blackfriars Edition, 60 vols. (New York: McGraw-Hill, 1964-1981). The text suggested is to be found in this edition in 1:5-41
VII. The Late Middle Ages (chapter XIII):
   A. Duns Scotus, various selections:
      1. LCC, 10:428-36
      2. Kerr, pp. 122-23
   B. Ockham, *On the Power of the Pope*, selections: LCC 10:437-42
   C. Marsilius of Padua, *Defender of the Peace*, selections: Barry, 1:479-90
   D. Eckhart, *Sermon on the Eternal Birth*
      1. LCC, 13:177-185
      2. R. B. Blakney, *Meister Eckhart: A Modern Translation* (New York: Harper and Row, 1941), pp. 109-17
   E. John Hus, *On Simony*, 1-4: LCC, 14:196-222

Index of Subjects and Authors

Principal references are in bold type; references to footnotes are in italics; all other references are in roman type.

Abelard, 165, **167-74,** 175, *178,* 179, 181, 183, 229, 313
Acacius of Constantinople, 79-82
Acephaloi, 81
Act and potency, 264-65
Active intellect, 234; unity of, 237, 240, 251, 260, 285, 287-88, 289, 290
Adam, 43-46, 62, 135, 145, 182
Adam, K., *23, 52*
Adam of Saint Victor, *178*
Adelmanus, *152*
Adeodatus, 16, 24, *25*
Adoptionism, **109-12,** 125
Adso of Luxeuil, 146
Aeneas of Gaza, 91, 92
Aeneas of Paris, 129, *205*
Aevum, *268*
Agnosticists, 81-82
Agobard of Lyon, 108, *112,* 126
Aktistists, 81
Al-Farabi, 186, 234-35, 265
Al-Ghazzali, 186, 235, 265

Al-Kindi, 234
Albert, K., *189*
Albert the Great, *189,* 231, 241, 257, **258-60,** 280, 281
Albigenses, 156, **192-93,** 222, 229
Albizu, J. L., *312*
Alcuin of York, 108, 110, *123,* 129, 146
Alesanco, T., *37*
Alexander III, *174,* 181
Alexander IV, 233
Alexander VI, 306
Alexander of Aphrodisias, 291
Alexander of Hales, *178,* 232, 244, **248-49,** 250, 254, 255
Alexander, P. J., *199, 200*
Alfonso VIII, 229
Alfred the Englishman, 186
Allegorical interpretation, 21, 70, 215, 217
Allegro, C., *130*
Almagno, R. S., *256*
Alonso, M., *185, 186*

Alvarez Turienzo, S., *41*
Amalarius, *119*
Amalric of Bena, 131, 136, 189, 240
Amalricians, 189-90
Amann, E., *57, 60, 82, 85, 88, 110, 114, 128*
Ambrose, 20, 21, 24, 28, 65, *71*, 113, 140
Ammann, A. M., *297*
Amolo of Lyon, *116*
Amorós, L., *249, 252*
Ampe, A., *325*
Analogia entis, 271
Analogy, 269-71, 308
Anastasius of Constantinople, 198
Anastasius Sinaita, 98
Anastos, M. V., *200*
Ancelet-Hustache, J., *324*
Anderson, M. E., *274*
Angels, 42, 63, 73-74, 93-94, *135*, 180, 238, 246, 264, 273-74, *288*
Anhypostatic union, 278
Anorios, *301*
Anselm, 148, **158-67**, 171, 172, 248, 266, 313, 316
Anselm of Laon, 168, 175, 183
Anthropology, 135, 145-46, 180, 274-75, *314*
Antiochene Christology, 100-101, 103, 217-18
Antweiler, A., *161*
Aphthartodocetism, 81, 98
Apokatastasis, 136
Apologia de Verbo incarnato, 181
Apostles' Creed, 130
Apostolic succession, 49, 50
Arabs, 90, 91, 103, 104, **105-6**, 148, 197, 233-37

Argerami, O., *240, 247, 250*
Arianism, 56, 70, 126
Aristippus, Henry, 233
Aristotle, 67, 68, 69, 98, *182*, 186, 189, **233-42**, 244, 246, 247, 248, 250, 251, 252, 254, 257, 258, 260, 261, 273, 274, 275, 277, 284, 285, 286, 301, 315
Armenia, Church of, 104-5, 219, 302
Asterios Gerostergios, *206*
Atto of Verceil, 146
Auer, J., *314*
Augustine, **15-55**, 57-65, 70. 71, 72, 73, 113, 114, 115, 116, 120, 122, 124, 125, *127*, 130, 135, 145, 154, *163*, 248, 272, 280, 326, 328
Augustine of Canterbury, 71
Augustinianism, 57-65, 71-74, **243-56**, 311
Averroes, 106, 186, 234, **235-37**, 241, 242, 250, 252, 284, 285, 288
Averroists, 236, 242, **284-91**
Avicenna, 186, **234-35**, *246, 247*, 265, 285
Avignon, Papacy in, 226, 304-5, 316, 331
Azevedo, Diego de, 229-30

Babai (Nestorian patriarch), 101
Babai the Great, **102-3**
Bacon, Roger, 230, 241, *248, 255*
Bailleux, E., *44*
Bainton, R. H., *29*
Baker, Augustine, *324*
Baker, D., *240*
Balic, K., *307, 312, 313*

Ball, J., 44
Bandinelli, Roland: see Alexander III
Baptism, 33, 47, 51-52, 62, 63; infant, 187
Bar Berika, Ebedjesu, 299
Bar Hebraeus, Gregory, 301
Bar Isho'dad of Merv, Theodore, 217-18
Bar Koni, Theodore, 217
Bar Nun, Isho, 217
Bar Senaja, Elijah, 216-17
Bar Sushan, I., 219
Baraut, C., 190
Barbarian invasions, 28
Bardy, G., 56, 69
Barion, J., 37
Barlaam, 295-96
Baron, H., 176
Baronius, 143
Barrett, H. M., 67
Barsumas, 101, 102
Barth, K., 161
Barth, T., 308, 309
Basel, Council of (A.D. 1431-1449), 305
Basiliscus, 78-79
Baur, F. C., 17
Baur, L., 240
Bazán, B. C., 240, 287
Beatus of Liebana, 110-11
Beck, H. G., 293, 294, 295, 296
Becket, Thomas, 225
Bede, 71, 107
Behrends, F., 148
Beierwalters, W., 130
Belisarius, 85
Ben Adi, Yahya, 219
Benedict of Nursia, 74, 191
Benson, R. L., 157
Benz, E., 232

Béraudy, A., 120, 121
Berengar, 120, 148, 150-56
Bergeron, M., 67
Bernard, 168, 169, 172-73, 175, 185, 224-25, 248, 254
Bernard of Chartres, 182
Bernard of Constance, 185
Bernard Sylvester, 182, 183
Bernath, K., 274
Bertagna, B., 321
Bertola, E., 240
Bertolini, O., 141
Bérubé, C., 256
Bettoni, E., 251, 308, 309, 314
Betzendörfer, W., 158
Beyene, Y., 301
Bianchi, L., 240
Bidawid, R. J., 216
Biel, Gabriel, 323-24
Bieler, L., 130, 145
Bissen, J. M., 252, 312
Bizet, J. A., 325
Blakney, R. B., 324
Blume, H. D., 45
Boehner, P., 248, 318
Boethius, 66-68, 145, 260, 261
Boethius of Dacia, 288-89, 290
Bogomil, 214
Bogomilism, 192, 213, 214
Bohemian Brethren, 333
Bohlin, T., 29, 31
Bolgar, R. R., 75
Bolgiani, F., 23
Bonano, S., 119
Bonansea, B. M., 307, 309
Bonardi, P., 325
Bonaventure, 172, 232, 233, 241, 244, 248, 249-55, 281, 287, 289, 315
Boniface VIII, 225-26
Bonné, J., 260

Bonnefoy, J. F., *313*
Bonner, G., *15*, 26, *29*
Bonzi da Genova, U., *324*
Borak, H., *309*
Bordoy, M., *37*
Boris of Bulgaria, 213-14
Borst, A., *192, 193*
Bosogne, F., *63*
Boyer, C., *23, 37*
Bozóky, E., *192*
Bradwardine, *328*
Brady, J. M., *39*
Bréhier, E., *64*
Brethren of the Common Life, 325
Bridges, J. H., *247*
Brlek, M., *313*
Broekaert, J. D., *74*
Brons, B., *93*
Bronswijk, A. C., *332*
Brown, P., *15*
Bruder, K., *67*
Bukowski, T. P., *287*
Bulgarians, 197, 205, 206, **213-14**
Burt, D. X., *54*
Buytaert, E. M., *169*

Cadaveric Council, *143*
Caesarius of Arles, *61*
Caggiano, E., *312*
Cajetan, Tomas de Vio, *269*
Callaey, P. F., *256*
Callus, D. A., *185, 240, 275*
Calvinism, 188
Campbell, J., *275*
Campbell, R., *158*
Campbell, S., *74*
Canal, J. M., *119*
Candidus, 127
Capanaga, V., *23, 41*

Capelle, G. C., *189*
Capone-Braga, G., *44*
Cappadocians, 98, 130
Cappuyns, M., *58, 61, 122, 124, 127, 130, 135, 145*
Carlyle, A. J., *184*
Carreras, J., *314*
Carton, R., *67*
Casado, F., *38*
Cassian, *see* John Cassian
Cassiodore, **69-71**
Cathari, *see* Albigenses
Catherine of Genoa, *324*
Catherine of Siena, *324*
Cayré, F., *23, 37*
Celibacy, 207
Cerularius, Michael, 207-8, 210, 211, *214*
Chadwick, H., *65*
Chadwick, O., *58*
Chakmakjian, H. A., *302*
Chalcedon, Council of, 76-81, 85, 87, 88, 89, 90, 98, 100, 101, 103, 104
Chappuis, G., *67*
Charlemagne, 107, 108, 109, 110, *123*, 128, 142, 203-4
Charles Martel, 107, 108
Charles the Bald, 108, 115, 117, 119, 123-24, 130, 137, 143
Charlesworth, M. J., *159, 160, 161*
Chartres, school of, 182-83
Châtillon, J., *175, 290*
Chéné, J., *58, 60*
Chenu, M. D., *157, 249*
Chesnut, R. C., 77
Chevallier, P., *95*
Chiocchetti, E., *314*
Chollet, A., *288, 291*
Christ, P. S., *237*

Christodulos (patriarch of Constantinople), *218*
Christology, 49, 72, **76-91,** 95-100, 102, 103, **109-12,** 136-37, 166-67, 171-72, 180-81, 193, 199-200, 203, 217-18, 219, 253, 278, 299-300, 301, 311-13
Church; and state, 184-85, *204,* 223-26; visible and invisible, 28, 50, 331; *see also* Ecclesiology
Cicero, 16, 28
Circumcelliones, 28
Cities, 220, 229
Clarembaud of Arras, 182, 183
Clark, J. M., *324*
Clarke, E. G., *217*
Claudianus Mamertus, 64, 70
Clement V, 316
Clement of Smolensk, 215
Coccia, A., *39, 317*
Coelestius, 30, 32-33
Cohen, A., *239*
Collins, J., *67*
Communicatio idiomatum, 82, 95, 98, 103, 111-12, 278
Conceptualism, 170
Conciliarism, 305, 317, **321-24**
Concupiscence, 45
Confessions, 16, 23, 40
Connolly, R. H., *102*
Connoly, G. J., *248*
Conrad II, 144
Consolamentum, 193
Constance, Council of, 305, 328, 333
Constans II, 90
Constantine, 27; Donation of, 336
Constantine V, 198, 207

Constantine VI, 203
Constantinople, Council of (A.D. 553), **84-88**
Constantinople, Council of (A.D. 681), 90
Constantinople, Council of (A.D. 869-870), 206
Contradictory Conference, 84, 96
Copleston, F., *36, 39, 69, 247,* 315
Coptic Church, 104, 218
Coulbeaux, E., *301*
Courcelle, P. P., *23*
Courtenay, W. J., *319*
Couturier, C., *51*
Craemer-Ruegenberg, I., *258, 260*
Creation, **38-39,** 40, 91, 92, 133-34, 136, 145, 180, 182-83, 193, 219, 237, 238, 239, 250, 272-74, 316; eternal, 133, 252, 259; *see also* World, eternity of
Cresi, A., *314*
Creytens, R., *282*
Cristiani, M., *115*
Crocco, A., *67, 171, 190*
Crombie, A. C., *240*
Cuervo, M., *259*
Cyprian, 28, 29, 50, 51
Cyril I of Alexandria (St. Cyril), 77, 78, 79, 87, 278
Cyril II (patriarch of Alexandria), *218*
Cyril of Turov, 215

D'Ailly, Pierre, *321,* 322, 323, 333
D'Alès, A., *65*
D'Alverny, M. Th., *186*
Da Milano, I., *187*

Dagens, C., *71*
Dahmus, J. H., *327*
Dal Pra, M., *130*
Dales, R. C., *288*
Daly, L. J., *323*
Damasus, 65
Damerau, R., *321*
Damiata, M., *317*
Daniel de Morley, 186
Dante, 221
David of Dinant, 189, 190, 240
Davids, J. A., *65*
De Andrés Hernansanz, T., *290*
De Courcecault, R., *312*
De Gandillac, M., *157*
De Ghellinck, J., *179, 180*
De Lagarde, G., *323*
De Mattos, G., *260*
De Montclos, J., *151*
De Plinval, G., *29, 31, 32, 51*
De Sesma, L., *314*
De Vaux, R., *189, 247*
De Vooght, P., *321, 329, 333*
De Vries, G., *301*
De Vries, J., *275*
De Vries, W., *300*
Debongnie, P., *324, 325*
Décarreaux, J., *107*
Decret, F., *17*
Decretals, 184
Deification: see Divinization
Delhaye, P., *125*
Delly, E. K., *218*
Demetrius of Lampe, *213*
Demons, 42, 43, 73-74
Descartes, *161*
Deusdedit, 185
DeVaux, R., *185*
Devisse, J., *113*
Devotio moderna, 325
Di Stefano, A. E., *41*

Di Vona, P., *323*
Díaz, M. C., *75*
Dickson, C., *247*
Didier, J. C., *151*
Diepen, H. M., *85*
Diesner, H. J., *66, 75*
Dietrich of Niem, 322
Díez Ramos, G., *172*
Diodore of Tarsus, 102, 103
Dionysius the Areopagite: *see*
  Pseudo-Dionysius
Dioscorus, 76, 80, 104
Disdier, M., *58*
Divinization, 92, 94, 209
Docetism, 65
Dominic, 192-93, **229-30**
Dominicans, 193, **229-31**, 247,
  257-83
Dominion, 330-31, 332
Donatism, **26-29,** 49, 51, 52, 105
Donatus, 27
Double truth, 236, 286
Doucet, V., *248*
Douie, D. L., *255*
Dualism, 18, 41, 65, 193, 202
Ducharme, L., *260*
Dufeil, M. M., *232*
Duin, J. J., *287*
Dunphy, W., *283*
Dura-Europos, *198*
Durand of Troarn, *152*
Durand, William, 225
Duvernoy, J., *192*
Dvornik, F., *206*

Ecclesiology, **49-50,** 69, 94, 317,
  321-22, 331
Eckhart, John, 324, 325
Edessa, school of, 101
Ekert, W. P., *258*
El-Ehwany, A. F., *234*

Elders, L., *266*
Elert, W., *88*
Elg, A. G., *60*
Elipandus of Toledo, **109-12**
Emerson, R. K., *146*
Encyclion, 78
Endura, 193
Enhypostaton, 97-98
Ennesch, C., *192*
Ephesus, Council of (A.D. 431),
    30, *58,* 100
Epiphanius, 131
Epping, A., *309*
Erasmus, *31*
Ernst, W., *320*
Eschatology, 54-55, 146, 180,
    269
Essence and existence, 265, *283*
Ethiopia, Church of, 104, 300-
    301
Eucharist, 51, 52-53, **119-23,**
    146, 147, 149, **150-56,** 176-77,
    183-84, 189, 193, *213,* 300,
    301, 321, 331-32; as sacrifice,
    73, 120, 122, 222; unleavened
    bread, 207, 208, 294
Euclid, 186
Eudes of Stella, 187
Eusebius Bruno, *152*
Eustratius of Nicea, 212
Eutyches, 76, 80
Evans, D. B., *96*
Evans, G. R., *161, 172*
Evil, 21, **41-42**
Evolution, theory of, *39*
Exemplarism, 39, 252

Fachler, F. P., *309*
Fahey, J. F., *120*
Faith; and reason, 239, 259,
    261-63, 286, 290, 315, 316,

317, 319, 326, 329; and works,
    48
Fakhry, M., *235*
Fall, 44, 135
Faustus of Milevis, 19, 20
Faustus of Riez, 58, 59-60, 63, 64
Feckes, C., *259*
Fedotov, G. P., *215, 297, 298*
Felix III, *80,* 140
Felix of Urgel, **109-12**
Femiano, S. B., *23*
Ferguson, J., *29*
Ferrara-Florence, Council of
    (A.D. 1439), 293, 294, 302
Ferrari, L. C., *19*
Fetten, T., *312*
Filioque, 125, **127-30,** 145, 164,
    165, *204,* 205, 208, 294, 295
Fishacre, Richard, 230, *247*
Flint, V. J., *183*
Flórez, R., *40*
Florus of Lyon, 112, 116-17
Fontaine, J., *75*
Forget, J., *247*
Formosus, *143*
Forms, plurality of, 238, 245-46,
    255, 260
Fortin, E. L., *64*
Fournier, P., *190*
Franceschini, E., *241*
Francis, *172,* **231,** 248, 254
Franciscans, 188, 192, **231-33,**
    247-56, 282-83, **306-16**
Frank, I. W., *324*
Fraticelli, 305
Fredegisus of Tours, 126
Free will, **42-43,** 44, 46, 92, 113,
    204, 209, 243, 272, 287
Frend, W. H. C., *17, 26, 77*
Frivold, L., *105*
Froland of Senlis, *152*

Fuhrmann, H., *140*
Fulbert of Chartres, **148-50**
Fulgentius of Ruspe, *61,* 113, 115

Gabriel, A. L., *227*
Gaianites, *81*
Galen, 186
García Villoslada, R., *143*
Gardet, L., *235*
Garnerius of Rochefort, *190*
Gaughan, N. F., *283*
Gaunilo, 161-63
Gauthier, L., *235, 236*
Gauthier, R. A., *240, 285*
Gautier of Saint Victor, 178
Gazzana, A., *269*
Geiben, C., *240*
Gelasius, 140-41, 184
Genakoplos, D. J., *293*
Gennadius, *59,* 64
Gennadius of Novgorod, 298
George of Arabia, 219
Gerard of Abbeville, 233, *255,* 282
Gerard of Cremona, 186, 233
Gerard of Florence, 144
Gerardo de Borgo San Donino, 233
Gerbert of Aurillac: *see* Sylvester II
Gerhoch of Reichersberg, *181*
German of Constantinople, 196, 198, 200, 203, *204*
German II of Constantinople, 294
Gerrity, B., *275*
Gerson, Jean de, 322, 333
Geyer, B., *158, 260*
Gezo of Tortona, 146
Gibson, M., *67, 113, 154*

Gilbert de la Porrée, 173, 178, 181, 182, 183, 190, 191
Gilbert, P., *159*
Giles of Lessines, *260*
Giles of Rome, 283
Gill, J., *294*
Gilson, E., *37, 68, 69, 145, 170, 175, 183, 234, 235, 236, 237, 247, 260, 283, 288, 309, 311, 314, 316,* 319
Giorgianni, V., *29*
Giuliani, S., *266*
Glaver, Rudolf, *192*
Glez, G., *224*
Glorieux, P., *247, 283, 285*
Gnosticism, 18, *192*
God; existence of, **159-63,** 239, 245, 251, *255,* 266-67, 277, 309-11; knowledge of, 132-33, 251, 308; language about, 269-71; nature of, 21, **37-38,** 93, 132-33, 163, 251-52, 267-71, 311; vision of, 55, 127
Godfrey de la Vendome, 224
Godfrey of Fontaines, 283
Godfrey of Saint Victor, 178
Goheen, J., *273*
Goichon, A. M., *235*
Gonnet, J., *187*
González, Domingo, 186
González, E., *266*
González, S., *139*
Gothic art, 220-21
Gottschalk, **112-15,** 116, 122, 126
Goy, R., *176*
Grabmann, M., *171, 255, 259, 288*
Grace, 30, 32-33, **46-49, 57-63,** 74, 180, 243, 320; infused, 49; irresistible, 47, 63, 72

Graf, G., *218*
Grane, L., *169*
Great Western Schism, 305, 317, 321, 323, 327, 330
Gregory I, the Great, 70, **71-74**, 113, 115, 141-43, 243
Gregory II, 198
Gregory III, 198
Gregory VII, 144, *151*, 184, 185, 207, 226
Gregory IX, 227, 231, 240
Gregory Acindynus, *296*
Gregory of Catina, 185, 225
Gregory of Datev, 302
Gregory of Nyssa, 64, 131
Gregory of Rimini, 319, *321*
Gregory of Sinai, 295
Gregory, T., *135, 319*
Griffe, E., *192*
Grion, A., *324*
Grodet, P., *71*
Grondijs, L. H., *17*
Groote, Gerard, 325
Grosseteste, Robert, 240, *255*
Gruber, L. M. de J., *67*
Grumel, V., *96, 99, 200, 203*
Grundlach, M., *114*
Guardini, R., *23*
Guichard of Lyon, 187
Guitmund of Aversa, 155, 156
Guitton, J., *40*
Gunther, R. T., *241*
Gustavsson, L. R., *113*
Guy, J. C., *58*
Guy of Ferrara, 185
Guy of Osnaburg, 185

Haacke, R., *78, 86*
Habbel, J., *269*
Hadrian I, 110, 198
Hadrian II, 206

Hadrumentum, monks of, 57
Haendler, G., *204*
Hamelin, A. M., *249*
Hansen, J., *259*
Harkins, C. L., *256*
Harnack, A. von, *52*
Haugh, R., *206*
Hausherr, I., *209*
Hayden, D., *169*
Haymo of Auxerre, *122, 145*
Haymo of Halberstadt, 122-23, *145*
Haymo of Hirschau, *122*
Haymo of Telleia, *122*
Hegel, *161*
Heinzer, F., *99*
Heiric of Auxerre, 144-45
Heitz, J., *24*
Hell, 116, 137
Heloise, 168, 169
Henana, schism of, 103
Hendrikx, E., 24
Hennephof, H., *198*
Henoticon, 79-82, 140
Henry IV, 184
Henry Bartholomew of Susa, 225
Henry of Ghent, 307, 308, *314*
Henry Suso, 325
Heraclius, 89
Hergenröther, J., *206*
Herman, E., *103*
Hero, A. C., *296*
Heseltin, G. C., *328*
Hessen, J., *37*
Hesychasm, 210, **295-96**
Heynck, V., *283*
Hilarion of Kiev, 215
Hilary of Arles, 58
Hildebrand: see Gregory VII
Hill, K. D., *240*

Hilton, Walter, *324*
Hincmar, **112-17,** 119, 124, 126, 131
Hippocrates, 186
Hirsch-Reich, B., *190*
Hissette, R., *290*
History, 53-54, 66, 176, 190-92, 215, 287
Hocedez, E., *255, 283, 312*
Hödl, L., *282*
Hoeres, W., *311*
Hofmann, F., *49*
Holy Spirit, 49, **127-30,** 165, 180
Holzapfel, H., *231*
Honorius (Pope), 89-90
Honorius III, 190
Honorius of Augsburg, 185
Hormisdas, 80, 83
Horn, G., *209*
Horst, L., *217*
Hrosvitha, 147
Huftier, M., *44*
Hugh of Chartres, 152
Hugh of Fleury, 225
Hugh of Saint Victor, **176-77,** *181,* 183, 185, 225, 248, 250
Hugh of Strasbourg, *260*
Humbert, 144, 156, 207, 208
Hundred Years' War, 305
Hurley, M., *329*
Hus, John, 305, 306, 327, **332-33**
Hussey, J. M., *210, 212*
Huyben, J., *325*
Hylomorphism, 238, 245-46, *247,* 252, 260, 264, 273, 274
Hypostatic union, 312

Ibas of Edessa, 84-88, 101
Ibn al'Assal, F., *300*
Ibn al'Assal, J., *300*

Ibn al'Muqaffa, A., *218*
Ibn Gabirol, 186, **237-38,** 246
Ibn Kabar, A.-B., *300*
Ibn Tarik, G., *218*
Iconoclasm, **197-204**
Ignatius of Antioch, 83
Ignatius of Constantinople, 205-6
Ildefonsus of Toledo, *128*
Illumination, 36, 245, *247,* 250, *255,* 260, 276, 307, *314*
Images, **197-204**
Imago Dei, 64, 135, 145, 150, 301
Individuation, 252, 260, 264, 273-74, 288
Indulgences, *331,* 333
Initium fidei, 57, 60, 62
Innocent I, 30, 31
Innocent III, *141,* 192, **222-25,** 226, 229, 231
Innocent IV, 231, 232, 240, *247*
Inquisition, 192, **226-27**
Investitures, 156, 158, 184-85
Irenaeus, *312*
Irene, 198-99
Iserloh, E., *321*
Isidore of Seville, 75
Iudicatum, 85

Jacob Baradaeus, 104
Jacob, E. F., *325*
Jacob of Edessa, 219
Jacobites 103, 104, 218-19, 301
Jacquin, A. M., *158*
Jaeger, C. S., *167*
Jalics, F., *58*
James, B. S., *172*
Janavaschek, L., *172*
Jaspert, B., *74*
Jay, E. G., *266*
Jay, P., *55*

Jean de la Rochelle, 232, *249*
Jeauneau, E., *145, 157, 182, 183*
Jerome, 30, *31, 65, 71*
Joachim of Fiore, 181, 189, **190-92**, 222
Joachimism, 231-32, *255*, 321
John II, 84
John VIII, 206
John XXI, 290
John XXII, 283, 325
John Cassian, 34, 58, 73
John Chrysostom, 58
John Duns Scotus, 255, *283*, 304, **306-16**
John Italos, 210, 211
John of Cournailles, *181*
John of Damascus, 196, 198, 201-2, 203, *204*
John of Gaunt, 327
John of Harran, *219*
John of Jandum, 291, 323
John of Parma, 192, 231-32, 249
John of Saint Giles, 230
John of Salisbury, *182*, 183, 185, 225
John of Spain, 186
John Peckham, 255, 282
John Philoponus, 91, 92
John Ruysbroeck, 325
John Scotus Erigena, 108, 112, 115-17, *120*, 122, *124*, **130-37**, 144, 145, 150, 151, 189, 190
John Tauler, 324-25
John the Deacon, *71*
John the Grammarian, 204
John the Teuton, 225
Johns, C. T., *324*
Jolivet, J., *173*
Jolivet, R., *41, 273*
Jordan, M. D., *282*

Judaism, 215, 222; philosophers, 237-39
Judaizers (Russian sect), 298, 299
Jugie, M., 77, *78, 80, 81, 82, 89, 218, 219*
Julian of Eclanum, 33
Julian of Halicarnassus, 81, 82
Junglas, J. P., *96*
Justin (emperor), 80, 83
Justinian, 83-88
Justus, *73*

Kaelin, B., *37*
Kannengiesser, C., *165*
Kant, *161*
Kawerau, P., *301*
Keleher, J. P., *52*
Kelly, J. N. D., *52*
Kempf, F., *224*
Kempis, 325
Kendzierski, L. H., *273*
Kennedy, L. A., *260*
Khaliq, A., *235*
Kilwardby, Robert, 241, *247, 255*, 282
Kilzer, M. C., *74*
Kleineidam, E., *273*
Klein, A., *324*
Klostermann, R. A., *298*
Klubertanz, G. P., *269*
Knowledge, theory of, **34-37**, 38, 69, 177, 183, 237, 245, *246, 247*, 250, *255*, 259-60, 275-77, 307-8, *314*
Knowles, D., *324*
Koch, J., *283*
Kolping, A., *161*
Konrad, R., *146*
Kottje, R., *113*

Kovach, F. J., *258, 260*
Kozma, *214*
Kreuzer, G., *90*
Kristeller, P. O., *137, 318*
Kuksewicz, K., *285*
Künzle, P., *275*
Küry, U., *129*
Kurz, L., *73*
Kutzli, R., *192*
Kvacala, J., *332*

Labourt, H., *216*
Lacroix, B., *66*
Ladner, G., *204*
Ladomerszky, N., *208*
Laistner, W., *69*
Lambot, D. C., *113, 124*
Lamirande, E., *52*
Lamotte, J., *54*
Landgraf, A. M., *247*
Lanfranc, *120,* 147-48, **150-56,** 158
Langton, Stephen, *247*
Lateran Council, Fourth (A.D. 1215), 181, 190, 191, **222-23,** 230
Lateran Council, Second (A.D. 1139), 187
Lateran Council, Third (A.D. 1179), 192
Laun, J. F., *328*
Law, natural, 277-78
Lawrence of Spain, 225
Layer, A., *258*
Lebon, J., *78*
Leff, G., *317, 318, 328*
Lemay, H. R., *182*
Leo III, 110, 129, 142
Leo IX, 144, 207
Leo III (emperor), 197-98, 200
Leo IV (emperor), 198

Leo V (emperor), 199, 202
Leo VI (emperor), 208
Leo of Ochrid, *214*
Leonardi, C., *145*
Leontius of Byzantium, *81,* 85, 86, 92, **96-98,** 99
Lértora, C. A., *240*
Leuthard of Chalons, *192*
Lewis, E., *323*
Libertini, C., *314*
Licinianus of Cartagena, *64*
Lindbeck, G. A., *318, 321*
Lindberg, D. C., *241*
Lindgren, U., *148*
Little, A. G., *232, 306*
Little, E. F., *173*
Liturgy, 71, 333; *see also* Sacraments
Logos, 36
Lollards, 328, 332
Longpré, E., *255*
Lorenz, R., *61*
Loserth, J., *332*
Lothair I, *123*
Lothair II, 117, 146
Louis of Bavaria, 317
Louis the Pious, *112,* 126, 127
Lucenti, P., *137*
Lull, Ramon, *256*
Lupo, T., *325*
Loscombe, E., *178*
Luther, 320, *324*
Lyon, Council of (A.D. 1274), 250, 294
Lytkens, H., *269*

Macarius, II (Coptic patriarch), *218*
Macarius (monk), 124-25
MacDonald, A. J., *147, 151, 152, 154, 155, 184*

Macek, J., *332*
McEvoy, J., *240*
McGill, A. C., *161*
McGinn, B., *190*
Macha, J., *294*
McIntyre, J., *158*
MacKinney, L. C., *148*
McLeod, F. G., *102*
MacQueen, D. J., *58*
MacQuinn, J., *40*
McWilliams, J., *260*
Madoz, J., *59, 65*
Maimonides, 237, **238-39**
Maisonneuve, H., *226*
Makdour, I., *234*
Malebranche, N., *36*
Malnory, A., *61*
Maloy, R., *119*
Mandonnet, P., *285, 287*
Manegold of Lautenbach, 155
Mani, 18
Manichaeism, **17-20,** 31, 41, 42, 44, *192,* 193, 214
Manieres, J. E., *131*
Mann, F., *45*
Manselli, R., *186*
Map, Walter, 187
Marchasson, Y., *165*
Marcionism, *192*
Marić, J., *95*
Marius Victorinus, 22, 64
Markus, R. A., *266*
Marsh, Adam, 232
Marsilius of Padua, 323
Martin, E. J., *198*
Martin of Braga, 74
Martínez, A., *273*
Martínez, J. M., *306*
Martins, M., *323*
Mary, 102, 173, *219,* 301; immaculate conception, *61,* 253,

279, 313-14; perpetual virginity, *61, 98,* **117-19,** 279
Mathon, G., *23, 63*
Matter and form, *255,* 279
Matthew of Aquasparta, 255
Matthews, A. W., *23*
Maurer, A., *288*
Maximus the Confessor, 89, 92, **98-100,** 131
Mayer, V., *313*
Mazzarella, P., *255*
Melchites, 104, 196
Melitionites, Constantine, *294*
Mendicants, **229-33;** *see also* Dominicans, Franciscans
Merits, 48
Meyendorff, J., *295*
Michael II, 199
Michael VIII Paleologus, 293
Michael Cerularius: *see* Cerularius, Michael
Michael Italicus, 212
Michael of Antioch, *219*
Michael Scotus, 186
Michaelites, *301*
Michaud-Quantin, P., *288*
Michelangelo, 337
Michelet, M., *324*
Migetius, 110
Migliore, P., *312*
Mingana, A., *216*
Minges, P., *312*
Moereels, L., *57*
Molnar, A., *187, 332*
Molnar, E. C., *333*
Monasticism, 25, 58, 71, 74, 98, 143, 145, 157, *172,* 173, 191, *219,* 220, 222, 229-33, 297
Monergism, **88-89,** 98-99
Monica, 24

Monophysism, **77-84,** 87, 88, 90, 95, 100, 103, **104-5, 218-19, 300-302**
Monotheism, **88-91,** 98-99, 200
Montagnes, B., *269*
Moorman, J. R. H., *232*
Morin, G., *122*
Morra, E., *251*
Mozarabs, 109
Muckle, J. T., *185*
Mundhenk, J., *274*
Muñiz, P., *274*
Muñoz Delgado, V., *290*
Murray, M. V., *283*
Muzzey, D. S., *232*
Mysticism, 94, 172-73, 177, 209-10, 211, 215, 221, 244, 247-48, 252-54, *256,* 295-96, 306, **324-27**

Nardi, B., *288*
Narses, **101-2,** 103
Nau, F., *299, 301*
Naumann, B., *137*
Nédoncelle, M., *67*
Nelson, J., *113*
Neoplatonism, 20, 21, 22, 23, 24, 39, 42, 53, 63, 91, 93, 125, 177, 238, 244, *283,* 285
Nerses III Glaietzi, *219*
Nestorianism, 86, 96-97, **100-103,** 110, 111-12, **216-18, 299-300**
Nestorius, *58,* 77, 80, 102, 103
Neumann, B., *283*
Newell, J. H., *182*
Nicea, Council of (A.D. 325), *138*
Nicea, Council of (A.D. 787), 199, 200, 203, 204
Nicephorus, 199
Nicetas Stethatos, *209*

Nicholas I, 117, 205, 206
Nicholas III, 294
Nicholas of Cusa, 326
Niobites, 82
Nisibis, school of, 101
Nitschke, A., *258*
Nominalism, 68, 69, 150, 164, 165, **317-24,** 326, 329

O'Connell, P., *208*
O'Connor, W., *59*
O'Daly, G. J. P., *45*
O'Meara, J. J., *130, 137, 145*
Oakley, F., *324*
Oberman, H. A., *318, 320, 324, 326*
Obertello, L., *67, 69*
Ockham, William of, 317-18, *321,* 322-23, 326
Odo, abbot of Cluny, 145
Odo of Beauvais, 124-25
Odo of Tournai, 181-82
Odo Rigaud, 232, 249
Olphe-Gaillard, M., *58*
Optatus of Milevis, 49-50, 51, 52
Orange, Synod of, **61-62**
Origen, 87, 217
Ormanian, M., *302*
Oromí, M., *252*
Orosius, 30, **65-66**
Ort, L. J. R., *17*
Orthodoxy, Feast of, 199
Otlo of Saint Emmeran, 155
Otto I, 144
Otto III, 144
Ozment, S., *326*

Palamas, Gregory, 295
Palamism: *see* Hesychasm
Pantheism, 136, 189, 325

Papacy, **139-42**, 184-85, 206-7, **222-26,** 300, 304-6, 321; infallibility, 90, 336
Parent, J. M., *182, 183*
Parente, E., *312*
Paris, Council of (A.D. 1210), 189, 190, 240
Parsufa, 102, 103
Partee, C., *255*
Paschasius Radbertus, 118-22, 146, 154
Patch, H. R., *67*
Patschovsky, A., *187*
Paulicians, *192,* 219
Paulinus of Aquileia, 108, 110
Pegis, A. C., *274*
Pelagianism, **29-34,** 44, 46, 51, 61
Pelagius (monk), **29-32,** 57, 58
Pelagius (pope), *88*
Pelland, L., *61*
Pelster, F., *282*
Penance, 73, **137-39,** 172, 173, 320, *331,* 332
Pennington, M. B., *173*
Pentarchy, 208
Pérez de Urbel, J., *65*
Périer, A., *219*
Perino, R., *163*
Perler, O., *39*
Perseverance, 47
Person, **67-78,** *178*
Peter III of Antioch, 208
Peter Bruys, 187
Peter Damian, 155, 156
Peter de Trabibus, 255-56
Peter Lombard, 174, *176,* **178-81,** 190, 228, 249, 280
Peter of Auvergne, 283
Peter of John Olivi, 255, *256*
Peter of Poitiers, *178,* 181

Peter of Tarantaise; see Innocent IV
Peter, patriarch of Alexandria, *80*
Peter the Devourer, 181
Peter the Fuller, *78,* 79, 83
Peter the Venerable, 169, *187*
Petit, L., *302*
Petrobrussians, 187
Pezet, M., *187*
Phantasiasts, *81*
Phelan, G. B., *158*
Philip the Fair, 225
Philippen, L. J. M., *187*
Philosophy and theology, **91-92,** 115-16, 131, 148-49, 154, 156, 164, 173, 177, 205, 210, 211-12, 219, 233-42, 244-45, 250-51, *255,* 257, 259, 261-63, 280-81, 285-86
Photius, *92,* 129, **205-7,** 208
Piazzoni, A. M., *176*
Pilkington, J. G., *16*
Pippin, 107, 108
Piret, P., *99*
Pius V, 283
Pius IX, 314
Planzer, D., *325*
Platero Ramos, J. A., *64*
Plato, 35, 36, 67, 69, 98, 182, 247, 280
Platonism, 35, 37
Plotinus, 21, 36, 39, 280
Poor Lombards, 188
Porphyry, 21, 68
Portalié, E., *15, 33, 36, 38, 45, 55*
Poschmann, B., *139*
Potentia Dei absoluta, **318-20**
Poverty, 187, 188, 231, 233, *255,* 323
Powicke, F. M., *240*

Predestination, 32-34, 57-63, 72, 74, **112-17,** 131, *204,* 219, 243, 271-72, *321, 328,* 331
Prete, S., *29*
Priscillian, 65, 226
Priscillianism, 65-66
Proclus, 285
Procopius of Gaza, 91, 92
Prosper of Aquitaine, 58, 60-61, 113, 115
Providence, *287,* 289
Prudentius of Troyes, 112, 114, 116, 117
Psellus, Michael, 208, **210-12**
Pseudo-Dionysius, 64, 91, **93-96,** 131, 132, 135, 177, 219, 244, 247, 253, 258, 280
Pseudo-Isidore, 184
Pseudo-Ockham, *319*
Puech, H. C., *17, 19*
Purgatory, 54-55, 73

Rabanus, Maurus, 112-15, 122, *123*
Rahman, F., *234*
Rahner, K., *139*
Ramírez, S., *283*
Ramos y Loscertales, J. M., *65*
Rangheri, M., *146*
Rarain, B., *298*
Rashdall, H., *227, 232*
Ratramnus of Corbie, 112, 114-26, 129, 151, *205*
Raymund of Toledo, 186
Realism, 69, 125, 165, 167, 175, 182, 189
Rebolla, A., *275*
Redding, J. P., *62*
Reeves, M., *190*
Remigius of Auxerre, 145-46, 148
Renaissance, 305-6

Resurrection of the body, 91, 92
Richard of Middleton, 255
Richard of Saint Victor, **177-78**
Richards, J., *71*
Riché, P., *75*
Ridolfi, R., *333*
Riedl, J. O., *283*
Riva, C., *45*
Rivera, J. F., *186*
Rivière, J., *312*
Robert of Courçon, 240, *247*
Robert of Melun, *181*
Robert of Retines, 186
Robert the Bulgarian, 227
Robson, J. A., *328*
Roché, D., *18*
Rodnite, H. E., *182*
Rohner, A., *259*
Roland of Cremona, 230
Rolle, Richard, *324*
Rondet, H., *51*
Roos, H., *288*
Roquebert, M., *192*
Roques, R., *93*
Roscelin, 163-65, 167, 168, 169, 170, 175
Russian theology, **214-16, 197-99**
Rutledge, D., *94*
Ryan, J. K., *309*

Sabbath, 299, 300, *301*
Sabellianism, 65, 109-10, 126
Sacraments, 29, **51-53,** 93, 176, 180, 219, *247,* 279-80, 298, *300*
Sáenz de Argadona, P. M., *65*
Saint Victor, school of, 174, **175-78,** 179, 247
Sajó, G., *288*
Samuel the Moroccan, 156

Sánchez Sorondo, M., *274*
Santi, C., *301*
Santiago-Otero, H., *183*
Sarkissian, K., *105*
Sassen, F., *286, 288*
Savonarola, Girolamo, 306,
  333-34
Scheltens, G., *309*
Schlieben, R., *69*
Schmaus, M., *309*
Schmidt, C., *192*
Schmieja, H., *287*
Schmitt, F. S., *161*
Schneider, T., *282*
Schneyer, J. B., *176*
Scholarios, Georgios, *296*
Scholastic method, 171, 221,
  228-29
Schürmann, R., *324*
Schurr, V., *67*
Sciacca, M. F., *45, 54*
Scriptures, style of, 126
Scythian monks, controversy of
  the, 82-84, 96
Seeberg, R., *72, 73, 316, 321,
  322*
Seiller, L., *312*
Selge, K. V., *187*
Seminal reasons, 39, 247
Semi-Pelagians, 34, **57-63,** 65
Senteler, J., *275*
Sentences, Four Books of, **178-81,**
  228, 249
Sergius of Constantinople, 88-
  90
Servatus Lupus, 112, 114
Severus of Antioch, **77-78**
Sewter, E. R. A., *210*
Shahan, R. W., *258, 260*
Shannon, A. C., *226*
Sharenkoff, V. N., *214*

Sharif, M. M., *234*
Sharp, D. E., *241, 255*
Sheikh, M. S., *235*
Sheldon-Williams, I. P., *131*
Siger of Brabant, 242, 281, 282,
  284-88, 290
Sigismund, 333
Sillem, E., *266*
Simeon of Bulgaria, 213-14
Simeon the New Theologian,
  209, 295
Simon of Tournai, 225
Simonis, S., *119*
Simony, 185, 304
Simplician, 20, 24
Sin, 180; original, 33, **43-45,** 69,
  169, 172, 173, 182
Sisinius, 17
Sizoo, A., *23*
Skepticism, 20, 21, 35
Sleva, V. E., *274*
Smits, C., *58*
Socrates (historian), 70
Södeberg, H., *192, 193*
Sophronius of Jerusalem, 89, 98
Sorbon, Robert, *247*
Sotericus Panteugenos, *213*
Soul, **63-65,** 72, 123-25, 146,
  219, 238, 245-54, 264, 274,
  287-88; immortal, 92, 314,
  316; incorporeal, 123-24; in-
  dividual, 124-25, 274; origin,
  45, 72, 182; pre-existent, 35;
  transmigration, 19, 193, 212;
  see also Active intellect
Spedalieri, F., *161*
Speroni, Hugo, 187
Spinka, M., *332*
Spirituals (Franciscans), 192,
  232, *255,* 317, 321
Spiteris, J., *213*

Springer, M., *258*
Starnes, C. J., *67*
Stephanites, *301*
Stephen IV, *143*
Stephen of Niobe, 82
Stercoranism, *213*
Sternmüller, F., *285*
Stoicism, 39, 45
Strigolniks, 298-99
Strijd, K., *165*
Suarez, F., *269*
Substance and accident, 263-64
Suidas, Nicetas, 208
Sulpitius Severus, 65
Sylvester II, 144, **147-48**

Tanquelm, 187
Tarasius, 198-99
Tatakis, B., *92, 209, 210, 212, 297*
Teetaert, A., *255*
Teilhard de Chardin, P., *312*
Tekeyan, P., *219*
Tempier, Stephen, 282, 289-90
Temple, S. F., *147*
Tentler, T. N., *320*
Tertullian, 44, 63
Theodora (Justinian's wife), 84, 85
Theodora (regent), 199, 205
Theodore II Lascaris, 294
Theodore of Mopsuestia, 84-88, 102, 217
Theodore of Pharan, *88*
Theodore the Studite, 196, 199, 202-3
Theodoret, 70, 84-88
Theodoric, 67, 70
Theodosius, 140
Theodulf of Orleans, 108, 129
Theopaschism, *79,* 82-84, 96

Theophylact (archbishop), *214*
Theotokos, 86, 102, 112
Thery, G., *189*
Theirry of Chartres, 182
Thomas Aquinas, *37, 161,* 181, *189,* 231, 232, 241, 245, *252,* 253, 254, *255,* **261-81,** 282, 285, 287, 289, 290, 308
Thomas, R., *167*
Thomism, *247,* 261, **281-83,** 307, 309, 315
Thomson, J. A. F., *328*
Thomson, S. H., *328, 332*
Thomson, W. R., *329*
Thondrachians, 219
Thonnard, F. J., *39*
Thouzellier, C., *186*
Thunberg, L., *99*
Tibiletti, C., *58, 60*
Tierney, B., *321*
Time, **40-41,** 268
Timothy I (Nestorian patriarch), 216
Timothy II (Nestorian patriarch), *300*
Timothy Aelurus, *78*
Tisserant, E., *300*
Toledo, Council III of, *139*
Toledo, translators of, 185-86
Torres, C., *65, 66*
Tradition, 329-30
Traducianism, 45, 72
Transubstantiation, 149, 155-56, 184, 187, 222, 317, *321,* 331-32
Tresmontant, C., *240*
Trinity, 67-68, 72, 82, 99, 125-30, 133, 134, 160, 163-65, 168, 173, 178, 180, 181, 182, 190, 191, 217, 252-53, 329
Trinkaus, C., *318, 326*

Trisagion, 79
Tummers, E., 44

Ullman, W., 140, 141
Ulrich of Strasbourg, 260
Unam sanctam, 225-26
Universals, 66-69, 125, 145, 148, 150, 164, 165, 169-70, 175, 181-82, 183, 189, 211-12, 237, 265-66, 328-29
Universities, 157, 227-29
Univocity of being, 309
Urban II, 156, 157

Vaca, C., 23
Vacarius, 187
Vailhe, S., 81
Valerius of Hippo, 25
Valla, Lorenzo, 335, 336
Van De Vyrer, A., 69
Van den Basselaar, J. J., 69
Van den Brink, J. N. B., 119, 120
Van der Lof, L. J., 52
Van der Vekené, E., 226
Van Eupen, T., 139
Van Opdenbosch, J., 119
Van Rooy, H., 273
Van Steenberghen, F., 234, 240, 241, 252, 266, 284, 285, 286, 287, 288, 291
Van Zijl, T. P., 325
Vanneste, J., 93
Vanni-Rovighi, S., 260, 274, 314
Varangot, O. A., 269
Vaschalde, A., 102
Vasiliev, A. A., 197
Veccus, John, 293
Velasco, R., 272
Verbeke, G., 234
Verbraken, P., 73

Verdeyen, P., 325
Verger, J., 173
Verhelst, D., 146
Verona, Council of (A.D. 1184), 188
Verwiebe, W., 40
Veuthey, L., 252
Vielhaber, K., 113
Vigilius, 85, 86-88
Vignaux, P., 319, 321
Vincent of Lérins, 58, 59
Vine, A. R., 101
Visser, D., 167
Vitalis, 57, 83
Vives, J., 66
Völker, W., 95
Vollert, C., 287
Voluntarism, 245, 255, 311, 314, 315, 316, 318
Von den Steinem, W., 128
Von Ivanka, E., 274
Vranken, G., 44

Waldensians, 186, 187-88, 333
Waldo, Peter, 187-88
War, just, 28-29
Weatherbee, W., 182
Wéber, E., 259
Weber, E. H., 254
Weilner, I., 325
Weingart, R. C., 172
Weinstein, D., 333
Weisheipl, J. A., 258, 260
Wendelborn, G., 190
Wenin, C., 170
Wheeler, M. C., 263
White, D. S., 206
Wieland, G., 259
Wigram, W. A., 77
Willgard of Ravenna, 147
William of Auvergne, 246

William of Auxerre, 240, *247*
William of Champeaux, 167-70, 175, 183
William of Conches, 182, 183
William of La Mare, 255, 282, 283
William of Saint Amour, 232-33, 282
Williams, P. L., *172*
Willis, G. G., *28, 29, 52*
Wilmart, A., *124*
Wilniewczye, M., *165*
Wilpert, P., *288*
Wilshire, L. E., *282*
Wippel, J. F., *263, 282, 283*
Wittmann, M., *238*
Wolfelm of Brauweiler, 155
Wolter, H., *187*
Workman, H. B., *327*
World: eternity of, 92, 212, 235, 236-37, 239, 240, *246, 247, 255,* 259, 273, 282, 287, 289, 290
Worms, M., *237*
Worringer, W., *221*
Wycliffe, John, 306, **327-32**

Yazid II, *197*

Zacharias of Mytilene, 91, 92
Zahringer, D., *50*
Zananiri, G., *205, 293, 294, 297*
Zangara, V., *24*
Zavalloni, R., *274*
Zeiller, J., *17*
Zeno (emperor), 79-80, 140
Zimmermann, A., *258, 259*
Zinn, G., *176*
Zosimus, 30
Zsamoyta, C. S., *274*